CW00924402

Arbitration in the International Energy Industry

Consulting Editor **Ronnie King**

Consulting editor
Ronnie King, Ashurst LLP

Managing director
Sian O'Neill

Arbitration in the International Energy Industry
is published by

Globe Law and Business Ltd
3 Mylor Close
Horsell
Woking
Surrey GU21 4DD
United Kingdom
Tel: +44 20 3745 4770
www.globelawandbusiness.com

Printed and bound by CPI Group (UK) Ltd, Croydon CR0 4YY

Arbitration in the International Energy Industry

ISBN 9781787422247
EPUB ISBN 9781787422254
Adobe PDF ISBN 9781787422261
Mobi ISBN 9781787422278

MIX
Paper from
responsible sources
FSC® C013604

Table of contents

Introduction

Ronnie King
Ashurst LLP

Describing a collection of essays as 'practical' may be thought rather predictable. No publisher would present a work which set out to be impractical. In this case, however, 'practical' is an apt description, as the text deals with issues that industry participants encounter in practice and gives guidance on how best to approach those particular aspects. It is also practical in the sense that it is written by practitioners with very extensive experience – experience being the source of their personal expertise. All of the contributors have had significant exposure in their professional work to the topics on which they have been invited to contribute. It has been my pleasure over the years to work with or against most of our contributors. I have very much enjoyed the opportunity given to me by the publishers to coordinate the contribution of chapters for this book.

The first chapter deals with contract terms relating to arbitration and allied topics. Dyfan Owen and James MacDonald address an important first step in securing the right type of dispute resolution process that the parties desire for their contract. They help to explain the desirability of keeping the drafting simple, but also explain the significance of choice of governing law and venue. Peter Ashford then tackles the costs question, highlighting the role that corporate counsel can play and reminding us of the scope for parties to affect the overall costs by gripping the procedure early on and taking care to keep the process proportionate. It is clear from industry experience that cost is a major area of dissatisfaction; Peter suggests that this is something which, with planning, can be much better managed.

The interrelationship between arbitration and other forms of alternative dispute resolution (ADR) is considered by Georgia Quick and Luke Carbon. 'Stepped' dispute resolution has become ubiquitous in certain business situations, including infrastructure construction. Arbitration is perceived as involving a lower rate of settlement than national court litigation, which may be understandable given political considerations which are not encountered so frequently in national dispute resolution – itself more likely to be seen in national court than arbitration. Understanding how best to maximise opportunities for amicable settlement through ADR or negotiation in the context of arbitration is a very valuable tool to limit cost and preserve relationships.

Rachael Bewsey writes from her perspective as a client. Her comments may strike a chord. Arbitration practitioners – good ones, at least – aim to make the process understandable and to strip out the mystique and jargon found in national court systems. Close collaboration between corporate counsel and external legal teams can make material differences to cost, transparency, cordial working relations with witnesses and prospects to identify and nail down settlement opportunities.

The oil industry is well served by the Association of International Petroleum Negotiators (AIPN). Many of the contributors to, and readers of, this book will be familiar with the AIPN and its work in producing model contracts. Its forms are used by several industry participants. Jennifer Smith and Imad Khan address AIPN dispute resolution wordings. There is also a contribution from Tim Martin, one of the best-known AIPN flag bearers, who gives us his insights in relation to oil sector arbitration in the Middle East, a topic of which he has extensive personal experience.

Contributions on two of the most fertile areas of dispute – gas pricing and construction – follow, from Matthew Saunders and Ghislaine Lawless and from Rob Palmer and Patrese McVeigh, respectively. Once again, these contributions come from practitioners who have had a number of arbitrations concerning the subject on which they write. In each case the reader is alerted to nuances particular to the type of dispute.

Nicholas Lingard and Emily Stennett write on joint venture disputes. The sector is distinguished by the almost universal use of joint ventures to explore for and exploit discoveries. The format of contracts among parties to a venture tends to follow similar patterns, of which provision for arbitration to resolve disputes is one. Nicholas and Emily highlight some important dynamics which result from the underlying commercial bargain. The importance of liquefied natural gas is noted by the contribution from Ben Giaretta. The industry is familiar with some of the areas for disagreement in relation to this part of the energy market. Ben focuses his comments on plant-related problems.

Tom Sprange and Ben Williams write on investment treaty disputes, of which they have significant professional experience. The question of state relations is well understood as a practical issue of utmost importance during contract formation and project implementation. The energy sector has played a big part in the evolution of investor protection and has been a significant user of investment treaty claims. Tom and Ben address this important subject in an industry context.

Neil Cuninghame and Max Strasberg consider the arbitration of competition law claims. This is perhaps an unexpected subject, competition law being encountered at national regulatory or economic community level. However, increasing numbers of referrals to arbitration allege conduct that gives rise to competition breaches and acceptance that such issues may be arbitrated between private parties. Neil and Max have acted on material claims of this nature and write based on experience.

A common observation is that lawyers are interested in issues of liability and are at home when considering issues of breach of contract and assigning of legal responsibility, but are less helpful – to put it mildly – when it comes to calculating damages. An accountant's eye is brought to this subject by Adrian Howick who, along with his colleagues, has assisted corporates to evaluate the level of damages which might be capable of being proved. In practice, parties need input from both lawyers and accounting experts to assess what losses are legally claimable and how much of those can be linked to the breach by a counterparty. Adrian shares his perspectives as an accountant involved in arbitration damages assessments.

The no longer novel question of funding is dealt with by Tom Glasgow and colleagues from funder IMF Bentham. They explain the nature of what may be available and how the economics work. Funding has been used in the sector, particularly for investment treaty work. There are indications of its use extending into the commercial claims sector, with some portfolio funding being undertaken by solvent claimant corporates.

Finally, Rajinder Bassi and Jon Newman deal with enforcement. Sector participants have generally been lucky when it comes to awards being honoured, at least in the context of joint venture disputes. This may lull parties into assuming that they will not have to take proceedings to enforcement. Rajinder and Jon address what can happen should that be required.

I hope very much that you find the contributions lively and informative, and will agree that they are practical in each of the senses suggested above.

Finally, I wish to acknowledge my gratitude to my colleague Michael Weatherley for his considerable assistance in bringing this publication together and his good-humoured patience in attending to my requests.

Effective arbitration clauses

James MacDonald
Dyfan Owen
Ashurst LLP

1. The importance of arbitration clauses

When negotiating contracts, dispute resolution is not always at the forefront of the minds of the contracting parties. However, given the complexity and value of contracts and the volatile nature of the industry in recent years, disputes often arise between contracting parties in the energy industry. When they do, it is important that the contract provides a clear dispute resolution mechanism so that time and cost are not wasted determining the appropriate forum and jurisdiction for the resolution of disputes. For a number of reasons (including ease of enforcement, procedural flexibility and confidentiality), arbitration is the preferred means of resolving international disputes in the energy sector. This chapter outlines the different options available for arbitration and the key considerations that should be taken into account when drafting an arbitration clause.

2. Pre-drafting considerations

An effective arbitration clause should be tailored to the transaction and the parties. Therefore, before putting pen to paper, it is important to consider at the outset when the arbitration clause may be triggered and whether there are any specific matters that the clause ought to address.

For these purposes, the parties should consider the following key factors.

- The nature and value of potential claims:
  - What could be subject to dispute?
  - What may be claimed? Money? Other assets?
- The complexity of potential claims:
  - Is the claim likely to involve technical matters?
  - Will expert evidence be required?
  - Will evidence be provided in written or oral form?
- Speed:
  - How quickly is a decision required?
  - Is there an ongoing contract to be performed?
- Location:
  - Where are the relevant parties located?

- (For the purposes of enforcement), where are the parties' assets located?
- Where are there adequate facilities to host an arbitration?
- Language:
  - What language should be used?
  - Will there be arbitrators, experts and counsel of suitable expertise who can conduct the arbitration in the specific language?
- Multi-party issues:
  - Are there more than two parties to the contract or involved in the same project?
  - Are there likely to be several related disputes taking place at the same time?
- Pre-arbitration:
  - Are pre-arbitration alternative dispute resolution (ADR) measures, such as mediation, desirable?
  - Would other forms of dispute resolution, such as expert determination, be more appropriate for certain disputes?

Some of these issues give rise to distinct drafting points in their own right and others inform decisions on, for example, which arbitral rules should be chosen. While it is difficult for parties to predict accurately the types of dispute that may arise under a contract, there is value in giving some consideration to the questions set out.

3. Drafting the clause

A number of specimen arbitration clauses are available, either from arbitral institutions or from industry bodies. These clauses provide a good starting point when drafting an arbitration clause and, if only a simple arbitration mechanism is required, may require little amendment. In fact, a number of the issues that arise in respect of arbitration clauses do so because the clauses negotiated between parties are not clearly, unambiguously drafted. This can be avoided by using simple, straightforward, tried and tested wording. However, even when seeking to draft a simple, straightforward arbitration clause or to adopt a specimen clause, it is important, in order to ensure its effectiveness, to give thought to the following key issues:

- the scope of the arbitration clause;
- the seat (or legal place) of the arbitration;
- the rules that will apply to the arbitration;
- the number and method of appointment of arbitrators; and
- the choice of law.

3.1 Scope of the arbitration clause

An effective arbitration clause should clearly identify the disputes that are to be referred to arbitration.

(a) Types of disputes

Commercial parties will usually want all disputes to be determined in a single forum. To achieve this, the arbitration clause should be broadly drafted and cover all disputes. National courts usually accept that wording such as 'all disputes arising out of or in connection with this contract' covers both contractual and non-contractual disputes.

If parties wish certain types of disputes (eg, technical disputes) to be resolved through other means (eg, expert determination), they should make that clear in their contract.

(b) Clear reference to arbitration

In *Anzen Limited v Hermes One Limited*[1] the Privy Council held that an arbitration clause which provided that "any party *may* submit the dispute to binding arbitration" (emphasis added) did not prevent a party from submitting the dispute to the competent courts rather than to arbitration. While this approach has not been followed in all jurisdictions,[2] it remains best practice to use language such as 'must' or 'shall', if the parties wish to avoid disputes as to whether parties are entitled to litigate rather than to arbitrate a dispute.

(c) Hybrid arbitration clauses

Some parties may prefer to have the option of being able to compel a counterparty to arbitrate, while also retaining the right for themselves to bring a claim in the courts. Clauses that provide such options are known as 'split' or 'hybrid' arbitration clauses. These clauses may also include a mechanism providing one or both of the parties with the right to determine which procedure will apply once a dispute arises. These clauses are increasingly common in financing agreements and security documents, as they provide lenders with greater flexibility when bringing claims against borrowers. However, such clauses should be treated with caution, as in some jurisdictions they have been found to be invalid on the basis that they do not contain a proper reference to arbitration or are considered contrary to public policy (ie, on the basis that only one party has the option to choose between litigation or arbitration).

---

1   (British Virgin Islands) [2016] UKPC 1.
2   See *Pipeline Services WA Pty Ltd v ATCO Gas Australia Pty Ltd* [2014] WASC 10.

3.3 Where should the arbitration take place?

This is also known as the 'seat' of the arbitration. An arbitration clause should specify the legal place or seat of the arbitration. The seat of the arbitration is critical, as this determines:

- the procedural law that will apply to the arbitration (eg, if the seat is in London, the Arbitration Act 1996 will apply);
- whether the dispute is arbitrable in that country (eg, in many jurisdictions disputes involving family matters or insolvency cannot be arbitrated);
- the extent to which the courts of the seat can intervene in the arbitration (eg, to determine an objection to jurisdiction or to grant interim measures in support of the arbitration);
- the extent to which third-party funding for the arbitration can be obtained and will need to be disclosed;
- whether the arbitral award can be challenged or appealed; and
- the enforceability of the arbitral award (some countries will enforce awards under the New York Convention only if the award is made in the territory of another contracting state).

The seat of arbitration is an important consideration. For example, in the first round of Egypt's solar power feed-in-tariff programme, the Egyptian government insisted on Egypt being the seat of arbitration for disputes under the power purchase agreements to be entered into with investors. This led to a number of international investors withdrawing their interest, because of unwillingness on the part of funders to agree to locally seated arbitration.

In some jurisdictions, public procurement laws restrict the dispute resolution options available for contracts with government authorities or state-owned enterprises. For example, in the United Arab Emirates, contracts with Dubai government entities cannot provide for arbitration outside of Dubai or be governed by a law other than Dubai law, unless an exemption is granted.

Where parties do have the freedom to choose the seat of the arbitration, consideration should be given to both the applicable arbitration law in the seat and the general attitude of courts in that seat to arbitration. For this reason, popular seats include England, France, Sweden, Singapore, Switzerland and New York. These jurisdictions are recognised as arbitration friendly and their courts have limited scope to interfere with the arbitral process.

The United Nations Commission on International Trade Law (UNCITRAL) has developed the UNCITRAL Model Law on International Commercial Arbitration, which provides a 'best practice' example which countries can adopt for their arbitration law. As described in the explanatory memorandum to the UNCITRAL Model Law: "it covers all stages of the arbitral process from the arbitration agreement to the recognition and enforcement of the arbitral award and reflects a worldwide consensus on the principles and important issues of international arbitration practice."

Legislation based on the UNCITRAL Model Law has been adopted in 80 countries.[3] In some other countries, such as England, legislation has been introduced which, although not directly based on the model law, incorporates many elements of the model law. If parties are considering choosing an arbitration seat that does not have an arbitration law based on the model law, they should investigate the potential effect of the local law on an arbitration and take note of any mandatory procedures that may need to be complied with. For example, the law may contain specific requirements in respect of notifying a defendant on the commencement of an arbitration or could permit an appeal on a point of law.

If enforcement may be required in a country that is not a signatory to the New York Convention, consideration should also be given as to whether any other regional or bilateral treaties could be relied upon. While most countries are signatories to the New York Convention, there are some exceptions, such as Libya. However, while Libya is not a signatory to the New York Convention, it is a signatory to the Riyadh Arab Agreement for Judicial Cooperation (also known as the Riyadh Convention), which provides for the reciprocal enforcement of arbitration awards between contracting states.

3.4   Which rules should be used?

Arbitration rules set out the detailed procedure for how an arbitration should be conducted. Parties can draft the arbitral rules themselves, but to save time and cost, the usual practice is to adopt pre-existing rules. By specifying, in the arbitration clause, the rules which will apply to the arbitration, the parties effectively incorporate those rules into their contract by reference. This gives the parties a clear agreed procedure to follow if a dispute arises.

Arbitral institutions each have their own rules, which should be used if the parties want their arbitration to be administered by a particular institution. However, there are also *ad hoc* arbitration rules which can be used for arbitrations conducted without the support of an arbitral institution. Therefore, before deciding on which rules to refer to in an arbitration clause, it is first necessary to consider whether the arbitration should be *ad hoc* or institutional.

(a)   Ad hoc *or institutional?*

Ad hoc arbitration is arbitration which the parties manage themselves. No arbitral institution oversees the process or supervises the conduct of the

---

3   These include Australia, Canada, Egypt, Germany, Hong Kong, India, Japan, Mexico, Nigeria, Korea, Russia, Singapore, Spain, Scotland and certain states in the United States (including California and Texas). For a full list, see www.uncitral.org/uncitral/en/uncitral_texts/arbitration/1985Model _arbitration_status.html.

arbitrators and the parties. The parties can draw up their own rules; however, it is more common for parties to leave the rules to the discretion of the arbitrators or to adopt rules specifically prepared for *ad hoc* arbitration, such as the UNCITRAL Arbitration Rules.

Institutional arbitration is arbitration conducted under the supervision of a specialist arbitration institution. The role of the institution typically includes:

- assisting with the appointment of arbitrators;
- intervening as appropriate (eg, to replace arbitrators if required);
- providing administrative support throughout the arbitration (in particular, with payment of arbitrators); and
- for some institutions, scrutinising the award of the arbitrators.

There are advantages and disadvantages to *ad hoc* and institutional arbitration:

- A good *ad hoc* arbitration can be tailored specifically to a dispute, after the dispute arises. The parties can frame their own methodology for resolving the issues between them. However, reaching agreement in relation to procedure after a dispute has already arisen can be difficult and this can lead to delays.
- Conversely, *ad hoc* arbitrations are more susceptible to obstructive parties that seek to frustrate the arbitration proceedings (although once an arbitrator or tribunal is appointed, there is much less scope for this). Institutional arbitration is better suited to avoiding such tactics.
- Costs may be harder to control in *ad hoc* arbitration. By contrast, leading institutions such as the International Chamber of Commerce (ICC) and the London Court of International Arbitration (LCIA) provide schedules of fees which enable parties to estimate how much the proceedings will cost.
- The reputation of a leading arbitration institution may make it easier to enforce an arbitral award in certain jurisdictions. Both the ICC and the LCIA have significant name recognition globally, lending authority to any award issued in their names.

Contract negotiators often favour institutional arbitration. It provides a 'safety net' in the event of anything going wrong, such as a difficult party refusing to participate in the process. In addition, the comfort provided by the oversight of an institution is likely to make the arbitration exercise more certain and less stressful. That said, as with any aspect of the dispute resolution procedure, circumstances may dictate a different approach. Thus, many of the disadvantages of *ad hoc* arbitration are less of a consideration in contracts between sophisticated parties with long-term aligned interests, such as major oil and gas companies.

(b)   *Institutional arbitration: choosing the institution*

There are numerous institutions to choose from and there is no magic formula for selecting between them. Sometimes parties are influenced by differences in the rules themselves, sometimes by familiarity and sometimes by their opinion of the international acceptability or reputation of a given institution and/or its cost and speed. Examples of some of the institutions are set out below:

- the American Arbitration Association and its international body, the International Centre for Dispute Resolution;
- the Hong Kong International Arbitration Centre;
- the International Court of Arbitration of the ICC;
- the LCIA;
- the Dubai International Financial Centre-LCIA Arbitration Centre;
- the Singapore International Arbitration Centre (SIAC); and
- the Arbitration Institute of the Stockholm Chamber of Commerce.

Copies of the rules and recommended wording for arbitration clauses are published by the above institutions on their websites.

The choice of seat often dictates which institution is chosen. Arbitration institutions at or near the seat of arbitration are usually best placed to appoint the best arbitrators in that location. This helps to reduce costs and increase efficiency in the arbitral process. It is also convenient to have an institution with an office in or near the same time zone as the arbitration hearing.

When comparing the different institutions and their rules, the following questions may help to determine which institution to choose:

- Do the rules cater for the specific needs of the parties?
- What is the reputation and experience of the institution?
- How much institutional involvement will there be?
- How many arbitrators should there be in default of agreement?
- What will the fees and costs be and how are they calculated?

3.5   Number and appointment of arbitrators

An arbitration clause will usually specify the number of arbitrators and the method of their appointment. However, arbitration rules will include a default position that will apply if the parties have not agreed on the number of arbitrators or the method of their appointment.

Arbitration is typically conducted by one or three arbitrators; to avoid deadlock, an even number of arbitrators should be avoided. Arbitration with a sole arbitrator will be less costly and should involve less delay. However, in high-value international disputes, such as those that often arise in the energy sector, it is usual to provide for the appointment of a tribunal of three arbitrators. By providing for three arbitrators, this also allows each party to nominate an arbitrator and for a 'neutral' third arbitrator (the president) to be appointed either by agreement between the two party-nominated arbitrators or by the supervising institution.

An arbitration clause can provide that the number of arbitrators depends on the value of the claim, so that lower-value disputes can be resolved more efficiently and with less cost. This may be suitable where there is a likelihood of both low-value and high-value disputes arising from a contract. However, value is not always a good guide to complexity and having a specified limit may unhelpfully encourage parties to artificially 'fix' the claim (either above or below the threshold). Where institutional arbitration is used, an alternative is to allow the institution to determine the number of arbitrators after consulting with the parties. For example, the ICC's arbitration rules provide that where the parties have not agreed on the number of arbitrators, the ICC shall appoint a sole arbitrator unless it appears to the ICC that the dispute warrants the appointment of three arbitrators.

If *ad hoc* arbitration is used, it is important to consider specifying an 'appointing authority' which will appoint the arbitrators if the parties are unable to reach agreement. The relevant rules used may contain a default mechanism. A number of authorities offer an appointing service, including most of the arbitral institutions and the Permanent Court of Arbitration.

It is possible for parties to specify, in their arbitration clause, the qualifications that an arbitrator should have. Qualifications should be defined carefully; too narrow a definition may make it impossible to identify an available arbitrator, while too wide a definition may give rise to satellite disputes or a finding that the appointed tribunal had no jurisdiction to act. Often, the most important quality for an arbitrator is familiarity with arbitration process and procedure, although industry knowledge may be helpful. It is also not advisable for parties to specify a named arbitrator, because if such person were unable or unwilling to act when a dispute arose, the arbitration clause would be incapable of being performed.

Under most institutional rules, the right to appoint an arbitrator is lost in a multi-party situation, unless specific provision is made in the arbitration clause. Therefore, if the parties anticipate that any dispute will involve multiple parties and provision has been made for all such parties to be joined in the same arbitration, consideration should be given as to how the appointment mechanism will work and it may be sensible to leave the appointment to the arbitral institution chosen.

3.6   Choice of law

Choice of law clauses are, strictly speaking, separate from arbitration clauses, since these set out the applicable (or 'governing') law regulating the parties' rights and obligations, by which substantive questions are to be judged. In contrast, an arbitration clause sets out the mechanism by which a dispute is to be resolved. However, choice of law clauses are often combined with arbitration clauses, so parties may have to consider this when drafting the arbitration clause. Also, in some circumstances, it may be important for parties to appreciate the distinction between the governing law of the contract, the procedural law of the arbitration and the law applicable to the arbitration clause.

(a)   *Governing law of the contract*

The governing law of a contract can be pivotal not only to its formation, interpretation and validity, but also to the question of what remedies can be awarded by the arbitrators. Parties are generally free to choose any governing law, even if it does not have a connection to the parties or the subject matter of the contract. For example, in the energy sector, it is common for parties to choose English law as this is considered to offer greater predictability and there is a significant body of case law arising from disputes in the energy sector. However, when contracting with government entities there may, for legal or political reasons, be a requirement that local law be used.

It is always advisable to specify the governing law when drafting the contract. Where the parties do not select a governing law, the choice will be made for them by the arbitrators, often by reference to the applicable conflict of laws rules in the seat of the arbitration. This may lead not only to uncertainty, but also to time and cost being spent arguing at the outset of any dispute over what law should be applied. It is also important that parties accurately describe the governing law they intend to apply (eg, 'English law' rather than 'UK law').

(b)   *Law applicable to the arbitration clause*

An arbitration clause in a contract is considered to be a separate agreement from the contract in which it resides – this is known as the principle of 'separability'. This means that the arbitration clause can survive if the contract is terminated or found to be void, which allows for claims arising out of a terminated or void contract to still be referred to arbitration. It is generally assumed that where no separate choice of law for the arbitration clause is made, the governing law of the contract as a whole is also the governing law of the arbitration clause.

However, difficulties can arise where the governing law of the contract is different from the seat of the arbitration – for example, if the contract is governed by English law but the seat is Paris. In those circumstances, disputes can arise. The outcome of such disputes can be significant, as the validity of the arbitration agreement is determined by reference to the law governing the arbitration agreement. In order to avoid such disputes, it is recommended either to include in the arbitration agreement a governing law provision (where the parties want the governing law of the arbitration agreement to follow the law of the seat), or to extend the contract governing law provision so that it also covers the arbitration agreement (where the parties want the governing law of the contract to also be the law applicable to the arbitration clause).

(c)   ***Procedural law***

The procedural law in an arbitration is different from the governing law of the contract – this is the law by which the arbitration will operate (eg, the UNCITRAL Model Law). It is possible, but rare in practice, for parties to specify in the arbitration clause that the procedural law will be for an arbitration arising out of the contract. Without this being specified, the procedural law is normally assumed to be the law relating to arbitration in the seat of the arbitration. Indeed, it is not advisable to specify in the arbitration clause a different procedural law from the procedural law in the seat of the arbitration, since this may give rise to conflicts that the local courts will have to resolve.

4.   Other considerations

4.1   Procedural questions

Parties rarely stipulate expressly the approach to specific procedural questions in arbitration clauses and under most sets of arbitration rules the arbitrators have considerable procedural discretion. However, as arbitration is a flexible process, the parties can, if they wish, agree on how the arbitration will be conducted. For example, if the parties would like to reduce time and cost, they can provide that only written submissions will be made to the tribunal.

The extent of document disclosure can also be an important procedural issue that can significantly affect cost and time. Where there are parties from different backgrounds, depending on their perspective, they may be concerned that there may be either too little or too much disclosure. In many instances experienced arbitrators will endeavour to bridge the gap between different legal systems and between the parties' expectations; but if the parties prefer more certainty on this issue, they may wish to consider specifying in the arbitration clause that questions of document disclosure will be governed by the International Bar Association's Rules on the Taking of Evidence in International Commercial Arbitration, which steers a compromise course.

4.2   Language

The parties should specify the language of the arbitration, as this will be the language of the written and oral submissions and any hearings. The language of the arbitration should normally be the language of the contract, since there will often be issues of contractual interpretation. Specifying the language in the clause will avoid time-consuming arguments over what the language should be once a dispute arises.

4.3   Excluding rights of appeal

In most jurisdictions, there are only limited grounds on which an arbitration award can be appealed. Parties can exclude (as far as is permitted by the laws of the relevant jurisdiction) the right to appeal on a point of law, in order to ensure that the award is final and binding. Institutional rules may already provide for this;[4] but if not, or if the arbitration is *ad hoc*, the parties will need to consider whether they want to achieve greater finality by excluding rights of appeal. If they do, express provision must be made in the arbitration clause itself. Stating that the award is to be final, binding and conclusive will not suffice.[5]

4.4   Confidentiality

If confidentiality is considered to be important, an express confidentiality agreement should be included, along with a remedy for breach of the same. Although in a number of jurisdictions, confidentiality of the arbitration proceedings and the award is implied both during the arbitration and in any related court proceedings, there are exceptions. The procedural law of the seat, together with any applicable rules, determines whether and to what extent confidentiality provisions apply and should always be checked. If in doubt, it is prudent to include an express confidentiality agreement in the clause.

4.5   Tiered dispute resolution clauses

While parties may wish to provide for arbitration as their final and binding dispute resolution procedure, they may wish to include in their contract procedures aimed at encouraging resolution of the dispute before it reaches that stage. These ADR procedures are well suited to contracts in the energy sector, which are often long-term contracts where the efficient and relatively amicable resolution of disputes can ensure the preservation of relationships.

The drafting of these 'stepped' or 'tiered' clauses varies significantly, from simple clauses to complex procedures. The Association of International Petroleum Negotiators international operating agreement, for example, offers a menu of optional dispute resolution methods which parties can select. The mechanisms commonly used in such clauses include:

- structured negotiation – this can take place at varying levels within the organisations or between senior management or at board level if necessary; and
- mediation – the mediator (a neutral person) facilitates a settlement between the parties by suggesting ways in which a compromise might be reached.

4   For example, both the LCIA and ICC Rules exclude rights of appeal as permitted by law.
5   *Shell Egypt West Manzala GmbH v Dana Gas Egypt Ltd* [2009] EWHC 2097 (Comm).

In drafting such clauses, it is important that they:

- contain a clear process;
- make it clear whether the ADR process is mandatory;
- make it clear when the process is triggered;
- incorporate a timeframe – the drafting should make it clear when one stage ends and another begins; and
- readily identify individuals with specific roles (eg, a mediator). Common practice is to refer to a body or institution as the appointing body in respect of such individuals.

4.6 Multiple parties

Disputes in the energy sector, particularly construction disputes, often involve multiple parties and multiple contracts. In the event of a dispute, there may therefore be claims under several different contracts.

Litigation can cope well with situations such as these, as judges will usually have power under the relevant court rules to compel parties to resolve related claims in a single set of proceedings. Traditionally, arbitration does not provide that option, as it is a consensual dispute resolution mechanism between contracting parties. Arbitration proceedings may be commenced only against other contracting parties.

It is possible that if a multi-party, multi-contract dispute arises, all of the parties may agree to have matters resolved in a single arbitration, but this is fairly rare. Instead – and unless express provision for consolidation has been made in the arbitration clause – parties wishing to consolidate are reliant on the applicable law (which in some instances provides for consolidation of arbitration without consent) or the arbitration rules selected. A number of institutions now provide for consolidation of related disputes and joinder of third parties in their arbitration rules.

If there are multiple parties or multiple contracts, it is therefore important to consider this when drafting arbitration clauses. Possible options include:

- ensuring that related contracts have, at the very least, identical arbitration clauses with reference to an institution which has rules that provide for joinder or consolidation; or
- including bespoke drafting which expressly provides for joinder and consolidation of all related disputes on a project or between multiple parties.

5. Conclusion

In referring disputes to arbitration, the parties are opting to have their disputes resolved privately instead of going to court. Unlike in litigation, the jurisdiction of an arbitral tribunal depends on the parties' arbitration agreement. It is therefore important that the arbitration agreement be clearly drafted. A badly drafted arbitration agreement can lead to expensive and time-consuming litigation over its meaning and effect, can jeopardise a party's prospects of enforcing the award and can mean that a party ends up having to litigate in the courts which it intended to avoid by agreeing to arbitration in the first place.

The optimal approach and wording of any arbitration clause will vary, depending on the type of contract and the identity of the counterparty. However, the options should always be carefully evaluated, since the inclusion of an effective arbitration clause plays an important role in protecting the commercial interests of parties in energy sector transactions.

Time and cost efficiency

Peter Ashford
Fox Williams

1. Introduction

The holy grail of an efficient arbitral process is sought by many and found by few. The parties, their counsel and the tribunal must all accept partial blame for that state of affairs, yet it is relatively easy to fix. Efficiency can be achieved, but it does not simply descend on the reference like some divine blessing. It must be sought and worked for. As Benjamin Franklin said, "By failing to prepare, you are preparing to fail."[1]

International arbitration is quite different from domestic court practice, in that – almost by definition – the parties have different cultural backgrounds. That may feed into different expectations of a dispute resolution process. There may be a mismatch of experience about the process and much the same might apply to the counsel engaged. Still further, the same might be said of the tribunal.

To make matters still more fluid, the various institutional rules say very little about how a reference is to be conducted – there is no 'playbook' – so even experienced parties, counsel and tribunals may have different experiences, preferences and expectations. Pulling all of that together into a coherent process has obvious problems.

The arbitration process could be described as 'flabby'. It is out of condition, lazy and complacent. Far too often, the process has unnecessary steps that are poorly focused and indulgent. The tribunal can fulfil the role of conditioning coach: to challenge the approach that the parties and their counsel may wish to take, to see whether it could be slimmed down and made more efficient. The parties and their counsel may get away with things that would not be permitted under the rigorous eye of a court, and some of that rigour may need to be carried across to international arbitration. Tribunals must be bold in using the powers that they undoubtedly have.

There are, however, a number of opportunities to get it right and these are addressed below.

---

[1] The quote is widely attributed to Franklin, although it appears that John Wooden said it first. It could also be dated back to Proverbs 16:20: "He who plans a thing will be successful…" To similar effect is Eisenhower: "A plan is nothing, planning is everything."

2.   The agreement to arbitrate

Many dysfunctional arbitration references (and hence delays, costs and inefficiencies) stem from poorly worded clauses.[2] When entering into the substantive contract, time and effort should be put into getting the agreement to arbitrate clause right. If the clause is multi-tiered,[3] make sure that each stage is clearly expressed and sufficiently certain to be enforced; and if there are conditions precedent from the previous tier, make sure that these are clearly expressed.

Determine whether you want to state the number of arbitrators and, if so, how many there should be.[4] Make a clear choice of law election and provide for the seat, language and a choice of law for the (separate) agreement to arbitrate.

3.   First procedural meeting

While there are a number of stages when the opportunity to bring time and cost efficiency arises, the first procedural meeting (FPM) is both the first and the most important. It is an absolutely vital stage in the proper and efficient administration of the reference. It is often the first opportunity for members of the tribunal to meet face to face; for the parties to meet each other since the dispute took on its formal dispute resolution process; for counsel and the parties to meet each other and the members of the tribunal. It is a golden opportunity for all involved to understand what is involved in the reference and how the parties wish the reference to be conducted.

By this stage, there will be at least a request for arbitration and an answer/response. Those documents might give sufficient detail for the claim (or the claim and defence may have been fully presented in correspondence prior to the request), or may leave the tribunal floundering as to what the real issues are. Although it may be necessary for the issues to be fully pleaded out subsequent to the FPM, it is important that sufficient materials are exchanged (and provided to the tribunal) in advance of the FPM, so that all involved can identify the issues involved, as only then can the reference be properly managed. That does not mean that the pleadings must be in place before the FPM: as above, the request and answer or pre-reference correspondence may be sufficient, or the parties could draw up a list of issues.

Some issues that may require specific mention, discussion and resolution are discussed below. They all derive from potentially diametric views that the parties and their counsel may have to the approach that ought to be adopted; and the issues raised are designed, so far as possible, to dispel potential misunderstandings. The efficient conduct of proceedings depends upon the

---

2   Although, of course, the clause is, by a legal fiction, considered to be a separate agreement.
3   For example, that arbitration can only follow negotiation, senior management meetings and mediation.
4   The choice is effectively between a sole arbitrator or a three-person tribunal. A sole arbitrator will be quicker, cheaper and generally more efficient. That must be balanced by the risk of entrusting a single person to make final decisions.

parties, usually through their respective counsel, having a common understanding as to the process to be followed. It will not, for example, be efficient if the perception of issues or the approachs to document production and witness preparation are different, or if the experts are asked to opine upon different questions on different material.

The United Nations Commission on International Trade Law (UNCITRAL) Notes on Organising Arbitral Proceedings are a useful source of guidance. While they do not pretend to provide all the answers, they do pose most of the questions and a study of the notes is a helpful reminder of the issues that can arise at the FPM.

3.1 Attendees

The attendance of appropriate senior representatives of the parties at the FPM is a matter of some debate; some practitioners favour it and others do not (those in the latter camp often consider that it avoids grandstanding by counsel), but the clearly preferable view is in favour of attendance. While there is unlikely to be resolution of any substantive issues at the meeting by the tribunal – the purpose of the meeting being procedural rather than substantive – nevertheless, the attendance of senior representatives enables a better understanding by those representatives of the issues and the time and cost of the process. This may itself promote settlement, but certainly ought to promote efficiency; at least, it should promote understanding of the process and, in part, of the opponent's case. A common understanding of what the issues are by parties, counsel and the tribunal is a key to efficiency. If everyone is 'singing from the same hymn sheet', the reference is likely to be smoother and more efficient. Time and money are wasted when parties (or counsel) are at cross-purposes. For example, when directing witness statements, there ought to be consensus as to which issues require witness testimony, and conversely which do not (perhaps because the evidence – for example, as to what the drafter of a contract intended it to mean – is inadmissible).

General counsel or other senior decision makers of the parties should play a vital role in the FPM – regrettably, few do. It is, after all, their (employer's – that is, the parties') reference, not that of their external counsel. It is they who should decide, of course with the benefit of advice from counsel, how the reference should proceed. The advocacy will be done by their counsel but their presence enables the party, through its representatives, to react to what the other party and the tribunal may suggest and make suggestions as to how the reference might be conducted.

In particular, there will in nearly every reference be real options as to how to manage the process, from the more modest (eg, how document production should be managed – some approaches more expensive in time and costs than others) to the more fundamental (eg, whether some or all of the issues should be determined on a 'documents only' basis or with a full evidentiary hearing).

Accordingly, the parties should be at the centre of the decisions on procedure. To enable wide-ranging debate as to the appropriate procedure, counsel should be ready, willing and able to discuss the time and cost implications of alternative procedures. Indeed, the tribunal ought to advise counsel to be ready to discuss, in broad terms, the potential range of budget costs for different procedural options. Most references can, to a greater or lesser extent, be undertaken on an expedited basis (also known as a 'quick and dirty' basis), or a full 'no stone left unturned' or 'Rolls Royce' basis.

3.2 Counsel

The identity of all members of the counsel team should be notified to the tribunal at the outset of the reference (some details, but not necessarily all, are usually given in the request for arbitration) and updated as changes are made. This is not simply for record purposes; it is rather intended to address the issues that can arise (eg, a conflict as between counsel and members of the tribunal).[5] The problem is particularly acute in England and other jurisdictions where there is a divided profession (eg, solicitors and barristers who appear both as counsel and as arbitrators). The identity of solicitors is usually overt and they are normally the address for service and on the record. The involvement of barristers, however, may not be overt. Although barristers are members of a particular 'set' or 'chambers', they are independent, self-employed and not in partnership with other members of the same set (although they will share expenses (including a marketing function that promotes the set)). This can give rise to concerns that there is a conflict of interest (or more strictly, an appearance of bias) in having members of the same set both being a tribunal member and appearing as barrister (counsel) representing a party. The external perception, especially in countries that do not have barristers (or a divided profession), is that the tribunal member and the barrister are from the same firm or business unit, and that there is an inevitable conflict.

3.3 Formalities

It is wise to obtain agreement to such things as:

- the formal submission to arbitration;
- whether any particular institutional rules apply and, if not, whether any should apply;
- whether the International Bar Association (IBA) Rules on the Taking of Evidence in International Arbitration, the IBA Guidelines on Party Representation in International Arbitration and/or the IBA Guidelines

---

5   Note the problems that arose in *Hrvatska Elektroprivreda dd v Slovenia*, ICSID Case ARB /05/24 (late appointment of counsel – a barrister from the same set as the arbitrator – created reasonable doubt as to impartiality and independence of the tribunal and counsel was removed); but see also *Rompetrol v Romania*, ICSID Case ARB/06/3.

on Conflicts of Interest in International Arbitration should be adopted, whether formally or as guidance for the tribunal;

- the seat of the arbitration;
- the language stipulated or to be adopted;
- confirmation that no change of name of any party has occurred;
- the address for service/communication;
- whether there are any issues as to the appointment of the tribunal; and
- whether there are any issues as to the jurisdiction of tribunal.

Should any of these matters arise late in the process, it is likely to be when a dispute has arisen and hence agreement is unlikely.

3.4 Directions to address the issues

Somehow at the FPM, what is required to be done to enable the tribunal to decide the issues must be agreed or ordered. Some issues may require extensive document production, long witness statements and the opinions of experts. Others might simply require submissions. If the parties (and their counsel) have not done the analysis of the issues in this way, it is suggested that it is the duty of the tribunal to do so – or at least to offer some thoughts on what is needed for a final determination.

The tribunal itself has a heavy burden to address this at the FPM. Simply making standard directions without an understanding as to what is necessary to determine the issues is arguably a dereliction of duty. Some arbitrators have a *pro forma* set of proposed directions which they have developed over time. Such *pro forma* directions are not necessarily a bad thing, as they often set out suggested approaches to common issues in arbitration. It is important that both arbitrators and parties approach such suggestions as a matter for discussion and parties should not rush to adopt them to be seen to agree with the tribunal.

An agenda of items to be raised at the FPM will often be circulated by the chairman. Although such an agenda will inevitably presuppose various procedural steps, nothing should be seen as 'standard' and hence necessarily required. The advantage of arbitration should be the flexibility of the process and its ability to respond to the claims, defences, facts and issues presented. The key to saving time and cost is to craft a procedure to the unique features that are before the tribunal. It is for that reason that an investment of time and money at the stage of the FPM can pay dividends later in the process – it will ensure that the appropriate preparatory work has been undertaken and with a common understanding of its aim and purpose. Simply because something has always been done a particular way does not mean that it must always be done that way.

3.5 Address for service

If a party refuses to participate further with the reference, an agreed address for service makes it far easier to proceed on the basis that notifications (eg, for an evidential hearing) have been given to an agreed address for service. On that basis, the tribunal may be willing to proceed if notice has been given to the party to the address so notified. This modest step avoids potentially lengthy and costly steps which may have to be taken to ensure that the defaulting party has had proper notice.

3.6 Bifurcation

The parties and the tribunal will consider whether it is appropriate to take any disputed jurisdiction, or any other issue, as a preliminary issue. Many tribunals will consider bifurcating liability and quantum, and that is a norm in many respects.

3.7 Procedure for reference

One of the key features of the FPM will be to set a timetable for the procedural steps. This will include:

- pleadings or memorials;
- whether there should be a list of issues;[6]
- document production;
- statements of witnesses;
- experts' reports;
- pre-hearing briefs;
- oral/evidentiary hearing; and
- post-hearing briefs.

3.8 Expectations as to behaviours

Especially if the parties are of differing cultures and/or are inexperienced in international arbitration it can be very helpful to spell out some expectations as

---

6   Tribunals are likely to be assisted by the compilation of a list of issues identifying the issues on the face of the pleadings, but whether the expense is justified needs considering. Any disputed application (eg, for document production) should be by reference to that list. The list will further determine the issues that ought to be addressed in witness statements and experts' reports, and will dictate those issues that the tribunal should determine in its award. The list can be amended as necessary with the consent of all parties and the tribunal.

7   The UNCITRAL Notes on Organising Arbitral Proceedings provide a useful checklist of what might be considered confidential:

The material or information that is to be kept confidential (eg, pieces of evidence, written and oral arguments, the fact that the arbitration is taking place, identity of the arbitrators, content of the award); measures for maintaining confidentiality of such information and hearings; whether any special procedures should be employed for maintaining the confidentiality of information transmitted by electronic means (eg, because communication equipment is shared by several users, or because electronic mail over public networks is considered not sufficiently protected against unauthorized access); circumstances in which confidential information may be disclosed in part or in whole (eg, in the context of disclosures of information in the public domain, or if required by law or a regulatory body). (Paragraph 32)

to how the parties and their counsel should behave. Such expectations might address:

- confidentiality;[7]
- serving documents;[8]
- retention of documents;[9]
- meeting and conferring regarding documents, especially electronic data;[10]
- pleadings and document production witness statements;[11]
- experts;
- evidentiary hearing;[12] and
- submission of unscheduled briefs and other documents.[13]

4. Timeframe

Experience indicates that doing something intensively uses less time in aggregate than if the task is spread over a longer period. That militates in favour of a short timetable (including the timeframe for an award).

The International Chamber of Commerce (ICC) Expedited Procedure Rules[14] have reduced fees and the key features are as follows:

- a sole arbitrator;

---

8   Again, the UNCITRAL notes are helpful:

Among various possible patterns of routing, one example is that a party transmits the appropriate number of copies to the arbitral tribunal, or to the arbitral institution, if one is involved, which then forwards them as appropriate. Another example is that a party is to send copies simultaneously to the arbitrators and the other party or parties. Documents and other written communications directed by the arbitral tribunal or the presiding arbitrator to one or more parties may also follow a determined pattern, such as through the arbitral institution or by direct transmission. For some communications, in particular those on organizational matters (eg, dates for hearings), more direct routes of communication may be agreed, even if, for example, the arbitral institution acts as an intermediary for documents such as the statements of claim and defence, evidence or written arguments. (Paragraph 34)

9   The parties are expected to retain all material documents and not to destroy anything that may be material to the issues the tribunal must determine. This may involve suspending the effect of document destruction policies, especially those relating to computer records. Failure to comply may result in an adverse inference being drawn by the tribunal.

10   If the parties expect electronic data (e-discovery or e-disclosure) to be material in the reference, they are expected to meet and confer to consider what agreements can be reached as to:
- what data is stored where;
- whether any data is stored in a medium that is not readily accessible;
- whether document production can be limited by reference to custodian, keyword searches and otherwise; and
- the format in which any production is given.

If the parties are unable to agree, recourse should be had to the tribunal at the earliest opportunity.

11   Statements should be the words of the witness and it is proper (subject to whatever ethical or other rules bind counsel) for counsel to assist in the drafting of a statement. It should remain the evidence of the witness and not what counsel might want a witness to say. The witness will be expected to verify the truth of the statement on oath or affirm that it is true.

12   Witnesses will be examined by the party calling them and then cross-examined on their statements, including by reference to any document on the record. Witnesses may be prepared for giving evidence by an explanation of the process, the key issues the tribunal is asked to determine and the key documents on the record, but they should not be coached in what to say or how to respond to questions. Mock cross-examination on the facts of this case is likely to be regarded as a breach of this behaviour.

13   The right should be reserved to refuse to admit to the record any brief or submission that has not been directed to be filed and served.

14   Applicable to arbitration agreements from 1 March 2017 and for amounts of less than $2 million – or the parties can opt in.

- speedy appointment of the sole arbitrator;
- FPM within 15 days of the arbitrator's receipt of the file;
- no terms of reference;
- no new claims after the appointment of the arbitrator;
- greater latitude on procedural matters;
- hearings by video or phone; and
- an award within six months of the FPM.

These are all helpful mandates and it will be interesting to see the take-up. They must still be married to appropriate attitudes.

5. Pleadings/statements of claim and defence

If the request and answer do not provide a sufficient agenda for the reference (and parties in simple cases should be encouraged to ensure that the request and answer are sufficient to stand alone), then pleadings will be necessary.

The 'look and feel' of pleadings is a matter for the individual pleader, but some discussion – for example, as to the extent to which the tribunal would find the pleading of evidence helpful or unhelpful, the extent to which documents should be attached and whether propositions of law or cases/authorities[15] should be pleaded – might remove differing perceptions as to what each party might receive from the other and what the tribunal might find of assistance. In some instances, guidance might be helpful.[16]

It is unlikely that the tribunal would consider it appropriate to make an order as to such matters as the format of pleadings, as this is very much a matter of style and the parties should, within reason, be permitted to present the case as they wish. However, clarity of expectation is likely to be helpful.

One of the most useful suggestions for economy is to have responsive pleadings incorporated in a single document. Although the document can become unwieldy, the concept is to have an assertion in the claim directly answered (by being adjacent – either immediately below or to one side in tabular form). This makes analysis of any pleading easier because the responsive parts are contained in a single document rather than having to manage, for example,

---

15 Note that, for example, the LCIA Rules provide that pleadings contain all "legal submissions on which it relies" – see LCIA Rules 2014, Articles 15.2, 15.3, 15.4 and 15.5.

16 For example, parties may prepare pleadings as they see fit; however, parties should adhere to the following principles:
- Material facts are to be asserted and in general it will not be appropriate to plead evidence in any detail;
- Key documents (eg, contracts, formal notices and the like) may be annexed to pleadings, but not evidential documents unless likely to be determinative of a key issue;
- Propositions of law may be asserted, but legal argument should be avoided unless likely to be determinative of a key issue;
- Pleadings should be concise statements from which the tribunal can readily ascertain the issues between the parties; and
- The parties should consider the benefit of responsive pleadings with each document incorporated with the preceding one.

claim, defence and cross-claim, reply and defence to cross-claim, rejoinder and reply to cross-claim and rejoinder to cross-claim. In this form (especially tabular), issues can be more readily identified and stated. Such a format may be potentially helpful for commercial representatives of the parties and in-house counsel who are not specialist disputes lawyers, as it enables the reader to track a particular issue without cross-reference to a variety of source materials.

Another option, which has some support, is to have statements of case that comprise formal pleadings, documents, witness evidence and potentially expert evidence, all served together. The claimant serves its statement of case/claim and the respondent serves its statement of case/defence. The claimant might serve reply and the respondent a rejoinder – both following the composite format. This tends to work best in fairly formulaic disputes, such as pricing disputes, rather than more fact-sensitive commercial disputes. It is also the format that is most commonly used in ICC arbitration practice and is widely recognised internationally by practitioners from many jurisdictions.

6.   Summary disposition

Much ink has been spent in writings over whether a tribunal has the power to grant 'summary judgment'. The term 'disposition' is preferred to 'judgment', as the latter is too closely aligned to court process. The clear consensus now appears to be that a tribunal does have the power to dispose of a reference without necessarily having a full evidential hearing after document production, witness statements and expert reports, and with each witness giving live evidence. Certain institutional rules put the question beyond debate by the inclusion of specific powers for arbitrators to deal with cases on such a basis. It may be done overtly as a summary disposition (ie, that there is no viable claim or defence, as the case may be), or framed as an issue that is bifurcated or otherwise dealt with separately and in advance of other issues. The concern over a summary disposition is whether that would give a due process defence to enforcement under the New York Convention.

A summary process in court can be appealed and so has an in-built system of checks and balances. The same cannot be said for a dispositive award. Furthermore, a respondent might be slow to 'come to the party': it might be taken by surprise by the commencement of the reference and slow in fully instructing counsel. It may be unfair if a respondent were forced to fully defend itself at a summary disposition stage when it was not ready to do so. Where parties have agreed to arbitration under institutional rules which provide expressly for summary disposal, courts called on to enforce awards made on a summary basis may be more likely to accept that due process has been followed than if the summary process has been adopted by arbitrators in face of the objection of one of the parties and in the absence of an express power to deal on a summary basis.

7.   Document production

Document production issues could merit a book of their own, but issues regarding the production of all documents, whether helpful or not, and the approach to e-discovery could properly be raised and resolved at the FPM.[17]

The first question to be addressed is whether any form of document production is, in fact, necessary. Are there issues of disputed fact that document production might assist? Conversely, are the issues ones of law (including the proper meaning of the contract) that document production will not assist? Have the parties attached to the pleadings all the documents that might be required?[18] The answers to these and similar questions might well prompt the answer as to whether further document production is required.

If further document production is required, the usual default is to adopt the IBA Rules on the Taking of Evidence in International Arbitration. This involves, at least the potential for, the following rounds of production:

- voluntary production of documents relied upon;
- voluntary production in response to requests from opponent; and
- tribunal-ordered production

This can be made more efficient by having the document requests (the so-called 'Redfern schedule') before the voluntary production, so that there is one round fewer. What must be borne in mind is that each production will involve a search of some sort (depending on how and how comprehensively the data was collected in the first place). Repeated searches are inefficient.

8.   Witnesses of fact

In some jurisdictions, witnesses who are directly related to a party – for example, directors or owners of a corporation – are considered of little assistance (or credibility), as opposed to neutral witnesses such as bystanders or expert witnesses. In other jurisdictions, it is expected that such directly related witnesses not only will give evidence, but also are likely to be the witnesses with the most material evidence. Others will see it as entirely proper for all witnesses to have the same weight. Equally, some jurisdictions see cross-examination as an affront, but most tribunals will expect it and accept it as the more likely route to the truth.

Some tribunals may wish to question witnesses themselves in advance of any questioning by the parties or prefer that all questions be put through the tribunal – this can be very cumbersome and is best avoided. The parties are likely to have a better understanding of the issues and are better situated than the tribunal to raise the relevant questions without significant preparation. This

---

17   Document production in arbitration is a process quite distinct from discovery. If there are disputes over the extent of document production, tribunals will expect the parties to confer and seek to agree a suitable protocol.

issue of fundamental approach cannot be left to chance and must be addressed well in advance. Again, it is a matter of managing expectations.

Whether witnesses are sworn or must otherwise affirm the truth of their evidence is another matter upon which expectations may differ. Some will expect only a judge to have the ability to administer an oath.

Furthermore, whether witnesses should be present solely for their own evidence and should withdraw at other times (when other witnesses are giving evidence) is a matter of differing opinion. Some tribunals will prefer witnesses to not see other witnesses give evidence, so that their evidence is not tainted by what a prior witness may have said. Other tribunals will be willing to have all witnesses present throughout the proceedings, so that any ambiguity in the evidence may be cleared up.

All of these issues should be addressed at the FPM or otherwise at an early stage in aid of the efficient conduct of the reference.

Aside from those practicalities, the focus on the issues upon which factual evidence will assist the tribunal and preventing prolix statements will also aid efficiency.

9. Experts

Expert evidence can often appear as though the respective experts are no more than 'passing ships in the night' who may be from different disciplines, rely on different materials, have different instructions, opine on different subjects and reach diametrically different conclusions. Needless to say, this is highly inefficient.

First, experts must acknowledge a duty to the tribunal that overrides any duty to the party by which they are instructed.[19]

Secondly, expert evidence should be restricted to what is necessary. Obviously, what may be necessary in one case will not be necessary in another. Identifying the issue(s) that the experts will opine upon, and doing so with precision, will ensure proper focus by the parties, counsel and the experts themselves.

Thirdly, the experts should invariably be from the same discipline. A surveyor should not be met by a structural engineer; a forensic accountant should not be met by an economist. If there are to be different disciplines, this should be appreciated from the outset and all parties should be clear. To be met with a surprise as to the discipline of the opposing expert is similarly inefficient, and the tribunal may well be faced with an application from each side to adduce

---

18   Institutional rules may address this – see, for example, LCIA Rules 2014, Articles 15.2, 15.3, 15.4 and 15.5, which provide that the claim, defence and any cross-claim, reply and defence to cross-claim and reply to defence to cross-claim should be served with "all essential documents".

19   Experts will be expected to acknowledge a primary duty to assist the tribunal rather than the party on whose behalf they are retained. Experts will ordinarily be expected to meet and seek to narrow issues between them and identify in a suitable manner those issues upon which they agree and those on which they do not, and should expect that the tribunal may require their evidence to be given by witness conferencing.

expert evidence in the same discipline as its opponent, thereby doubling the number of experts.

Fourth, to build upon the identification of the issue(s) on which the experts will opine, a common set of documents should be provided to the experts and, to the extent possible, a common set of instructions. The instructions can be framed in (multiple) alternatives to cater for each party's alternative bases of putting the case. Such instructions (and the bundle of common documents) can be settled at a 'meet and confer' with counsel and experts from each side.

Fourth, the experts should meet and confer to narrow issues between them. Such meetings should take place both before and after their reports are served. Meeting before reports avoids experts taking a position in a report from which they find it difficult to resile. Similarly, meeting after reports are exchanged to further narrow differences and to draw up a joint statement explaining where the experts differ, and why, helps to narrow and identify the issues. Consistent with an overriding duty to the tribunal, these meetings and the joint statement should have assisting the tribunal as their objective.

Following these suggestions should ensure that the need for supplemental reports (or worse, additional experts) is minimised.

Finally, consideration should be given to 'hot-tubbing' the experts, which can be a more efficient use of time. This must be balanced by the concern that 'hot-tubbing' can work in favour of the expert who is more eloquent, assertive or polished over the expert who might have the better technical skills.

10. Arrangements for evidentiary hearing

To ensure a smooth running of the evidentiary hearing, arrangements must be made for a venue, a transcript, and translations and interpretation.

Precise timetabling or an agreement to 'chess-clock' the parties may also aid efficiency.

11. Post-hearing arrangements

Lawyers from a common law litigation background are familiar with oral closing statements which are delivered after all evidence has been heard and typically after a very short delay either on the day itself or the following morning. Oral closings feature much less in arbitration practice. Tribunals will normally invite or direct the parties to submit post-closing statements or briefs. These can be directed to be served simultaneously or sequentially, and may or may not provide for a right of reply. Details of costs must also frequently be submitted.

Experience suggests that it is best to wait until the hearing itself before fixing all arrangement for post-hearing briefs. Again, the time limit for submissions affects costs and a short timeframe will save money. It is also important for the parties and the tribunal to police the length of submissions to make the documents focused and manageable. It is also very helpful for the tribunal to lay down clearly what it wants the submissions to deal with.

12. Conclusion

The questions of cost and duration of arbitration are two of the main difficulties which parties experience in relation to arbitration. In contrast to national court procedures, which the parties and the judges can do little to influence, arbitration empowers parties and tribunals to craft an efficient and proportionate approach to the case at hand. The selection of arbitrators known to practise efficiency and active client and counsel attention to each procedural step can cut costs materially, accelerate the process and enhance the experience of parties and the reputation of arbitration as a means of fair and affordable dispute resolution.

Alternative dispute resolution

Luke Carbon
Georgia Quick
Ashurst

1.   Alternative dispute resolution in the international energy sector

The international energy sector, together with the related construction industry, has for many years been noted as forming "the largest portfolio of international commercial and state investment disputes in the world".[1]

Energy projects generally involve a variety of public and private stakeholders, significant investment and programmes that span years (if not decades). In recent years, as the energy sector has consolidated, there are also fewer project proponents. It follows that commercial relationships in the energy sector are increasingly important and long-lasting. These relationships can span projects, borders, legal systems and cultures.

It is unsurprising, then, that the energy sector produces unique challenges for dispute resolution and that parties would prefer to seek out alternatives to more formal dispute resolution mechanisms such as litigation or arbitration. This chapter considers alternative dispute resolution (ADR) procedures in detail, looking at the applicability and suitability of particular processes in the resolution of energy disputes. At a high level, ADR can offer greater flexibility and control on the part of the parties, privacy, confidentiality, greater efficiency, less formality, lower legal costs and better opportunities for preserving legal relationships.

2.   Alternative to what?

An ADR process was traditionally understood to be some dispute resolution process that did not involve traditional court processes. While there is some debate as to which forms of dispute resolution fall within the broad definition of 'ADR processes', commonly accepted examples include negotiation, mediation, early neutral evaluation and dispute boards, as well as a number of others that are examined later in this chapter.

Expert determination, although more formal and often binding, is generally considered to be a form of ADR. In the past, arbitration was often considered to

---

1   AT Martin, "Dispute resolution in the international energy sector: an overview", *Journal of World Energy Law and Business*, vol 4, no 4, 2011, p332.

fall within this definition simply on the basis that it provides an 'alternative' to litigation. However, in many respects, it is akin to litigation. While arbitration has many known benefits, it is still a formal and relatively involved dispute resolution procedure. Arbitration is therefore not considered to be a form of ADR for the purpose of this chapter. In any event, expert determination and arbitration are considered in detail in other chapters and so are afforded only passing mention here.

ADR processes are generally utilised in one of the following three scenarios:

- as a result of a compulsory (court-ordered or legislated) process;
- pursuant to a contractual process; or
- as part of an *ad hoc* process.

While ADR processes can be binding or non-binding, the ADR processes focused on in this chapter are generally non-binding.

3.   Compulsory ADR

In respect of compulsory ADR, a focus on improving active case management techniques has seen a increased use of ADR processes in pre-litigation and as part of court processes. Court-ordered ADR is required by both legislation and court rules in a number of jurisdictions. This is recognition of the effectiveness of ADR to resolve even the most intractable disputes.

Pre-litigation requirements generally oblige parties to take genuine and reasonable steps to resolve the dispute by agreement (ie, before commencing proceedings) or to narrow the issues in dispute. The use of an appropriate ADR process is encouraged. Some Australian courts even have the power to refer matters for ADR (usually mediation) with or without the consent of the parties.[2] In England, an unreasonable refusal to mediate could result in court sanctions (although the courts cannot compel parties to mediate).[3] In many jurisdictions, ADR is a required step for particular types of disputes. By way of example, Italy has mandatory mediation for finance disputes (including disputes concerning insurance, banking and financial contracts).[4]

4.   Contractual ADR

Contractual ADR is the most common form of ADR employed in the energy sector and the form which may give rise to the greatest benefits, but also some pitfalls. The principle of freedom of contract gives parties the right to agree to any method of dispute resolution that they consider appropriate in the circumstances.

---

2   For example, Section 26(1) of the Civil Procedure Act 2005 (NSW); Section 53A of the Federal Court of Australia Act 1976 (Cth).
3   *Halsey v Milton Keynes General NHS Trust Steel v Joy* [2004] 1 WLR 2002. See also Ashurst, *Quickguides: Commercial Mediation*, www.ashurst.com/en/news-and-insights/legal-updates/quickguides---commercial-mediation/.
4   Legislative Decree 28/2010 (Italy).

Contractual ADR processes commonly form one or more layers of a tiered dispute resolution clause. Courts will generally enforce contractual dispute resolution clauses that are sufficiently clear, provided that they are not against public policy or contrary to any specific legislation prohibiting a form of ADR.

In comparison to *ad hoc* ADR processes, which are agreed to by the parties when a dispute arises and are discussed below, contractual ADR processes are generally less flexible (having been agreed at the time of entry into the parties' contract). Accordingly, they may not be as well suited to the resolution of the specific issues that ultimately arise. Their inclusion in a contractual dispute resolution mechanism can nevertheless be an impetus for amicable dispute resolution and may assist in alleviating any potential concerns with regard to being the first party to propose an alternative method of resolving a dispute (and any perception of weakness in doing so).

As noted elsewhere, ADR commonly forms a part of multi-tiered dispute resolution clauses in energy contracts. Different standard form contracts employ different ADR mechanisms for dispute resolution, although there are some common features. Three examples are provided in Table 1 on the next page.

5.   *Ad hoc* **ADR**

Regardless of their contractual arrangements, parties can agree at any stage of a project or a dispute to participate in any form of ADR process in an effort to resolve the issues between them. This is colloquially referred to as '*ad hoc* ADR'. *Ad hoc* ADR can be the most effective process to resolve a dispute because it may be specifically tailored to the particular dispute that has arisen and the relationship the parties find themselves in at that time. The downside is whether, at the time a dispute has arisen, the parties can sensibly agree on the optimal form of ADR, rather than seeking to obfuscate any process to improve their own position. In some circumstances, the contract between the parties may, as a compromise, expressly provide for *ad hoc* ADR. Although it is provided for in the contract, the actual choice of and participation in that process are entirely consensual.

6.   **Common ADR processes**

The majority of ADR processes involve a neutral third party. Negotiation is the obvious exception to this. The precise role of a neutral in the resolution process depends on the method chosen by the parties and any other agreement that has been reached between them with respect to the applicable procedure to be followed. Where a neutral is involved, he or she will be required, in all circumstances, to be impartial and independent of both parties in order to ensure party confidence in the process.

In contrast to court proceedings, parties seeking to resolve a dispute by way of ADR have the ability to select the most appropriate neutral to facilitate

Table 1. Table of ADR mechanisms in three different standard form contracts

Industry	Standard form contract	Structure of ADR mechanism
Oil and gas projects	Conditions of Contract for Engineering, Procurement and Construction Turnkey Projects (the Silver Book), published by the International Federation of Consulting Engineers (FIDIC) (2nd edition, 2017)	• Claims are first referred for determination by the employer's representative (ER). Once a claim has been submitted, the ER will consult with the parties to encourage them to reach an agreement. If no agreement is reached, the ER will make a fair determination which is final and binding unless a notice of dissatisfaction is issued. • If a notice of dissatisfaction is issued, claims are referred to a standing dispute avoidance and adjudication board (DAAB), which will decide the dispute. • If either party is dissatisfied with the decision of the DAAB, it must issue a further notice of dissatisfaction (failing which the decision will become final and binding). • Following the issue of the further notice of dissatisfaction, the parties must again attempt to settle the dispute amicably through negotiation. • If this step is unsuccessful, the matter may be referred to international arbitration under the International Chamber of Commerce (ICC) rules.

continued on next page

Industry	Standard form contract	Structure of ADR mechanism
Petroleum	Association of International Petroleum Negotiators Model Joint Operating Agreement 2012	• Senior executive negotiations (optional provision). • Mediation (optional provision). • ICC pre-arbitral referee procedure (optional provision). • Arbitration. • Expert determination (optional provision for specified disputes).
Mining services	Model Mining Services Contract produced by the Australian Mining Petroleum Law Association (Version 4, 2013)	• Two initial levels of negotiations culminating in good-faith negotiations between the chief executive officers of both parties. • If negotiations fail, the dispute must be referred to mediation. • Once the agreed period for mediation expires, a party may refer the matter to expert determination (where the contract permits) or commence court proceedings.

resolution of the particular dispute. It may be that the issues in dispute require a neutral with specific expertise, be it legal or technical. As the parties may find reaching an agreement as to the identity of the neutral difficult once a dispute arises, it is sensible to ensure that there is an agreed method set out in the contract by which the neutral can be appointed in the absence of agreement by the parties. Energy contracts commonly specify a particular professional institution to undertake the nomination of the neutral on behalf of the parties. Parties should take care in choosing a nominating institution and ensure that that institution will in fact undertake a nominating role. The inclusion in a contract of a body as a nominating authority that does not make appointments could render the relevant contractual clause inoperable.

It is common practice, once the third-party neutral is appointed, for the parties and the neutral to execute an agreement (usually in the form of a tripartite agreement) to govern the relationship between them. This agreement usually:

- identifies the boundaries of the neutral's role and responsibilities;
- defines the issues requiring resolution; and

- sets out the compensation payable by the parties for the services to be rendered by the appointed neutral.

The agreement will also often contain an agreed confidentiality regime to apply to the process.

As mentioned above, most of the ADR processes reviewed in this chapter are non-binding on the parties (sometimes referred to as facilitative, evaluative and advisory ADR processes). The role of the third-party neutral in these processes is to assist the parties towards finding a mutually acceptable resolution to the issues in dispute. The neutral has no power to impose a solution on the parties, though in some processes he or she may be given the power to provide a non-binding view which may be highly persuasive.

In contrast, arbitration and expert determination (also referred to as contractual adjudication) are considered to be binding or determinative forms of ADR. Statutory adjudication, a method of ADR that is at first instance binding on the parties, is considered later in this chapter.

An illustration of a range of ADR methods is set out in Figure 1, from the least adjudicative/binding method (negotiation) to the most adjudicative/ binding method (adjudication).

7.   Facilitative, evaluative and advisory ADR processes

One advantage of non-binding ADR is that, ultimately, the solution reached is not imposed on the parties. Another important advantage is that successful ADR can produce early settlement and hence result in significant cost savings. Therefore, the parties are more likely to assume ownership of the process. In consequence, there is a significantly greater likelihood that the agreed solution will be implemented in practice. While the outcome of ADR processes generally represents a compromise between the parties, a mutually negotiated and agreed solution is less likely to result in either party perceiving itself as the 'loser' in the process.

More broadly, consensus-based processes are seen by some as a tool for societal preservation. For example, in China, there exists a general preference for processes such as mediation. Some have suggested that this is because of the emphasis in Confucian philosophy on the need to preserve harmony in society which, in the context of disputes, means "compromise, yielding, and non-litigiousness".[5] Furthermore, despite challenges implicit in investor-state disputes in the oil and gas industry in Asia, mediation, for example, has increasingly been identified as a preferred method to settle disputes.[6]

Some common examples of non-binding ADR processes are explored below.

---

5   AFM Maniruzzaman, "Resolving International Business and Energy Disputes in Asia – Traditions and Trends", *Transnational Dispute Management*, March 2011, p6.
6   A Jennings, *Oil and Gas Exploration Contracts* (Sweet & Maxwell, 2002) p22.

Figure 1. Illustration of a range of ADR methods, from the least adjudicative/binding method to the most adjudicative/binding method

Informality and autonomy

Negotiation: referral of the dispute to senior management; may be a precursor to other forms of dispute resolution in a tiered resolution process.

Mediation: facilitated negotiation; non-adjudicative but may be court ordered.

Facilitation: similar to mediation (although arguably allows for the facilitator to assume a broader role); often adopted where there are two or more parties.

The parties control the process and determine the outcome.

Conciliation: a more evaluative process; a conciliator can be required to provide parties with advice.

Mini-trial: a structured dispute resolution process; combines conciliation with executive negotiation; intended to expose senior executives to the strengths and flaws within their cases.

Early neutral evaluation and expert appraisal: evaluative ADR processes, intended to aid the parties in assessing the risks where the matter cannot be settled.

Dispute review boards: a panel of impartial experts (typically between one and three) appointed by the parties under the contract.

A third party takes a more active role in assisting the parties to reach a negotiated and agreed solution.

Adjudication: contractual adjudication/expert determination; statutory adjudication arising out of 'construction contracts' in some jurisdictions.

Med-arb: where mediation has not resulted in settlement the mediator assumes the role of the arbitrator and determines the dispute.

The parties lose control and a third party determines the dispute.

Formality and third-party control

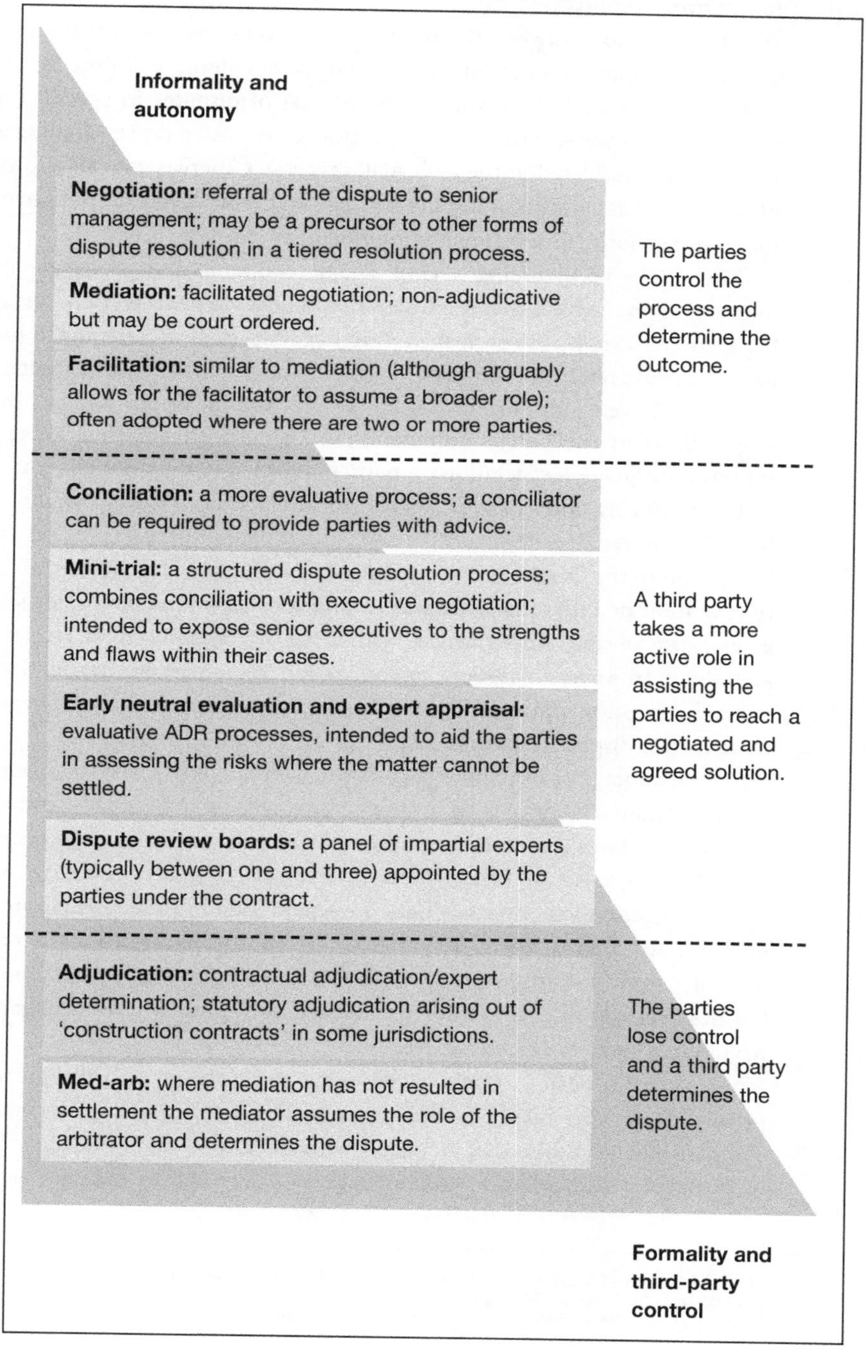

7.1 Negotiation

(a) Key features and issues

Direct negotiation between the parties is most often used as a first step in an escalating dispute resolution clause and is a common feature in energy contracts. It ordinarily consists of the referral of disputes to specified senior management representatives of each party as a single-step process (failing which the dispute is escalated to the next ADR process). Otherwise, it can also consist of subsequent referrals of a dispute through to higher levels of management if initial discussions fail to reach a resolution.

The utility of including a contractual requirement to negotiate can be questioned on the basis that it is a step that is likely to be taken on a consensual basis, in any event. However, including negotiation as a prerequisite to more formal dispute resolution processes can act to circumvent any sensitivity that a party may have to proposing it as an option, due to concerns as to how that may reflect on the party's confidence in its case. In addition, there is an increasingly greater expectation on parties, reflected in the development of pre-action protocols and court processes, to attempt to resolve disputes before initiating proceedings. Notably, in the launch of its Initial Report on Dispute Resolution in the Energy Sector, the International Centre for Energy Arbitration (ICEA)[7] indicated that there was very strong support for mandatory negotiation as an early dispute ADR process, with 83% of respondents in favour of its adoption.[8] However, including an obligation to undertake negotiation in a dispute resolution clause will result in some delay to the commencement of more formal dispute resolution steps.

The advantage of structured negotiation is that it takes the dispute out of the hands of those who have been intimately involved 'at the coalface' and who, as a result, may have entrenched positions with regard to the issues in dispute. As such, the objective of negotiations undertaken at higher levels within the relevant organisations is to facilitate the separation of disputed issues from any emotion attached to them, in order to enable the parties to focus on their mutual commercial interests in resolving the dispute and continuing their business relationship. In order to achieve this purpose, the obligation to negotiate should be non-delegable.

Negotiation ensures that the existence and content of a dispute remain private. It is also relatively inexpensive form of dispute management in comparison with other ADR processes, with suitable levels of flexibility capable of being provided for in a structured clause. However, in order to achieve a

---

7   The ICEA is a joint venture of the Scottish Arbitration Centre and the Centre for Energy, Petroleum and Mineral Law and Policy at the University of Dundee.
8   ICEA, *Dispute resolution in the Energy Sector Initial Report* (2015) p5.

result, negotiation requires the full cooperation and commitment of both parties to the resolution of the dispute.

Negotiation is not generally a binding form of dispute resolution, although it may result in the execution of a binding agreement to reflect the outcome of the parties' discussions. In order to ensure that an agreement to negotiate is contractually binding, there must be no uncertainty as to when the negotiations should be taken to have failed – that is, the clause should provide a set timeframe for negotiations to occur and a clear indication of when the parties will have the right to pursue the next dispute resolution step. In some legal systems, an agreement to negotiate may be regarded as enforceable to some extent and parties can be required to demonstrate that they have engaged in good-faith efforts to settle by negotiation.

(b)   Appropriate use

Negotiation should be kept in mind at all stages of a dispute. However, it is likely to be most effective either at the time the disputed issue first arises (before the parties have formed entrenched views on the matter, so making a commercial settlement potentially easier) or following a mediation or other structured ADR process, which provides the parties with an opportunity to better understand their respective positions (without having been put to the expense of court proceedings). Going through this process can often expose strengths and weaknesses in the parties' positions and provide greater impetus for settlement. At this time, it can also be strategically beneficial to move the negotiations to senior personnel who have not been involved in the matter previously and can view the relevant facts and positions dispassionately.

7.2   Mediation

(a)   Key features and issues

Disputes have been mediated for time immemorial. In more recent times, mediation has become recognised as the ADR "method of choice in the business community".[9] Although it can take many forms, mediation is essentially facilitation by a trained, impartial third party who helps the parties to resolve their dispute.[10] In mediation, the focus is on the parties' interests and objectives, rather than on their strict legal entitlements.[11] Mediation affords parties a high level of control and flexibility over the process, which can be adapted to suit the circumstances of the parties and the dispute.

---

9   AT Martin, *op cit*, p 337.
10 T Sourdin, *Alternative Dispute Resolution* (Thomson Reuters, 5th edn, 2016) p76.
11 See A Redfern and M Hunter, *Law and Practice of International Commercial Arbitration* (Sweet & Maxwell, 4th edn, 2004) p37; R Fisher and W Ury, *Getting to Yes: Negotiating Agreement Without Giving In* (Penguin Books, 1983) pp41–44.

Mediators each have their own approach and no two mediations will be the same. In this regard, it is important to select the appropriate mediator for a particular matter. For example, a mediation may take place in a day or over the course of several weeks; it may involve joint and separate sessions, or expert conclaves (where both parties' experts may meet with the mediator in the absence of the parties); and the parties' legal representatives may be involved. Nevertheless, in general, mediation is a more consensual, less evaluative process than either facilitation or conciliation. The mediator is not usually required to express an opinion as to the issues in dispute (though mediators will often share privately with each party what they see as potential weaknesses in its case); rather, the mediator aids the parties in reaching their own resolution. Although the parties control the process, in some circumstances they may wish the mediator to take on a greater evaluative role. Evaluative mediation – employing a mediator with specific technical expertise to make recommendations (which are not binding, but may provide guidance) – can be an appropriate technique in the context of energy project disputes.

Mediation is used extensively, on a domestic level, in many jurisdictions. It is employed less at an international level – principally as a result of the unregulated nature of the process, which consists, to a large extent, of *ad hoc* procedures that are not globally recognised.[12] In practice, there can be a cultural disconnect between parties to international contracts in their perception and understanding of mediation processes too. Some authors have identified a clash between East and West: whereas western societal norms are principally individualistic, Eastern societies tend to adopt a collectivist approach to life and society.[13] In practical terms, this may play out in the status afforded to, and the use of, ADR at an international level. For example, consensus-based ADR is the preferred method of resolving disputes in many countries in the Middle and Far East and the Asia-Pacific region. And in China, mediation has been a primary method for dispute resolution for centuries, rather than as an 'alternative' to litigation.[14] This is reflected in the incorporation of mediation and other forms of ADR in international contractual dispute resolution clauses in these jurisdictions. In addition, mediation does not share some of the other features of arbitration that make it so popular on an international level, including having in place applicable infrastructure to ensure enforceability of decisions internationally.

That said, mediation practice has started to develop at an international level. In 2014 the ICC issued the ICC Mediation Rules, which replaced the outdated

---

12 P Deane, W von Kumberg, M Leathes, D Masucci, M McIlwrath, L Mooyaart and B Whitney, *Making Mediation Mainstream: A User/Customer Perspective*, http://imimediation.org/making-mediation-mainstream, p2.
13 AFM Maniruzzaman, *op cit*, pp5-6.
14 Legislative instruments providing for mediation-arbitration have been enacted in a significant number of jurisdictions across Asia. See further *ibid*, p18.

2001 Amicable Dispute Resolution Rules and set out parameters for the conduct of mediation proceedings in an attempt to create a holistic approach to dispute resolution techniques. In 2016 the Vienna International Arbitral Centre (VIAC) published the Vienna Mediation Rules, which cover mediation proceedings and arbitration proceedings administered by VIAC. An updated version of the Vienna Mediation Rules was published in January 2018. The European Union has also implemented the Directive on Certain Aspects of Mediation in Civil and Commercial Matters 2008,[15] with the objective of "facilitat[ing]...access to alternative dispute resolution and ... encouraging the use of mediation".[16]

In 2015 the United Nations Commission on International Trade Law (UNCITRAL) Working Group II (Arbitration and Conciliation) asked member states to consider the desirability and feasibility of a New York Convention-style instrument for the cross-border recognition and enforcement of agreements reached through mediation or conciliation. In early 2018 the working group finalised its work in preparing a draft Convention on International Settlement Agreements (resulting from mediation). The draft convention was considered by UNCITRAL at its General Assembly in late June 2018, at which time the General Assembly approved its final form. The General Assembly recommended that the convention, to be known as the Singapore Convention on Mediation, be open for signing as soon as practicable in 2019. As at the date of writing, the final convention has not yet been published. The draft convention states that "each Contracting State shall enforce a settlement agreement in accordance with its rules of procedure and under conditions laid down in this Convention".

A number of other institutions also provide model mediation clauses and guidance, including recommended rules on mediation procedures and administering mediations. Some well-known examples include:

- the Centre for Effective Dispute Resolution and the London Court of International Arbitration in the United Kingdom;
- the International Centre for Dispute Resolution in the United States; and
- the Australian Dispute Centre and the Australian Centre for International Commercial Arbitration in Australia.

These institutions also offer support and administrative facilities for domestic and international mediation.

In light of the above, it is highly likely that mediation practice will continue to develop and that mediation will increasingly be used as a sophisticated ADR procedure to resolve disputes in the energy sector.

---

15   European Parliament and Council, Directive 2008/52/EC of the European Parliament and of the Council of May 21 2008, http://eur-lex.europa.eu/LexUriServ/LexUriServ.do?uri=OJ:L:2008:136:0003:0008:En:PDF.
16   See Article 1. However, the directive has not resulted in the consistent and widespread use of mediation: see G De Palo, L D'Urso, M Trevor, B Branon, R Canessa, B Cawyer and L R Florence, *"Rebooting" the Mediation Directive: Assessing the Limited Impact of Its Implementation and Proposing measures to Increase the number of Mediations in the EU* (European Parliament, Committee on Legal Affairs, 2014).

Typically, any outcome achieved through mediation is not binding unless and until the parties record their agreement in an executed settlement document, which can then be enforced if required.

A mediation may be the first time the parties are exposed to an independent view as to their respective strengths and weaknesses, particularly if they have not been properly advised by their solicitors. In preparing for mediation, the parties may also, for the first time, be forced to turn their minds to the real issues and consider what they can really hope to achieve.

(b)   *Appropriate use*

Mediation is a useful method of dispute management and resolution at any stage throughout the life of a dispute, whether incorporated in a stepped contractual dispute process or agreed to by the parties once a dispute arises. Generally conducted on a without prejudice or confidential basis (noting that privilege is not a recognised concept worldwide), mediation allows the parties to have a free and open dialogue on the issues. It should be considered as an option particularly in circumstances where the monetary value of a dispute does not justify the time and expense of more formal proceedings, or where the parties put a high value on the maintenance of their relationship. When dealing with a counterparty from an Asian or Middle Eastern background, it may also be a culturally sensitive consideration.

In general, mediation is used as a fairly early step in a multi-tiered dispute resolution clause. As such, mediation can often occur before the parties have fully explored and defined the issues in dispute. Similarly, in circumstances of court-ordered mediation, a reference to mediation may occur at the beginning of the dispute resolution process; while in some countries courts direct mediation after pre-trial procedures have been completed, but before the trial preparation has begun. While mediation can be a useful resolution mechanism at this early stage (particularly in relation to less complex disputes), consideration should also be given to the use of mediation at the later stages of a dispute once the parties have a better understanding of their respective positions and the strengths and weakness of their case. This can be a strong impetus for settlement.

Mediation may not be suitable for very complex or technical disputes (often arising in the energy sector) which require both expert technical and legal analysis. While it is possible, as mentioned above, to have a mediator adopt an evaluative role, parties should consider at the outset whether this is likely to be required in order to ensure that they appoint a mediator with the right expertise. More complex matters may require greater involvement by the neutral and parties should consider whether an alternative process (eg, conciliation, expert determination or arbitration) is more appropriate in the circumstances.

Perhaps more importantly, the parties should look for a mediator who has sufficient experience as a mediator (rather than some other dispute processes), who understands the commercial context in which both parties are operating and who has sufficient gravitas to gain the mutual confidence of the parties. This need not be a retired judge, although some retired judges do adapt well to the role of mediator or may be suitable in certain disputes. Experienced mediators can deploy effective techniques to facilitate the parties reaching a settlement that they would be unable to see their way to without guidance.

Similar considerations apply for the procedure to be adopted. Parties should consider what will be appropriate in each circumstance and not necessarily adopt the procedure that they adopted in their last mediation, including whether representation by counsel is necessary, the role of position papers and opening statements, the involvement of experts and the role of clients. Experienced mediators should test the appropriateness of the procedures that the parties may have proposed in pre-mediation conferences.

There may also be a tension between the parties as to whether evidence, including expert reports, must be exchanged before the dispute can be resolved. If a party has a strong evidential position, it may propose the exchange of technical evidence ahead of mediation. On the contrary, a party which has a weak evidential position may propose attending mediation before the exchange of technical evidence, with a view to resolving the dispute before any formal dispute process is commenced. Some parties may not even be prepared to successfully mediate until discovery of some sort has taken place.

The need to properly crystallise the dispute needs to be weighed against the costs involved in these more formal dispute stages. It may also mean that even where an earlier, more exploratory mediation (perhaps required as part of a tiered dispute resolution clause) has been unsuccessful, it can still be productive to consider mediation at a later stage. Given the relatively minor costs of a mediation, it is not prohibitive to consider subsequent mediations.

Mediation has obvious benefits in the energy sector due to the long-term contracts and long-lasting relationships found therein. Many mediations that do not settle 'on the day' settle soon afterwards (or at least sooner afterwards), or result in benefits such as exposing weaknesses, narrowing issues, corralling multiple defendants, ventilating grievances or demonstrating resolve.

7.3 Mediation-arbitration/arbitration-mediation

(a) Key features and issues

Mediation-arbitration (med-arb) and arbitration-mediation (arb-med) offer a halfway house between mediation and arbitration. Med-arb allows the mediator of an unresolved dispute to assume the role of an arbitrator in relation to all or particular issues that remain in dispute between the parties. On the other hand, arb-med allows the arbitrator of an unresolved dispute to assume the role of a mediator in relation to all or particular issues that remain in dispute between the parties. They are referred to collectively as 'med-arb' hereafter.

Med-arb has the advantage of certain procedural and time-related efficiencies, in that it removes any requirement to engage a separate arbitrator in circumstances where the mediation is unsuccessful.

Med-arb has been adopted in consumer, labour and administrative tribunals in, for example, Australia[17] and Canada.[18] It is extensively utilised in China and across other parts of Asia in commercial contexts – and is specifically contemplated in arbitration legislation in Hong Kong, China, Singapore, Japan and India. It is also contemplated in the procedural rules of some of the arbitration and mediation centres in these jurisdictions. However, the adoption of the procedure for the resolution of commercial disputes, including in the energy sector, has been significantly less concerted in western commerce.

This perhaps justifiable apprehensiveness to adopt med-arb is mainly due to concerns that arise from the conflicts inherent in the dual mediator/arbitrator role. This dual role may discourage candour during the course of mediation and inhibit the likelihood that the parties will be able to achieve a mediated outcome of their dispute. The mediator/arbitrator may have previously held private sessions with the parties and could be in possession of confidential or without prejudice information as a result. This also gives rise to questions of procedural fairness – whether the mediator should disclose any knowledge that he or she has, to allow each party to respond – and also to apprehended bias. In some jurisdictions, apparent or actual bias may give rise to grounds to challenge the appointment of an arbitrator.

The potential for bias issues to arise in the context of med-arb was highlighted in *Gao Haiyan v Keeneye Holdings Ltd*.[19] While an arbitration award rendered following a mediation process conducted by the arbitrator was ultimately upheld, some mediation meetings were called into question and were the subject of various rounds of appeal.

In Australia, the uniform domestic Commercial Arbitration Acts deal with the potential issue of (apparent and actual) bias by permitting med-arb and arb-med only in circumstances where provision has been made in the relevant arbitration agreement or where the parties subsequently consent to it. In addition, an arbitrator who has previously acted as a mediator is not permitted to conduct subsequent arbitration proceedings in relation to the same dispute unless all parties consent in writing. Further, the uniform acts provide that the arbitrator (previously the mediator) is under an obligation to disclose to the

---

17   See, for example, Section 27D of the Commercial Arbitration Act 2010 (NSW).
18   See, for example, Section 35 of the Arbitration Act (RSA 2000).
19   [2012] 1 HKLRD 627.

parties all confidential information that the arbitrator considers to be material before the arbitration proceedings commence and which was obtained from one party during mediation proceedings.

While legislative amendments of this nature assist with alleviating concerns of bias, there remains apprehension that parties to a med-arb or med-arb process may withhold important information from the mediator for fear that it be used against them in any arbitral proceedings. This has the unfortunate result of rendering the mediation process itself much less effective. It is also recognised that participation in these processes can provide unsuccessful parties with a potential opportunity to challenge any award on the basis of apprehension of bias or public policy grounds.

(b)   Appropriate use

For the reasons outlined above, the use of med-arb is likely to be met with some resistance by clients (and their lawyers) from common law backgrounds, who are more likely to prefer the engagement of a different arbitrator if a mediation is unsuccessful. Nevertheless, med-arb does provide a number of advantages to participants and may be considered appropriate in a complex dispute if mediation is unsuccessful.

7.4   Facilitation

(a)   Key features and issues

The process of facilitation is in many ways fairly similar to mediation; however, it is characterised by greater flexibility and arguably allows for the facilitator to assume a broader role than is customary for a mediator. While a facilitator, like a mediator, must remain impartial, the level of facilitator intervention in the process may depend on the approach adopted by the particular neutral. Nonetheless, the roles of both facilitators and mediators remain limited to advising on or determining the process, rather than the content, of the discussion.

Some believe that a facilitator has a "much wider contributory role than that permitted to a mediator because of the different dynamics and procedures that apply" to a facilitation.[20] In this regard, facilitation frequently involves more than two parties (such that the requirements of a great number of stakeholders must be considered), and can be employed in a number of different circumstances to identify and define issues for resolution, at which point the facilitation may conclude or alternatively continue further to explore options for reaching a solution.[21] Whereas the intended outcome of a mediation is most

---

20   R Charlton, *Dispute Resolution Guidebook* (Law Book Company Information Services, 2000) p265.
21   *Ibid*, p263; Australian Disputes Centre, Facilitation Overview, www.disputescentre.com.au/facilitation/.

often the resolution of a dispute, the goals of a facilitation may be the resolution of specific problems or the need to accomplish certain tasks.[22] A facilitator's role can extend to setting a programme for fact finding and the holding of meetings, focusing the participants on agreed objectives and, where appropriate, making suggestions as to alternative ways to approach an issue.[23]

(b)   *Appropriate use*

Facilitation should be considered in more complex matters, where several stakeholders are involved and/or a number of steps need to be taken (with guidance provided as to those steps and a timetable for completion), in order for the parties to progress to resolution. It may be appropriate in circumstances where significant fact finding is required to be undertaken in order for the parties to fully appreciate their respective positions and be capable of reaching a settlement.

This form of ADR is less suitable for simple disputes that do not require the time input or more extensive intervention of the appointed neutral.

7.5   Conciliation

In contrast to mediation, conciliation is more often regarded as an evaluative process,[24] in that a conciliator is generally required to provide the parties with advice as to potential options for resolution, their view on the issues in dispute and possible terms of settlement. It is not unusual for a conciliator to possess legal qualifications or have expertise that is relevant to the dispute between the parties.

The role of a conciliator has been described broadly to encompass, among other things:

- the identification of systematic issues giving rise to disputation;
- the power to issue recommendations and directions;
- the assessment of the parties' genuine attempt at settlement; and
- the facilitation of a mutually acceptable agreement.[25]

The process of conciliation is often considered to be less formal than the classical mediation model.[26] The process need not necessarily be governed by a particular set of rules; however, a number of international institutions offer comprehensive procedural rules to assist parties in managing a conciliation. Examples include:

- the UNCITRAL Conciliation Rules 1980;

---

22   Australian Disputes Centre, *op cit.*
23   R Charlton, *op cit*, pp265-266.
24   T Sourdin, *opt cit*, p191.
25   D Bryson, "'And the leopard shall lie down with the kid: a conciliation model for workplace disputes'", *Australian Dispute Resolution Journal*, vol 8, no 4, 1997, pp245-246.
26   D Spencer, *Principles of Dispute Resolution* (Lawbook Co, 2011) p127.

- the UNCITRAL Model Law on International Commercial Mediation and International Settlement Agreements Resulting from Mediation 2018 (which replaced the Model Law on International Commercial Conciliation 2002);[27]
- the Institute of Civil Engineers Mediation/Conciliation Procedure 2012;
- the ICC Mediation Rules 2014 (which may be used for "whatever settlement procedure" the parties consider appropriate); and
- the Institute of Arbitrators and Mediators Australia's Conciliation Rules.

There are significant inconsistencies between the definitions applied to conciliation across jurisdictions, which has led one critic to complain that "nobody is sure what it means".[28] Further, there are differing views as to whether conciliation is becoming an irrelevant or outdated form of ADR. However, another author alludes to a possible resurgence in interest.[29]

(b) Appropriate use

Parties may choose to adopt conciliation in circumstances where it is considered that greater input from the neutral is required. In particular, it may be appropriate in circumstances where the parties consider that a non-binding view expressed by a qualified expert (either technical or legal) neutral would be beneficial in the settlement of their dispute.

It is important, however, that the parties carefully consider the appointment of a conciliator and ensure that they are satisfied with the relevance and level of that person's expertise. Even in circumstances where any opinion or recommendations expressed by the conciliator are non-binding, it will be difficult for a party to resile from the expressed position in any ongoing conciliation or negotiations.

In circumstances where the parties are of the view that a binding outcome is preferable, consideration should also be given to other ADR processes that may be more suitable.

7.6 Mini-trial

(a) Key features and issues

The mini-trial or 'information exchange' is a structured dispute resolution process which combines a form of conciliation with executive negotiations. The purpose of a mini-trial is to expose senior executives to the strengths and the

---

27 In amending the model law, UNCITRAL decided to use the term 'mediation' instead of 'conciliation', in an effort to adapt to the actual and practical use of the terms. This change in terminology has no substantive or conceptual implications.
28 A Speaight QC, "Conciliation – the case against" (speech delivered at the International Conference of the Society of Construction Law, London, 7 October 2008), www.myscl.org/publications_7_1_12.pdf.
29 AFM Maniruzzaman, *op cit*, p10.

flaws in their cases, such that they have an understanding of their likely position should the dispute escalate to litigation.

During a short hearing, the parties' lawyers present a truncated version of their clients' cases to senior representatives of both parties. A third-party neutral chairs the hearing and subsequently assists the party representatives in negotiations to resolve the dispute. The extent of the neutral's role in the process can differ depending on the agreement of the parties. In addition to facilitating the negotiations and encouraging resolution, the neutral may be required to advise on substantive legal issues or to provide the parties with a non-binding opinion as to the likely result should the case go to court. In this respect, the neutral's role is akin to that of a conciliator.

In the main, mini-trial clauses are brief and refer to a particular procedure by which the parties agree to be bound.[30] Although there is some variation between the specificity of requirements, mini-trial procedures generally provide for the following:

- appointment of a neutral adviser or umpire by agreement;
- exchange of documents before the information exchange session, including:
  - written statements summarising the issues;
  - briefs and documents or other exhibits on which the parties intend to rely (and which are also provided to the neutral adviser); and
  - discovery between the parties (the scope of which may be prescribed by the relevant procedure), pursuant to which documents discovered may by agreement be used in subsequent litigation;
- exclusion of the rules of evidence (some rules of privilege may apply);
- the neutral adviser's opinion to address issues of facts and law; and
- legal counsel to present the 'best case' for each side at the settlement session.

Mini-trials are utilised primarily in the United States and Canada, but not commonly in the energy sector.[31]

The most significant advantage of the mini-trial compared to other forms of ADR is the degree of preparation required, which becomes useful if a resolution is not reached.[32] Parties also retain a greater degree of involvement and control over the outcome than in more adjudicative processes; and the hearing affords both parties the opportunity to hear the other's position and to assess the relative strengths and weaknesses of their positions.

---

30   For example, see the model mini-trial clauses drafted by the International Institute for Conflict Prevention and Resolution and the Oslo Chamber of Commerce.
31   A Redfern and M Hunter, *op cit*, p40.
32   Dispute Prevention and Resolution Services Department of Justice, *Dispute Resolution Reference Guide*, (revised edn, 2006), www.justice.gc.ca/eng/rp-pr/csj-sjc/dprs-sprd/res/drrg-mrrc/05.html.

However, there are a number of perceived disadvantages of engaging in a mini-trial process.[33] First, the relatively high costs involved mean that expenditure has been wasted if the parties could have resolved the dispute through mediation. Furthermore, the process of preparation is similar to preparing for a trial and is not focused on cooperation, which may further polarise the parties' positions. Finally, active participation by senior management is often required, which can be a time-consuming and wasteful use of management time in circumstances where progress is slow or commitment by the parties is lacking.

(b)   Appropriate use

Parties may wish to make use of the mini-trial process in circumstances where substantive legal issues are involved or extensive evidence is required to be presented, but they do not wish to undertake a more formal process such as arbitration or litigation. It may also be appropriate in circumstances where limited discovery would be of assistance to the parties in properly understanding their respective cases. As noted, this process exposes the parties' senior executives to the respective strengths and weaknesses of their cases, which can encourage settlement.

However, mini-trials are an expensive and time-consuming method of ADR and may not be appropriate in many cases where parties either do not require or do not wish to be put to the expense of extensive documentary evidence or discovery. It may be that a form of mediation or facilitation is sufficient to resolve the issues in dispute.

7.7   Early neutral evaluation and expert appraisal

(a)   Key features and issues

Early neutral evaluation and expert appraisal are both evaluative ADR processes. While they differ in application, both aid the parties in assessing the risks to which they may be exposed in circumstances where the matter cannot be settled.

Early neutral evaluation has become increasingly popular in recent years, as demonstrated by the provision for early neutral evaluation in the English courts[34] and in the schemes offered by institutions and organisations.[35] It provides for the parties to present their cases, including the evidence on which

---

[33]   Dispute Prevention and Resolution Services Department of Justice, *op cit.*
[34]   Early neutral evaluation is expressly provided for in the Civil Procedure Rules (see Rule 3.1(2)(m)) and is offered in the Chancery Division, Commercial Court and the Technology and Construction Court.
[35]   For example, the Chartered Institute of Arbitrators, the Centre for Effective Dispute Resolution and the London Court of International Arbitration have early neutral evaluation schemes. See also Ashurst, *Quickguides: Early Neutral Evaluation*, www.ashurst.com/en/news-and-insights/legal-updates/early-neutral-evaluation/.

they rely, to a neutral dispute resolution practitioner in an attempt to resolve the dispute before further escalation of the issues. The neutral's role is to evaluate the respective strengths and weaknesses of the parties' positions and to provide an initial non-binding assessment of the potential outcome should the matter become the subject of litigation. The neutral may then assist the parties in formulating a sensible approach to resolution.

Expert appraisal involves a primarily factual investigation by an expert with particular knowledge of the issues in dispute, following which the expert produces an opinion as to the likely position and advises the parties as to the manner by which a desirable outcome might be achieved.[36] It differs from neutral evaluation in that the opinion provided is usually focused on specified issues within the expertise of the practitioner, rather than the entirety of the dispute.[37] The process is similar to an expert determination, although the opinion expressed by the expert is not binding on the parties.

(b) Appropriate use

The effectiveness of these processes depends heavily on the extent of preparation by the parties before presenting their cases. Thorough preparation is required so that the neutral or expert has the necessary information to ensure that any assessment that he or she makes of the likely outcome is meaningful and reflects the actual issues in dispute. As such, neutral evaluation and expert appraisal can be costly methods of ADR (eg, in comparison to mediation).

They may, however, prove useful in circumstances where the parties are deadlocked in relation to a particular issue or dispute. In that case, the provision of an evaluation of the merits from a highly regarded neutral practitioner or expert can be extremely persuasive and may provide a basis on which the parties can move towards resolution.

7.8 Dispute boards

Dispute boards have already gained widespread acceptance in the infrastructure sector, but may have equal application in the construction or operation of energy projects and joint ventures. Generally speaking, there are two distinct types of dispute boards – dispute boards that issue:

- binding determinations (often referred to as 'dispute adjudication boards' or 'dispute resolution boards'); or
- non-binding recommendations (often called 'dispute review boards' or 'dispute advisory boards').

---

36   National Alternative Dispute Resolution Advisory Council, *Dispute Resolution Terms*, www.nadrac.gov.au/
      www/nadrac/nadrac.nsf/Page/What_is_ADRGlossary_of_ADR_Terms#EE.
37   R Charlton, *op cit*, p348.

These terms, however, are often used interchangeably and without regard to the exact powers and function of the board in question (which will be determined by the terms of the relevant contract). Dispute boards may also be standing (in the sense that they play a role throughout the term of the parties' contract) or *ad hoc* (in the sense that they may be brought into existence as and when required by the parties).

A dispute board will generally consist of a panel of between one and three impartial experts that undertakes a dual dispute avoidance and dispute resolution role.[38] While the functions of a dispute board will depend on its powers as agreed between the parties, they commonly include:

- holding regular meetings;
- identifying pressure points;
- offering informal views;
- establishing procedures;
- suggesting solutions;
- conducting informal hearings; and
- making recommendations for the settlement of disputes before they gain momentum.[39]

The primary advantage that arises from the implementation of a dispute board is that it promotes communication. Issues can be dealt with as they arise and the parties can discuss them with an impartial third party. In addition, the effectiveness of the dispute board will turn on the technical expertise that board members maintain, combined with the board's day-to-day familiarity with the project.

Dispute boards are ordinarily comprised of members with diverse expertise, so that they can deal with a wide range of issues. For example, a board may be comprised of a lawyer, an engineer and a quantity surveyor. And unlike 'external' third-party experts, a dispute board's insight and day-to-day familiarity with the project can result in issues being identified at an earlier time and resolved in a more efficient way.

By promoting communication, offering informed views and issuing non-binding recommendations (or determinations), dispute boards can encompass a combination of other ADR processes. They are often engaged with in an attempt to avoid disputes or to assist with the resolution of disputes in alternative ways. To that end, parties should be open to utilising dispute boards in *ad hoc* ways outside of their ordinary role under the relevant contract.

Issues can arise, though, where a dispute board's role is ill defined and where

38 P Loots and D Charrett, *Practical Guide to Engineering and Construction Contracts* (CCH Australia Ltd, 2009) p312.
39 D Jones, *Building and Construction Claims and Disputes* (Construction Publications Pty Ltd, 1996) p159.

the lines are blurred between impartial expert and adviser. The parties may consider that a dispute board which has been involved throughout the course of the project and been privy to without prejudice communications should not finally determine any dispute that is the subject of those communications. Likewise, a dispute board that already has a predisposed view of a matter may be unsuitable to resolve a dispute in respect of it. In short, dispute boards walk a fine line in their dual role and the parties should ensure that this dual role remains clearly delineated as the project and disputes evolve.

Dispute boards are often criticised for being expensive. They no doubt are. However, their expense should be weighed against the prospect of avoiding disputes and resolving those that may arise efficiently. Much will depend upon the nature of the project and the likely issues anticipated. A significant challenge for dispute boards is that there are seldom mechanisms in place to replace or reconstitute them. It is likely that a party which considers that a dispute board frequently takes a different view from its own will become disenfranchised with the process and seek to replace the dispute board or otherwise to seek to avoid using it.

The enforceability of dispute board decisions is also an issue that is largely unsettled internationally. Once obtained, a dispute board decision may be enforced as a binding decision as an expert determination would. However, a dispute board decision, is not final where a notice of dissatisfaction is given within the timeframe provided in the contract.[40] The status of a dispute board decision that is the subject of arbitration or litigation is generally unclear. However, authorities in Singapore have found that a failure to comply with a dispute board decision can be referred to arbitration; but the decision can also be enforced as a standalone award, pending the outcome of the arbitration.[41]

(b)   Appropriate use

Dispute boards are perhaps most effectively used on long-term projects, where the cost of retaining them is proportionate to the project value. They can be applied successfully to resolve technical disputes quickly and efficiently, which allows the project to continue unimpeded. They are generally not appropriate for the resolution of disputes that involve significant legal issues or low-value projects.

Regardless of their form or powers, dispute boards will ultimately be of greatest utility if they are engaged with genuinely by the parties and used to determine disputes as and when they arise. That engagement should always be tempered, however, to allow for the dispute board to perform its ultimate function of providing an impartial determination.

---

40   See, for example, Clause 21 of the FIDIC Silver Book.
41   *PT Perusahaan Gas Negara (Persero) TBK v CRW Joint Operation* [2015] SGCA 30. The courts in South Africa have also held that parties are "obliged to promptly give effect to a decision by a DAB", as this is taken to give effect to the intentions of the parties: see *Tubular Holdings (Pty) Ltd v DBT Technologies (Pty) Ltd* 2014 (1) SA 244 (GSJ).

8. Determinative ADR

8.1 Adjudication

Expert determination or adjudication, one of the most prominent forms of ADR in the energy sector, is examined in another chapter. These processes involve the preparation of relatively brief submissions and a determination by a neutral third party. Statutory adjudication of disputes arising out of a 'construction contract', as defined in the relevant legislation, is in place in the United Kingdom, Singapore and Australia,[42] and is therefore of relevance to energy projects, which frequently involve a construction phase. However, certain construction contracts are excluded from the statutory regime (eg, contracts for drilling for or extracting oil, natural gas or minerals).[43]

The aim of security of payment legislation is to provide statutory rights of adjudication to contractors and subcontractors in relation to disputes relating to non-payment by principals. The policy rationale for the process is the transfer of payment risk up the chain and the alleviation of contractors' cash-flow concerns[44] by ensuring that they are "entitled to receive, and... recover, progress payments promptly".[45]

The relevant statutory processes are highly detailed and, in contrast to contractual adjudication or expert determination, are in no way flexible, in that prescribed timeframes and processes must be complied with. The nature and application of the legislation are outside the scope of this chapter. However, given the potential applicability to the construction phase of certain energy projects undertaken in these jurisdictions, brief mention has been made. Advice should be obtained if parties are intending to operate in these regions.

9. ADR clauses: enforceable or not?

There is some debate as to the enforceability of ADR processes as a part of contractual dispute resolution – that is, whether agreed ADR processes in a multi-tiered dispute resolution clause can be conditions precedent to the taking of the next step.

Although the enforceability of an agreement to participate in ADR will depend on the terms of the contract in question, courts will generally give effect

42 See the Housing Grants, Construction and Regeneration Act 1996 (United Kingdom); the Building and Construction Industry Security of Payment Act 2006 (Singapore); the Building and Construction Industry Security of Payment Act 1999 (NSW); the Building and Construction Industry Security of Payment Act 2002 (Vic); the Building and Construction Industry Payments Act 2004 (Qld); the Building and Construction Industry Security of Payment Act 2009 (Tas); the Building and Construction Industry (Security of Payment) Act 2009 (ACT); and the Building and Construction Industry Security of Payment Act 2009 (SA).

43 See, for example, Section 105 of the Housing Grants, Construction and Regeneration Act 1996 (United Kingdom) and Section 5(2) of the Building and Construction Industry Security of Payment Act 1999 (NSW).

44 D Jones, *Commercial Arbitration in Australia* (Lawbook Co, 2013) p29.

45 *Probuild Constructions (Aust) Pty Ltd v Shade Systems Pty Ltd* (2018) 351 ALR 255 at [36]. See also *Maxcon Constructions Pty Ltd v Vadasz* (2018) 351 ALR 369.

to the terms of the agreement, provided that the terms of the agreement are sufficiently certain.

The issue of whether an agreement to participate in ADR procedures is binding on the parties has arisen in the context of applications to stay proceedings on the basis that the condition precedent to commencing those proceedings had not been achieved. In *Channel Tunnel Group Ltd v Balfour Beatty Construction Ltd*,[46] the House of Lords granted a stay of proceedings that were brought, according to the court, in breach of an agreed method of resolving disputes. Lord Mustill considered that the parties, having negotiated a carefully drafted dispute resolution clause (which provided that, in the first instance, any dispute or difference arising would be referred to a panel of experts before arbitration), should be held to their bargain. The agreed ADR procedure should be followed, no matter whether the parties subsequently found "their chosen method too slow to suit their purpose".[47]

In *Cessnock City Council v Aviation and Leisure Corporation Pty Ltd*, the Supreme Court of New South Wales granted a stay of proceedings that were brought, according to the court, in breach of a binding alternative dispute resolution provision. In this case, Justice Hammerschlag said that: "The starting point is that the parties should be held to their bargain. It is for the party opposing the stay to show good reason why the action should proceed and the onus is a heavy one."[48]

Notwithstanding the apparent willingness of the courts to honour the terms of parties' agreements, courts have also highlighted the need for ADR clauses to be clear and sufficiently certain. In *Tang Chung Wah (aka Alan Tang) v Grant Thornton International Limited*,[49] the English High Court found that the agreement lacked sufficient definition and certainty to constitute enforceable conditions precedent. In this case, the court criticised the agreement as being "too equivocal in terms of the process required and too nebulous in terms of the content of the parties' respective obligations to be given legal effect".[50]

In *Aiton Australia Pty Ltd v Transfield Pty Ltd*,[51] referring to an Australian Law Reform Commission review, the court noted that it considered the following to be applicable to all stages of a dispute resolution clause: "The process established by the clause must be certain. There cannot be stages in the process where agreement is needed on some course of action before the process can proceed because if the parties cannot agree, the clause will amount to an agreement to agree and will not be enforceable due to this inherent uncertainty."[52] In this case, the court considered that the absence of a

---

46   [1993] AC 334.
47   *Ibid* at 353.
48   [2012] NSWSC 221 at [31].
49   [2013] 1 All ER (Comm) 1226.
50   *Ibid* at [72].
51   (1999) 153 FLR 236.
52   *Ibid* at [252].

mechanism for apportioning the mediator's costs (mediation being only the first step in the dispute resolution clause) caused particular difficulties in this regard.

As previously mentioned, the courts may also refuse enforcement of an ADR provision in circumstances where it is found to be against public policy. A dispute resolution clause may be considered to be against public policy in circumstances where it is found to oust the jurisdiction of the court. This issue was considered in the context of an expert determination clause in *Baulderstone Hornibrook Engineering Pty Ltd v Kayah Holding Pty Ltd*.[53] However, the findings regarding ouster were the subject of subsequent criticism in *Straits Exploration (Australia) Pty Ltd v Murchison United NL*,[54] where the clause under consideration was ultimately distinguished from that in *Baulderstone* in that it preserved and potentially widened the court's jurisdiction to review any expert determination.

In addition to the above, the inclusion in project contracts of a requirement to participate in ADR processes 'in good faith' is quite common. The content of such an obligation is the topic of much debate. Nevertheless, good faith as a concept is reflected in the legal norms of many countries, including in Europe, the Middle East and the United States. However, the remedy for breach of such an obligation is unlikely to be more than procedural (eg, an order requiring the parties to attend a meeting) and therefore may be of little value.

The above reinforces the need to ensure absolute clarity in the drafting of multi-tiered dispute resolution clauses in order to ensure both that the parties' intentions are properly reflected and that the clauses are enforceable.

10. Significance of ADR in the energy sector

Increasingly, trends in the energy and resources sector are shaping global economies. The scarcity of resources worldwide, combined with exponential growth in energy consumption, only highlights the importance of current energy projects. These projects are not conducted in a vacuum; they impact on a variety of different stakeholders, with their own interests and agendas, and are frequently of significant political import. In consequence, disputes arising from such projects are many and varied in nature.

Given the complexity and highly technical nature of most energy disputes, litigation and arbitration proceedings can be lengthy, expensive and disruptive – not only to the progression of a project, but also to the underlying business relationships upon which the success of the project lies. Arbitration is an excellent dispute resolution process. It has distinct advantages over litigation, most notably privacy and the enforceability of awards. However, it is generally relatively expensive and time consuming – much like litigation. It is also an

---

53   (1997) 14 BCL 277.
54   (2005) 31 WAR 187.

involved process that is best used after a dispute has crystallised, once positions have been taken and the relevant facts are essentially known to the parties. Save for emergency or expedited arbitrations, arbitration does not allow for the real-time resolution of disputes. It does little to maintain relationships as, despite party autonomy in arbitration, ownership of the resolution of the dispute really passes to the arbitrator/s who determine the legal issues put to them. And while an arbitration should finally determine the dispute between the parties, the parties' relationship may be irrevocably damaged. In addition to the issues that arise from arbitrations, litigation exposes the parties to public scrutiny and can cause concerns with respect to the disclosure of confidential commercial information. Litigation in common law jurisdictions also risks potentially adverse precedent resulting from proceedings between parties.

As a result, ADR as a dispute management and resolution tool is a particularly crucial consideration for energy sector participants. Among the benefits that ADR can provide are increased privacy, greater control over the process and flexibility of procedure, and the ability to choose an ADR mechanism that is relevant to the particular circumstance and the issues in dispute. ADR also provides the parties with an opportunity to select a neutral with relevant energy sector expertise to guide the dispute resolution process. Further, the parties determine the scope of the neutral's role and the extent to which any recommendations or determinations of the neutral will be binding on the parties.

ADR provides participants with the opportunity to manage and resolve disputes before they escalate. This has significant time and cost implications, and can assist parties with the maintenance of critical business relationships without delay to project timelines.

Practical tips from an in-house lawyer's perspective

Rachael Bewsey
Ophir Energy plc

1. Introduction

The significance of the role that in-house counsel can play during international arbitration proceedings is often understated. As the key interface between the company, its representing counsel and external parties, in-house counsel have a major role to play over the course of any dispute. Disputes in the energy industry that proceed to arbitration will often be hotly contested and both parties are likely to have engaged top-quality law firms to represent them. The difference between a successful outcome and an unsuccessful outcome may hinge on small margins.

In-house counsel can play a critical role in ensuring that the company and its representing counsel are as well prepared as possible to commence or defend proceedings, that the proceedings are conducted as efficiently and cost effectively as possible, and that proceedings are conducted on the basis of the company's commercial priorities. External counsel will usually advise on the legal merits of different options and work on presenting the best possible case based on each option. However, it will be in-house counsel's understanding of the company's objectives that will ultimately determine the most appropriate course of action.

This chapter is intended to provide practical tips for energy sector in-house counsel who find themselves performing this crucial role. It follows each stage of the international arbitration process, from drafting the arbitration agreement to dealing with the final award.

2. Setting the stage: the arbitration agreement

It is often the case that in-house counsel in the energy industry will have to deal with disputes arising from contracts that have been drafted many years prior. This will likely mean that the in-house lawyer tasked with managing the dispute will not have been involved with the drafting of the contracts.

Such drafting usually occurs during extensive negotiations which may involve numerous stakeholders, including governments, regulators and multiple parties of different nationalities. In such a scenario, there may have been intensive negotiations around the governing law of the contract; however, the mechanics of any dispute resolution process may have been less closely discussed or even regarded simply as boilerplate, with little or no consideration as to their application. This is often because negotiators of a contract tend to be focused on the positive outcomes of the project or agreement, and consideration of a future dispute will occupy less of their attention.

In-house counsel should ideally have their first opportunity to affect the outcome of any future arbitration at the drafting stage. Where possible, in-house lawyers should take the opportunity during the contract negotiation and drafting to reiterate to the negotiating team the possibility of a dispute during the life of the contract and the importance of drafting the best possible dispute resolution provisions. Armed with a clear understanding of the commercial priorities of the company, the in-house lawyer should be able to assist with the drafting of specific and tailored dispute resolution clauses. For example, limits on the duration, time and cost of arbitrations can be discussed, drafted and agreed to ensure that potential future disputes are conducted as efficiently and cost effectively as the circumstances of the dispute allow. This may include selecting arbitration rules which allow for expedited proceedings in appropriate circumstances or agreeing to the application of evidential rules that place limits on document production (eg, the International Bar Association Rules on the Taking of Evidence in International Arbitration).

If a dispute resolution clause has been drafted to capture clearly and concisely the intentions of the parties in the event of a dispute, then the parties have a reliable basis upon which to proceed with the various stages of the dispute resolution process. This avoids issues arising between the parties regarding the proper procedure or the jurisdiction of the arbitral tribunal to hear certain disputes, which in turn can lead to substantial delays and additional costs in determining the parties' intentions under the contract, even before the formal dispute resolution process begins.

Accordingly, the arbitration agreement in any contract provides in-house counsel with an opportunity at the beginning of a commercial agreement to ensure that the intended dispute resolution process is clear and workable should a dispute arise.

Where in-house counsel do not have this opportunity, the arbitration agreement presents the first point of analysis when seeking to determine the manner and process for resolving a dispute. It may also indicate that certain preliminary issues need to be resolved if the arbitration agreement is unclear or ambiguous.

3.   Initial stages of a dispute

3.1   Relationship dynamic and communication

At the outset, it is important that in-house counsel are aware that a dispute has arisen. In some industries and corporate environments, there may be a perceived tension between the operations or commercial teams and the legal or contract management teams. The objective of the operations or commercial teams will often be to get on with the job and avoid destabilising relationships with parties with whom they will very likely have to continue to work. Informing lawyers of a dispute in many instances will be perceived as a significant escalation of the matter and consequently, in-counsel are not always informed when a dispute initially arises.

Additionally, from the onset of a dispute where operating teams, commercial teams or even senior management are involved, there may be other priorities, such as where an incident involves the health and safety of personnel or equipment. In-house counsel will have to coordinate between these different groups, as well as bringing in external counsel, where appropriate, to assist with the assessment and management of the dispute.

It is therefore vital to have good relationships with all functions in your company so that, in the event of any circumstance affecting the rights and obligations of the company, you are informed sooner rather than later. Creating good rapport and a culture of involving the legal department in the routine activities of the company is something that can be worked on well in advance of the initial stages of a dispute. It is important to stress that early engagement with the legal department will help, not hinder, the progress and resolution of a dispute.

In the energy industry, there are typically multiple parties to the contracts under which a dispute arises, and it is not unusual for a dispute to be brought against the whole joint venture or contractor parties in a PSC regime. Consider the different parties and how they fit into the structure of the contractual arrangement, as well as how these parties fit into the structure of their respective organisations. Importantly, consider how and to what extent they may fit into the dispute resolution process. In the event that there is a dispute involving the joint venture, the operator's in-house counsel will need to take a more managerial role, beyond that of the usual operating and subcommittee levels, ensuring that all parties are focused on the tasks at hand and that appropriate levels of information are shared in order to ensure that both the company's and the joint venture's legal interests are adequately considered and appropriately preserved.

At the outset of a dispute, set up a working team and create clear lines of communication and responsibilities. It is also important to have lines of secure communication with the legal teams of joint venture partners on the same side in a dispute. The parties should be encouraged to direct correspondence through the legal teams of each respective party. A virtual data room for past and future correspondence will also be helpful.

Depending on the terms of the agreement, joint venture partners may also have rights to appoint their own external counsel, so it is worth considering and seeking approval of your choice of counsel (at least from the respective in-house legal teams) early on. However, you should not rush to seek formal approval of your choice of counsel from partners if such approval is not required. Notwithstanding absence of conflict, parties may seek to limit your selection (eg, to exclude firms which work on a regular basis for your company or to encourage you to select counsel with whom they have a specially close relationship, but with whom you have not had material experience). When appointing external counsel on a dispute brought against the joint venture, remember that external counsel will have to carry out conflict checks against all partners in the joint venture. In relation to counsel selection, it is important to consider that the preparation of the case is likely to involve significant interaction with external counsel over what can be a relatively long period (as compared with typical timeframes for a commercial negotiation). You should satisfy yourself that the personal chemistry will work between your team, other internal or joint venture stakeholders and the external law firm.

In some situations, the dispute could be between joint venture partners or between the operator and non-operators. In such cases, it is important to consider how the dispute teams may be compartmentalised in order to allow the operating committee and sub-committee representatives to maintain functioning relationships even while a dispute is ongoing.

Similarly, if a dispute has arisen with a government entity, it is also useful to have a team to deal with the dispute separately from the day-to-day working team to avoid ongoing conflict and escalating tensions.

3.2 Wording of the contract

Once you are aware of a dispute, it is first important to be thoroughly familiar with the contract or contracts to which the dispute relates. It is crucial to ensure that the procedures set out in the dispute resolution clause are followed precisely and in their entirety. If the dispute resolution provisions provide for consultation or mediation as a preliminary step to arbitration, ensure that all such consultation or mediation procedures are followed. It is also extremely important to ensure that all dispute notices are drafted and served in accordance with the terms of the notice provisions, particularly all timeframes provided for in the contract. A failure to follow the procedure could result in serious adverse consequences for the subsequent conduct of the dispute, including potentially being barred from disputing a particular issue at all. Accordingly, in-house counsel should consider the preparation of a schedule or reference guide to ensure that notices and timelines required in the contract are adhered to when a dispute arises.

Additionally, consider whether the dispute resolution clause prevents or allows for other interlocutory remedies, such as injunctions, and whether such remedies should be exercised in court or through a particular arbitral institution. For example, where an aggrieved party wants to stop a particular breach of contract from occurring or continuing, the relevant contract should be consulted to determine the appropriate forum for the interlocutory application. Make sure that when advising on the likelihood of success of such remedies, all obstacles and legal issues are considered fully. Senior management will often assume there is a right to an interlocutory remedy, so it is vital to assess and understand the precise rights of the company early on and manage expectations accordingly.

Where the in-house lawyer is working for the operating company of a joint venture, make sure that the relevant operator responsibilities and limitations on dealing with disputes concerning the joint venture are carefully reviewed. There may be prior approvals or operating committee affirmative votes that are required to authorise the operator to conduct or settle disputes on behalf of the joint venture. In older operating agreements, such clauses are often poorly drafted and lack clear guidance on such issues. Considering the wording of such clauses as well as prompt communication with other members of the joint venture is therefore an important step.

If the dispute resolution procedure provides for arbitration, consider the type of arbitration involved, particularly whether the arbitration is intended to be *ad hoc* or institutional. Arbitration agreements are often drafted based on the relative development of the rules and procedures of the various arbitral institutions. Whereas arbitration agreements drafted prior to 1999 often referred disputes to *ad hoc* arbitration, the current tendency in Southeast Asian oil and gas contracts (for example) is to provide for institutional arbitration, such as under the rules of the Singapore International Arbitration Centre. It is worth taking the time to understand the type of arbitration to which the dispute will be subject, the rules that may apply and the procedure that will be followed. It is likely that internal stakeholders will want to understand the requirements and timeliness associated with the particular procedure; therefore, a 'roadmap' for resolution of the dispute which addresses the basic steps and the time for completion should be prioritised.

3.3 Evaluating the merits of the case

Once the wording of the contract has been analysed, in-house counsel should do a full evaluation of the merits of the dispute and conduct a full risk assessment in order to determine the likelihood of success. Subject to the terms of the dispute resolution provision, the decision to commence arbitration proceedings should in principle be taken only when all avenues for settling the dispute amicably have been explored and exhausted. In-house counsel are usually in a much better position to assess this compared to external lawyers, as they are usually more familiar with the company, its management and their priorities.

When evaluating the merits of a dispute, it is also important to update management regularly on the progress of the process and its costs, and thereby manage the expectations of senior management. Once external counsel are engaged and the arbitration process commences, it is often the case that each side will be more entrenched in its position. This is likely to increase the longer the arbitration process carries on and as the costs of the process continue to mount. While a particular company's inclination and ability to settle a particular dispute will almost always be completely determined by the particular circumstances of the parties and the dispute itself, in-house counsel should remain alert to opportunities to settle the dispute, as set out further below.

3.4 Information control

If not already in place, a management-approved protocol should be established to control the flow of information during proceedings. The protocol should ensure that there is a chain of communication and a clear list of personnel who are involved and who should be updated. In-house counsel will usually be responsible for ensuring that those who need to be informed and involved are adequately updated. Similarly, those who are not required to be involved should not receive information unnecessarily, as managing the information and the discussions occurring within the company during the dispute resolution process overlaps heavily with privilege issues, discussed below.

Setting up a virtual data room for the documents and evidence relating to the dispute can be very helpful. If you have engaged external counsel, they should be able to arrange this for you. This will be useful over the course of arbitration proceedings, such as during disclosure. It will also save a lot of time and expense, as documents can be searched for in one place or location.

Password protect all documents and possibly all correspondence. This is especially important if the dispute is to be dealt with confidentially, as is typically the case with arbitration. This can also minimise the risk of privilege being inadvertently waived.

Similarly, the information control protocol should refer to the use of social media (Facebook, WhatsApp or other messaging platforms) by requiring that no one discuss any aspect of the dispute on social media (at least without prior approval). In particular, WhatsApp messages have become a common form of inter and intra-company communication in some industries and can be very difficult to track. It is imperative that no discussion on any areas of the arbitration occurs over such platforms, unless first approved by counsel and/or management.

3.5 Privilege

Privilege is one of the most important and possibly contentious issues in a dispute. The complexity and continuing development of the law on privilege often mean that non-lawyers (and even some lawyers) do not fully appreciate when privilege applies, when it does not and when it will be deemed to have been waived. Privilege is something that should be kept in mind by in-house counsel at all times, but it becomes vitally important during a dispute, particularly at the very beginning where the lines between what is in dispute and what is not are unclear, and where correspondence between certain personnel dealing with the issue may not attract privilege and subsequently be disclosed during the proceedings. In-house counsel, in conjunction with their representing counsel, should constantly be reminding the company, and if necessary fellow joint venture partners, of how to maintain privilege where necessary and how to ensure that privilege is not inadvertently waived. As a general rule, all substantive communication regarding the issues in dispute should be done through the in-house or external counsel.

There are also some procedures that can be implemented in a company to ensure that privilege is not lost. For example, stress the importance of not documenting opinions about the dispute, especially from those not qualified as lawyers or involved. Additionally, ensure that where possible, in-house counsel instruct, or at the very least are consulted in the instruction of, any kind of expert. Consider also the timing and content of advice that is shared between parties to a dispute. Finally, encourage regular face-to-face meetings or calls, with as little note taking as possible by anyone other than the lawyers who are advising.

As privilege is a notoriously tricky area of law, concise guides on privilege (eg, as in the form of a flowchart or checklist) can be distributed to those involved in the dispute to minimise the risk of privilege being lost. It may also be useful early on to request that external counsel meet with those involved in the dispute to provide training on privilege.

3.6   Preservation of documents

After an initial review of the dispute, all potentially relevant documents need to be located and, if possible, consolidated. It is important to take the lead in managing this process, as outside counsel can only work with the documents they are provided with. There may also be significant cost savings in having the initial process managed in-house as much as possible, rather than having external counsel sift through vast amounts of documentation to extract what is relevant. Depending on the circumstances, however, it may be more cost and resource efficient if the support teams of external counsel manage this.

Additionally, all potentially relevant documents need to be preserved. There should be document preservation and destruction policies in place in the company, reinforcing that all forms of communication and documentation should be preserved where a dispute is likely or has arisen, and must not be destroyed once a dispute has commenced. This overrides any usual commercial practice to destroy documents after a set period. It is important for in-house counsel to ensure timely communication of the need to preserve documents. Failure to do so can lead to criticism and raise suspicions in relation to destruction of evidence.

3.7 Settlement negotiations

At the initial stage, as well as throughout the dispute, in-house counsel should endeavour to find scope for a compromise to be reached between both parties. Settling the dispute has the obvious advantage of being far less expensive in terms of time and cost than pursuing the arbitration through to award. Further, a settlement may also preserve the business relationship between the parties, and allow for the project or enterprise to carry on for the benefit of all involved. As in-house counsel should have a deep understanding of the company – such as the board's general appetite for risk, commercial objectives and priorities – in-house counsel should be constantly alert to the possibility of settling the dispute and heavily involved in any settlement negotiations. In-house counsel should be especially proactive in seeking settlement opportunities on arbitration cases, as unlike many national court litigation systems, arbitration does not build in mediation opportunities.

4. Formal dispute – preparation

4.1 Costs and budgets

Over the course of dispute proceedings, in-house counsel are generally required to manage the dispute resolution budget and report to internal management, joint venture partners and possibly a relevant industry regulator. A company will usually want to recover its expenditure by claiming costs back after (or as part of) an award on the merits. The other side will also usually aim to prevent such costs from being recovered. It is therefore likely that all time recorded will be reviewed and audited thoroughly; accordingly, it is important that all time spent on the matter and other costs such as disbursements or consultant fees incurred by the company are recorded meticulously and specifically. Such costs may also require justification later, so it is good practice to keep detailed narratives of the tasks and why the costs were necessarily incurred.

In a production sharing contract type regime, it is worth setting up a separate time-recording code so as to better justify internal time for joint venture audits. Further, it could also be useful in detailing internal time spent, which may increase the likelihood of being able to claim internal costs in or following an eventual successful award on the merits.

With respect to budgets, in-house counsel will need to have a comprehensive, realistic and up-to-date estimate of all aspects of the costs of the dispute. For example, these will likely include the fees and costs of external counsel, independent experts and the specific costs associated with the arbitration process (eg, hire of a hearing venue, transcribers and interpreters, and even the cost of food and refreshments provided at the venue). Practically, it is a good idea to agree internally, and with representing counsel, certain costs upfront, such as flights and hotel accommodation. This allows expectations of such costs to be managed more easily and updated where necessary. Including a percentage internally for contingency is prudent as costs can often be underestimated, regardless of the best intentions of in-house and external counsel.

Dispute resolution budgets will inevitably change from time to time, due to unexpected issues that may arise during an arbitration. As proceedings progress, either party may adjust its case theory or arbitration strategy in reaction to the arguments put forward by the other side. This may lead to new issues being disputed or interlocutory procedural steps which subsequently increase the time and cost of achieving a final award. Such issues may not have been in the scope of the fees arranged with external counsel at the outset, and the dispute resolution budget should be reviewed and amended if additional procedural issues arise. Ensure monthly invoicing from external counsel and advisers; and have regular discussions around costs in order to assess whether the estimates are still reasonable or should be revisited and adjusted accordingly.

In this respect, in-house counsel can bring to bear cost-saving discipline throughout arbitration proceedings, and may have suggestions on more innovative and cost-saving ways of approaching tasks. When agreeing with external counsel and advisers on the approach and cost of the arbitration proceedings, in-house counsel can play a pivotal role in encouraging innovative solutions to arbitration activities which are traditionally considered to be the most time and cost intensive, such as document review and disclosure.

4.2 Selecting the arbitrator

The process of identifying and nominating an arbitrator is another important step in ensuring the best possible outcome in any arbitration. Different arbitrators will have differing levels of experience, will come from different legal traditions and backgrounds, and will have certain experiences that will inform their approach to the resolution of your dispute. Research on particular arbitrators should include a review of the institutions of which they are members, their professional history and their level of experience in the conduct of international arbitrations. Further, if a tribunal is constituted, the arbitrators will need to interact with each other throughout the proceedings. The amount of influence that arbitrators have on each other will therefore depend on their personality, professional standing and credentials. Candidates' availability is also something which should be considered and they should ideally not be distracted by other matters during crucial periods in the arbitration.

Throughout the nomination and appointment process, in-house counsel should continue to be involved so as to ensure that the arbitrators who are eventually appointed to the tribunal are best suited to understand the intricacies and nuances of the energy industry and the issues in dispute. Similarly, the arbitrators must be of a calibre so as to ensure that all parties will be assured of their professionalism, impartiality and fairness.

In arbitration proceedings, where awards are not publicly available, the reputations of arbitrators will usually come by word of mouth. It is therefore important to engage external counsel with deep exposure to a variety of arbitrators and wide experience of arbitration. Recent efforts by organisations such as Arbitrator Intelligence to increase transparency and accessibility of information in this area are certainly welcome.

4.3   Experts

Start considering the use of an expert as early as possible. Expert evidence in arbitration proceedings, particularly in the energy industry, is often critical in clarifying or interpreting particularly complex or idiosyncratic issues which underlie the dispute. An expert who can clearly and simply explain to the tribunal the technical bases for a party's position may prove to be decisive to the outcome of the award. As with the selection of arbitrators, before expert are selected, they should be assessed on their independence and ability to provide the specific evidence required to assist the tribunal in its understanding and analysis of the facts of the case.

When approaching the selection of an expert, it is important to bear in mind that the personalities of experts and how well they come across when presenting their findings can make a difference in terms of establishing credibility before the tribunal. Having an opinion tested under cross-examination can be challenging and the prospective expert's experience under such circumstances is very important. Keep in mind that sometimes the best technical experts may not react well under such circumstances.

While they must remain independent, experts should also be subject to cost control measures similar to external counsel, such as prior approval of team members and regular cost reviews. If external counsel are managing this, it is important to be updated on the cost and progress that the experts are making during arbitration proceedings. It goes without saying that an expert's remuneration should be in no way dependent on the outcome of the proceedings or performance. A standard hourly-rate fee structure is usually preferable.

4.4   Witnesses

Witness evidence will often be crucial in proving a party's case. A knowledgeable, reliable and presentable witness to the facts, matters and circumstances of the dispute can prove to be an important factor in persuading a tribunal of one party's position over the other.

In-house counsel should keep in mind that witnesses who have the necessary knowledge or background on the matter in dispute may have departed the company, or may be involved in subsequent projects or activities on the other side of the world. Where possible, in-house counsel should attempt to prepare written witness statements as early as possible, or at the very least request from management that these individuals be made available for proceedings even when they have moved on from the company.

For current employees, consider whether they might be open to giving oral evidence at the hearing and be subject to cross-examination. As when considering the right expert, due consideration should be given to whether the employee will be able to present the case effectively under intense and potentially hostile scrutiny. No matter how competent an employee is in the office, the realities and pressure of a hearing mean that he or she may not be suitable as a witness. An employee who becomes flustered or forgetful under cross-examination may undermine the position being taken in the case, or prevent the case from being presented in the best light. Additionally, consider cultural differences which may prevent an employee from being an effective witness. An employee may not wish to give evidence against a national regulator, for example. This assumes an element of choice in who the company presents as fact witnesses. In all cases, it is an important part of external counsel's role to identify witnesses whose evidence is necessary to establish facts that are not capable of proof without such witnesses' participation. In complex disputes, with several issues and involving long time periods of contract performance, parties can mistakenly try to have one witness testify over a range of issues in relation to some of which he or she lacked direct involvement.

The process of witness selection and preparation for hearing may be time intensive, so make sure to allocate enough time. For witnesses who are still employees, ensure that they have sufficient time to prepare their witness statements, away from the pressures and demands of their daily tasks. Ensure that they are available to attend the oral hearings and are available for discussions with representing counsel when required. If reply witness statements are exchanged, this will add a further burden on the witness and further allowances should be made for him or her to adequately prepare a reply.

5.   During arbitration proceedings

After a tribunal has been appointed, there will usually be a preliminary hearing between the parties before the proceedings properly commence. This is to allow the arbitrators an opportunity to meet the parties and to establish the procedure that will be used for the conduct of the arbitration. As this will set in place the procedures for how the arbitration will be conducted, in-house counsel should be actively involved in the process and agree with external counsel a schedule beforehand to propose to the tribunal.

Once the formal arbitration process begins, in-house counsel may be tempted to allow the external counsel representing the company to take over the proceedings. This may be especially true of counsel who come from a more commercial background and are less experienced in the dispute resolution process. It is important, however, for in-house counsel to continue to take an active role in the conduct of the proceedings. It is not unusual that representing counsel will continue to rely on in-house counsel for tactical and strategic decisions which require the company's commercial imperatives to be considered. In-house counsel can contribute to the conduct of proceedings by providing input on how certain points can be effectively put before the tribunal.

When organising the logistics for the hearing, ensure that costs of company attendance at the arbitration (eg, travel, accommodation, food) are documented meticulously. This will assist the tribunal in awarding these costs subsequently.

6.   After the arbitration hearing

The award may take some months to be drafted and delivered to the parties. External counsel should be consulted in order to ensure that internal stakeholders are suitably informed of the likely timeline for receipt of an award and whether the award is expected to be partial or complete.

Once the award has been given, engage with external counsel quickly. In cases where in-house counsel disagree with the award, seek advice as to whether the award can be challenged and consider whether this is a commercial decision requiring input from senior management. In most instances, an arbitral award can be challenged only on very limited grounds. Therefore, similar to preparing for the start of arbitration proceedings, conduct a full and objective evaluation as to the likely success of a challenge, what the company is trying to achieve at the end of the challenge and the estimated costs of the potential challenge.

Finally, consider issues of enforcement of the award regardless of the outcome. In most cases, statistics indicate that the losing party will answer the award voluntarily. Figures of over 90% voluntary compliance are frequently cited. However, where enforcement is required, instructing local counsel in the jurisdiction where the award is sought to be enforced is usually required.

7.   Conclusion

In summary, the role of in-house counsel during any dispute – whether or not formal proceedings are commenced – is pivotal in ensuring that whatever the outcome, the company suffers the least detriment (or extracts the greatest benefit), both financially and reputationally.

The 2017 AIPN Model Dispute Resolution Agreement

M Imad Khan
Jennifer Smith
Hogan Lovells

1. Introduction

Since 1990, the Association of International Petroleum Negotiators (AIPN) has produced model contracts for use in a wide range of agreements related to the international energy industry – joint operating agreements, farmout agreements, gas sales and gas transportation agreements, and liquefied natural gas (LNG) master sales and purchase agreements, to name a few.[1] The AIPN's objective is to create tools "that serve as the starting point for negotiations and significantly decrease the time it takes to finalize a deal".[2] The AIPN forms are widely accepted and used within the industry. This is unsurprising, given that the drafters of these model contracts hail from the AIPN membership, which is comprised of more than 4,000 individuals from more than 110 countries, and includes representatives from host governments, academic institutions, international oil and gas companies, national oil companies and law firm practitioners.

Of the almost 20 AIPN model contracts available, the majority include some form of arbitration clause.[3] However, because the AIPN model contracts were developed over time and by different committees, their approach to arbitration varies. In 2002 the AIPN board of directors recognised the need to provide users with a model for the arbitration agreement itself to reconcile the various approaches.[4] To that end, the board formed a committee to draft a model dispute resolution agreement.[5] The committee produced the 2004 AIPN Model International Dispute Resolution Agreement ('2004 clause'), the goal of which was to facilitate the "fair, speedy, efficient, and cost effective resolution of disputes".[6]

1   AIPN, History, available at www.aipn.org/about-aipn/history/.
2   AIPN, Model Contracts, available at www.aipn.org/model-contracts/.
3   See, for example, AIPN 2002 Model Form Joint Operating Agreement in Oil and Gas Joint Ventures, Article 18; 2006 AIPN Model Contract Gas Sales Agreement, Article 23; 2006 AIPN Model Form International Unitisation and Unit Operating Agreement, Article 20; 2012 AIPN Model Contract Master LNG Sale and Purchase Agreement, Article 15; 2014 AIPN Model Unconventional Resource Operating Agreement, Article 18.
4   2004 Model International Dispute Resolution Agreement, Guidance Notes at 2.
5   *Id.*
6   2017 AIPN Model Dispute Resolution Agreement, Guidance Notes at 2.

While the 2004 AIPN Model International Dispute Resolution Agreement has been lauded as providing "good precedents for international energy agreements and some excellent reference works for drafting dispute resolution clauses",[7] arbitration law and procedure have evolved since 2004. In recent years, arbitral institutions have amended their rules and adopted measures to promote efficiency and to address common concerns in international arbitration. For example, in October 2016 the London Court of International Arbitration (LCIA) adopted new rules on the appointment of emergency and replacement arbitrators. In 2016 and 2017 the Singapore International Arbitration Centre (SIAC), the United Nations Commission on International Trade Law (UNCITRAL) and the International Chamber of Commerce (ICC) released new rules giving parties the option of applying for expedited procedures.

While arbitral institutions were adopting amendments to the arbitral procedure, the AIPN formed a new committee to update the 2004 clause. Over a period of many months, the AIPN drafting committee obtained input from a broad range of international arbitration specialists, transactional lawyers and experts.[8] Their work culminated in the 2017 Model Dispute Resolution Agreement (MDRA), with a greatly expanded menu of alternative and optional provisions designed to address various scenarios encountered by contract negotiators and to provide guidance as to when particular provisions may be appropriate. Along with the 2017 MDRA, the committee produced Guidance Notes containing additional background and explanatory information that detail the circumstances in which some provisions should be considered. The overall objective is to provide negotiators with "maximum flexibility" in drafting the dispute resolution provisions.

The 2017 MDRA is more comprehensive and much heftier than its 2004 predecessor in at least three ways. First, it is prepared in a different format, with greater detail throughout. Second, it contains more detailed notes as to how to apply its provisions. And third, it contains more 'alternative' provisions, with explanations as to when they should be considered for use. Many matters that the 2004 clause left the various sets of arbitration rules to supplement are now delineated in the 2017 MDRA. To borrow a food service metaphor, issues that were formerly part of a 'combo' are now 'a la carte', providing greater flexibility in drafting the clause.

The drafters of the 2017 MDRA undoubtedly recognised that a well-drafted arbitration clause facilitates a more efficient arbitration by reducing the likelihood of litigation and avoiding costly and time-consuming disputes over the clause itself. Indeed, the Guidance Notes to the 2017 MDRA emphasise that

---

7   Tim Martin, *International Dispute Resolution*, Independent Petroleum Assoc of Am 5 (2011).
8   The 2017 committee was chaired by Tim Martin and Jennifer L Price. The 2017 model AIPN clause may be downloaded from the AIPN website at www.aipn.org/forms/store/ProductFormPublic/international-dispute-resolution-agreement.

a clearly drafted arbitration clause is essential to give effect to the parties' intent to use arbitration for dispute resolution and to avoid court intervention.[9]

This chapter explains the application and significance of key components of the 2017 MDRA. Section 2 offers an overview of the various dispute resolution options and alternatives; sections 3 to 8 explore in greater detail the various elements of the model arbitration agreement and expand upon various points that the contracting parties should consider; and section 9 addresses the role of expert determination in international dispute settlement and international arbitration.

2. The 2017 AIPN Model Dispute Resolution Agreement: an overview

The 2017 AIPN Model Dispute Resolution Agreement is designed to be employed in one of four ways:

- a dispute resolution clause incorporated within an international petroleum agreement;
- a standalone master or umbrella dispute resolution agreement to be incorporated by reference in multiple related international petroleum agreements;
- an agreement between the parties as to dispute resolution after a dispute arises; or
- a dispute resolution agreement to be used in other AIPN model contracts in lieu of the clause suggested in the model contract itself.[10]

Parties thus may incorporate the AIPN Model Dispute Resolution Agreement in their contracts before any dispute arises or rely on this model agreement after a dispute arises.

The drafters first provide a fundamental choice between two different approaches to arbitration clauses: the "Basic Model Arbitration Agreement," which is simple and concise and allows parties flexibility in moulding the arbitral process after the arbitration is initiated; and the "Detailed Model Arbitration Agreement", which provides various options and alternatives to tailor the arbitration clause more specifically to the parties' needs at the time of contracting. Both models are part of the 2017 MDRA.

The drafters also provide "Optional Arbitration Provisions" that parties may wish to include in their arbitration clause, such as emergency and expedited arbitration procedures, guidelines for the disclosure of documents and rules for the taking of evidence.[11] Additionally, they offer a multi-step dispute resolution

---

9   2017 AIPN Model Dispute Resolution Agreement, Guidance Notes at 13.
10 2017 AIPN Model Dispute Resolution Agreement, Guidance Notes at 1.
11 These optional provisions additionally address the following topics: interim relief, damages, declaratory relief, costs, fees, interest, other forms of remedies, joinder of parties, consolidation of parallel arbitrations, confidentiality, waiver of sovereign immunity and means of providing notice during the arbitral process. 2017 AIPN Model Dispute Resolution Agreement at 11-18.

framework in which negotiation and/or mediation could occur before the arbitration stage.[12] Many of these optional arbitration provisions are addressed by designated arbitration rules and therefore may not be necessary to include in an arbitration clause; parties, however, may find them useful in *ad hoc* arbitrations or where the designated rules are silent on such topics. The Guidance Notes to the 2017 MDRA should be consulted for further details about these additional model provisions.

3. The AIPN's Basic Model Arbitration Agreement

The AIPN's Basic Model Arbitration Agreement consists of a single paragraph that contains the essential elements of an effective and enforceable international arbitration agreement:

- an express agreement between the parties to submit disputes to arbitration;
- a definition of the scope of the arbitration agreement (ie, the types of disputes that are subject to arbitration);
- designation of the arbitral regime and/or rules that will govern the procedural aspects of the arbitration;
- the seat of the arbitration;
- the language of the arbitration; and
- the number and method of appointing arbitrators.[13]

These short and typically standardised clauses have the benefit of being tried and true, particularly if parties adopt the model clause without change. If the parties intend to have one of the more established arbitral institutions administer the arbitration, the Basic Model Arbitration Agreement should be perfectly sufficient, as designated arbitral rules will provide the necessary details for the arbitral process.[14]

4. The AIPN's Detailed Model Arbitration Agreement

By contrast, the Detailed Model Arbitration Agreement expands upon the Basic Model Arbitration Agreement and provides various alternatives to craft a bespoke arbitration agreement that more specifically addresses the dispute resolution preferences of the parties.[15] The drafters address such issues as multiple contracts, various methods of arbitrator appointment, multi-party arbitrations and arbitrator qualifications.

---

12   *Id* at 18; 2017 AIPN Model Dispute Resolution Agreement, Guidance Notes at 51.
13   See Gary B Born, "International Arbitration and Forum Selection Agreements: Drafting and Enforcing" ¶ 3 (2016) (listing critical elements that must be addressed in most every international arbitration clause); *Nigel Blackaby, J Martin Hunter, Constantine Partasides, Alan Redfern and Hunter on International Arbitration* 96-97 (2015).
14   A number of the AIPN's model contracts utilise a version of this Basic Model Arbitration Agreement. See, for example, 2012 AIPN Model Contract Master LNG Sale and Purchase Agreement, Article 15.2.1.
15   2017 AIPN Model Dispute Resolution Agreement at 5; 2017 AIPN Model Dispute Resolution Agreement, Guidance Notes at 14.

Regardless of which model suits the contract, the parties will need to answer at least four questions before adapting the model to their contract:

- whether the arbitration should be administered or conducted *ad hoc*;
- the legal framework that will govern the arbitration, determined by the seat of the arbitration and the governing law;
- the scope of the arbitration agreement; and
- the selection of arbitrators.

A discussion of these considerations follows.

5.   Administered versus *ad hoc* arbitration

The 2017 MDRA provides model provisions for both administered and *ad hoc* arbitration. The 'administered rules' clause designates an arbitral institution (eg, the International Centre for Dispute Resolution, the ICC or the LCIA)[16] that not only administers the arbitration, but also publishes the arbitration rules that will govern the procedural aspects of the arbitration. The 2017 MDRA's basic administered arbitration clause reads:

Any dispute, claim, or controversy of any nature arising out of or relating to this Agreement, including but not limited to its formation, existence, performance, interpretation, breach, validity, or termination ("Dispute"), shall be resolved by final, binding arbitration [by three arbitrators] [by a sole arbitrator] in accordance with the _____ [designate international arbitration rules] ("_____ Rules"), in _____ [specify language to be used]. The seat of the arbitration shall be _____ [City, Country]. [Judgment on the award may be entered by any court of competent jurisdiction.][17]

The second option is an *ad hoc* (non-administered) rules arbitration, for parties that wish to use an established set of arbitration rules but without administration by a particular arbitral institution. This alternative provides:

Any dispute, claim, or controversy of any nature arising out of or relating to this Agreement, including but not limited to its formation, existence, performance, interpretation, breach, validity, or termination ("Dispute"), shall be resolved by final, binding arbitration [by three arbitrators] [by a sole arbitrator] in accordance with the _____ [designate international ad hoc arbitration rules] ("_____ Rules"), in _____ [specify language to be used]. The [designate arbitral institution] shall be the appointing authority. The seat of the arbitration

---

16   The 2018 Queen Mary Survey reaffirmed that the five most preferred arbitral institutions are the ICC (https://iccwbo.org/about-us/who-we-are/dispute-resolution/), the LCIA (www.lcia.org/), the Hong Kong International Arbitration Centre (www.hkiac.org/), the SIAC (www.siac.org.sg/), and the Arbitration Institute of the Stockholm Chamber of Commerce (www.sccinstitute.com/). 2018 Queen Mary International Arbitration Survey at 2, www.arbitration.qmul.ac.uk/media/arbitration/docs/2018-International-Arbitration-Survey---The-Evolution-of-International-Arbitration-(2).PDF; see 2015 Queen Mary International Arbitration Survey at 2, www.arbitration.qmul.ac.uk/docs/164761.pdf.

17   2017 Model Dispute Resolution Agreement at 4-5.

shall be _____ *[City, Country]. Judgment on the award may be entered by any court of competent jurisdiction.*[18]

Ad hoc arbitrations are conducted under the rules agreed by the parties, which are typically the UNCITRAL or International Institute for Conflict Prevention and Resolution Arbitration Rules. When selecting this alternative clause, it is important that the parties choose not only the rules under which the arbitration shall be conducted, but also the institution that shall serve as the appointing authority for the arbitrators should the parties be unable to agree.

Administered arbitration and *ad hoc* arbitration both have their advantages. Administered arbitration can offer additional predictability and stability because it is governed by institutional procedures, which should enhance the arbitral process by keeping the arbitration (and the arbitrators) on track. For example, institutional administration can assist with deciding which rules apply, the language of the arbitration, the seat of the arbitration, whether and how to consolidate proceedings, challenges to the constitution of the arbitral tribunal, and issues relating to the removal and replacement of arbitrators.[19] Some commentators and practitioners are also of the view that awards rendered under the auspices of a leading arbitral institution carry greater weight in national court enforcement proceedings than an *ad hoc* award.[20]

Administered arbitrations are more prevalent than *ad hoc* arbitrations. According to the 2015 Queen Mary survey, 79% of respondents indicated that their arbitrations over the past five years were administered by arbitral institutions, which is consistent with the same survey's findings for 2006 (73%) and 2008 (86%).[21] Administered arbitrations, however, come at a cost. Because administering arbitration involves supervisory functions, arbitral institutions charge a fee for this service in addition to the fees and expenses of the arbitrators themselves.

Ad hoc arbitrations, on the other hand, can provide more flexibility in shaping the arbitral process to satisfy the needs of the parties at the time of the dispute. In the authors' experience, *ad hoc* arbitrations can run very smoothly, without the need for court intervention, where a strong and experienced arbitral tribunal is empanelled and where sophisticated multinational parties and arbitration counsel are involved. If the parties recognise the need to cooperate in the process to resolve the dispute efficiently and effectively, and are not otherwise incentivised to delay the proceedings, an *ad hoc* arbitration may be appropriate.[22]

---

18   *Id*; 2017 AIPN Model Dispute Resolution Agreement, Guidance Notes at 14.
19   For a more comprehensive description of the types of services provided by arbitral institutions, see Rémy Gerbay, *The Functions of Arbitral Institutions*, 55 Int'l Arb L Lib 55-116 (2016).
20   Gary B Born, "International Arbitration and Forum Selection Agreements: Drafting and Enforcing" ¶ 62 (2010).
21   The 2015 Queen Mary University of London's International Arbitration Survey at 21.
22   *Nigel Blackaby, J Martin Hunter, Constantine Partasides, Alan Redfern and Hunter on International Arbitration* 43 (2015).

Indeed, there are numerous examples of high-profile, high-dollar disputes arising under long-term oil concession agreements that were resolved through *ad hoc* arbitration.[23] *Ad hoc* arbitration may also provide the parties with additional comfort as to the confidential nature of the proceedings, as it involves fewer people. Parties, however, should be aware that some local laws prohibit *ad hoc* arbitration. Chinese law, for example, does not recognise *ad hoc* arbitration: under China's arbitration law, failure to designate an arbitral institution invalidates the arbitration agreement.[24]

There are some perceived disadvantages to *ad hoc* arbitration as well, especially where the parties are represented by persons who lack the requisite expertise to set up the framework for an *ad hoc* arbitration or where the parties fail to cooperate. If an *ad hoc* arbitration lacks pre-established rules and procedures, it may also result in unnecessary delays and increased costs. *Ad hoc* arbitration can also necessitate more court intervention than an administered arbitration – for example, where the parties have difficulty empanelling a tribunal or where a party may be recalcitrant or obstructive. Finally, the discussion regarding arbitrators' fees can be awkward, as parties and their counsel will not wish to upset an arbitrator who is in the position of ultimately determining the outcome of the dispute. While examples of extortionist tactics in fee discussions are rare, they do exist and parties should take this into consideration when turning to *ad hoc* arbitration.

6. Legal framework: seat of arbitration and governing law

In addition to the gateway determination of administered versus *ad hoc*, the two most important decisions in international arbitration are the seat of the arbitration and the choice of governing law; both provide the legal framework for the arbitration. This is true whether the parties adopt the AIPN's Basic Model Arbitration Agreement or its Detailed Model Arbitration Agreement.

Arbitration does not exist in a legal vacuum. It is regulated by a web of laws that govern:

- the merits of the parties' dispute, including the existence, validity, enforceability and interpretation of the parties' contract, as well as the law that governs any non-contractual claim;

---

23   See, for example, *Sapphire Int'l Petroleum Ltd v National Iranian Oil Co*, 13 ICLQ 1011 (1963); *Tx Overseas Petroleum Co v Government of the Libyan Arab Republic*, 17 ILM 3 (1978); *British Petroleum Co (Libya) v Government of the Libyan Republic*, 53 ILR 297 (1979); *Libyan American Oil Company (LIAMCO) v Libyan Arab Republic*, 17 ILM 3 (1978).

24   See Arbitration Law of the People's Republic of China, Decree 31, Arts 16, 18 (31 August 1994). See also Kun Fan, *Arbitration in China: A Legal and Cultural Analysis* 2.2.2(B) (2013). As China is a party to the New York Convention, however, its courts will enforce arbitral awards resulting from *ad hoc* arbitrations conducted outside of China and recognise the validity of the arbitration agreement "on a case by case basis in the event that the laws of the country where the *ad hoc* arbitration was conducted recognized *ad hoc* arbitration". *Id* (internal citation omitted). Hong Kong's Arbitration Ordinance, by contrast, defines 'arbitration' as "any arbitration, whether or not administered by a permanent arbitral institution" [1 June 2011] LN 38 of 2011, Art 2(1).

- the parties' arbitration agreement, including its existence, validity, enforcement and interpretation;
- the arbitral proceeding (ie, the procedural law or *lex arbitri*); and
- the conflict of law rules applicable to selecting each of the three foregoing laws.[25]

These issues inevitably consume the most time and attention in negotiating an arbitration clause.

6.1 The seat of the arbitration

While the choice of seat is less important in determining the framework for the arbitration agreement, it can be very important in establishing the framework for the proceedings and awards. Practically, the arbitral seat dictates the logistical consequences for arbitral proceedings, such as travel options, availability of hearing venues, facilities, translators, court reporters and other services important to the conduct of the arbitration. The seat of arbitration can also affect the willingness of arbitrators to participate. The arbitral seat has greater importance than these practicalities, however, as it also determines the procedural law or the legal framework that governs the arbitral proceedings, as well as the location of the courts that would hear applications relating to the arbitration (eg, challenges to arbitrators, applications to stay concurrent proceedings) and actions to annul or set aside the arbitral award. In short, the arbitral seat has significant legal effect.

The 2017 AIPN Model Dispute Resolution Agreement Guidance Notes list five important ramifications related to the choice of arbitral seat.[26]

First, the place or seat of the arbitration determines the enforceability of the award under the New York Convention, which applies to the recognition and enforcement of foreign arbitral awards and the referral by courts to arbitration.[27] To date, there are 159 parties to the New York Convention.[28] The arbitral seat is usually (but not always) the place where the arbitral award will be 'made' for the purposes of the New York Convention, which has significant legal consequences for the enforceability of an arbitral award outside the country in which it was rendered. If a state is a party to the New York Convention, awards issued within its territory will generally be subject to the convention's pro-enforcement rules in other contracting states. However, if the state where the award is issued is not a party to this convention, the award may well not enjoy

---

25   Born, *International Commercial Arbitration* 2618 (2014).
26   AIPN Model Dispute Resolution Agreement, Guidance Notes at 28–29.
27   Convention on the Recognition and Enforcement of Foreign Arbitral Awards, 10 June 1985, 330 UNTS 3.
28   A list of the contracting states to the New York Convention is available at www.newyorkconvention.org/countries. The Queen Mary Survey noted that the five most preferred and widely used seats are London, Paris, Hong Kong, Singapore and Geneva. See 2018 Queen Mary International Arbitration Survey at 2.

its many benefits; instead, such awards will be subject to domestic arbitration laws when enforced abroad.[29]

Second, the place of the arbitration determines where the arbitral award can be set aside. National courts of the seat of the arbitration are usually the only place with jurisdiction to annul or set aside an international arbitral award. This is because the extent of judicial review of an arbitral award is considered to be primarily a matter of national law. Therefore, selecting a seat of the arbitration with the desired level of judicial review is an important consideration.[30] Most national arbitration statutes treat international arbitral awards as binding, with *res judicata* effect.[31] Indeed, the UNCITRAL Model Law, which has been adopted in 80 states and in a total of 111 jurisdictions, provides for the presumptive validity of international arbitral awards.[32] Other jurisdictions that have not adopted the UNCITRAL Model Law, such as the United States, also have national laws that show great deference to arbitral awards.[33]

Third, because the law of the seat normally determines the national arbitration law governing the arbitration proceedings – *lex loci arbitri* – parties should be careful to select a site for arbitration that has a developed law on arbitration, along with a judiciary that respects and promotes the right to arbitrate disputes. In other words, the seat of the arbitration should have both national arbitration legislation in place and courts that have demonstrated that they are supportive of international arbitration.[34]

This is important because the national courts are sometimes requested or required to intervene in aid of arbitration. Procedural concerns relating to the selection, qualifications and removal of arbitrators may be heard by the courts. Similarly, disputes over the extent of the arbitrators' power to order provisional measures, order disclosure of documents or resolve jurisdictional disputes may end up in court. Even issues related to choice and conduct of counsel in an arbitration may be addressed by the national courts. Thus, selecting a seat whose national legislation and judiciary support and facilitate the arbitral process is essential.[35]

Fourth, it is generally understood that the parties acquiesce to personal jurisdiction in the chosen seat's national courts for purposes of judicial actions related to the arbitration, including requests for interim relief from the courts

---

29   Born, *International Commercial Arbitration* 2055 (2014).
30   *Id* at 2056.
31   See International Law Association, *Interim Report: Res Judicata and Arbitration* (2004) (discussing the application of the principle of *res judicata* in various jurisdictions including English common law, US common law and European civil law).
32   UNCITRAL Model Law on International Commercial Arbitration, Article 34. For the current status of the UNCITRAL Model Law, see www.uncitral.org/uncitral/en/uncitral_texts/arbitration/1985Model_arbitration_status.html.
33   *First Options of Chicago, Inc v Kaplan*, 514 US 938, 943 (1995) (interpreting the Federal Arbitration Act adopted in 1925, before the UNCITRAL Model Law was adopted in 1985).
34   Born, *International Commercial Arbitration* at 2055.
35   *Id* at 2055-56.

in aid of arbitration. Availability of such judicial assistance to support arbitral proceedings is yet another consideration that should be factored into the choice of the seat of the arbitration.

Fifth, selecting a seat may result in the waiver by a host state or state-owned company of its sovereign immunity for purposes of the jurisdiction of the courts at the seat.

In addition to the considerations outlined above, parties frequently insist that the arbitral seat be 'neutral' – that is, the home jurisdiction of neither party.[36] Parties understandably do not want their counterparty's national courts to be responsible for overseeing the arbitral process or for considering annulment applications. As the AIPN Guidance Notes point out, this is especially true in the oil and gas industry, where parties may "display a degree of skepticism about choices of jurisdictions of the opposing parties".[37] Parties to international oil and gas contracts generally designate a neutral seat, if for no other reason than to avoid the perception that there is any tactical advantage in the arbitral process or enforcement of the resulting arbitral award.

It is always prudent to check the restrictions, if any, of the national arbitration law of the chosen seat before finalising the arbitration agreement. There have been instances, for example, where a party has been unpleasantly surprised to learn, after a dispute arose, that the national laws of the seat mandate the nationality, gender or religious affiliation of the arbitrators. Historically, there were a number of examples of this type of restrictive arbitration legislation, from Saudi Arabia to Ecuador.[38] While many of these types of laws have been repealed and replaced with laws preserving a party's right to appoint an arbitrator of its choice, other nuances within such legislation may be equally undesirable. The United Arab Emirates' 2016 amendment to its arbitration law underscored the need for such a review. Although the UAE courts have generally been perceived as supportive of international arbitration, legislation adopted in 2016 raised the potential for criminal liability of arbitrators in some circumstances.[39] This, in turn, prompted some arbitrators to decline appointments in UAE-seated arbitrations. Recently, however, the UAE again amended its law to exclude arbitrators from the scope of its application, thereby removing any criminal liability for arbitrators.[40]

While the seat of the arbitration is important and should be given much consideration, the drafting of this aspect of the arbitration clause is quite

---

36 Julian DM Lew, *Achieving the Dream: Autonomous Arbitration*, 22 Arb Int'l 179, 180 (2006) ("In every international arbitration, parties and arbitrators are invariably from different jurisdictions. The place of arbitration is frequently selected as a neutral country").
37 AIPN Model Dispute Resolution Agreement, Guidance Notes at 29.
38 Implementing Regulations of the Arbitration Law, Royal Decree 7/2021/M of 09/08/1405H, 27 May 1985, §3 (Saudi Arabia); General Organic Code of Processes, Article 127 (Ecuador).
39 Federal Decree Law 7/2016, Article 257.
40 Federal Decree by Law 24/2018.

simple. The AIPN Basic Model Arbitration Agreement suggests the following straightforward language: "The seat of arbitration shall be _____ [City, Country]." The AIPN Detailed Model Arbitration Agreement suggests the following language[41]:

> Unless otherwise agreed by all Parties to the Dispute, the seat of arbitration shall be _____ [City, Country]. If the Parties agree [or the Tribunal/Arbitrator orders], [the Tribunal/Arbitrator] may hold hearings in other locations without changing the seat of arbitration.

This additional language permits the parties (or the tribunal itself), after a dispute has arisen, to select a location for the hearings different from the legal seat. In practice, this can happen with some frequency and depends on the circumstances of the case (eg, the location of work site, witnesses, counsel or tribunal). Changing the hearing location can reduce the cost burden and time expended on resolving the parties' dispute, without changing the application of the national laws of the seat to the proceedings.

6.2 Governing law

Because parties that enter into arbitration agreements desire enhanced certainty and predictability concerning their legal rights, they will generally agree upon the applicable substantive law that governs the merits of the parties' dispute.[42] Absent such agreement, arbitrators possess broad powers to select, interpret and apply choice-of-law rules in determining the applicable substantive law.[43] This power of the arbitral tribunal is limited, however, where parties have expressly chosen the law applicable to the merits of the dispute. International arbitration conventions, national laws and institutional arbitration rules unequivocally affirm and give effect to the parties' freedom to select the substantive law that governs the underlying contract.[44]

As noted in the 2017 AIPN Model Dispute Resolution Agreement's Guidance Notes, "[t]he choice of law is very important because it may affect the

---

41 2017 AIPN Model Dispute Resolution Agreement at 10.

42 According to a survey conducted by the ICC, in its cases filed in 2012, the contracts at issue contained choice-of-law clauses in 88% of cases (84% in 2011). ICC, *2012 Statistical Report*, 24(1) ICC Ct Bull 5, 13 (2013).

43 Marc Blessing, *Choice of Substantive Law in International Arbitration*, 14 J Int'l Arb 39 (1997). This deference to the tribunal is recognised by arbitration rules such as the 2010 UNCITRAL Rules, Article 35(1), and ICC Rules, Article 21(1); international conventions such as the European Convention on International Commercial Arbitration, Article VII(i), ratified by 31 states; and the UNCITRAL Model Law, Article 28, which has been adopted in 76 states and by 107 jurisdictions.

44 See Permanent Bureau, Hague Conference on Private International Law, *Consolidated Version of Preparatory Work Leading to the Draft Hague Principles on the Choice of Law in International Contracts*, Preamble ¶ 1 (October 2012) (affirming the importance of the principle of party autonomy on the choice of law in international contracts); International Centre for the Settlement of Investment Disputes (ICSID) Convention, Article 42 ("[t]he Tribunal shall decide a dispute in accordance with such rules of law as may be agreed by the parties"); UNCITRAL Rules, Article 35(1) (providing that "tribunal[s] shall apply the rules of law designated by the parties as applicable to the substance of the dispute"); ICC Rules, Article 21(1) ("[t]he parties shall be free to agree upon the rules of law to be applied by the Arbitral Tribunal to the merits of the dispute").

enforceability of certain contractual provisions, provide some unintended benefit or remedy, or allocate legal duties and responsibilities in a manner significantly different than another jurisdiction".[45] The governing law clause should be separated from the dispute resolution clause, to ensure that there is no ambiguity between the substantive law that governs the parties' duties and obligations under the contract and the procedural law that governs the arbitral process. If the parties intend the same law to apply to both the underlying contract and the dispute resolution clause, this too should be clearly stated in the contract. This is important because the arbitration agreement in a contract is separable from the underlying agreement, and therefore a governing law clause that does not explicitly apply to the arbitration agreement may not be considered applicable to the arbitral process.

The 2017 AIPN Model Dispute Resolution Agreement provides two alternatives for the governing law clause: a 'standard governing law' clause, and a 'consistent with international law' clause.[46] The 'standard governing law' clause provides:

The substantive laws of _____ [designate state/country], exclusive of any conflicts of laws rules that could require the application of any other law, shall apply to the determination of [disputes, claims, or controversies of any nature arising out of or relating to this Agreement, including but not limited to its formation, existence, performance, interpretation, breach, validity, or termination] [Disputes (as defined in this Agreement)] between or among the Parties.

The 'consistent with international law' clause provides:

The substantive laws of _____ [designate state/country], to the extent consistent with international law, as defined in Article 38 of the Statute of the International Court of Justice and exclusive of any conflicts of law rules that could require application of any other law, shall apply to the determination of [disputes, claims, or controversies of any nature arising out of or relating to this Agreement, including but not limited to its formation, existence, performance, interpretation, breach, validity, or termination] [Disputes (as defined in this Agreement)] between or among the Parties. To the extent the laws of _____ [designate state/country] are not consistent with international law, then general principles of international law shall prevail.

These alternatives have much in common: they both apply the laws of the selected jurisdiction, provide an opportunity to refine the term 'dispute' (ie, the scope of the agreement), and exclude the provisions of the selected jurisdiction that relate to conflicts of law. This conflicts-of-law exclusion prevents the conflicts rules of the selected jurisdiction from applying the law of another jurisdiction.[47]

However, the alternatives differ in one significant way. The 'consistent with international law' phrase applies the law of the selected jurisdiction, but only

---

45   2017 AIPN Model Dispute Resolution Agreement, Guidance Notes at 4.
46   *Id.*
47   *Id* at 3.

"to the extent consistent with international law, as defined in Article 38 of the Statute of the International Court of Justice".[48] Article 38(1) of the Statute of the International Court of Justice is "widely recognized as the most authoritative statement as to the sources of international law" and codifies three main sources of international law: treaty, customary international law and general principles of international law.[49]

Practitioners most frequently select the 'standard governing law' clause where the contracting parties are not affiliated with a sovereign. If contracting with a state-owned entity, however, it may be preferable to utilise the 'consistent with international law' alternative. In many countries, state-owned enterprises play a key role in strategically important sectors such as energy and utilities, and frequently partner with foreign companies in the form of business agreements. Many state parties may prefer or even be legally required to choose the law of their country as the law applicable to the underlying agreement.[50] In such cases, a provision that applies to the law of the state party "to the extent it is consistent with international law" can guarantee non-state parties some recourse to legal protections beyond those afforded by the law of the party state. In other words, it provides the private party, which may have little negotiating leverage with regard to the choice of a set of national laws other than those of the state party, with an additional layer of legal protection pursuant to rules of international law.

Use of the 'consistent with international law' alternative is designed to limit the application of the substantive law agreed upon between the parties by requiring that the governing substantive law, at a minimum, also be consistent with treaty law, rules of customary international law and general principles of international law. At the same time, where the governing law is not consistent with international law, general principles of international law shall prevail.[51]

General principles of international law "have been understood as general rules on which there is international consensus to consider them as universal standards and rules of conduct that must always be applied and which, in the opinion of important commentators, are rules of law on which the legal systems of the States are based".[52] For example, in the *Chorzow Factory* case of 1928,

---

48   2017 AIPN Model Dispute Resolution Agreement at 4.
49   See Malcolm Shaw, *International Law* 54-86 (2009); Vaughan Lowe, *International Law* 36-53 (2011).
50   2017 AIPN Model Dispute Resolution Agreement, Guidance Notes at 5.
51   2017 AIPN Model Dispute Resolution Agreement at I(B). Notably, this clause differs slightly from the 'consistent with international law' clause found in the 2012 AIPN Model International Joint Operating Agreement, which suggests the following alternative language for the applicable law clause:
       The laws of _____, to the extent consistent with international law, shall govern this Agreement for all purposes. To the extent the laws of _____ are not consistent with international law, then international law shall prevail.
52   *Inceysa Vallisoletana SL v Republic of El Salvador*, ICSID Case ARB/03/26, Award, 2 August 2006 ¶¶ 226-227; see also Vaughan Lowe, *International Law* 36-53 (2011). General principles of international law are well-recognised principles across legal systems, determined "through a process of comparative law whereby features common to domestic legal systems are established. Although formally equivalent to treaty and custom, they are frequently used to fill gaps left by these two sources". Christoph Schreuer *et al*, *ICSID Convention: A* 607-608 (2009).

which concerned the seizure of a nitrate factory, the Permanent Court of International Justice held as a matter of general principles of international law that "any breach of an engagement involves an obligation to make reparation".[53] Other examples of general principles of international law include the probative value of indirect evidence and the principle of estoppel.[54]

If practitioners wish to include treaty law and customary international law – rules of international law to be deduced by examining consistent and widespread state practice[55] – and give arbitral tribunals the broadest base of law upon which to draw, it is advisable to use the following language:

To the extent the laws of _____ [designate state/country] are not consistent with international law, then principles of international law shall prevail.

7.   Defining the scope of the dispute to be arbitrated

Parties will also need to determine which disputes the agreement will cover. The 2017 MDRA provides three alternative provisions:

- The first definition of scope applies to disputes arising under a single contract;
- The second is a master dispute resolution agreement to apply to disputes arising under any of a set of related agreements; and
- The third applies to disputes that arise after an agreement is made.[56]

The second alternative builds on the language of the first, which reads: "'Dispute' means any dispute, claim, or controversy of any nature arising out of or relating to this Agreement, including but not limited to its formation, existence, validity, interpretation, performance, breach, or termination."[57] Drafting international arbitration clauses this broadly is recommended if the intent is to encompass all disputes with any connection with the parties' dealings. Courts interpret broad-form arbitration clauses in states that are supportive of arbitration as covering all disputes with a plausible factual relation

---

53   *Factory at Chorzow (Germany v Poland)*, Merits, 1928 PCIJ (ser A) No 17, at 29 (13 September); see also Shaw at 79.
54   *Corfu Channel (UK v Albania)*, Merits, 1949 ICJ 4, at 18 (9 April) (discussing probative value of indirect evidence); Ian Brownlie, *Principles of Public International Law* 638 (1979) (finding that there is "considerable weight of authority support[ing] the view that estoppel is a general principle of international law").
55   See *Military and Paramilitary Activities (Nicar v US)*, Judgment, 1986 ICJ at p 98 (27 June). Likewise, in *Kuwait v Iran*, the UN Compensation Commission held that environmental loss suffered by a state occasioned by the acts of another state is compensable as a matter of custom. "Criteria for additional Categories of Claims", UN Compensation Commission, Governing Council, 5th Session ¶ 35 at 8, UN Doc S/AC.26/1991/7/Rev.1 (1992). Other principles include the precautionary principle of sustainable development, stakeholders' participation and partnership; and the duty to conduct comprehensive environmental impact assessment. See *Responsibilities and Obligations of States Sponsoring Persons and Entities with Respect to Activities in the Area*, International Tribunal for the Law of the Sea, Advisory Opinion of 1 February 2011 at ¶ 135.
56   2017 AIPN Model Dispute Resolution Agreement at 5–6.
57   *Id* at 5.
58   See *Mitsubishi Motors Corp v Soler Chrysler-Plymouth, Inc*, 473 US 614, 624 (1985).

to the parties' agreement or dealing; therefore, disputes touching upon matters covered by the contract fall within the scope of a broad-form arbitration clause.[58]

8. Arbitrator selection

8.1 Number of arbitrators

Determining whether one or three arbitrators is appropriate involves three primary considerations: cost, time and confidence.[59] While multiple arbitrators may increase the arbitration's cost and duration, it is more common to opt for three arbitrators in disputes with a significant monetary value. Parties' confidence in the arbitration's binding result can be bolstered due to the perception that three arbitrators will correct for biases or prevent mistakes that may occur with a sole arbitrator's decision. Diversity of experience, training and nationality can also lead to a more robust assessment of the evidence. In addition, with a sole arbitrator, the parties do not typically have a role (or at least not as great of a role) in the selection of the tribunal.

Although some commentators promote the benefits of a sole arbitrator, a three-arbitrator tribunal is generally preferable, especially because either the process to select one arbitrator may prove difficult or parties may lose faith in the arbitral process if a sole arbitrator is imposed by an appointing authority. The value of a three-member tribunal is particularly important in energy-sector arbitrations, given the high dollar amount that is typically in dispute.[60] And notably, a recent LCIA *Cost and Duration: 2013-2016* report determined that it is the complexity of the case, and not the number of arbitrators, that increases costs and length.[61] Of course, many considerations will influence the decision as to the number of arbitrators – speed, cost and diversity, to name a few – and will require careful thought.

8.2 Appointment of arbitrators

Although arbitration rules generally provide for a method of appointing arbitrators, the 2017 MDRA provides alternatives for the parties to specify their

---

59 2017 AIPN Model Dispute Resolution Agreement at 7. The 2017 AIPN Model Dispute Resolution Agreement presents another alternative: the parties agree initially on one or three arbitrators, but retain the option to reconsider their mutual decision after a dispute arises. Another alternative is for the parties to decide on the number of arbitrators based on the value in dispute. Because parties frequently disagree on the value of the dispute, this alternative provides that the arbitral institution or appointing authority shall make that determination if the parties cannot agree.

60 For disagreement with this perspective, however, see Jennifer Kirby, "With Arbitrators, Less Can be More: Why the Conventional Wisdom on the Benefits of having Three Arbitrators may be Overrated", 26 J Int'l Arb 337 – 355 (2009); see also Jan Paulsson, "Moral Hazard in International Dispute Resolution", 25 ICSID Rev 339, 348 (2010) ("The original concept that legitimates arbitration is that of an arbitrator in whom both parties have confidence. Why would any party have confidence in an arbitrator selected by its unloved opponent?").

61 LCIA, *Costs and Duration: 2013-2016* at 3, 7 (2017).

own method of appointment.[62] If the parties have agreed to select three arbitrators, the MDRA clause provides that each party shall nominate an arbitrator and those arbitrators shall nominate a third arbitrator.[63] If the party-selected arbitrators fail to do so, the arbitral institution or appointing authority shall appoint the third member.[64]

With regard to specific qualities possessed by the arbitrators, most of the major sets of arbitration rules already require that arbitrators be suitably qualified and of a nationality different from that of either party.[65] Should the parties wish to stipulate to these requirements separately, the 2017 MDRA provides two alternatives.[66] Both alternatives share the following language: "Arbitrators shall be qualified by education, training, or experience to resolve matters in the nature of the Dispute. The Arbitrators shall be fluent in the language(s) of the arbitration."[67] The MDRA alternatives differ only in that the first applies the nationality rule to a sole arbitrator and the second applies it to a panel.[68]

9. Expert determination

The 2017 MDRA also provides suggested language for an 'expert determination' clause, whereby some specific issues will be referred to an independent third-party expert for resolution. The expert determination process is best suited to resolve discrete and well-defined types of disputes, such as technical, accounting, valuation, oil and gas reserve estimates, and construction evaluations. Used this way, expert determination can be a management tool to clarify the origin and root of disagreements by focusing the parties' attention on key issues, allowing them to avoid further disputes.[69]

The value of an expert determination is in its relative low cost and speed, resulting from the deep knowledge of the particular issue that the decision-maker brings to the table.[70] Another advantage is the flexibility that the expert typically has with regard to the methods for obtaining the information needed to make the determination.

The disadvantage of the process is that an expert's decision is not enforceable in the same way as an arbitral award. The determination of an expert is considered binding only as a matter of contract and must be enforced

---

62   2017 AIPN Model Dispute Resolution Agreement at 9.
63   *Id*.
64   *Id*. If there are more than two parties, the 2017 AIPN Model Dispute Resolution Agreement provides that all claimants together shall nominate one arbitrator and all respondents together shall nominate one arbitrator.
65   2017 AIPN Model Dispute Resolution Agreement, Guidance Notes at 24.
66   2017 AIPN Model Dispute Resolution Agreement at 9–10.
67   *Id*.
68   *Id*.
69   Jean-François Guillemin, *Reasons for Choosing Alternative Dispute Resolution*, in Jean-Claude Goldsmith *et al*, *ADR in Business: Practice and Issues across Countries and Cultures* I 21, 37-38 (2006).
70   Julian Lew *et al*, *Comparative International Commercial Arbitration* 1-34 (2003).

as a breach of contract where the determination is not carried out voluntarily.[71] Another disadvantage is that side disputes can and often do arise as to the expert's 'jurisdiction' and the scope of the issues that the parties intended for the expert to resolve. In short, while the clause is usually intended to save the parties money and time, in practice, once disputes arise they rarely fit into the nice, neat 'issue bucket' that the drafters envisioned. Instead of streamlining the resolution, the parties can inadvertently end up in a quagmire, arguing about what issues should be resolved by whom and in what forum.

The AIPN committee, recognising these limitations, recommends that if an expert determination provision is desired, "extreme care in defining the issues subject to expert determination" should be taken.[72] The difficulty in defining the scope of expert determination is particularly tricky at the time of contracting, as it is often difficult to predict the nature of specific disputes and their amenability to expert determination.

The AIPN committee recommends that the scope be appropriately limited both by precise description in the clause and by reference to the particular contract clauses. Precisely defining the scope of issues subject to expert determination can also help to avoid any jurisdictional battles relating to the authority of the expert to resolve a dispute.[73]

The AIPN drafting committee correctly cautions that expert determination is independent of and not a substitute for arbitration or court proceedings.[74] Even if the parties choose to submit some issues for expert determination, it is important that the contract also includes a dispute resolution clause – whether the chosen forum is arbitration or court – as further legal proceedings may be necessary to enforce the expert's decision. It is also most likely the case that an expert determination process will not be appropriate to resolve all of the possible disputes that may arise under the contract. Thus, a separate dispute resolution clause is also recommended to govern those issues not to be dealt with through expert determination.

---

71   As the 2017 AIPN Model Dispute Resolution Agreement notes: "Expert Determination is independent of arbitration and other alternative dispute resolution processes. Unlike an arbitration award, an expert determination is not directly enforceable in the courts of foreign jurisdictions. The decision of an expert is only binding contractually." 2017 AIPN Model Dispute Resolution Agreement at 21.

72   *Id.*

73   The 2012 AIPN Model Contract Master LNG Sale and Purchase Agreement is a good example of an expert determination clause that could benefit from a more precise definition as to those issues which are to go to an expert for resolution and those which are meant for the courts or arbitration. As drafted, 'expert' in the Model LNG SPA is defined only as "an independent expert appointed pursuant to Article 15.4 to resolve a Dispute of a technical nature". If using the Model LNG SPA, the parties should consider defining more concretely and narrowly the types of 'technical' disputes intended to be captured (or refer to specific contractual clauses that might be implicated). Similarly, the AIPN Model Form International Unitisation and Unit Operating Agreement defines 'expert' only as "the Person appointed as such pursuant to the provisions of [the expert determination clause]". While there are clauses in the Unitisation Model Contract referring to issues that would be resolved by an expert (eg, redetermination, procedures for metering and sampling, the decommissioning work programme and budget and appraised value), the expert determination clause itself could be improved by cross-referencing these contractual provisions, making it clear that these are the only issues that should be referred to an expert.

74   2017 AIPN Model Dispute Resolution Agreement at 21.

10.   Conclusion

The drafting committee of the 2017 MDRA did an admirable job in accomplishing its objectives to strike a balance between the complexities of international arbitration law and the need for straightforward, practical and effective guidance for those negotiating these contracts.

Parties should use the 2017 MDRA as a comprehensive guide and checklist to ensure that they consider all important elements of arbitral procedure. For petroleum contract negotiators who may be less experienced in international arbitration, it is always a good idea to seek the advice of experienced international arbitration counsel for guidance in drafting the arbitration clause. The 2017 MDRA drafting committee also sensibly recommends proceeding with caution, as the complexity and interdependence of several of the options can lead to confusion. If in doubt, utilise the short, simple provisions set forth at the beginning of the 2017 MDRA.

Regardless of whether parties are steeped in deep knowledge of the intricacies of international arbitration, the 2017 MDRA is a 'state of the art' tool for use in complex, international agreements, in the petroleum sector or elsewhere.

The authors would like to extend their gratitude to James Chalk, JD candidate, Harvard Law School 2018, for providing research assistance with this chapter.

Oil and gas arbitrations in the Middle East and North Africa

Tim Martin
Northumberland Chambers

1. Oil and gas in the Middle East and North Africa

In 1901 William Knox D'Arcy acquired an oil concession in Iran, on which he and his investors discovered oil in 1908. This discovery began the Anglo-Persian Oil Company (later called the Anglo-Iranian Oil Company), which became the foundation for the company known today as British Petroleum (BP). It was also the beginning of the oil industry in the Middle East. International oil companies (IOCs), which consisted predominately of American and British companies, acquired many other oil concessions throughout the Middle East and North Africa (MENA)[1] over the next 30 years. The IOCs' investments in the region during the first half of the 20th century resulted in the discovery of a significant majority of the world's proven oil reserves over a lengthy period, as shown in Table 1.

Table 1. Proven crude oil reserves (billions of barrels)[2]

	1980		1990		2000		2010	
	Barrels	% Total	Barrels	% Total	Barrels	% Total	Barrels	% Total
MENA region	396.0	58.0%	696.8	67.8%	748.1	59.5%	830.2	51.2%
Total world	683.4	100%	1,027.5	100%	1,258.1	100%	1,621.6	100%

As a direct result of these discoveries, IOCs acquired control over the vast majority of global petroleum supplies. This did not sit well with countries in the

---

1   The countries included in the MENA region are, in the Middle East, Bahrain, Iran, Iraq, Israel, Jordan, Kuwait, Lebanon, Oman, Qatar, Saudi Arabia, Syria, United Arab Emirates and Yemen; and in North Africa, Algeria, Egypt, Libya, Morocco and Tunisia.
2   *BP Statistical Review of World Energy.*

MENA region, which began their struggle to control their oil resources when Iran first nationalised the Anglo-Iranian Oil Company in 1951. A tumultuous period of coups, revolutions, deal making and nationalisations lasting several decades ensued.[3] During this period, countries in the MENA region were at the forefront of an anti-colonialist backlash, reflected in their increasing expropriation of oil concessions.[4] They sought economic independence by banding together and establishing the Organisation of the Petroleum Exporting Countries (OPEC) and issuing its Declaratory Statement of Petroleum Policy in 1960.

A major fallout from this struggle was a series of nationalisations by MENA host governments of the IOCs' investments in the region. This resulted in a dramatic reversal in control of the worlds' oil reserves from the IOCs to the national oil companies (NOCs) that host governments established to manage their petroleum reserves, as illustrated in Figure 1.

Figure 1. Control of world oil reserves: IOCs v NOCs

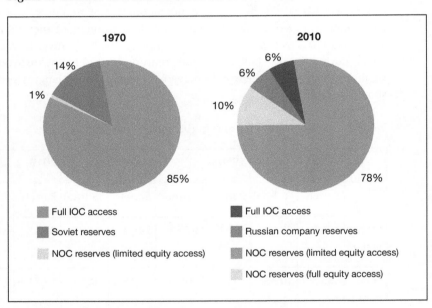

Sources: PFC Energy, Oil & Gas Journal, BP Statistical Review

2.   Historical MENA oil and gas arbitration cases

The IOCs responded to these nationalisations with a number of ground-

---

3   For a fascinating narrative of this period, see Daniel Yergin, *The Prize* (Simon & Schuster 1991).
4   See Joan E Shapiro and Jeffrey A Hart, *The Politics of International Economic Relations* (Wadsworth, 7th ed 2010) at 315, where they describe an increase in expropriations from 10 in 1968 to more than 80 in 1975.

breaking investor-state *ad hoc* arbitration cases between the 1950s and 1980s that established many of the key principles in international investment, arbitration and oil and gas law. Those cases included the following:

- *Petroleum Development v Sheikh of Abu Dhabi* (1951);
- *Saudi Arabia v Aramco* (1958);
- *Sapphire v NIOC* (1964);
- *BP v Libya* (1974);
- *TOPCO v Libya* (1977);
- *LIAMCO v Libya* (1977);
- *Kuwait v AMINOIL* (1982);
- *Amoco International Finance v Iran* (1985); and
- *Mobil Oil v Iran* (1987).

2.1 Petroleum Development v Sheikh of Abu Dhabi

Lord Asquith of Bishopstone was the sole arbitrator in the *ad hoc* arbitration of *Petroleum Development v Sheikh of Abu Dhabi*.[5] The agreement did not include a governing law clause. It merely stated that the agreement was intended to be applied in the spirit of goodwill and integrity, and to be interpreted in a reasonable manner. Faced with the decision on what law to apply in interpreting the agreement, Lord Asquith stated the following:

> *If any municipal system of law were applicable, it would* prima facie *be that of Abu Dhabi. But no such law can be reasonably said to exist. The Sheikh administers a purely discretionary justice with the assistance of the Koran; and it would be fanciful to suggest that in this very primitive region there is any settled body of legal principles applicable to the construction of modern commercial instruments.*

As a result, Lord Asquith rejected the use of *Shari'ah* and how it would determine damages. Instead, he applied the "modern law of nature", which closely resembled the English common law with which he was most familiar. This would be considered offensive language from today's perspective, but it needs to be placed in historical context. What Lord Asquith was describing for the first time was the evolving international arbitration practice of supplementing (or replacing) national law with international law and legal practice.

2.2 Saudi Arabia v Aramco

On 29 May 1933 the government of Saudi Arabia signed a concession contract with Standard Oil Company of California (Socal, which subsequently became Chevron). The concession contract granted the exclusive right to Socal in eastern Saudi Arabia to "explore, prospect, drill for, extract, treat, manufacture, transport, deal with, carry away and export petroleum … however … such right

---

5   *Petroleum Development Ltd v Sheikh of Abu Dhabi*, Award of September 1951, 18 *International Law Reports* 144 (1951).

does not include the exclusive right to sell crude or refined products ... within Saudi Arabia" for a period of 60 years. Socal found oil five years later in 1938, which began the development of the world's largest oil fields. By 1948, Socal had formed a consortium called the Arabian American Oil Company (Aramco) with three other large American oil companies – Standard Oil of New Jersey (Exxon), Socony-Vacuum (Mobil) and the Texas Company (Texaco) – to manage the concession contract. Among other agreements, Aramco entered into off-take contracts for the sale and transportation of crude oil and products from its concession to its shareholder companies and other buyers around the world.[6]

In 1954 Aristotle Onassis – who at the time owned one of the largest crude oil shipping companies in the world – obtained the approval of the government to form a company in Saudi Arabia called the Saudi Arabian Maritime Tankers Company (SATCO). The government then signed a shipping contract with SATCO to transport all the oil produced under the Aramco contract to foreign markets for a period of 30 years. Aramco refused to comply with the SATCO contract and did not allow Onassis to transport the crude oil produced from the concession. The Aramco agreement had an arbitration clause, which the parties revised to provide for an *ad hoc* arbitration[7] in Geneva, Switzerland with a three-member tribunal. The arbitration was held prior to the enactment of the New York Convention or the establishment of widely accepted international arbitration rules, such as the United Nations Commission on International Trade Law (UNCITRAL) Arbitration Rules. Since the Aramco contract did not provide for any particular procedural rules, the tribunal applied the law of nations to the procedural issues of the arbitration.

Saudi Arabia argued that Aramco was not entitled to the absolute right to transport oil beyond Saudi territorial waters, since that right was not expressly provided in the concession agreement. It further argued that even if Aramco was conferred such a right, it was in breach of the concession by transferring those rights to a third party (ie, its buyers). Aramco submitted that, by virtue of its agreement, it had the exclusive right to transport petroleum extracted by it to any place overseas and upon such terms as it chose.

There was no choice of law (or governing law) clause in the concession agreement. The tribunal therefore agreed that the law of Saudi Arabia governed the concession contract but that it was not prepared to fully apply *Shari'ah* because it determined that Islamic law was in an "embryonic state". Instead, the tribunal decided to reconstruct, in an abstract manner, the choice of law that reasonable persons would have intended to use in the concession agreement. As a result, the tribunal's decision on the choice of law provided that:

---

6   Stephen M Schwebel, *The Kingdom of Saudi Arabia and Aramco Arbitrate the Onassis Agreement*, Vol 3, No 3, *Journal of World Energy Law & Business*, at 245 (2010).

7   *Saudi Arabia v Arabian American Oil Company (Aramco)*, Award of 23 August 1958, 27 *International Law Reports* 117 (1963).

- The law of Saudi Arabia applied to the relationship between the parties;
- Gaps in the law of Saudi Arabia would be filled by principles from worldwide custom and practice in the oil business;
- General principles of law applied because the concession agreement had an international character;
- The sale and transport of oil as governed by custom and practice in maritime law and the international oil business would apply; and
- Public international law applied when certain matters could not be governed by the municipal laws of the State.

The Aramco contract specified that Aramco's exclusive right to sell the oil it extracted did not include the right to sell crude or refined products within Saudi Arabia. The tribunal therefore concluded, by reverse logic, that Aramco must have had the exclusive right to sell outside Saudi Arabia. In its final award, the tribunal upheld the validity of the Aramco contract and held that the SATCO contract was in conflict with it and thus not effective against Aramco.

Saudi Arabia accepted the tribunal's decision, even though it very much disliked the award. As a direct result of this arbitration award, Saudi Arabia prohibited its government entities from including arbitration clauses in their agreements, unless they got special permission from the head of the government. It also slowed down Saudi ratification of the New York and International Centre for the Settlement of Investment Disputes (ICSID) Conventions. In the end, Saudi Arabia resolved the matter in 1973 by re-negotiating the original concession with the Aramco shareholders so that it purchased the Aramco company from them over a 10-year period, resulting in Saudi Aramco, the world's biggest company.

2.3 *Sapphire v NIOC*

Sapphire Petroleums Ltd, a Canadian company, and the National Iranian Oil Company (NIOC) entered into a contract in 1958 to expand the production and exportation of Iranian oil. They set up the Iranian Canada Oil Company in Iran to carry out the contract on behalf of the parties. Sapphire started work on the concession and then claimed reimbursement of its expenses. However, NIOC refused to reimburse the expenses, arguing that Sapphire had not consulted NIOC before carrying out its operations. On 28 September 1960 Sapphire commenced an arbitration against NIOC and appointed an arbitrator. NIOC refused to appoint an arbitrator. Pursuant to the contract, Sapphire requested the president of the Swiss Federal Court to appoint a sole arbitrator who appointed Swiss Federal Judge Pierre Cavin in an *ad hoc* arbitration.[8] NIOC did

---

8   *Sapphire International Petroleums Ltd v National Iranian Oil Co (NIOC)*, Award of 15 March 1963, 35 *International Law Reports* 136 (1963).

not appear at the arbitral hearing. Sapphire claimed breach of contract and requested compensation for expenses, loss of profit and the refund of a $350,000 indemnity, provided by Sapphire as a bank guarantee that was cashed by NIOC.

The contract did not provide an express choice of governing law. The arbitrator stated that since the contract was both concluded and performed in Iran, the *lex loci contractus* and *lex loci executionis* pointed to the application of Iranian law. However, the arbitrator found that the concession agreement provided that the contract was to be performed according to principles of good faith and goodwill. There was therefore a negative intention to reject the exclusive application of Iranian law since Sapphire would not be protected against legislative changes if the contract was governed by Iranian law. By reference to the rules of good faith, the arbitrator held that it was in "the interest of both parties to such agreements that any disputes between them should be settled according to the general principles universally recognized and should not be subject to the particular rules of national laws".

The arbitrator held that Iran, as an expropriating state, must compensate the investor for actual loss suffered (*damnum emergens*) and lost profits (*lacrum cessans*). He included lost profits based on the principle of *pacta sunt servanda*, which requires that contract damages put the aggrieved party in the position that it would have been in if the contract had been performed.

The arbitrator found that the existence of both commercial quantities and damages was uncertain. Sapphire argued it had the right to compensation for loss of "chance" to discover oil. A geologist retained as an expert by Sapphire testified that the minimum loss Sapphire would suffer was its investment of $8 million and a maximum loss would be lost profits of $46 million. The arbitrator decided that the geologist's analysis did not fully account for all risks involved, such as exploring in a desolate region and the possibility of wars and price recessions, and therefore awarded actual damages of $650,874 and lost profits of $2 million.

2.4 *BP v Libya*

Muammar al-Qaddafi seized power in Libya in September 1969. He began squeezing oil companies in the country the following year by calling for an increase in the posted price. He then began expropriating their concessions. The first of three noteworthy arbitration cases against Libya was initiated by BP.[9] This was an *ad hoc* arbitration with a sole arbitrator who decided that Danish procedural law would govern the arbitration, since the seat of the arbitration was in Copenhagen.

---

9   *BP Exploration Company (Libya) Limited v Government of the Libyan Arab Republic*, Award of 10 October 1973 and 1 August 1974, 53 *International Law Reports* 297 (1979), V *Yearbook Commercial Arbitration* 143 (1980).

The concession agreement provided that it was governed by principles of the law of Libya common to the principles of international law, and in the absence of such principles by general principles of law, including those principles applied by international tribunals. The arbitrator noted that this excluded any single municipal legal system.

The arbitrator accepted BP's arguments that the concession was in the nature of a contract, which was concluded pursuant to legislation that contemplated a contractual relationship, and created a direct contractual link between BP and Libya. The arbitrator found that the nationalisation of BP's property, rights and interests constituted a fundamental breach of the concession and was a total repudiation of the agreement. He also found that the government's actions:

- were arbitrary and discriminatory;
- violated public international law because they were made for purely extraneous political reasons; and
- were confiscatory because no offer of compensation had been made since the nationalisation.

2.5 *Texaco Overseas Petroleum Co (TOPCO) v Libya*

Texaco and California Asiatic Oil Company initiated an *ad hoc* arbitration[10] against Libya when it nationalised their oil concession. The Libyan government did not participate in the arbitration. The arbitrator adopted international law to govern the procedural aspects of the arbitration.

The sole arbitrator adopted the approach taken in the *Aramco* case, holding that the state party was not subject to the law of another country and that the parties had the right to select the governing law. The arbitrator applied a "two-tier system" to determine the governing law, so that:

- principles of Libyan law applied to the extent common to international law principles; and
- in the absence of such commonality, general principles of law applied.

The sole arbitrator held that under the new concept of international law, contracts between states and private persons can be 'internationalised' and subject to public international law. He based this on the reference in the contract to international law and general principles of law. He also held that the concession agreement granted by a former government of Libya was of a contractual nature because it expressed an agreement of the wills of both the investor and Libya based on general principles of law.

The arbitrator decided that the Libyan government could not exercise its

---

10 *Texaco Overseas Petroleum Co (TOPCO) v Government of the Libyan Arab Republic*, Award of 19 January 1977, 53 *International Law Reports* 389 (1977), *IV Yearbook Commercial Arbitration* 177 (1979).

sovereignty to nationalise in violation of its specific commitments in the stabilisation clauses of the concession agreement, and that its nationalisation of TOPCO's investment amounted to a breach of the concession agreement.

2.6   Libyan American Oil Company (LIAMCO) v Libya

This was an *ad hoc* arbitration[11] with a sole arbitrator. The arbitrator held that the parties were free to select the law to govern their contractual relationship, and that any part of the Libyan domestic law that was inconsistent with principles of international law must be excluded. He also held that both Libyan and international law apply custom and equity, and that certain general principles of law were found in Libyan legislation and Islamic law, including the principle of sanctity of property and contracts, respect for acquired vested rights, prohibition of unjust enrichment and the obligation to pay compensation for expropriation.

The arbitrator concluded that compensation for nationalisation should include the value of all the tangible property seized, and that at a minimum, *damnum emergens* (the value of the nationalised property) should be compensated. He awarded LIAMCO the full amount of its claim for its interest in the physical plant and equipment for a value of $13,882,677.

The arbitrator determined that both Libyan and Islamic law allowed for the recovery of lost profits, and that classical international law allowed the recovery of lost profits for both wrongful taking of property and lawful nationalisations. However, he rejected compensation for lost profits if they were not "certain and direct", were doubtful and were not probably realisable.

Libya contended that for lawful expropriation, it owed only the net book value of the tangible assets seized. LIAMCO claimed lost future profits. The arbitrator described as "extreme" the compensation methods of net book value and recovery of full profits. Instead, the arbitrator held that "it would be reasonable and just to adopt a formula of 'equitable compensation' as the measure for the estimation of damages." The arbitrator concluded that it was "just and equitable to consider interest claimed not as usury (riba), but as compensatory equivalent of a discount rate".

2.7   Kuwait v Aminoil

Kuwait terminated the American Independent Oil Company's (AMINOIL) concession agreement and confiscated its assets in September 1977. As a result of the nationalisation of its assets, AMINOIL initiated an arbitration[12] against Kuwait, which resulted in the most cited case in state investment disputes.

---

11   *Libyan American Oil Company (LIAMCO) v Government of the Libyan Arab Republic*, Award of 12 April 1977, 62 *International Law Reports* 140 (1977), *VI Yearbook Commercial Arbitration* 89 (1981).
12   *Government of Kuwait v American Independent Oil Company (AMINOIL)*, Award of 24 May 1982, 66 *International Law Reports* 518 (1982), *IX Yearbook Commercial Arbitration* 71 (1984).

The tribunal referred to a "transnational law" in determining the applicable substantive law, which was domestic plus international law. The tribunal also determined that the purpose of the stabilisation clause in the concession contract was only to prohibit measures of a confiscatory nature. However, with respect to damages, the stabilisation clauses were held to create "legitimate expectations" that must be taken into account in assessing damages. The tribunal refused to find duress, which required that there must be "absence of any other possible course" or means used to obtain it was illegal.

The tribunal did not apply *Shari'ah* principles in quantifying damages. Kuwait argued for net book value as the standard for compensating AMINOIL, while AMINOIL proposed valuating its expropriated assets using the discounted cash flow (DCF) valuation method. The tribunal held that the DCF method was acceptable in principle, but applied a combination of methods based mainly on a going concern value. The tribunal awarded AMINOIL a depreciated replacement value of the fixed assets seized by Kuwait and a going concern value plus "reasonable rate of return" (ie, profits). The tribunal took into account a reasonable rate of return for AMINOIL, noting that it "had come to accept the principle of a moderate estimate of profits, and this constituted its legitimate expectation". As a result of this valuation approach, the tribunal awarded AMINOIL $179,750,764.

Finally, Kuwait argued that a number of negotiations and settlements during the period from 1971 to 1977 "had generated a customary rule valid for the oil industry – a *lex petrolea* that was in some sort a particular branch of a general universal *lex mercatoria*". The tribunal rejected Kuwait's argument on *lex petrolea*.

2.8 *Amoco International Finance v Iran*

A series of oil and gas arbitrations arose from the Iranian revolution of 1979 and the subsequent seizure of US owned assets in the country by the revolutionary Iranian government. US investors initially pursued their claims in the US courts. However, in order to resolve the hostage crisis of US citizens seized by Iranian students, the United States agreed under the Algiers Accord to terminate litigation against Iran in US courts, to release Iranian assets in the United States that had been frozen under a US Treasury licence and to establish the Iran-US Claims Tribunal to handle all US claims against Iran.

Amoco International Finance Corp made a claim[13] against Iran at the Iran-US Claims Tribunal for the expropriation of its 50% interest in the shares of Khara Chemical Co Ltd. The tribunal determined that the legality of expropriation must be determined by international law, rather than domestic

---

[13] *Amoco International Finance Corp v Government of the Islamic Republic of Iran*, Award 310-56-3 of 14 July 1987, 15 Iran-US CTR 189, 83 *International Law Reports* 500.

local law. The tribunal held that a clear distinction must be made between lawful and unlawful expropriations, since the rules applicable to the compensation to be paid by the expropriating state differ according to the legal characterisation of the taking.

The tribunal stated that in the absence of a stabilisation clause, a contract does not bar nationalisation and any such nationalisation is not unlawful. Since there was no express stipulation in the contract barring the state from nationalising the investment, the tribunal held that Iran did not act unlawfully in nationalising Amoco's interests. However, it decided that Amoco's interests constituted "property" or "interests in property" under the bilateral treaty between the United States and Iran, and were subject to compensation in the event of an expropriation.

Amoco proposed a DCF method of valuation in its damages claim. Iran claimed that net book value was "the normal standard of compensation in case of lawful expropriation, especially in the oil industry". The tribunal decided that because the DCF method allows projection of damages over a long period, it opened "a large field of speculation due to the uncertainty inherent in any such projection", and said it amounted to "a capitalization of hypothetical future earnings for all other elements of valuation".

The tribunal rejected both the DCF and net book valuations methods. Instead, the tribunal decided that for a lawful expropriation, the going concern value at time of dispossession was the proper measure of compensation; while for an unlawful expropriation, lost profits might be added to the calculation of damages.

2.9 *Mobil Oil v Iran*

Mobil Oil Iran Inc also made a claim[14] against Iran at the Iran-US Claims Tribunal. Its claim was under a under a sale and purchase agreement where its first sentence stated that it "shall be interpreted in accordance with laws of Iran". However, the tribunal held that the reference to Iranian law was "solely for interpretation of the Agreement", and that general principles of commercial and international law would be applied to all other issues in the dispute. The tribunal decided that it was not appropriate that the contract be governed by the law of one party, given the contract's international character.

The tribunal concluded that the legality of expropriation (including contractual rights) must be determined by international law and held that a claimed loss "cannot easily be ascertained with a degree of certainty necessary to allow finding that profits claimed were within legitimate expectations of parties". The tribunal therefore rejected the application of lost profits in the calculation of damages.

---

14   *Mobil Oil Iran Inc v Government of the Islamic Republic of Iran*, Award 311- 74/76/81/150-3 of 14 July 1987, 16 Iran-US CTR 3, 86 *International Law Reports* 230.

2.10 Summary of historical arbitration cases

The above historical oil and gas arbitrations from the MENA region were instrumental in establishing many of the key principles now used in investor state disputes. They illustrated how contracts between states and private parties can be 'internationalised' by making them subject to public international law and international arbitration. In doing so, the tribunals chose not to exclusively apply local law, which was primarily *Shari'ah*. The tribunals also established other key principles in international investment law, including:

- the sanctity of property and contracts;
- a prohibition on unjust enrichment;
- the right of states to expropriate investments;
- the requirement that in doing so, a state must compensate the investor for its loss; and
- the use of legitimate expectations in determining damages.

On the commercial side, there were no reported commercial oil and gas arbitration cases from the MENA region during this period. Those that did occur took place in US and English courts.[15] Reported MENA commercial oil and gas arbitration cases have only recently emerged.

3. Recent MENA oil and gas arbitration cases

3.1 Commercial arbitrations

The International Chamber of Commerce (ICC) International Court of Arbitration is one of the leading commercial arbitration institutions in the world. Its caseload is a good indicator of trends in the international arbitration world. A review[16] was conducted of oil and gas arbitration cases at the ICC court that arose from the MENA region between 1988 and 2012. There were 450 oil and gas arbitrations in total at the ICC Court during that period, of which only 11 were from the MENA region.[17] That was less than 3% of all ICC oil and gas arbitration cases. There was no correlation between this number and the amount of oil and gas reserves in the MENA region.[18]

---

15 An example is the series of *Hunt v BP* cases that dealt with a farm-in and joint operating agreement in 1960 between Nelson Bunker Hunt and BP on Concession 65 awarded to Hunt by Libya in 1957. Each party initiated various claims in the United States and English courts after the Libyan government nationalised BP's interest in 1971 and Hunt's interest in 1973: *Nelson Bunker Hunt v BP Exploration Company (Libya) Ltd*, 492 F Supp 885 (1980), 580 F Supp 304 (1984), 756 F 2d 880 (5th Cir 1985), and *BP Exploration Co (Libya) v Hunt* [1979] 1 WLR 783 (High Court), [1982] 1 All ER 925 (Court of Appeal), [1983] 1 WLR 232, [1983] 2 AC 352.

16 A Timothy Martin, "ICC Oil and Gas Cases in the MENA Region" *ICC ICArb Bulletin*, Vol 25, Issue 2 (2014) 21.

17 *Id* at 21. The 11 cases are reviewed and analysed in detail in the above article. Redacted versions of the cases are provided in the same issue of the *ICC Bulletin*.

18 Countries in the MENA region had up to 67% of the world's crude oil proven reserves and up to 52% of the natural gas proven reserves in the world during that time period. See *BP Statistical Review of World Energy (1988–2012)*.

The amounts in dispute ranged from between $4 million and $10 billion. There was one state investment dispute involving a production sharing contract, while the remaining 10 cases were commercial disputes between companies involving:

- three seismic/drilling contracts;
- three construction infrastructure claims; and
- four sales contracts for crude oil, natural gas or liquefied natural gas.

There were no joint venture disputes involving either a joint operating agreement or joint venture company.

3.2   Investor-state arbitrations

The World Bank was involved in the settlement of the nationalisation of the Anglo-Iranian Oil Company after the overthrow of Iranian Prime Minister Mohammed Mosaddeq in 1953.[19] As a result of this and other nationalisations, the World Bank established ICSID in 1966 to provide a neutral forum to resolve investor-state disputes of this nature.[20] Even though ICSID developed into the "premier international investment arbitration facility in the world",[21] handling most of the world's investor-state disputes, it has registered very few oil and gas disputes from the MENA region. And the few that it has registered have only occurred in the last decade.

As of August 2017, ICSID had 642 concluded and pending cases in its registry, with 151 of those cases coming from the oil, gas and mining sector, which made up 23.5% of ICSID's caseload. Within that sector, 10 cases were from the MENA region, eight from the oil and gas sector and two from the mining sector. Of those eight oil and gas cases, two cases had the same parties, resulting in one of them being withdrawn, leaving a total of seven oil and gas cases from the MENA region. This resulted in oil and gas cases from the MENA region making up 4.7% of the total ICSID caseload from the oil, gas and mining sector.

The earliest MENA oil and gas case was registered at ICSID in September 2007. The parties settled that case with the tribunal registering the settlement without ruling on the merits. The next case was discontinued without an award. There are three cases pending without an award. The result is that there are only two ICSID oil and gas awards from the MENA region at this time. The seven oil and gas cases are listed in Table 2.

19   Antonio R Parra, *The History of ICSID 21* (Oxford, 2nd ed 2017).
20   *Id* at 87.
21   *Id* at 267.

Table 2. Oil and gas cases at ICSID

Case	Claimant(s)	Respondent(s)	Date registered and dispute	Status
ARB/16/7	Attila Doğan Construction & Installation Co Inc	Sultanate of Oman	March 2016 Oil and gas engineering and construction enterprise	Pending
ARB/14/4	Unión Fenosa Gas, SA	Arab Republic of Egypt	February 2014 Natural gas liquefaction operations	Pending
ARB/12/30	Lundin Tunisia BV	Republic of Tunisia	October 2012 Oil exploration and exploitation operations	Concluded: Dec 2015
ARB/12/11	Ampal-American Israel Corporation and others	Arab Republic of Egypt	May 2012 Natural gas export	Pending
ARB/11/7	National Gas SAE	Arab Republic of Egypt	March 2011 Gas pipelines construction and operation agreement	Concluded: April 2014
ARB/09/14	Mærsk Olie, Algeriet A/S	People's Democratic Republic of Algeria	July 2009 Exploration and production of liquid hydrocarbons	Concluded: Sept 2013 Discontinued
ARB/07/25	Trans-Global Petroleum, Inc	Hashemite Kingdom of Jordan	September 2007 Oil exploration concession	Concluded: April 2009 Settlement

4. Correlation between number of arbitrations and amount of reserves

The amount of proven oil and gas reserves is a good indicator of a country's long-term production rates and therefore the amount of its petroleum activity and related business transactions generated over a sustained period.[22] Long-term business activity and transactions inevitably generate disputes. One would therefore assume that there would be some correlation between the amount of proven oil and gas reserves and the number of oil and gas disputes over time from one region of the world to another. However, that is not the case with regard to the MENA region when compared to the rest of the world. It is not even close.

The MENA region has had between 50% and 67% of the world's proven oil reserves and between 40% and 50% of the world's proven gas reserves at different times over the last half century.[23] There has not been an equivalent percentage of investor-state or commercial oil and gas arbitrations coming out of the MENA region compared to the rest of the world during that period.

The ICSID statistics are a good reflection of the number of investor-state disputes in the world. Oil and gas cases from the MENA region made up less than 5% of the total ICSID global caseload from the oil, gas and mining sector – significantly less than the percentage of global oil and gas reserves located in that region. In contrast, Central and South America had less than 10% of the world's oil reserves for most of that period,[24] while generating approximately one-third of the world's oil and gas investor state disputes during the same period.[25]

Similarly, the ICC statistics are a good reflection of the number of commercial oil and gas arbitrations in the MENA region compared to the rest of the world. Given the confidential nature of most commercial arbitrations, it is not possible to accurately track every oil and gas arbitration, but the ICC

---

22   There is never a direct annual correlation because of geopolitical, economic, technological and logistical reasons over different periods. Examples are:
- Saudi Arabia's policy of maintaining 1 million to 2 million barrels of daily production in spare capacity to stabilise global markets;
- economic sanctions imposed upon Iran;
- regional conflicts in Libya, Iraq and Syria;
- technology advances in fracking and horizontal drilling in the United States; and
- pipeline constraints.

      However, over time, there is generally a correlation between proven oil and gas reserves with a similar percentage of global production, revenue and business activity.

23   These percentages change over time with technology advances, fluctuating oil prices and what companies can reasonably recover based upon existing economic and operating conditions at the time of the estimate.

24   *BP Statistical Review of World Energy (1980-2010).* The percentage of proven oil reserves was between 4% and 7% between 1980 and 2007. The reserve estimates for Venezuela began to increase significantly in 2008 as a result of recognising the economic viability of its heavy oil deposits based on the rapid increase in the oil price at that time, which resulted in Central and South America having an estimated 19% of the world's proven oil reserves by 2010. That percentage has subsequently dropped along with the dramatic drop in oil prices in 2014.

25   As of August 2017, ICSID had 151 cases from the oil, gas and mining sector. Fifty of them were from Central and South America.

database provides a good indication of where these arbitrations are occurring. The MENA cases were less than 3% of the total ICC oil and gas arbitration cases during that period. Once again, there was no correlation between the amount of oil and gas reserves located in the MENA region and the number of commercial oil and gas arbitrations generated from that region, compared to the rest of the world.

Why is there a disconnect between the large oil and gas reserves and related business activity in the MENA region and the relatively small number of oil and gas arbitrations it generates? Is it because investors in the region prefer not to use arbitration to resolve their disputes? There is some validity to this explanation, since there has been a long tradition in the MENA region for parties to use *sulh* (settlement) and *musalaha* (reconciliation) to settle their disputes, rather than the courts or arbitration. However, there could be a number of structural reasons for the relatively few oil and gas arbitrations in the region.

One factor is that IOCs were generally prevented from investing in major oil and gas fields in the region since the early nationalisations. Instead, it was the large NOCs that made those investments. No IOC investment meant that there could not be investor-state disputes in those countries. There have been a few investor-state arbitrations at ICSID over the last decade, but they have been in countries such as Tunisia, Oman, Jordan and Egypt,[26] which have smaller reserves and therefore a need to attract foreign capital and technology. There will be a few more in the future, but not on the scale seen since the historical cases described above.

There have been limited commercial oil and gas arbitrations in the region, for related reasons. The large NOCs – such as Saudi Aramco, NIOC, Kuwait Petroleum Corporation and Abu Dhabi National Oil Company – dominate petroleum activity in their respective countries. They are the only game in town. Consequently, service, equipment and infrastructure providers wanting to build long-term business operations are inclined to settle with the NOCs rather than arbitrate. Similarly, the big NOCs want reliable and quality contractors to be there when they need them. They can do that only by encouraging mutually beneficial, long-term relationships, which would preclude disputes.

The large NOCs use sophisticated contracts that lock in counterparties with detailed obligations. These contracts often require the use of local courts, local arbitration institutions or *ad hoc* arbitration under national arbitration laws, rather than international arbitration institutions. Finally, many of the commercial contracts generated by NOCs and performed in-country stipulate that the governing law is the domestic law of that country. In the MENA region,

---

26   There was one investor-state arbitration at the ICC during that period, which was between Hunt Oil and Yemen.

that law is either *Shari'ah* or based upon it. That choice of law has an impact on the dispute process and the kinds of damages awarded.

5.   The role of *Shari'ah* in MENA oil and gas arbitrations

The historical oil and gas arbitrations described above 'internationalised' the contracts in dispute by making them subject to either public international law, general principles of law, general principles of commercial and international law, principles of good faith and goodwill, transnational law, custom and practice in the oil business, or a combination thereof, rather than applying the law of the jurisdiction where the investment was made. Many of the disputed contracts did not specify a particular governing law. When the contracts did reference local domestic law, the tribunals would restrict its application by concluding that since the contracts were international in nature, they should apply international law and practice. That approach may no longer be the case going forward, particularly if there is a governing law clause in the contract that clearly specifies local law, which is either entirely or partially based on *Shari'ah*.

Arbitration has a long history in the Islamic world. The *Qur'an*, and therefore *Shari'ah*, approves of arbitration. The Prophet Mohammed acted as an arbitrator in tribal disputes, including one regarding the Black Stone in the *Ka'ba*, which is located in Mecca. However, after losing the investor-state disputes described above, many of the MENA countries rejected the use of international arbitration, in particular for contracts with the government. That has begun to change over the last decade. These governments have moved from outright hostility to gradual acceptance of international arbitration by ratifying the New York Convention and by basing their national arbitration laws on the UNCITRAL Model Arbitration Law.

As a result, many of the national arbitration laws in the MENA region now:

- confer a right on parties to manage the dispute resolution process without interference from the courts;
- provide greater flexibility in the choosing of arbitrators, arbitral rules, institutions, the seat of arbitration, the governing law and the language of the arbitration; and
- accept the principles of separability and competence-competence.

Even though these national arbitration laws now accept international practice, they still explicitly or implicitly require the arbitration process and award to be *Shari'ah* compliant. That is not always straightforward, since the interpretation and application of *Shari'ah* principles will vary from one jurisdiction to another within the MENA region. Despite that variance, parties and arbitrators dealing with a dispute connected to the MENA region should nevertheless understand and apply *Shari'ah* principles to the arbitration process and the arbitral award.

Shari'ah provides that contracts are divine in nature and that there is a sacred duty to uphold them except for matters that *Shari'ah* has deemed void or unenforceable. Contracts are therefore usually strictly enforced as drafted in Islamic courts. The general rule of contract under *Shari'ah* is "all is permitted unless specifically prohibited". Under Islamic law, parties are therefore free to enter into any contract they wish and will be bound by its terms, except for certain matters prohibited by *Shari'ah*, which are typically *haram*, or forbidden. The most important prohibitions are *gharar* (uncertainty or speculation) and *riba* (interest or usury).

Shari'ah requires certainty in contracts, and thus forbids transactions comprising an element of uncertainty or *gharar* relating to the object of the contract, its consideration or the time allowed for performance of the parties' respective obligations. *Shari'ah* also prohibits *riba*, which literally means 'an excess'. *Riba* is interpreted differently in different Islamic jurisdictions. In Saudi Arabia, it means interest of any kind. Other Islamic jurisdictions are more flexible on what constitutes *riba*. Other prohibitions include *jahala* (uncertain or unclear terms), *ghabn* (deceit, such as large discrepancies from the market price), *khataa* (mistake), and *wa'ad ta'aqud* (a future promise or an 'agreement to agree').

Parties can claim damages under *Shari'ah*. However, it takes a more restrictive approach in determining the amount of damages than what international companies are accustomed to in common law or civil law jurisdictions. Islamic courts have traditionally only awarded damages that arise as a direct consequence of a breach of contract. This is because *Shari'ah* will only restore a party to the position it was in before the breach, not to where it would have been had the obligations been performed. Otherwise, this would be speculative in nature, which is not enforceable under *Shari'ah*.

As a result, consequential, indirect, punitive and speculative damages are not typically awarded in Islamic courts. This restriction can extend to future lost profits, which can result in much smaller damage awards in those courts. Simply being foreseeable may not be sufficient to make a damages claim legitimate. A party must prove the damages it actually suffered. It cannot rely upon a claim of what may be foreseen in the future, which under *Shari'ah* is considered speculative and unearned in nature.

Liquidated damages may be unenforceable in an Islamic court if they are considered a penalty. There is no exact equivalent term or legal concept for 'liquidated damages' under *Shari'ah*. The closest corresponding term is 'penalty clause' or 'agreed compensation' for damages. Despite that general restriction, various Islamic jurisprudence schools have allowed the inclusion of liquidated damages clauses in contracts if the parties have specifically agreed to such terms. In such circumstances, both parties are expected to adhere to the terms of the clause as compensation for breach of the contractual obligation.

However, they may still be required to show that the calculations underlying the liquidated damages do not equate to a penalty.

In addition to the requirements of *Shari'ah*, parties need to be aware of the many procedural hurdles that exist in these countries to have international arbitration awards recognised and enforced in local MENA courts, including the following.

5.1 Special power of attorney

Countries such as the United Arab Emirates[27] and Qatar[28] require that a signatory to an arbitration agreement be in possession of a special power of attorney that entitles it to agree to an arbitration clause. Failure to comply with this requirement may lead to an arbitral award being annulled.

5.2 Signing and attesting awards

Some jurisdictions, such as the United Arab Emirates, require arbitrators to sign every page of an arbitral award containing the reasoning and dispositive sections, and to sign their awards while physically located in the country.[29] Failure to do so could result in the award being annulled.

5.3 Submitting awards to local courts

The Saudi Arbitration Law[30] requires arbitral tribunals to deposit their original award and an Arabic translation from a Saudi accredited translation agency at the Saudi competent court within 15 days of issuance of their award to the parties. Failure to do so could result in the award not being recognised and enforced in Saudi Arabia. This is different from international arbitration practice (and Article 36(2) of the UNCITRAL Model Law), where an award is typically filed in the court by the party seeking to enforce the award (not by the arbitration tribunal) and only at the point of time when one of the parties wants to enforce it, not when the tribunal issues it.

5.4 Witness oaths

A number of jurisdictions[31] in the MENA region require arbitral tribunals to swear in witnesses appearing before them according to specific oath requirements under their respective codes of civil procedure or arbitration laws. Failure to swear in a witness using such formulistic oaths may result in the annulment of the award.[32]

---

27   UAE Civil Procedure Code, Articles 58(2) and 203(4).
28   Qatar Commercial and Civil Procedure Code, Articles 72(1) and 190.
29   UAE Civil Procedure Code, Articles 205(2) and 212(4).
30   Saudi Arbitration Law, Royal Decree M/34 dated 24 Jumada 1433H, corresponding to 16 April 2012G, Articles 43 and 44.
31   UAE Civil Procedure Code, Article 211; Syria Law 4 of 2008, Article 32(2); Qatar Commercial and Civil Procedure Code, Article 200; and Jordan Law 31 of 2001, Article 32(d).
32   *Bechtel v Department of Civil Aviation of the Government of Dubai*, Petition 503/2003, 15 May 2005, Dubai Court of Cessation.

5.5 Attributing award

Some local courts have set aside foreign arbitral awards on the basis that they were not rendered in the name of the country's ruler and as such were contrary to domestic public policy.[33]

Over time, such procedural obstacles will diminish in significance as arbitration laws and courts in the MENA region learn to adapt to international arbitration practice and their treaty obligations. However, international practitioners will need to be aware of these procedural challenges in the short term.

---

33   Petition 64/2012, 12 June 2012, Qatar Court of Cassation.

Gas pricing disputes

Ghislaine Lawless
Matthew Saunders
Ashurst LLP

1. Introduction

Gas – whether natural gas or liquefied natural gas (LNG) – has traditionally been sold under long-term sale and purchase agreements (SPAs). These contracts typically last for fixed periods of 10 to 25 years (or more), or are linked to the life of a particular gas-producing field. In either case, the contracts will normally (although not universally) contain a pricing formula, intended to allow for fluctuations in pricing. At least for continental European contracts, there have traditionally been two major contract 'models': Groningen or Troll, with multiple variations of these.

In Europe, over the last decade or so, these contracts and in particular their pricing formulae have been the source of many disputes between sellers and buyers of natural gas – so much so that 'gas price arbitration' has become a specific field of specialisation for arbitration lawyers. Now, the 'perfect storm' of economic, political and technological factors that caused these European disputes has seemingly largely passed. There is good reason, however, to think that familiar-looking clouds may be gathering over the LNG market in Asia.

While there are differences in commercial standards and negotiation styles between the European and Asian LNG markets, parallels can usefully be drawn and the study of the history of one market may lead to a greater chance of success in the other, as regards both contract renegotiations and disputes. The question of what lessons can usefully be drawn from the European gas price wars is the subject of this chapter.

2. Natural gas and the LNG markets

A gas producer must put significant capital into obtaining its gas, often with significant reliance upon bank finance. To support such capital investment, the producer needs a guaranteed income stream. However, the gas producer will not be satisfied with security alone – it knows that gas prices will fluctuate and that economic circumstances will change over the course of a long-term contract. Increasingly in Europe, pricing has been influenced by demand for power generation and the impact (or anticipated impact) of new sources of supply, compounded by the development of fracking technology, especially in North

America (increasingly seen as a significant LNG exporter, whereas only a few years ago it had been seen as a market for LNG exports from Gulf exporters). If gas prices go up, the seller will want that to be reflected in the price that it receives. The gas buyer, of course, wants security of supply, but also needs to make sure that it can sell the gas on (or convert it to power) at a price which allows it to make a profit.

Before the liberalisation of the European gas markets, a state-owned gas supplier might have had a monopoly on gas, but it still needed to compete with coal and oil as sources of power and so needed to price competitively. In the early days of the European natural gas markets, a buyer could change between burning gas or burning oil (before the days of fuel-specific efficient burner technology), so there was some practical logic in basing the price of gas on that of oil, as a competing fuel.

Two methods were used to try to strike a balance first between the buyers' and sellers' competing interests, and second between the parties' conflicting needs for stability and for the contract to flex and change with the economic circumstances. Those mechanisms are indexation and 'price re-opener' clauses.

2.1 Indexation

In the early days of the gas market, the state-owned utility was the dominating presence. National gas markets were dominated by monopolies or small oligopolies of importers which contracted with foreign gas producers on a long-term basis. Gas pipelines carried imported gas in one direction only, from its point of delivery. There was no real market competition, so there was no recognised 'market price' for gas that could be used for indexation on a regular basis.

Instead, indexation was carried out by applying a multiplier to a fixed price. The multiplier was typically calculated by reference to an inflation rate and a weighted average of a 'basket' of fuel prices. In continental Europe, prices of Brent crude (or another crude oil) were often the largest or even the only item in that 'basket'. Other items might be the electricity price, the coal price or similar. There were even reported instances of Central European price formulae referencing the price of wood as a competing fuel! Generally, when oil prices went up, gas prices went up and vice versa.

The effect of swings in gas contract prices might be limited by parties opting to include 'top stop' or 'bottom stop' formulae in a contract. These stops allow price fluctuations to happen within a known range, giving both parties more certainty.

Alternatively, 'S-curve' calculations can be used. An S-curve calculation uses one of three different calculations, depending on where the current comparator fuel price (eg, Brent crude) is in a given range. Where the comparator fuel price is at the top or bottom of the range, the gas price rises or reduces more slowly. For example, a $1 increase in the price of a barrel of Brent crude might increase the price of a unit of gas by $0.50 or by $0.75, depending on the previous day's price. This can assist both buyers and sellers of gas: buyers benefit from a slower rise in the gas price when Brent crude prices are high and sellers benefit from a slower decrease in the gas price when Brent crude prices are low.

2.2 Price re-opener clauses

As well as an indexation formula, many long-term gas contracts contained a 'price re-opener' or 'price review' clause. These clauses can be activated when a 'trigger event' takes place. The trigger event may simply be automatic (eg, the expiry of a three-year interval over a 25-year contract). An automatic trigger event allows the parties to know and plan for a price adjustment. Too-frequent reviews would potentially cause significant price instability and remove the advantages of a long-term SPA for both parties.

There may also be provisions in a contract for special trigger events. There is no standard for these trigger events. They might be objective events, such as the fall of the price of an indexation benchmark below a given point. Another example would be if the buyer's rate of return fell below a defined 'acceptable' level. Special trigger events could also be subjective, such as the 'significant' or 'material' impact of a particular input or factor on the pricing of the gas. There is also commonly an occasional right to seek a price review outside of the established cycle through deployment of a 'joker'.

Separately from price review clauses, some gas sales agreements have included 'hardship' clauses. Hardship clauses operate akin to a contractual *force majeure* provision, as a path to changing contract terms which may go beyond just price (eg, potentially including longer times for payment, the extension of credit or prepayment being made to the seller). Under certain civil legal systems, a right to seek variation of contractual terms where hardship can be established may also be provided for under the applicable governing law. Perhaps one of the best-known examples is Section 36 of the Swedish Contracts Act (although it is commonly very difficult to apply such a provision successfully where contracts were negotiated between sophisticated commercial entities, rather than in a consumer context).

Problems commonly arise in the operation of price review clauses when it is unclear whether the trigger event threshold has been met. These can be the result of poor drafting, but clauses are often deliberately drafted in broad and general terms in an attempt to foster the flexibility necessary to deal with unforeseen events. Of course, this breadth in drafting also allows for arguments over commercial and legal interpretation.

Recent experience has shown that the greater the difference between long-term contract pricing and prices available on spot markets, the greater the incentive to 'take every point' and dispute issues such as whether a trigger point has been met.

Once triggered, price re-opener clauses oblige the parties to review the gas price formula and set certain parameters for that process – for example:

- the process by which the parties should negotiate;
- the methodology for reviewing the price under the contract; and
- the scope of that review (eg, is it only as to price or may other terms also be reviewed, such as volume flexibility?).

3. The 'perfect storm'

From early 2009 onwards (concurrent with the global financial crisis), the number of disputes developing out of price review processes grew significantly, fuelled by the significant differences between long-term contract and spot pricing. It became apparent that despite the inclusion of indexation mechanisms, many long-term gas SPAs were no longer working for parties. Numerous disputes arose as contracts were deemed to be economically unviable, in certain instances to the extent of threatening the solvency of the parties.

The key elements that caused this 'perfect storm' in the European gas industry were as follows:

- The market was liberalised, driven by the EU Third Energy Package and enforcement steps by national regulators. Gas markets became much more interconnected. Gas trading hubs were developed and infrastructure was built which made the spot trading of gas more feasible. At these hubs, gas-to-gas competition took place and so 'market prices' developed and became applicable across more of the European market.
- Energy from new, renewable sources came to the market, supported by preferential governmental policies such as subsidised feed-in tariffs. This increased the energy supply, imposing downward pressure on gas prices.
- The economic slowdown following the financial crisis caused energy demand across Europe to drop, resulting in reduced demand for gas. For example, factories cut energy-intensive production as demand for their output disappeared.
- Fracking and other unconventional gas extraction methods were developed. Again, this increased the supply of gas coming to the market – and the effect of its development in North America meant that the potential of Europe receiving LNG exported from the United States focused minds on potential for further downward price pressure.

As a result, spot market prices for gas effectively 'decoupled' from oil prices. Existing indexation formulae (based on oil prices) were no longer seen as effective. Gas buyers sought to use price re-opener clauses to reconfigure the existing contractual arrangements – primarily in relation to price, but also in relation to the volume of gas to be sold.

Most European gas price contracts provided for a multi-stage dispute resolution process, typically comprising:

- the occurrence of a trigger event;
- service of a notice from one party to the other;
- negotiations between the parties; and
- referral of the dispute to arbitration in the absence of amicable resolution.

The scale of 'delta' between spot and market meant that resort to arbitrations was in many instances inevitable.

These disputes mainly focused on the extent to which the trigger threshold and any other preconditions to price review had been met, and how (if at all) the price should change as a result.

4. The Asian LNG market

The Asian LNG market still largely uses long-term SPAs (typically 20 years or longer), attributable to the large capital outlay needed to extract/produce the gas, and to liquefy and transport it. Long-term LNG SPA contracts feature oil price indexation rather than gas hub pricing. They also commonly include take-or-pay and destination clauses (which effectively restrict the buyer's ability to sell on or divert gas exceeding its requirements to a new destination). In many respects, therefore, the Asian picture resembles the pre-liberalised European natural gas market.

Unlike natural gas, which moves through pipelines, LNG is cryogenically cooled into a liquid state and transferred in containers by specialist ships. While this permits more flexible transit than natural gas, transporting LNG over long distances is very expensive (much more expensive than transporting oil over the same distance), as is regasification for internal delivery within a country by pipeline. This arguably limits the extent to which the LNG market can liberalise in similar fashion to natural gas markets, which are based on pipeline transit.

The large geographic dispersion of market transactions and the aforementioned high transport costs have meant that it has not been easy to date to index LNG contract prices to a 'market price' in Asia. Oil is not a true alternative to LNG, so LNG contract pricing based on oil price indexing can present problems for parties.

In 2016 observers remarked that the LNG market had slipped into supply and demand imbalance and that it was likely to remain there.[1] This was caused by a slowdown in Asian demand, coupled with a rapid increase in new LNG export capacity in net exporting countries such as Australia following

---

[1] N Fulford and R Pereira (2016) "LNG pricing – all change!", *Global Gas Analytics* July 2016, http://gaffney-cline-focus.com/files/Articles/GCA_InterfaxArticle-LNGPricingAllChange.pdf.

technological advances which allowed cheaper and faster production of liquefaction factories and tankers. The result was an oversupply in the market. At the time of writing, however, Asian LNG prices have hit a seasonal four-year high as the Chinese push to increase the proportion of power generated from gas in China (decreasing dependence on coal) takes effect.[2] At the same time, oil and coal prices are high, supporting indexed prices. Current demand levels are concerning LNG buyers in Japan and Korea, and are expected to increase further in winter (LNG demand usually spikes in cold weather).

It is fair to assume that if the Asian LNG market becomes seriously unbalanced in either direction, parties will seek to trigger price review clauses. For example, buyers might seek either to reduce the amount they are paying for LNG under an existing long-term contract or to increase profitability by way of greater flexibility in terms of take-or-pay or destination clauses, or both. This may give rise to an increase in disputes as sellers seek to resist such changes.

Valuable strategic lessons for parties facing a dispute may be taken from the arbitrations which have taken place in recent years in the European market. As explained in more detail below, the outcome of many of these European disputes was the adjustment of gas prices by arbitration tribunals. While the legal regimes governing LNG disputes may often not be European (it is relevant that European civil law regimes may be more conducive to 'adjustment of the contractual bargain' in terms of price review than common law regimes), it is useful to understand how similar problems were addressed by arbitrators in those disputes. Occasionally, quite unexpected outcomes were reached, where a tribunal revised a pricing formula in a significant way or altered other terms of the contract. Some European civil law regimes – for example, those in Scandinavia – allow for the adjustment of a contractual bargain where changes which were unforeseeable at the time the contract was entered into are considered to have caused 'unreasonable hardship' to a party. In certain rare circumstances, a contract may even be declared ineffective.

The results of those European gas price disputes have sometimes come as a surprise to parties which were not necessarily expecting the arbitrators to listen to two proposed pricing structures, but then invent a 'third way' of their own devising. Even if there are significant differences as between legal regimes, there is a strong possibility that arbitrators who can demonstrate experience in the slew of European gas price re-opener claims over recent years may find themselves put forward as strong choices for appointment in Asian LNG disputes, and it would come as no surprise if they were to adopt a similar *modus operandi* to Asian disputes.

---

2   E Terazono (2018) "LNG market enjoys 'China moment' as prices rally", *Financial Times* 2 June 2018, www.ft.com/content/045e81b8-642e-11e8-a39d-4df188287fff.

5. Lessons to be drawn

5.1 Before a dispute arises: triggering a price review

In general, and certainly where the 'triggering party' anticipates resistance to its request for a price review, it is vital that the request be both formally and substantively valid.

(a) Is the price review request formally valid?

A request will be formally valid when it complies with any timing, content and notice requirements set out in the contract, as well as any potential pre-conditions.

The triggering party must be careful to adhere to any time limits set out in the contract. It is sensible to set diary reminders in advance of any windows in which a price review can validly be triggered in order to avoid missing the opportunity to do so.

The triggering party should also check whether any outstanding price review requests have been left open and unresolved, which could potentially prevent a new review being validly triggered.

The content of any request must strike a balance between complying with contractual requirements (eg, where reasons must be given for the request – a common feature of price review clauses) and allowing some room for manoeuvre and subsequent development of arguments. Where the contract is silent on what should be included, a (broad) description of the circumstances causing the request could sensibly be included to frame discussions.[3] Later, it may be desirable to add further detail or further justifications for the review.

Similarly, the party objecting to the price review will want to make clear that its stated objections are not exclusive and may be expanded on later.

It is not usual for a price review clause to require parties to set out their requested new price formula in the trigger notice and not doing so will allow the requesting party additional time to refine the formula in negotiations. However, if omitted without any saving wording, it may provide a means for the objecting party to challenge the validity of the notice. A balance must be struck.

Where the wording of a contract does not give specific guidance as to the level of detail or the extent of the reasoning to be given in the trigger notice, it is useful to refer to the parties' practice in previous price reviews.

(b) Is the price review request substantively valid?

As well as establishing whether the relevant market conditions are grounds for

---

3   Final Award in Case 9812 (August 1999), quoted in M Polkinghorne and SM Volkner (2003) "Price Re-Openers In Long Term Gas Supply Agreements", in JM Gaitis (ed). *The Leading Practitioner's Guide to International Oil and Gas Arbitration* 531–532.

a price review, the triggering party must check the contract carefully to ensure that its reasons constitute acceptable justification.

Again, using diary reminders for price review request windows can allow a party to prepare supporting evidence in advance of serving the request itself. This allows a swift and informed response to be given if the non-triggering party objects to the request. Keeping a weather eye on market developments and ensuring that they can be suitably evidenced is equally important.

5.2 Obligations to negotiate

Where an SPA provides that the parties must negotiate (and in particular, where the obligation is a part or precondition of a staged dispute resolution mechanism), the European gas price arbitration experience tells us that this obligation cannot safely be ignored by the parties.

Even where a contract is vague as to the need to negotiate in good faith, or does not mention it at all, some civil law regimes will imply a contractual obligation that the parties do so. By contrast, some common law regimes will regard an agreement to negotiate as an 'agreement to agree' (and therefore as unenforceable) and are less likely to imply a good-faith provision into a contract.

Nevertheless, it is well worth avoiding the risk of even a loosely worded obligation to negotiate being treated as a precondition to arbitration, with the result that a constituted tribunal is found later to lack jurisdiction.

Parties should therefore take advice early as to what they are required to do under the dispute resolution provisions in their contract, and ensure that they do not proceed to arbitration or the next stage of the tiered dispute resolution mechanism until they are confident that they may safely do so. It would be unwise to fight an arbitration only to discover at the end that the arbitrator has no jurisdiction because the stages of the dispute resolution process set out by the contract were not properly completed.

Where negotiations do take place, it can be prejudicial to a party if it is later shown to have adopted in those negotiations a different position from that which it takes before an arbitral tribunal. It is therefore important that discussions be carried out on a without prejudice basis (ie, they cannot be referred to or relied upon by the parties in subsequent proceedings – although advice should be taken as to whether the legal regime that would ultimately govern an arbitration respects such principles). This should be stated expressly before and at any negotiations to resolve the dispute.

Notes should also be kept of the discussions, so that where the discussions do not benefit from without prejudice privilege, there is a record of the position(s) taken and inconsistency can be avoided. Relevant and timely input from legal and technical experts will be of paramount importance.

5.3   Trigger events

Experience tells us that a party is unlikely to be able simply to assert that the trigger threshold for a price review has been met. It is probable that some measure of support will be needed and this should include a clear position as to the relevant market where the gas is being marketed. Where the contract lacks clarity on this point, expert evidence will be needed.

5.4   Confidentiality and privilege

Pricing formulae are by their nature extremely commercially sensitive. It is advisable to check to what extent the contract provides for the arbitration to be confidential. If there are any doubts or concerns, early engagement with the tribunal and counterparty to the dispute to address concerns as to confidentiality and commercial secrets will avoid unpleasant surprises later.

To give an example, where a buyer is requesting a supply price reset on the basis that it cannot make a profit selling gas on, it will need to provide evidence of confidential sales data. Perhaps, however, a subsidiary company of the seller competes with the buyer, making the buyer particularly reluctant to share its sales data. Early engagement might allow the parties to agree for the buyer's portfolio of sales to be audited by an independent auditor.

Issues to consider include the following:

- Will documents provided to lawyers, expert witnesses and to the tribunal remain confidential?
- Where documents are ordered by the tribunal to be produced, to what degree can they be treated as confidential and will concerns as to commercial secrecy be an effective defence against production?
- To what extent will the proceedings – and in particular the award, which may contain a record of any evidence submitted (including key provisions of the contract itself) – be confidential?

To assist in establishing and maintaining both confidentially and legal privilege (which protects certain categories of sensitive documents from compulsory production), legal counsel should be instructed early on and advice should be taken on the extent to which documents are circulated within the business. Fully involving legal counsel early in the process of a gas price arbitration can protect a party by allowing it to make fully informed and correct decisions on the treatment and creation of documents. Getting these decisions right will pay dividends should the dispute proceed to an arbitration in which document production orders are made. This is an area where both parties to the dispute may share similar concerns as to preserving confidentiality, so 'confidentiality club' type arrangements may well be mutually attractive.

5.5 Economic evidence

It is important to gather and carefully analyse the economic evidence in support of any claim or defence before beginning a price review. In the first instance, it is essential to understand whether the economic evidence supports the need for a price review before beginning the lengthy and expensive process of bringing a case for one. This can be difficult in an opaque market.

Further, having the right expert team in place as early as possible will be a significant advantage for any party in a gas price arbitration. There is a finite number of suitably qualified individuals who are experienced in giving evidence before international tribunals.

It is therefore important to identify and instruct suitable experts early on. This is particularly the case where an expert witness with recent experience of industry practice is needed. Faced with evidence from an experienced commercial practitioner with expertise in contract management or negotiation against a consultant economist who has spent little time at the 'coalface', arbitrators may find the former more compelling. The most compelling expertise for a tribunal is often that of 'doing' over many years in the industry.

It is also relevant that, where International Chamber of Commerce (ICC) arbitration rules are adopted, 'trade usages' are expressly to be taken into account by the tribunal per Article 21(2) of the ICC Rules.

5.6 Selecting an arbitrator

In the context of a gas pricing dispute, care should be given to the choice of arbitrators and, in particular, the selection of a chairperson. Gas pricing disputes often involve complex economic principles as much as they do questions of law, and it is important to have an arbitral tribunal which can understand and assess the arguments being made on these principles. Equally, as explained above, experience of the gas sector can be very useful and may be preferred by a selecting party.

Parties should be aware, when selecting counsel or arbitrators, that those individuals with considerable experience in dealing with gas price arbitrations are likely to have gained that arbitration experience in civil law European forums. In fact, there is a distinct group of lawyers, arbitrators, economists and other practitioners with shared experience of European disputes and the complex economic principles that may be involved. Against this background, it is important for a party to understand what its chosen arbitrator or chairperson's experience might be, and how that might influence the approach taken to its dispute, in terms of both procedural issues and the award itself.

Civil law principles have achieved greater prominence in the resolution of gas price disputes, being part of the dominant legal systems in the primary jurisdictions for such disputes. This is because the (common law) UK gas market was liberalised earlier than its continental neighbours under the Thatcher government. As a result, fewer common law gas pricing disputes were seen when gas and oil prices decoupled.

Arbitrators and lawyers working on gas price arbitrations in Europe are commonly thought to have been significantly influenced by civil law principles and practices (including common law practitioners, such as the authors of this chapter). Of course, many arbitrators will have come from civil law backgrounds in the first place, but those arbitrators with a common law background who have sat in many civil law proceedings will naturally have had their point of view widened, and may be more open to different ways of doing things than they might otherwise have been. They may even subconsciously see a civil law approach as the norm in a gas pricing dispute and take an unexpected approach to document production.

Further, a tribunal's understanding of the extent of its jurisdiction to amend the contract (beyond the immediate scope of the price re-opener mechanism) may tend towards a (potentially more interventionist) civil law approach, even where the governing law of the SPA is common law.

In this regard, perhaps the most controversial aspect of the European gas price arbitrations has been the tendency of some tribunals to decide that their jurisdiction goes beyond a mere adjustment to the price of gas under the contract. The most famous instance of this is the *Atlantic LNG* case.[4]

In *Atlantic LNG*, the seller was to deliver its gas mostly to receiving terminals in Spain, but the buyer had the option to sell some gas on to its terminal in Boston. Regardless of where the cargoes went, the pricing was based on the price of LNG in Spain. This became a problem for the seller when US gas prices rose and Spanish gas prices dropped, causing the buyer to require all its gas to be delivered to Boston by the seller. The seller triggered the price review clause, which required only that a "fair and equitable" price be set. The tribunal's award provided for a new, unrequested, dual-price structure which was tied to either New England or Spanish LNG prices, depending on where the majority of the LNG cargoes were delivered.

In other cases, tribunals have looked at other elements of the price formulae in an attempt to make a fair and equitable award – for example, changing the elements in the 'basket' of fuel price references or moving a contract from oil price-linkage to hub pricing. This arguably amounts to rewriting the parties' contractual bargain for them and is therefore outside the tribunal's jurisdiction. In the worst-case scenario, parties are left with an amended contract which has a pricing formula outside the bounds of normal industry practice and is potentially unworkable.

Issues particularly worthy of consideration by parties considering whom to appoint to hear their gas pricing dispute include the following:

---

4   *Atlantic LNG Company of Trinidad & Tobago v Gas Natural Aprovisionamientos SDG SA*, UNCITRAL, Final Award dated 17 January 2008.

- What view is the arbitrator likely to take of his or her jurisdiction in a gas price dispute?
- What approach is the arbitrator likely to take to document production?
- How comfortable is the arbitrator likely to be with adjusting anything beyond price in the pricing formula?
- How far might the arbitrator be comfortable in applying governing law hardship regimes or even competition law mechanisms as a route to adjusting the contractual bargain?

Where possible, a party (or its counsel) should look into any published awards to which the arbitrator has been party, or any articles or books to which he or she has contributed. This is an area where legal counsel can assist, as they will be engaged with the arbitration community and may have previous experience of an arbitrator and their practices and views. Where experienced experts have been instructed early on, their input can also be very valuable.

6. Conclusion

For two decades after the introduction in Europe of Troll and Groningen model long-term gas sales contracts, arbitrations to determine price revision were all but unheard of. That has changed dramatically in the past few years and at least some of the ingredients that led to disputes in the European gas market appear also to feature in recent Asian developments. A little learning from history may prove invaluable for all concerned.

EPC and construction disputes

Patrese McVeigh
Rob Palmer
Ashurst LLP

1. Introduction

Construction projects continue to evolve in scope and complexity, challenging the limits of engineering, design and construction in remarkable ways. Nowhere is this better demonstrated than in the energy sector, where technically complex projects in remote and often hostile locations are constructed under ever-increasing pressures of time. Frequently, work on these projects is tendered out on an engineering, procurement and construction (EPC) basis.

Quality, time and cost objectives do not usually sit well together. EPC contracts provide the framework for managing risks by, for the most part, shifting the risk of delivery to the contractor, albeit at a potential price premium.

This chapter provides an overview of the structure of EPC contracts, typical time, cost and quality-related obligations, the nature of typical claims and the processes for resolving any consequent disputes.

2. EPC and other construction contracts

2.1 EPC contracts

An EPC contract is, as the name suggests, an agreement for the provision of all detailed design and engineering for a particular project (or part of a project), the procurement of all equipment and services, and the construction work itself. EPC contracts are used extensively throughout the oil, gas, petrochemical and resources industries, which typically involve large-scale, complex projects.

The exact form of an EPC contract will vary depending on a number of factors, such as:

- the particular industry;
- the level of sophistication of the project parties;
- the owner's level of involvement or integration with the contractor team; and
- the history between the owner and contractor.

Phases of work covered, however, are:

- engineering and design, typically involving the development of the design concept into detailed specifications and procedures, technical drawings and material lists for the purposes of construction. Importantly, this may not require the contractor to start from scratch. In the context of EPC contracts, it is not unusual for the contractor to have the benefit of an initial feasibility study and concept design for delivery of the project (sometimes referred to as the 'front end engineering design' or 'FEED');

- procurement, typically involving purchase of the goods and services required to deliver the project. This is often a significant task, requiring a well-managed and organised system of tendering for certain works, critically assessing all bids received for those works and selecting a successful supplier or contractor; and

- construction, typically involving the management/supervision of suppliers and subcontractors, and performance of physical construction work. Essential to this phase are efficient and effective collaboration between multiple parties and coordination of disparate and time-dependent activities. The programme or schedule of activities cannot be rigid, however; it must be flexible enough to change and adapt to various hurdles and unforeseen circumstances as construction progresses.

No matter what the size of a construction project, it will likely involve a complex structure of contractual relationships between multiple parties. Under an EPC contract, the owner (also sometimes referred to as the principal or employer) will engage a main contractor to complete the works. The main contractor will then often engage other professional consultants (eg, engineers, architects, project managers, surveyors), as well as specialist subcontractors in order to complete the works.

There can be additional layers of complexity where the owner finances the project through debt and equity arrangements, where government or state-owned entities are involved, or where the owner is an agent or manager of a partnership or joint venture made up of entities with competing or conflicting interests.

There are many variants of this type of contract. For example, EPCM contracts are also frequently used on large-scale energy projects and typically involve a management contractor taking on management responsibility (but not delivery risk) for a project. These are, however, beyond the scope of this chapter.

2.2 Standard forms

For large-scale energy projects, contracts are frequently prepared on a bespoke basis. However, there are a number of standard form contracts available for the parties to use, including the New Engineering Contract (NEC) the International Federation of Consulting Engineers (FIDIC) and the CREIN/LOGIC forms.

There are a number of advantages in using standard form contracts, including drafting efficiencies and greater certainty in drafting (as the clauses have often been interpreted by the courts or arbitral tribunals). There are also disadvantages, in that the standard contracts are not 'one size fits all'; any perception that they are can lead to undesirable consequences.

3. Common areas of dispute

Major construction projects have a number of inherent risks. These can be grouped into the following broad categories:

- time-related risks;
- cost-related risks;
- quality-related risks; and
- political/economic risks.

3.1 Time-related risks and claims

EPC contracts generally set a date for the works to commence, as well as a date by which the works are to be completed. 'Completion' may take place for different parts of the works at different times, and may involve different stages (eg, 'mechanical' completion, followed first by a commissioning process and then by functional testing).

The contractor is incentivised to deliver a project by the stipulated deadline in a number of ways. Delivering the project on time means that the contractor will avoid having to otherwise pay the owner damages (often in the form of 'liquidated damages'). At times, a contractor may be additionally incentivised to complete works on time by the payment of bonuses.

Whether a project is completed on time is often of great commercial significance. Delays are not unusual, however, reflected by a myriad of potential causes of delay, such as:

- delays in obtaining permissions or approvals (eg, from government departments, local councils and landholders);
- delays in obtaining site access;
- poor or unrealistic scheduling of activities;
- design changes;
- delays in ordering materials and their delivery;
- shortages in manpower, equipment and/or materials;
- inclement weather;
- unforeseen ground conditions; and
- lack of funding.

(a) Extensions of time

While the contractor is responsible for achieving a completion date, in the event of a delay it may be entitled to an extension of time. Most EPC contracts include provision for a contractor to request an extension of time, typically requiring that the contractor submit a formal notice to the owner within a certain period of discovering that the works will be delayed and identify the reason for the delay. The contractor is likely to be entitled to an extension of time where the delay was caused by the owner or (perhaps) was outside the control of the parties.

The ability of a contractor to request an extension of time in circumstances where the delay was caused by the owner embodies an important principle of construction law, at least under English law and other common law systems: the prevention principle. This legal principle relevantly provides that:

- the owner cannot insist on the contractor completing the works by the date for completion where it has prevented the contractor from performing that obligation;[1] and
- in circumstances where the delay is caused by the owner and the contract fails to provide an entitlement to an extension of time, the contractor will be excused from having to complete the works by the date for completion and will instead be permitted to complete the works within a reasonable time (referred to as 'time at large'). A consequence of this is that the owner will be unable to claim liquidated damages for the contractor failing to complete the works by the date for completion.[2]

Most EPC contracts provide that where a contractor fails to achieve completion on time (by either the contracted date for completion or the relevant extended time for completion), an owner will be entitled to claim liquidated damages. Liquidated damages are a predetermined estimate of the damages that the owner will suffer if the works are not completed on time. The liquidated damages are often calculated as a daily rate referable to the contract price. Such provisions can be advantageous for both parties. For an owner, they remove the need to prove actual loss (which can be both time consuming and expensive). For a contractor, liabilities are capped and risk can be priced at the tender stage.

Aside from claiming liquidated damages, it may also be open for an owner to consider terminating the contract. EPC contracts may include an entitlement to terminate where delay in completion continues beyond the maximum period specified for liquidated damages.

(b) Schedules and delay analysis

It is often the case that any relevant delay is assessed having regard to a programme or schedule of works developed by the contractor for the purpose of

---

1   *Multiplex Constructions (UK) Ltd v Honeywell Control Systems Ltd (No 2)* [2007] BLR 195.
2   *Peak Construction (Liverpool) Ltd v McKinney Foundations* (1970) 1 BLR 114.

tracking the progress of works to achieve completion. Such a schedule should identify the activities required to achieve completion and the duration and sequence of those activities. This document may be approved by the owner or the contract administrator, and can be complex when there are sequences of connected events and multiple work fronts being carried out at the same time.

EPC contracts typically call for reporting of progress against the schedule and for the schedule regularly to be updated. In some cases, however, the connection between the schedule and reality can be tenuous.

A divergence between schedule and reality is measured using the technical discipline of delay analysis. At a basic level, this analysis involves examining a particular event and describing the impact that it had on the project works. Not all events will impact on the project works in a way that delays achieving the completion date, with disputes typically relating to whether (and to what extent) events have impacted on the sequence of activities that is necessary for achieving completion by the completion date (referred to as the critical path).

A number of different methods are used in delay analysis.[3] Each method has its own advantages and disadvantages, and may produce different results when applied to the same facts. Accordingly, selecting a method should involve careful consideration. However, in practice, parties can be limited by the information and evidence that is available to them. The main techniques are generally accepted to be as follows:

- 'Impacted as-planned': This method takes the original schedule and, at the time an event occurs, adjusts it to take into account the total estimated impact of that event on the project works. An advantage of this method is that it requires minimal records. A disadvantage is that impact of an event is only an estimate, not the reality.

- 'Time impact': This method involves taking an updated schedule and adjusting it with programming software to allow for the total estimated impact of that event on the project works. An advantage of this method is that it is considered to most closely reflect the position as at the time of the event. A disadvantage is that it depends on the reliability of the updated schedule, which can be costly to verify.

- 'Time-slice windows': This method involves using a series of schedules that each record the progress of the works for a particular period (eg, a month). Programming software is used to analyse the schedules and identify the activities that form the critical path. It also compares the status of those activities at the end of one schedule and the start of the following schedule (the 'window') to determine the extent of the delay. Following this, contemporaneous project records are used to reveal the event that is likely to have caused that delay. Utilising contemporaneous

---

3   Society of Construction Law Delay and Disruption Protocol (February 2017) (2nd Ed).

129

records is certainly a key advantage of windows methods. Similar to time-impact analysis, it can be costly where the series of schedules proves to be unreliable and needs to be verified.

- 'As-planned versus as-built windows': Rather than use a series of regularly updated schedules, this method involves using only those reliable schedules which are available in order to identify the activities that form the critical path, then comparing the planned completion dates against the actual completion dates of those activities to determine the extent of the delay. As in the time-slice windows method, contemporaneous records are used to identify the extent to which the event caused the delay.

- 'Collapsed as built': This method involves taking the schedule that has been updated to record all the project works (the final as-built schedule) and, in reverse chronological order, adjusting it by subtracting the estimated impact of a particular event on the project works. The modified schedule is expected to reveal when the contractor would have completed the project works, but for the delays. An advantage of this approach is that it starts with what actually occurred on site. However, this assumes the final as-built schedule is reliable and includes the necessary logic to enable this exercise.

- 'Retrospective as built': This method involves taking the final as-built schedule, identifying (retrospectively) the activities that form the critical path, then comparing the planned completion dates of those activities with the actual completion dates to determine the extent of the delay. Contemporaneous records are used to ascertain the event that caused the delay. Similar to the collapsed as built, an advantage to this approach is that it starts with what actually occurred on site. A disadvantage of this method is that it may not allow for changes to the criticality of certain activities.

3.2 Cost-related risks and claims

An EPC contract will specify the amount that the contractor is entitled to be paid for the project works (often defined as the contract price). The contract may adopt one of a number of methods to calculate the price.

The most common pricing method for an EPC contract is lump sum. A lump-sum contract is one where the parties agree on the payment of a stipulated sum for all the works before the works commence. This pricing methodology is consistent with the philosophy underlying an EPC contract of handing over responsibility and risk to a contractor; the contractor is expected to price that risk accordingly at tender stage.

While the pricing methodology in a contract may be relatively certain, the scope of work can frequently change. The scope of work often changes as the works progress to allow for different work methodologies and scheduling, and the omission or inclusion of work. Where those changes deviate from the original design or plan, there will be an impact on the contract price.

(a)   *Variations*

Given the impact on the contract price, disputes often arise as to whether there has in fact been a change or variation to the original design (as opposed to an instruction within the contemplated and priced scope of work). If there has been a variation, there is also often a dispute as to the value of that change. The pricing methodology adopted in the contract will generally inform how to assess the value of the variation in scope.

There are many ways in which the scope of work may change. These include instructions from the owner:

- to alter the original plans or design;
- to change work conditions or management;
- to vary certain methods and procedures;
- to vary the amount of work or materials required for the project; or
- to account for unforeseen physical conditions on site (where the risk of such conditions has not been allocated to the contractor).

An EPC contract typically will describe the way in which an owner may issue instructions in relation to the works. It will usually require the owner to issue an instruction in writing or, in the case of urgent instructions, may allow for the instructions to be provided orally and confirmed in writing at a later date.

The instruction may or may not entitle the contractor to an adjustment in the contract price. No entitlement will arise where the instructed work forms part of the scope of works, either expressly or by necessary implication. This will be, for example, where the contractor's design proves to be inadequate and has to be changed. In those circumstances, the contractor will be unable to recover any additional design costs it incurs.

On the other hand, an entitlement to an adjustment in the contract price may arise where the instructed works deviate from the original scope of works, design, plan or programme. This may be where, for example, the owner expressly includes extra works. A more complex example would be where the owner instructs the contractor to complete the same works, but in a reduced timeframe and, as a consequence, the contractor increases its labour force with a corresponding drop in productivity. A claim for costs of this kind is often referred to as a claim for disruption costs.

Instead of adding to the scope of works, the owner may omit works. This may be where, for example, the project has progressed in a way that makes certain items of work unnecessary. However, this power is usually limited in a way that prevents the owner from fundamentally altering the scope of works or deleting works and engaging another person to perform those works.

In addition to express instructions from an owner, an EPC contract usually will also stipulate the way in which a contractor should notify the owner of an entitlement to a variation. This may be necessary where the scope of works is varied as a result of unforeseen physical conditions, such as unexpected underground obstructions or unpredictable soil conditions, or where other outside factors necessitate a change.

(b) Valuation

If the parties accept there has been a change in scope, the change will need to be valued so that the contract price can be adjusted accordingly. Where the contract prescribes the way in which a variation is to be valued, the mechanism typically will be informed by the pricing methodology adopted in the contract. Where the works are not of a similar character to the work set out the schedule or in the context of a lump-sum contract, reasonable rates are generally appropriate.

Valuing a variation in the scope of work may be relatively straightforward. This will be where, for example, the change in scope of works is clearly defined and agreed, and its valuation is uncontroversial. More often than not, valuing variations and cost claims is complex and necessitates input from specialised experts, such as quantity surveyors.

3.3 Quality-related risks and claims

(a) Obligations as to quality

A contractor makes a number of promises in relation to the quality of its performance and the works when it agrees to take on a project. EPC contracts typically set out these promises in great detail, in the form of warranties, representations, undertakings and guarantees.

The promises will extend to the work for which the contractor is responsible – which, in the case of an EPC contractor, will include design, engineering, procurement, commissioning and testing activities.

At a basic level, typically the promises will collectively require the EPC contractor to carry out and complete the works in their entirety, using suitable materials, while exercising reasonable skill and care. In addition, the EPC contractor will frequently warrant that the completed works are reasonably fit for their intended purpose (eg, as stipulated in the contract), possibly for the duration of their expected life. This is different from carrying out the works with reasonable skill and care,[4] and in fact the obligations can co-exist.[5] By way of example, a contractor may design a specification with reasonable skill and care, but the works may nonetheless fail before the end of their expected life.

---

4   *Hancock v BW Brazier (Anerley) Ltd* [196] 1 WLR 1317.
5   *MT Hojgaard A/S v E.ON Climate and Renewables UK* [2015] EWCA Civ 407.

As can be seen, the promises may be expansive and, as a consequence, the risk of exposure to liability is high. An EPC contractor usually limits its potential overall liability by inserting a limitation or exclusion into the EPC contract. An EPC contract will typically limit the overall exposure to the contract price or a fraction thereof and exclude liability for certain kinds of loss, such as 'consequential losses'.

(b)   *Defective work*
Where these promises are breached, the consequences will depend upon how the contract or system of law treats such a breach. Depending on the nature and extent of the defect concerned, the associated costs can be significant and the question of whether work is in fact defective is a common source of dispute.

A defect may arise in a number of ways. In some cases, responsibility for a defect will be readily apparent. It may be that the contractor's design is deficient, in that the contractor prescribes a type or amount material that is wholly unsuitable for the project – for example, piping of an unsuitable thickness. Often, however, responsibility is less clear cut. What if, for example, the contractor has supplied defective materials in reliance upon design parameters supplied (but not verified) by the owner? In every case, a clearly delineated scope of responsibilities is key.

Defects can be categorised into patent and latent defects. The distinguishing feature is the time at which the defect is discovered. A patent defect is a defect that can be discovered on reasonable inspection. A latent defect is a defect that remains hidden from reasonable inspection and may not become apparent for many years.

At the time an owner certifies completion, there may be latent defects, but there should be no patent defects. In practice, however, defects requiring more than minor (*de minimis*) works will often remain unrepaired and the owner will request the contractor to repair the defects within a specified period post-completion. This may give rise to disputes as to when completion was in fact achieved.

It is common for EPC contracts to set aside a specified period post-completion for the contractor to remedy any defects. This is typically referred to as the 'defects liability period' or 'maintenance period'. During this period any defects identified during the defects liability period can be made good (although, in practice, it is often used to also repair defects existing at the time of completion).

If a defect is identified during the defects liability period, the owner may (or may be required to) notify the contractor of the issue and request the contractor to return to site to address it. This notice may not necessarily request the contractor to repair the defect. Frequently, the issue that is initially uncovered is later found to be a consequence or symptom of the actual defect. It may be that the initial notice requests the contractor to return to site to undertake a process of investigation and analysis to determine the nature and extent of the defect, so that the parties may make an informed decision as to the most appropriate next steps.

Depending on the options available under the EPC contract, the most appropriate next step may be for the owner to accept the defective work for a reduction in the contract price. Alternatively, it may be more appropriate for the owner to instruct the contractor to develop a rectification plan and carry out the necessary works. Instead of instructing the contractor to carry out this work, the owner may opt to engage a third party; however, this will be subject to the terms of the contract, which will often require that the contractor first be given the opportunity to rectify. It is often assumed that once the defects liability period expires, the contractor's liability for defects also ends – however, in the absence of provisions to the contrary, this may not be the case.[6]

Outside of the defect liability period, the owner's remedy for defective work often will sound in damages. The guiding principle for calculating contractual damages under most common law systems is to restore the owner, so far as money can do, to the position it would have been had the work conformed with the contract.[7] This may be the cost of repairing the defect. Alternatively, it may be the cost of reinstatement. The cost of reinstatement may be significant – so much so that it is considered unreasonable. In those circumstances, the more appropriate measure of damages will be the diminution in value or, if there is no diminution in value, loss of amenity.[8]

However, such remedies may be limited or excluded. It is common for the parties to agree to place a cap on the total amount of damages that may be recovered or agree to exclude certain types of loses, such as consequential loss. At times, the parties may codify the available remedies by way of a sole and exclusive remedy clause. Such limitations and exclusions will generally be interpreted strictly, but will nonetheless be relevant to assessing a damages award.

3.4 Political and economic risks and claims
Construction projects, particularly large projects, tend to be completed over a significant amount of time, often a number of years. Over that time, the relevant economic and political conditions will inevitably change.

Economic conditions may, for example, be influenced by changes in monetary and fiscal policies, the accessibility of finance, inflation or exchange rates. Political conditions will unsurprisingly change following a change in

---

6   *Hancock v Brazier* [1966] 1 WLR 1317 CA; *Pearce and High v Baxter and Baxter* [1999] EWCA Civ 789. See, also, *Keating on Construction Contracts* (10th Ed), [11-035].
7   *Livingstone v Rawyards Coal Co* (1880) 5 App Cas 25; *Robinson v Harman* (1848) 1 Exch 850.
8   *Ruxley Electronics and Construction Ltd v Forsyth* [1996] AC 344.

government. This goes hand in hand with shifts in policy, such as the appeal of certain infrastructure projects. There may also be legislative changes, such as amendments to labour laws making it more expensive to employ workers or the introduction of employment quotas.

These changes have the potential to increase or decrease the cost of completion, such as by making the price of labour more or less expensive. They could also increase or decrease the scope of work, such as by introducing a new carbon emissions regime that necessitates the development and implementation of a raft of procedures and protocols. They could also jeopardise the viability of an entire project – for example, where the government rolls out populist export controls that, in effect, reduce the anticipated rate of return for the project or, in circumstances where the government is involved in the project, simply backs out of its investment. Understandably, disputes can arise as to who should be responsible for bearing the risk of these changes.

EPC contracts usually contain a variety of mechanisms aimed at addressing the impact of economic and political changes on a project. One mechanism involves calculating the cost of the completed work at regular intervals with a formula that captures any relevant rise or fall in the price of certain activities and items. This would, for example, capture general inflation or specific rises in the cost of labour. This mechanism is commonly referred to as a 'fluctuations' clause (or a 'variation of price', 'variation in cost' or 'rise and fall' clause).

A so-called 'change in law' clause may entitle a contractor to claim additional time or cost where a project is affected by legislative changes that impact on project delivery. Eligibility is often limited to those changes that would not have been reasonably foreseeable at the time of entering into the construction contract.

While beyond the scope of this chapter, bilateral or multilateral investment treaties may also provide rights of redress in certain circumstances.

4. Dispute resolution processes

4.1 Dispute resolution mechanisms
The construction industry utilises a range of dispute resolution processes, from informal to formal and collaborative to adversarial. At the informal and collaborative end of the spectrum is negotiation. This involves an owner and contractor discussing the dispute among themselves and agreeing on a compromise that seeks to preserve each other's own interests.

Mediation is also commonly used in the construction industry. Similar to negotiation, mediation involves an owner and contractor discussing the dispute and agreeing on a compromise. Unlike negotiation, the discussion is guided by an independent third party, which can be particularly useful in breaking any deadlocks and ensuring that the discussion remains constructive. Mediations can be arranged through a mediation institute or on an *ad hoc* basis.

A dispute board is a project-specific dispute resolution process intended to provide an alternative to conventional dispute resolution mechanisms such as arbitration or litigation. Usually the parties will appoint a board (on either a 'standing' or an '*ad hoc*' basis) with jurisdiction to hear and advise the parties on issues and disputes as they arise. Typically, a board will comprise three independent members, who will issue either non-binding recommendations or binding decisions (depending upon the parties' agreement). Typically, contracts provide that even binding decisions can be referred on to arbitration or litigation.

In the case of specific technical disputes, an owner and contractor may consider referring the matter to expert determination. This involves the parties preparing submissions on their respective positions and providing the submissions to an independent expert for review and determination. This is best suited to disputes that involve a single issue of a technical, rather than legal, nature – for example, determining whether a particular material meets the relevant contractual specifications. In these circumstances, the parties may have greater confidence that the suitably qualified expert will determine the dispute correctly.

For international construction projects in the energy sector, arbitration tends to be the formal dispute resolution method of choice. Arbitration involves the owner and contractor presenting their respective cases to a panel of one or three independent arbitrators selected by the parties or by a specialist institution. The arbitral tribunal will consider the information presented to deliver a final and binding decision.

Alternatively, the parties may elect to refer disputes to the courts of a specified country, or to remain silent as to jurisdiction (in which case any dispute should be referred to the court having jurisdiction pursuant to the relevant conflict of laws rules). Court litigation involves the owner and contractor presenting their respective cases, in accordance with the rules and procedures of the court, to a judge or panel of judges, who will consider and weigh the evidence before delivering a final and binding judgment.

An EPC contract will typically specify the process which the parties have agreed to use to resolve any disputes. It may specify a single dispute resolution process, such as arbitration. However, frequently it will specify a customised range of processes ordered in tiers from least formal to most formal. It may specify, for example, that the parties are to attempt to resolve any dispute by negotiation and, if unsuccessful, by mediation, and, if still unsuccessful, by arbitration.

One advantage of a multi-tiered dispute resolution process is that it can direct the parties to engage in procedures, such as negotiation and mediation, that they may not otherwise have considered. When successful, resolving disputes through less formal means can have significant benefits, such as reducing litigation costs and preserving the relationship between the parties, which is particularly important when project works are continuing.

However, multi-tiered dispute resolutions processes also have a number of disadvantages. Less formal processes can be pointless, particularly when the project is nearing completion and the parties have become entrenched in their positions. In these circumstances, the process may only delay resolution of the dispute. Further, introducing layers of complexity into the dispute resolution process may not reduce the number of disputes being heard in the arbitration – it may have the opposite effect, especially where the process is not clearly drafted. Parties may dispute which process should be used for hearing a particular dispute, whether there has been compliance with the relevant pre-arbitral processes and the effect of any non-compliance. Such disputes will need to be heard before an arbitral tribunal or, at times, in separate proceedings before the relevant national court.

An owner and contractor should consider the advantages and disadvantages of the various dispute resolution processes before adopting any one process for the project. In practice, the simplest and clearest approach is often best.

4.2   Arbitration

Arbitration is consistently chosen by an owner and contractor as either the sole dispute resolution process or the ultimate dispute resolution process in a multi-tiered dispute resolution arrangement. This is particularly so for large cross-border construction projects. There are a number of reasons why this is the case.

One reason is the availability of construction expertise and experience. EPC contracts themselves can be technical and voluminous, and are more easily digested by those with experience in the industry. Construction disputes can also be technically complex, necessitating a high level of understanding of a range of disciplines, such as engineering, quantity surveying and accounting. Arbitration accommodates this by giving the parties the freedom to appoint arbitrators with expertise in construction law and the relevant technical disciplines.

Another reason is the flexibility of the proceedings. Traditional court procedures and processes do not always allow technical disputes, such as construction disputes, to be presented in a simple and effective way. Arbitration may not suffer the same limitations, in that the parties may in principle (if not always in practice) agree on the manner in which the case is presented, such as the number of pleadings, the rules of evidence, the extent of document disclosure and timing.

Another advantage of arbitration concerns confidentiality. Construction disputes often involve serious allegations attacking the inherent capabilities of the contractor or the good faith of the owner. Such allegations would ordinarily attract significant publicity and damage the reputation of the contractor, the owner and possibly the project itself. Arbitration limits this concern by keeping the proceedings private and, subject to applicable laws, confidential.

The neutrality of arbitration can also be a significant benefit. In cross-border matters, there may be a perception that the national court of the owner or the contractor may be biased against the alien entity. Arbitration removes this issue by allowing the parties to hold the proceedings in a neutral forum.

In the event that a construction dispute escalates to arbitration, a number of strategies can be used to make the process more efficient and effective. A full discussion of these is beyond the scope of this chapter; however, strategies might include the following:

- At the contract drafting stage, well before a dispute arises, the owner and the contractor should make sure that the dispute resolution clause has been properly and clearly drafted. This can limit the scope of, for example, jurisdictional challenges as to whether arbitration is the chosen forum;

- During the project stage, the owner and the contractor should be astute in their management of all project documentation, such as contract documents, project correspondence (including emails), site records and photos. This is often a substantial task in large-scale projects, but proper document management becomes invaluable when preparing for an arbitration; and

- At the dispute stage, parties should be as prepared as possible as early as possible. The owner and contractor should consider engaging and fully briefing legal counsel and any necessary technical experts early on for the purposes of understanding the strengths and weaknesses of their respective cases. This may assist in the settlement of some weaker disputes. It will also help the parties to work out what will be the clearest case theory that will resonate with the arbitrators and achieve a successful outcome.

Joint venture disputes

Nicholas Lingard
Emily Stennett
Freshfields Bruckhaus Deringer

1. Introduction

The term 'joint venture' (JV) is used to encapsulate many different forms of collaborative business relationships, from a contractual arrangement (eg, a joint production agreement) to the incorporation of a vehicle jointly owned by the parties to the venture. It has been said that: "Mergers, like marriages, can be legally defined and therefore readily counted. Alliances [JVs] are more like love affairs: they take many forms, may be transient or lasting."[1] Across those various forms, the key characteristic of a JV is the element of collaboration between parties to further a particular commercial goal.

So understood, JVs are the most common way of organising at least oil and gas investments, and many other investments in the energy sector. In many cases, projects in the energy sector are simply too large for a single company (even an international major) to finance alone. JVs may also enable entry to markets that would otherwise be inaccessible due to local content regulations (eg, by pairing with a local partner), or facilitate the sharing of specialised or local knowledge (eg, a small company with the technological expertise to pursue a particular project but not the capital, might partner with a larger company that can fund the project but does not have the internal know-how to implement the project alone). They can also be attractive in terms of risk sharing and market positioning. A recent study found that as much as 71% of upstream investment in oil and gas megaprojects is made through JVs.[2] Such are the benefits of investing through JVs in the energy sector that it is common for collaborative arrangements to be formed among parties that are otherwise competitors.[3]

Against this background – particularly once one factors in the market volatility and political instability familiar to investors in the energy industry –

---

[1]   *The Economist*, 15 May 1999, p109, cited in K Reece Thomas and C Ryan, *The Law and Practice of Shareholders' Agreements* (4th edn 2014), p271.
[2]   EY, *Joint ventures for oil and gas megaprojects* (2015), p1.
[3]   It has been observed that this collaboration among direct competitors is more of a widespread phenomenon in the energy industry than in other major industries: "It is difficult to imagine Coke and Pepsi negotiating a joint venture, but international oil companies (IOCs) do so frequently". T Martin and JJ Park QC, "Global Petroleum Industry Model Contracts Revisited: Higher, Faster, Stronger", (2010) Vol 3(1) *Journal of World Energy Law & Business* 4.

it is unsurprising that disputes among parties to an international JV in this sector are a frequent occurrence. They can arise at any stage in the life of the venture or before it has even fully crystallised (eg, it is not uncommon to see a dispute under a joint bidding agreement before the relevant concession has been awarded). The commercial success – if the parties have failed, for example, to properly define the manner in which profits are to be shared – as much as commercial failure of the venture can engender conflict. Often the JV will involve a long-term relationship between the JV partners (in many cases not only in the context of that particular investment, but also others), such that it might not be a single incident but a series of incidents that over time causes a rupture in the venturers' relationship.

Most of the time, given the commercial importance of continuing the relationship, parties will make efforts to resolve JV disputes without recourse to formal dispute resolution proceedings. However, when a disagreement does translate into formal proceedings, it likely will involve a high-stakes issue, with serious – perhaps existential – consequences for the JV, or indeed one of the parties to it. It is therefore essential that proper mechanisms are in place to resolve such disputes in a fair, efficient and effective manner.

The preferred method for the resolution of energy sector disputes, including in relation to JVs, is international arbitration.[4] A number of factors give arbitration the edge over litigation as a dispute resolution mechanism in this area.[5] It is trite to observe that large proportions of the world's proved oil and gas reserves – and, as a result, oil and gas investments – are found in countries where it can be difficult for foreign investors to do business.[6] In addition, energy JVs often involve parties of different nationalities and one party may be a state or state-owned entity. In such circumstances, a party is unlikely (and in some cases would be ill advised) to agree to litigate in the other party's home state. Arbitration offers the opportunity for neutrality. It also has the benefit of allowing the parties the flexibility to tailor the dispute resolution procedure best to fit their circumstances and, crucially, provides a robust framework for enforcement of awards rendered. These points are discussed further below.

---

4   PwC and Queen Mary University of London School of International Arbitration, *Corporate Choices in International Arbitration: Industry Perspectives* (2013), p7 (56% of energy-sector respondents identified arbitration as their preferred dispute resolution mechanism, 22% court litigation, 17% adjudication/expert determination and 5% mediation). See also London Court of International Arbitration (LCIA), *Facts and Figures – 2017 Casework Report* (2018), pp5 (24% of cases commenced under the LCIA Rules in 2016 related to the energy and resources sector), 11 (15% of the agreements underlying arbitrations under the LCIA Rules were shareholders' agreements, share purchase agreements and joint venture agreements)

5   See P Oxnard and B Le Bars, "Arbitration of Energy Disputes: Practitioners' Views from London and Paris", in Association for International Arbitration, *Alternative Dispute Resolution in the Energy Sector* (2009) 55, pp57–65.

6   At the time of writing, Venezuela holds the largest individual share of total proved oil reserves (though regionally the largest proportion is located in the Middle East); and Russia, closely followed by Iran, holds the largest proportion of proved natural gas reserves. BP, *BP Statistical Review of World Energy* (67th edn 2018), pp12, 26.

This chapter seeks to identify some of the most common pitfalls that may be encountered in the event that a JV dispute arises and to propose ways to mitigate the risk of ending up on the wrong side of it.

The chapter is organised as follows:

- section 2 discusses typical disputes arising in the JV context;
- section 3 discusses key aspects of arbitration clauses from the perspective of JV parties;
- section 4 considers particular issues arising in the context of multi-party and multi-contract JVs;
- section 5 discusses the significance of structuring decisions in the JV context; and
- section 6 addresses the practicalities of managing a dispute external to the JV.

2. Typical disputes in a JV context

The range of issues to which a dispute could relate in the JV context is vast and the grounds for disagreement are highly fact specific. Rather than attempting to chronicle all of them, this chapter considers, by way of illustrative example only, what is probably the most contentious stage in the life of a JV: the voluntary or forced exit of a party, which may or may not involve the termination of the JV itself.

Almost all JVs will come to an end eventually: many last only a few years.[7] If an exit goes badly, it could seriously affect the parties' relationship, reputations and, critically, value retained from the JV.[8] It is therefore surprising that, according to a recent survey of executives involved in JVs, only 19% of JVs had an exit strategy in place.[9]

So, what are a party's options in the event it decides not to continue in the JV? In the broadest terms, there are three:

- Walk away: The 'nuclear option' for a dissatisfied JV party is simply to down tools and end its involvement with the project. However, even if the exit is motivated by serious breach of contract by the other parties, this approach entails a high risk of a claim for repudiatory breach of contract or similar action being brought against the exiting party. It is generally not an advisable option.
- Exercise a contractual exit right or terminate: The JV agreement might include provisions enabling a party to exit the JV, force the exit of the JV

---

7   EY, *Joint ventures for oil and gas megaprojects* (2015), p1 ("[T]he average JV takes 18 months to establish, yet the vast majority survives less than five years, with some research papers suggesting the failure rate for these relationships is as high as 70%").

8   The importance of exit may be enhanced where a private equity investor – for which exit will typically be at the centre of its strategic planning – becomes involved in an energy JV. This has become increasingly common over recent years as oil prices have depressed.

9   Boston Consulting Group, *Getting More Value from Joint Ventures* (December 2014), p12.

partner or bring the venture to an end (eg, put or call options, deadlock provisions and/or specific termination provisions).[10] Parties should be aware, however, that an attempt to exercise such a right will often be met by a challenge from the other parties to the venture. Enforcing such rights through formal arbitration proceedings may take considerable time and delay the desired exit/termination. As is discussed further below, clear drafting can reduce the scope for a JV partner to frustrate the exercise of contractual exit/termination mechanisms.

- Negotiate an exit: Generally, the optimal approach commercially is for the parties to negotiate and agree the terms of a party's exit and/or the dissolution of the venture. However, this approach should not be viewed as distinct from the approach of exercising a contractual exit/termination right. Strategically, a party's negotiating position may be significantly altered if it can confidently point to a clear contractual provision that supports its right to take the desired action (or, from the other side of the table, make it clear that the party purporting to act is not entitled to do so). In hostile negotiations, parties may consider taking preliminary steps towards formal proceedings in order to enhance their leverage in the commercial negotiations, such as sending a letter before claim or even filing a request for arbitration.

The more thought the parties give to their rights to exit, force another party's exit and/or terminate at the outset of the venture, the more confidently they should be able to invoke (be it formally or in the context of commercial negotiations) the contractual mechanisms when the time comes to do so. There are many such mechanisms and endless variations thereon. This chapter highlights three that often arise in the disputes context: termination provisions, put or call options and forfeiture provisions.

2.1 Termination

One mechanism that a party might employ in appropriate circumstances is a termination clause. The exercise of a right to terminate is obviously a major step and often the subject of disputes. Relative to their importance and the complexity of the disputes to which they give rise, termination clauses are often not afforded sufficient attention at the drafting stage. Termination clauses generally permit a party to terminate the venture, or its interest in the venture, on specified conditions. The condition to exercise may be as simple as the giving of proper notice, without the need for any underlying trigger ('termination for convenience'); or it might additionally be tied to the occurrence of a particular event ('termination for cause'). Termination may also

---

10   See I Hewitt, *Hewitt on Joint Ventures* (6th edn 2016), ch 13.

arise as the result of, for example, a put or call option or default mechanism, as discussed below. Termination arising out of a particular triggering event is more likely to give rise to disputes between the parties than a straightforward termination for convenience, as there is simply more scope for challenge: has it adequately been established that the trigger event has in fact occurred? This is particularly the case when the trigger event involves default on the part of a non-exiting party. The less clearly defined the trigger event is, the easier it will be for the non-exiting party to dispute the fact that its conduct (or omission) constitutes such an event.[11]

Similarly, the procedure for invoking the termination clause should be clearly thought out and reflected in the agreement. For example, the parties should consider whether a defaulting party will be entitled to remedy a default once put on notice of it and, if so, what will constitute a sufficient remedy and what timeframe will be allowed to achieve it. Unduly complicated or restrictive procedures are best avoided, as they heighten the risk of an otherwise valid termination being delayed or defeated on a technicality.

Parties should also be sure to deal in their agreement with the consequences of the exercise of any termination right. The level of complexity that this entails will differ depending on the form of the JV: the termination of a contractual alliance will typically be more straightforward than the termination of a party's interest in an equity JV. In the latter category, additional considerations, such as the handling of the exiting party's interest in the JV company, will need to be factored in. In either case, if the underlying project will continue following one party's exit, the parties must decide, for example, how the assets contributed by the exiting party will be handled (ie, if they will be recovered by that party, the party continuing the project may need to negotiate transitional arrangements) and any new assets acquired or created by the JV company. If a JV agreement forms part of a web of contracts (eg, including transitional services agreements, secondment agreements, marketing agreements and so on), the parties should make clear what they intend to be the consequence of termination of the JV agreement for these various ancillary contracts: are they to stay on foot or will the termination of the JV agreement trigger the termination of some or all of the others? In this scenario it is important to ensure that the termination provisions across the suite of agreements work together. To take another example particularly pertinent to many energy JVs, a key concern for an operator/manager on termination will often be the payment of rehabilitation and decommissioning costs, which can be a significant financial outlay at the end of the life of the JV. A party taking on that role should consider whether it is adequately protected in the event that its coventurer(s) fail to meet a late-

---

11   Trigger events generally should not be linked to overambitious commitments made by either party (or commitments that may no longer be achievable further down the line due to a change in circumstances), or to a general non-material breach of the JV (eg, a failure to provide information).

stage cash call to cover such costs. One way to limit the operator/manager's exposure to counterparty credit risk could be by providing for the creation of a sinking fund.

2.2 Put or call options

In the case of an equity JV, the JV agreement might include an option for a party to 'put' its shares to the other party (ie, require the other party to purchase its shares in the JV company), or to 'call' the other party's shares (ie, require the other party to sell its shares to the 'calling' party).[12] Similarly, a buy-out option might be found in an unincorporated JV (ie, a right to acquire the other JV partner's interest for value).

This can be an onerous remedy, having the effect of forcing a party to buy or sell its interest in the JV, perhaps at a time and/or a price unsatisfactory to it. Accordingly, the exercise of these options in the context of a JV is often hotly contested.

As with termination clauses, the parties can minimise the risk of challenge by ensuring that the trigger event(s)[13] and procedures for invoking the option are clearly drafted and practically workable. For example, if regulatory or shareholder approval is likely to be required for completion of a transfer under any option, any time limits on exercise of the option and completion of the transfer should either be fixed at a sufficiently long period to accommodate fulfilment of that condition or provide for extensions of time if such consents are needed.

It is also critical in the context of a put or call option to consider how the price for the transferring interest will be calculated. This is a commercial question, which could be addressed by reference to any number of formulae.[14] The key issue, in the event that an option ends up being the subject of a dispute, is to ensure that the contract clearly shows how the parties wish to have their interest in the JV valued. Formulae should be closely tested to ensure that they will operate as intended. A vague or unworkable formulation may leave this key question to be answered by an arbitral tribunal, with neither JV party having any certainty as to how it will decide.[15]

---

12   For an example put and call option agreement, see I Hewitt, *Hewitt on Joint Ventures* (6th edn 2016), Precedent 16 in Part E, para E-16.

13   In view of the serious nature of the remedy, hair triggers should be avoided. It is generally preferable to limit buy-out triggers to financial default. If it is necessary to provide for non-financial default triggers, these should be qualified by materiality and have an adequate cure period.

14   For example, the price could be fixed at a set figure, by reference to a formula or by an independent third-party valuer. See I Hewitt, *Hewitt on Joint Ventures* (6th edn 2016), para 13-20.

15   Similar considerations should be taken into account when drafting provisions for pre-emption rights upon a party's voluntary exit. If a party wishes to sell to a third party, confidentiality restrictions may also be critical and should therefore be carefully thought out. Such restrictions can mean that additional consents are required from a JV counterparty in relation to a sale – if a party needs consent from its JV partner to give information to a potential purchaser and that consent is not forthcoming, this could block the sale or affect value.

2.3   Forfeiture

An alternative approach where a party wishes to end the JV for a fault-based reason is to force the defaulting party's exit from the venture through the exercise of a forfeiture provision. A forfeiture provision typically provides that under certain circumstances, a defaulting party must forfeit something – such as all or part of its participating interest in the JV – to the non-defaulting party.

Under a strict forfeiture provision, the defaulting party loses all of its rights to participate in the JV as soon as a default is fully confirmed.[16] It is commonplace for joint operating agreements (JOAs) to contain clauses allowing one party (usually the primary operator) to issue cash calls to its counterparty (or counterparties) in respect of that party's ongoing share of joint expenditure in the project. There will also often be a contractual right for the calling party to require the defaulting party to forfeit its interest in the project if the cash call is not met and is not remedied within time.

Although such provisions are common in energy JVs, a forfeiture provision need not require the defaulting party to give up its entire interest in the JV.[17] For instance, the Association of International Petroleum Negotiators (AIPN) published a Model International JOA in 2012, which contains several alternatives to complete forfeiture, such as the following:

- Withering option: This gives the non-defaulting party the right, in the context of an approved development plan, to obtain part of the defaulting party's participating interest in the specific exploitation area to which the default relates. That interest – or the 'withering interest' – is calculated by reference to a complex contractual formula.
- Enforcement of security: This type of provision allows the non-defaulting party to enforce a mortgage and/or security interest on the defaulting party's participating interest.

2.4   Enforceability

When drafting termination, call or put option, or – and especially – forfeiture provisions, parties should consider whether such a clause will be enforceable under the governing law of the contract in the event of a dispute. Under several legal systems, including English and New York law, a provision may be unenforceable if it is deemed to be a 'penalty'.

(a)   New York law

Under New York law, a liquidated damages provision – that is, a contractual provision that sets, in advance, the damages that will be owed to the non-

---

16   E Pereira, "Protection against Default in Long Term Petroleum Joint Ventures" (May 2012), The Oxford Institute for Energy Studies, p10.
17   *Ibid*, p10.

Figure 1. Exit/termination mechanisms: key drafting considerations

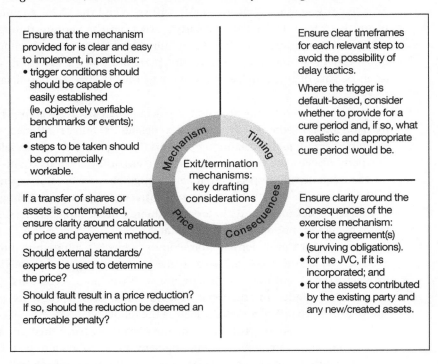

Ensure that the mechanism provided for is clear and easy to implement, in particular:
• trigger conditions should should be capable of easily established (ie, objectively verifiable benchmarks or events); and
• steps to be taken should be commercially workable.

Ensure clear timeframes for each relevant step to avoid the possibility of delay tactics.

Where the trigger is default-based, consider whether to provide for a cure period and, if so, what a realistic and appropriate cure period would be.

If a transfer of shares or assets is contemplated, ensure clarity around calculation of price and payement method.

Should external standards/experts be used to determine the price?

Should fault result in a price reduction? If so, should the reduction be deemed an enforcable penalty?

Ensure clarity around the consequences of the exercise mechanism:
• for the agreement(s) (surviving obligations).
• for the JVC, if it is incorporated; and
• for the assets contributed by the existing party and any new/created assets.

breaching party in the event of a breach – may be considered an unenforceable penalty if either:

- damages flowing from the breach could have been readily ascertained at the time of contracting; or
- the amount liquidated is "conspicuously disproportionate" to "foreseeable losses" that would result from a breach.[18]

A recent New York Court of Appeals decision has called into question whether a court should focus only on damages foreseeable at the time of contracting, or whether courts can also examine whether the liquidated amount is proportional to the actual damage suffered in the event.[19]

In the energy JV context, parties have argued that forfeiture provisions, or even call options that operated similarly to forfeiture provisions, are unenforceable penalties under New York law. For instance, in a JV for the construction and operation of a crude oil refinery, one party sought to exercise

---

18   *Bates Advertising USA v 498 Seventh,* 7 NY 3d 115 (2006); *Addressing Sys & Prods, Inc v Friedman,* 59 AD 3d 359, 359 (NY App Div 2009).
19   *172 Van Duzer Realty v Globe Alumni Student Assistance,* 24 NY 3d 528 (2014). See also G Banks, "Liquidated Damages: Is the Law Changing?", *New York Law Journal,* 26 January 2015.

a contractual call option to acquire its JV partner's interest in the venture following a call event (an uncured failure to supply crude oil or, in the alternative, to pay damages, as defined in the relevant agreement) by that partner.[20] The agreement set out two alternative formulae for calculating the purchase price, applicable at the option of the non-breaching party, in the event of a party's exercise of the call option (or the agreement's reciprocal put option). In the event, one of those formulae – the one which the non-breaching party in that case elected to apply – resulted in a purchase price of zero dollars. The dispute went to arbitration, in which the claimants (the breaching parties) argued that the call option operated as an unenforceable penalty under New York law. The tribunal accepted arguments raised by the respondents (the non-breaching parties) to the effect that:

- only liquidated damages provisions could be considered penalties under New York law (and then only in certain circumstances, as above); and
- the call option was not a liquidated damages provision, but rather operated as a termination provision.[21]

On that basis, the tribunal upheld the respondents' exercise of the call option.[22]

(b)   English law

The test for whether a contractual provision is an unenforceable penalty under English law is slightly different. In 2015, the Supreme Court in *Cavendish v Makdessi*[23] reformulated the test.[24]

The dispute concerned whether provisions in a share purchase agreement (SPA) under which a breaching party lost his right to certain payments for shares already sold to the non-breaching party and was compelled to sell his remaining shares to the non-breaching party at a discount constituted a penalty and were therefore unenforceable.

Under the SPA, Makdessi sold part of his shareholding in a company to Cavendish. In consideration for those shares, Makdessi was to receive four payments: the first two payments were fixed sums and the second two

---

20   *PDV Sweeny, Inc v ConocoPhillips Co*, Case 14-CV-5183 (AJN), Memorandum & Order, pp2–3 (SDNY, 1 September 2015).
21   *Ibid*, pp14-15.
22   *Ibid*, p15. The claimants petitioned the courts of New York (the arbitral seat) and the Second Circuit to vacate the arbitral award on the basis that the award was contrary to New York's public policy against penalty clauses. That application was rejected at first instance and on appeal. *Ibid*, p23. See also *PDV Sweeny, Inc, v ConocoPhillips Co*, Case 16-170-cv, Summary Order, (US Court of Appeals for the Second Circuit, 7 November 2016).
23   *Cavendish Square Holding BV v Talal El Makdessi* [2016] AC 1172.
24   Until a few years ago, the leading English authority on the law of penalties was *Dunlop Pneumatic Tyre Company Ltd v New Garage & Motor Company Limited* [1915] AC 79, which held that a clause providing for a payment of a sum of money upon breach of contract would be an unenforceable penalty if the sum payable did not represent a genuine pre-estimate of the loss likely to flow from that breach (at pp86–87).

payments were to be calculated in subsequent years based on the company's profitability. However, the SPA provided that if Makdessi breached certain restrictive covenants under the SPA, he would become a "Defaulting Shareholder" and would thereby:

- forgo his right to receive the second two payments; and
- at Cavendish's option, be required to sell his remaining shares at a price fixed under the SPA.

Cavendish and the company alleged that Makdessi had become a defaulting shareholder and thereby triggered the default provisions under the SPA. Makdessi argued that the default provisions constituted an unenforceable penalty.

As a starting point, the majority in the Supreme Court considered that where a contract is concluded between parties who were properly advised and had comparable bargaining power, "the strong initial presumption must be that the parties themselves are the best judges of what is legitimate in a provision dealing with the consequences of breach". In the light of this observation, the court determined that it should hold a clause to be an unenforceable penalty only if it "is a secondary obligation which imposes a detriment on the contract breaker which is out of all proportion to any legitimate interest of the innocent party in the enforcement of the primary obligation".[25] In other words, the court takes into account the non-breaching party's commercial interest in enforcing the contract, and considers whether the pre-estimation of loss is "unconscionable" or "extravagant" in proportion to that interest.[26] This reformulation arguably increases the likelihood that a forfeiture provision in an English law JV agreement would be deemed enforceable.[27]

For parties seeking to enforce the forfeiture clause, there are two broad drafting strategies which may mitigate the risk of its being held to be a penalty under the *Cavendish* test. First, the agreement should expressly record that the parties are each sophisticated commercial enterprises of comparable bargaining power which have engaged legal and/or financial advisers in relation to the

---

25   *Cavendish Square Holding BV v Talal El Makdessi* [2016] AC 1172, pp1204–1205.

26   *Cavendish Square Holding BV v Talal El Makdessi* [2016] AC 1172], p1278.

27   Even before *Cavendish*, some arbitral tribunals applying English law showed a willingness to enforce forfeiture provisions in a JV context. For instance, in one confidential proceeding (publicised by the International Chamber of Commerce in anonymised form), Companies A, B and C entered into a crude oil production sharing agreement, shared management agreement (SMA) and other agreements. The SMA provided for the sharing of costs and expenses, and for consequences should a party default on a required payment. In particular, if a party remained in default for more than 60 days after receiving a notice of default, it had to forfeit and assign its participating interest to a non-defaulting party. Company C conceded that it breached its obligations under the SMA and other agreements by, among other things, failing to issue timely letters of credit and make timely payments of cash calls, but argued that the forfeiture provision was an unenforceable penalty. Having considered the parties' commercial objectives and bargaining positions at the time of contracting, the tribunal concluded that the forfeiture provision was not a penalty: "On the contrary, it provides a fair and businesslike arrangement designed to preserve a project in a case of a specified default." *Company A v Company C* (ICC Case No 11663), Final Award, 2003, cited in AJ van den Berg (ed), *Yearbook of Commercial Arbitration* (2007) Vol XXXII 60, at 68.

negotiation and execution of the agreement. Second, the parties should set out (either in the body of the agreement or as an appendix):

- their agreement as to the legitimate interests that are served by performance of the cash call clause; and
- that the forfeiture clause is a common provision in agreements of this nature which serves as a reasonable and proportionate means to deter breach and to protect those legitimate interests of the parties.

3. Key aspects of arbitration clauses for JV parties

Although a dispute generally is not at the forefront of the parties' minds at the time that a JV is agreed, the importance of a well-drafted arbitration clause should not be underestimated. Where the JV is of an international nature – and particularly, as commonly occurs in the energy sector, if it involves a country whose legal system is perceived to be less developed, neutral or reliable than others' – early agreement on fundamental issues such as the mechanism by which the dispute will be resolved, where such procedure will take place and what law(s) will govern can eliminate potential further battles should the need to invoke that procedure arise. A well-drafted clause also allows the parties to have confidence in their ability effectively to enforce their rights under the contract. Ultimately, a contract is only as strong as its dispute resolution clause.

However, that the need for 'free drafting' of these important clauses is limited. Generally, where the parties agree to refer their dispute to institutional arbitration, or to *ad hoc* arbitration under the United Nations Commission on International Trade Law (UNCITRAL) Arbitration Rules, they will be best served by using a model clause promulgated by the relevant institution or UNCITRAL.[28] An example of such a clause, issued by the Singapore International Arbitration Centre (SIAC) is set out in Figure 2 on the next page.

In the remainder of this section, we highlight those procedural issues most pertinent to a potential dispute among joint venturers in the energy sector, which should be considered when negotiating an arbitration clause.

3.1 Seat

The 'seat' is the legal place of the arbitration. The law of the seat of the arbitration (together with the relevant arbitral rules, discussed below) will govern the arbitration itself, even if the substantive issues in dispute are to be

---

[28] Parties to a JV in the energy sector may also have reference to the dispute resolution provisions in industry standard form contracts. For example, the AIPN produces a range of model contracts tailored to the petroleum industry, which typically contain a standard form dispute resolution clause providing for international arbitration as either the sole or 'last resort' dispute resolution mechanism, together with a number of optional clauses. These optional clauses cover matters such as waiver of the right to appeal on a point of law, the form and content of the notice of dispute, the rules of the arbitration, the number of arbitrators and the method for their appointment and the language and seat of the arbitration.

Figure 2. SIAC Model Clause

> *Any dispute arising out of or in connection with this contract, including any question regarding its existence, validity or termination, shall be referred to and finally resolved by arbitration administered by the Singapore International Arbitration Centre ("SIAC") in accordance with the Arbitration Rules of the Singapore International Arbitration Centre ("SIAC Rules") for the time being in force, which rules are deemed to be incorporated by reference in this clause.*
>
> *The seat of the arbitration shall be [Singapore].**
>
> *The Tribunal shall consist of _____** arbitrator(s).*
>
> *The language of the arbitration shall be _____.*
>
> ** Parties should specify the seat of arbitration of their choice. If the parties wish to select an alternative seat to Singapore, please replace "[Singapore]" with the city and country of choice (e.g., "[City, Country]").*
> *** State an odd number. Either state one, or state three.*

Source: www.siac.org.sg/model-clauses/siac-model-clause

determined by reference to a different governing law.[29] A number of significant consequences flow from the selection of a particular seat.

First, the seat of the arbitration is relevant to the finality of the award. The seat is the only jurisdiction in which a party may apply to the courts to have the award annulled or set aside (in effect, invalidated). The law of the seat will typically provide the (usually limited) grounds on which an arbitral award may be annulled, and the courts of the seat will typically have jurisdiction to decide whether those grounds exist and warrant annulment.

Second, the seat of the arbitration is relevant to the enforceability of the award. Generally speaking, a party can seek to enforce an arbitral award in virtually any jurisdiction in which the counterpart holds assets, but the likelihood that the award will be enforced increases where the arbitral seat is located in a country that is a party to the United Nations Convention on the Recognition and Enforcement of Foreign Arbitral Awards (the New York Convention). The New York Convention provides a framework for the enforcement of foreign arbitral awards in contracting states, allowing only limited grounds for refusal. The convention applies to all foreign arbitral

29 N Blackaby, C Partasides, *et al*, *Redfern and Hunter on International Arbitration* (6th edn 2015), para 2.83, p99; paras 3.15-3.32, pp159–163; para 3.37, pp166 *et seq*.

awards, wherever made, but almost half of its signatories have made a reservation to the effect that its scope will be limited to awards made in another contracting state.[30] To maximise the chances of benefiting from the convention's robust enforcement provisions, it is therefore advisable to choose a New York Convention contracting state as the seat of the arbitration.

Third, the powers of arbitrators or the domestic courts of the seat to order specific or interim relief (eg, injunctions or specific performance) may vary depending on the law of the seat.[31] The availability of such remedies can be significant in a JV context, where urgent relief may be required to prevent loss to the JV company or a party that could not later be adequately compensated in damages. For example, if one party were to threaten to disclose confidential information regarding the JV company, the non-breaching party may, depending on the law of the seat, seek an order from the tribunal and/or the court restraining such conduct. As another example, a party that suspects its JV partner intends to sell its interest in, or an asset of, the JV could (again, depending on the law of the seat) seek to enjoin its partner from doing so pending the outcome of the arbitration. This issue is also discussed in the context of the selection of arbitral rules (see below).

Fourth, and relatedly, the law of the seat determines the extent of the powers afforded to local courts to supervise, regulate and/or intervene in the arbitration proceedings.[32] The risk of interference by domestic courts may be particularly pronounced in the context of JVs in the energy sector, as these often involve countries whose local courts may be perceived to be susceptible to bias or corruption, especially if one of the parties to the JV is a state or a state-owned entity. By contrast, that risk is comparatively low in jurisdictions such as England and Wales, New York and Singapore, where the rule of law is strong and courts and legislatures are generally supportive of arbitration.

When drafting an arbitration agreement, parties should bear in mind that the law of the seat will govern the arbitration proceedings, but may not necessarily be deemed to govern the arbitration agreement itself, including issues such as the interpretation of the arbitration agreement or the question of whether a party to the dispute has consented to arbitration.[33] This issue arises

---

30   At the time of writing, 159 states are parties to the New York Convention, 74 of which have made such a reservation. The full list is available at www.uncitral.org/uncitral/en/uncitral_texts/arbitration/NYConvention_status.html.

31   For example, English law specifically permits arbitrators to grant interim relief, specific performance (with the exception of contracts relating to land) and declaratory relief. Arbitration Act 1996, ss 39, 48(3), 48(5).

32   This could include frustrating the arbitration, such as by ordering a stay of the proceedings, or providing support to the arbitration – for example, by filling a vacancy in the composition of the tribunal absent another mechanism for doing so.

33   See, for example, *Arsanovia Ltd v Cruz City 1 Mauritius Holdings* [2013] 2 All ER (Comm) 1, pp7–14, 17 (holding that Indian law – the governing law of the shareholders' agreement – governed the parties' arbitration agreement, despite its designation of a London seat, and nullifying an arbitral award on the basis that the arbitral tribunal did not have jurisdiction over one of the parties under Indian law).

because of the principle of severability: if the remainder of the contract (including its governing law clause) is found void for some reason, its dispute resolution clause ought in principle to survive; which gives rise to the question of which law is to be used to interpret the dispute resolution clause.[34] Where the governing law of the contract is that of a jurisdiction other than the seat, the parties would be prudent to specify which law governs the arbitration agreement specifically. Notably, such an express election is absent from the SIAC Model Clause at Figure 2 above; it is a wise addition.[35]

3.2   Institutional or *ad hoc* arbitration and arbitral rules

The provisions of the law of the seat applicable to the arbitration proceedings do not typically include detailed procedural guidelines for the conduct of the arbitration proceedings. One of the attractions of arbitration over litigation is that parties are free to choose these themselves. They can elect either to tailor their own set of rules and proceed '*ad hoc*' – that is, without the involvement of an arbitral institution – or to conduct their arbitration subject to the rules of an established international arbitral institution (eg, the International Court of Arbitration of the International Chamber of Commerce (ICC), the London Court of International Arbitration (LCIA) or SIAC). Historically, some states and state-affiliated organisations have preferred *ad hoc* arbitration, without the involvement of an institution.

If the parties opt for 'institutional' arbitration, the selected institution will administer the proceedings pursuant to its institutional rules. The rules of the established arbitral institutions can generally be relied upon to be workable and effective, and tend to be regularly updated in consultation with experts in the field. By contrast, in an *ad hoc* arbitration, there is no institutional support or automatically applicable set of rules (though the parties can mitigate the risks involved with shaping their own procedure from scratch by adopting the UNCITRAL Arbitration Rules). In the context of an international JV dispute, the potential attractions of *ad hoc* arbitration (ie, the procedure may be quicker, cheaper and more flexible) will often be outweighed by the convenience of having the proceedings administered by a specialised institution and adopting a tried-and-tested set of rules. If the parties are unable to cooperate effectively,

---

34   See the decision of the Singapore High Court in *BCY v BCZ* [2016] SGHC 249, adopting the 'three-stage test' for determining the proper law of an arbitration agreement as elaborated by the English Court of Appeal in *Sulamérica CIA Nacional de Seguros SA v Enesa Engenharia SA* [2012] EWCA Civ 638:
- the parties' express choice of governing law;
- the parties' implied choice based on their intentions at the time of entering into the contract; or
- the system of law with which the arbitration agreement has the closest and most real connection.

35   By contrast, the various model arbitration clauses promulgated by the Hong Kong International Arbitration Centre contain the following wording: "The law of this arbitration clause shall be [...]" (or, for use in a standalone arbitration agreement, "The law of this arbitration agreement shall be [...]"). See Hong Kong International Arbitration Centre website, "Model Clauses", www.hkiac.org/arbitration/model-clauses.

using an *ad hoc* procedure may simply provide further opportunities for disagreement and delay.[36]

In deciding on a set of arbitral rules to govern their dispute, parties should be alive to the particular features that each set of rules offers. For example, as noted above, it may be important that the selected rules provide an option to apply for interim relief.[37] It may also be significant in the JV context – where the disputing parties will often have a continuing investment pending the resolution of their dispute – whether the relevant rules contain features designed to enhance the quick and efficient disposal of proceedings, which will be desirable if the dispute is disrupting the normal functioning of the venture. Examples of such features include emergency arbitrator proceedings,[38] expedited procedure[39] and summary dismissal of unmeritorious claims.[40]

3.3 The arbitral tribunal

Parties are recommended to specify in the arbitration agreement the number of arbitrators to be appointed to the tribunal and the process by which the arbitrators will be appointed. Most commonly, arbitration proceedings are heard either by a sole arbitrator or by a three-person tribunal[41] (typically with each party nominating one arbitrator and the third presiding arbitrator being appointed either by agreement or by the administering institution).

There are some advantages to referring a dispute to a sole arbitrator: most obviously, the cost will typically be lower and the decision making quicker.[42] But

---

36   See I Hewitt, *Hewitt on Joint Ventures* (6th edn 2016), para 14-12, p336. See also N Blackaby, C Partasides, *et al*, *Redfern and Hunter on International Arbitration* (6th edn 2015), pp42–57.
37   See ICC Rules of Arbitration 2017, Art 28; LCIA Arbitration Rules 2014, Art 25; SIAC Arbitration Rules 2016, Rule 30; UNCITRAL Arbitration Rules 2013, Art 26.
38   Emergency arbitrator proceedings enable parties to seek urgent temporary relief where they are unable to wait until the tribunal has been constituted. See ICC Rules, Art 29 and Appendix 5; LCIA Rules, Art 9B; SIAC Rules, Rule 30.2 and Schedule 1. According to the 2016 ICC Dispute Resolution Statistics, the average time taken to complete emergency arbitrator proceedings under the ICC rules was 18 days. The ICC also reported that over half of the applications under its emergency arbitrator procedure in 2016 related to the construction, engineering and energy sectors. See International Chamber of Commerce, "ICC Dispute Resolution Statistics" (2016), p33.
39   See ICC Rules, Art 30 and Appendix VI; SIAC Rules, Rule 5. The LCIA Rules do not provide for an expedited procedure, though a party can apply to the LCIA Court for expedited formation of the tribunal in cases of exceptional urgency. LCIA Rules, Art 9A.
40   See SIAC Rules, Rule 29. No express provision for summary dismissal is made in the ICC Rules, the LCIA Rules or the UNCITRAL Rules. However, an October 2017 update to the ICC's arbitration practice note stresses that, despite the absence of an express provision, "an application for the expeditious determination of manifestly unmeritorious claims or defenses may be dealt with, within the broad scope of Article 22 ['Conduct of the Arbitration']". ICC, "Note to parties and arbitral tribunals on the conduct of the arbitration under the ICC Rules of Arbitration", 30 October 2017, p10. Although not described as 'summary dismissal' as such in the note, the accompanying ICC press release referred to the possibility of the "*immediate* dismissal of manifestly unmeritorious claims or defences". ICC press release, "ICC Court revises note to include expedited determination of unmeritorious claims or defences", 30 October 2017 (emphasis added).
41   Article 12(1) of the ICC Rules, for example, requires that disputes "*shall* be decided by a sole arbitrator or by three arbitrators" (emphasis added).
42   The LCIA recently observed that while three-member tribunals typically handle larger cases, statistical analysis (from 2013 to 2016) shows that three-member tribunal cases are not proportionally more expensive or lengthy. LCIA, "Facts and Figures – Costs and Duration: 2013-2016", pp3, 16–17.

the norm is for three arbitrators, and in many cases for good reason: if a dispute is of high value (monetary or otherwise), involves parties from different jurisdictions (with the cultural, linguistic and legal differences that may follow), has a complicated and/or politically sensitive fact pattern and/or involves the interplay of different legal systems, a panel of three decision makers may be better placed to address these complexities and thus to render a better-quality award.[43] JV disputes in the energy sector often feature many, if not all, of those factors.

It is also advisable for the parties to agree in their arbitration agreement on the process for the selection of the arbitrator(s). Commonly (including under most major arbitral rules),[44] the favoured approach in a three-person tribunal scenario is for each party to nominate an arbitrator and the third presiding arbitrator to be appointed either by the two party-appointed arbitrators or by the administering institution.[45] Where the arbitration agreement provides for the appointment of a sole or presiding arbitrator by agreement of the parties or their appointees, this can often result in delay. It is therefore prudent to specify a deadline for such agreement to be reached, failing which the decision will be referred to an independent appointing authority (ie, the administering institution). Many institutional rules provide for such a deadline.[46]

JV parties should also give some thought to whether they wish to specify any characteristics that the arbitrator(s) determining any disputes between them should have. For example, if the JV relates to a highly specialised area, relevant qualifications or experience in that field may be necessary to properly grasp the issues in dispute. Commonly, where the parties are from different countries (in particular if one party is a state-owned entity or the JV is in a politically sensitive industry), the arbitration clause may specify that a sole or presiding arbitrator cannot be a national of the home state of either party. However, parties wishing to include specifications as to characteristics should bear in mind that if the criteria are too restrictive, obscure or ambiguous, there might be no or few candidates available at the time a dispute arises who satisfy the criteria, or ambiguity as to whether a proposed candidate qualifies – meaning that time and cost will be wasted in deciding how to resolve this dilemma.

---

43   See M Mangan, L Reed and J Choong, *A Guide to the SIAC Arbitration Rules* (2014), paras 7.03-7.06.
44   See, for example, ICC Rules, Arts 12(4)-(5); SIAC Rules, Rule 11; UNCITRAL Rules, Art 9. A notable exception is the LCIA Rules, which provide for the LCIA Court to appoint all three arbitrators, unless the parties agree to party nomination of arbitrators.
45   Particular issues can arise in relation to the constitution of the tribunal in the context of a multi-party JV, as discussed in section 4 below.
46   For example, ICC Rules, Arts 12(3) and (5); SIAC Rules, Rules 10.2, 11.2; UNCITRAL Rules, Arts 8(1), 9(2)-(3).

4.   Multi-party and multi-contract JVs

A JV in the energy sector commonly will not be limited to a single agreement between two parties, but rather will require a web of contracts covering different aspects of the project, in relation to various rights and obligations held by various entities.[47] It follows that disputes in relation to such a JV may erupt under multiple agreements, among multiple parties with potentially divergent interests.[48]

In this scenario, without careful management of the procedure, closely related disputes could end up being resolved by different tribunals in different proceedings, risking inefficiency and inconsistent results. It could also lead to disagreement among the various parties as to their respective procedural rights in the course of the arbitration (most obviously, the right to appoint an arbitrator), which could in some circumstances form the basis for a challenge to the validity of the award ultimately rendered.[49]

As observed in one of the leading commentaries on international arbitration, "[t]he difficulties of multiparty arbitrations all result from a single cause": the fact that arbitration is a contractually based mode of dispute resolution.[50] Unlike national courts, whose jurisdiction to resolve a given dispute is vested in them by the relevant state, an arbitral tribunal derives its jurisdiction solely from the consent of the parties to submit a given dispute to arbitration.[51]

Where there are or may be related proceedings among multiple parties or under multiple agreements, the most efficient approach may be for such proceedings to be heard together, by either:

- joining additional parties (eg, a joint venturer's parent company) to proceedings already on foot; or
- agreeing to bring two or more arbitrations, or claims arising under different contracts, in relation to the same or similar facts before the same tribunal (ie, consolidation of multiple contract disputes).

However, an application for joinder or consolidation can be complicated if the parties do not agree on this at the point when the dispute(s) arise.[52]

If the parties anticipate a preference for joinder or consolidation at the outset, they might sensibly address it in the arbitration agreement,[53] and/or

---

47   See DR Haigh QC and P Beke, "Multiple Contracts and Multiparty Energy Arbitration" in JW Rowley QC, D Bishop and G Kaiser (eds), *Global Arbitration Review: The Guide to Energy Arbitrations* (2015) 229, p230.
48   Nearly half of all new cases filed with the ICC in 2016 (43%) involved three or more parties, of which 23% involved more than five parties, with one case involving a staggering 46 parties. See ICC Statistics, p1.
49   See generally B Hanotiau, *Complex Arbitrations: Multiparty, Multicontract, Multi-Issue and Class Actions* (2006), pp197–208.
50   N Blackaby, C Partasides, *et al*, *Redfern and Hunter on International Arbitration* (6th edn 2015), p141.
51   See generally B Hanotiau, *Complex Arbitrations: Multiparty, Multicontract, Multi-Issue and Class Actions* (2006), pp7–48.

select a set of arbitration rules[54] and a governing law that provide for such procedural mechanisms.[55] In a multi-contract scenario where consolidation is preferred, parties should also ensure that key terms of the arbitration agreements (eg, the seat, the language, the governing law and the provisions regarding constitution of the tribunal) in the respective contracts are consistent, or at least compatible, with one another. Absent the express consent of all parties to the consolidation, this is a condition to consolidation of proceedings under different arbitration agreements in the major arbitration rules that contain specific consolidation provisions.[56] In addition to ensuring compatibility of the key terms – and of particular use where the chosen institutional rules do not contain liberal, or any, consolidation, joinder and/or multi-contract provisions – the parties to each of the relevant contracts can consent therein to a dispute being heard in the same proceeding as a related dispute arising under a different contract.

Where a JV arrangement is comprised of multiple agreements, parties may be tempted to create bespoke dispute resolution clauses tailored to each agreement, particularly where some of the agreements may require industry-specific technical analysis. For instance, in a JV for an oil refinery, in which one of the JV partners undertakes both to act as operator of the JV under one agreement and to supply oil to the venture under a separate supply contract, the JV or JOA may include an arbitration clause providing for a panel of three arbitrators under particular institutional rules, but the separate oil supply agreement may provide for baseball arbitration by one arbitrator in the event of, for example, a pricing dispute. This can have unintended consequences

---

52   For example, joinder of a party's parent company may be permitted under the French 'group of companies' doctrine (ie, "the arbitration clause expressly accepted by certain of the companies of the group should bind the other companies which, by virtue of their role in the conclusion, performance or termination of the contracts containing said clauses, and in accordance with the mutual intention of all parties to the proceedings, appear to have been veritable parties to these contracts or to have been principally concerned by them and the disputes to which they may give rise" (*Dow Chemical v Isover Saint Gobain* (ICC Case 4131), Interim Award, 23 September 1982, cited in P Sanders (ed), *Yearbook of Commercial Arbitration*, (1984) Vol IX, 131, p136). By contrast, English law takes a much more restrictive approach to this question and will 'pierce the corporate veil' only to prevent an abuse of corporate personality. *Petrodel Resources Ltd v Prest* [2013] UKSC 34. See also N Voser, "Multi-party Disputes and Joinder of Third Parties" in AJ van den Berg (ed), *50 Years of the New York Convention: ICCA International Conference* (2009) 343, pp370–381; G Born, *International Commercial Arbitration* (2nd edn 2014), pp2564–2613.

53   For suggested drafting of clauses providing for multi-party and/or multi-contract arbitration, see J Gillis Wetter, "A Multi-Party Arbitration Scheme For International Joint Ventures" (1987) Vol 3(1) *Arbitration International* 2, pp 6–10; DR Haigh QC and P Beke, "Multiple Contracts and Multiparty Energy Arbitration" in JW Rowley QC, D Bishop and G Kaiser (eds), *Global Arbitration Review: The Guide to Energy Arbitrations* (2015) 229, pp233–234; 242–246; B Hanotiau, *Complex Arbitrations: Multiparty, Multicontract, Multi-Issue and Class Actions* (2006), Appendix 2, pp313–338.

54   See, for example, ICC Rules, Arts 7-10; LCIA Rules, Art 22.1(viii)-(x); SIAC Rules, Rules 7-8.

55   Certain jurisdictions appear to allow national courts discretion to order consolidation even if the parties object, such as the Netherlands, New Zealand, certain Australian states and a number of US states. See DR Haigh QC and P Beke, "Multiple Contracts and Multiparty Energy Arbitration" in JW Rowley QC, D Bishop and G Kaiser (eds), *Global Arbitration Review: The Guide to Energy Arbitrations* (2015) 229, p239. See also G Born, *International Commercial Arbitration* (2nd edn 2014), pp2586–2589.

56   See ICC Rules, Art 10(c); LCIA Rules, Art 22.1(x); SIAC Rules, Rule 8.1(c).

where terms in the JV or JOA are related to or dependent upon the price or supply of oil to the JV. If the functional relationships between agreements with incompatible arbitration agreements are not carefully thought through at the time of contracting, it can result in expensive 'disputes within a dispute' as to whether two parallel but related proceedings can be consolidated once a dispute arises.

Similarly, the constitution of an arbitral tribunal can become more complicated outside of the classic bipartite proceeding. A well-known example of the difficulties that can arise where a dispute involves multiple parties whose interests are not aligned is the French Court of Cassation's 1992 decision in *Siemens v Dutco*.[57] In that case, two respondents (unrelated companies) were required jointly to appoint an arbitrator (which they did under protest), while the single party claimant had the opportunity to make its own selection. The French court upheld a challenge to the constitution of the tribunal on the basis that the respondents' right to equal treatment had been violated. The court further found that, as a matter of French public policy, the right to equality in the arbitrator appointment process cannot be waived in advance of a dispute arising (ie, in the arbitration agreement).

To avoid the type of situation that arose in *Dutco*,[58] parties to a multi-party JV could:

- agree to the appointment of a sole arbitrator (by agreement of all parties or by an independent appointing authority); or
- agree that, in a multi-party scenario, the multiple claimants and/or multiple respondents respectively will jointly appoint an arbitrator, but

---

[57] *BKMI Industrieanlagen GmbH & Siemens AG v Dutco Construction, Cour de Cassation* (1er Chambre Civile), Pourvoi N° 89-18708 89-18726, 7 January 1992. The claimant (Dutco) initiated arbitration against Siemens and BKMI, its counterparties in a consortium for the construction of a cement plant in Oman. The arbitration agreement provided for ICC arbitration and and a three-person tribunal. Dutco nominated its arbitrator when it filed its request for arbitration and the two respondents (unrelated companies with divergent interests) were ordered, under the ICC rules in force at the time (which were amended following the *Dutco* decision), jointly to appoint the second party-appointed arbitrator. They were unable to agree on the identity of that arbitrator, but eventually made a joint nomination under protest.

[58] The *Dutco* decision is a French law authority: different national courts might reach different decisions. It is nonetheless prudent to take steps to avoid ending up in this scenario where there would appear to be a real risk of an award being challenged.

[59] If the rules provide for the appointing authority to make a nomination in place of the multiple claimants/respondents which are unable to agree, while the other party's nomination is allowed to stand, this arguably is a violation of the right to equal treatment and could risk a challenge being brought along the lines of that in *Dutco*.

[60] For example, ICC Rules, Arts 12(6) ("Where there are multiple claimants or multiple respondents, and where the dispute is to be referred to three arbitrators, the multiple claimants, jointly, and the multiple respondents, jointly, shall nominate an arbitrator for confirmation pursuant to Article 13"); 12(7) ("Where an additional party has been joined, and where the dispute is to be referred to three arbitrators, the additional party may, jointly with the claimant(s) or with the respondent(s), nominate an arbitrator for confirmation pursuant to Article 13"); and 12(8) ("In the absence of a joint nomination pursuant to Articles 12(6) or 12(7) and where all parties are unable to agree to a method for the constitution of the arbitral tribunal, the Court *may appoint each member of the arbitral tribunal and shall designate one of them to act as president*. In such case, the Court shall be at liberty to choose any person it regards as suitable to act as arbitrator, applying Article 13 when it considers this appropriate" (emphasis added)). See also LCIA Rules, Art 8; SIAC Rules, Rule 12.

use arbitration rules that provide for all three arbitrators[59] to be appointed by an independent appointing authority in the event that the multiple claimants and/or multiple respondents cannot agree on a single candidate for their respective party-appointed arbitrator.[60]

5.   Structuring JVs: a dispute resolution perspective

While parties to an international JV will generally give careful thought to the structuring of that venture from a commercial and tax perspective, the consequences of the chosen structure from a dispute resolution perspective are all too often overlooked. These structural decisions can have game-changing consequences in the event that a dispute arises. Which legal regime will govern the parties' contractual relationship? By incorporating in a particular jurisdiction, have the parties subscribed to particular provisions of the law of that jurisdiction that are inconsistent with the terms of their agreement, rendering their contractual bargain as to certain issues unenforceable? Will an arbitration agreement be enforceable in respect of the issues that the parties may wish to refer to a tribunal? If the JV company and/or its assets are nationalised or harassed by the host state, will investment treaty protection be available? While these issues are unlikely to be at the forefront of the parties' minds at the outset of the venture, a party that considers these issues at the time the JV structure is being devised is far less likely to suffer an unpleasant surprise if a dispute arises.

5.1   Applicable law

The selection of the governing law of the contract(s) between the parties – that is, the identification of the legal regime that the parties intend to govern their rights and obligations under the contract and, depending on how the clause is drafted, their related non-contractual rights and obligations – is an important issue in any contract, but one that is particularly pronounced in the context of an international JV. JV parties in the energy sector often come from different countries with significantly different legal cultures, meaning that the parties' expectations as to how the contract between them will function and – at the most basic level – what its terms mean may not automatically align. If a local JV party wishes to choose the local law of the place of the venture as the governing law, the non-local party should consider, with local counsel, the implications of this for any future disputes.

In selecting a governing law,[61] a number of factors should be taken into consideration by a JV partner. On a practical level, a party should have regard to

---

61   In some jurisdictions, local law constrains the parties' freedom to make an election of governing law by requiring that a contract be governed by local law if all contracting parties are locally incorporated (even if those locally incorporated entities are subsidiaries of foreign companies). Recent court decisions suggest that this is the law in India, though there is some ambiguity as to the scope of the rule. See *TDM Infrastructure Private Limited v UE Development India Private Limited*, (2008) 14 SCC 271; *Bharat Aluminium Co v Kaiser Aluminium Technical Services, Inc* (Civil Appeal 7019 of 2005, Indian Supreme Court, 6 September 2012).

how accessible the relevant legal system is (ie, whether key authorities are publicly available and easily accessible in a language that it and its team work in) and how familiar (or not) it and its team (including preferred external counsel) are with the legal norms they are selecting. A range of technical considerations are also relevant to this decision. For example, does the legal system in question recognise legal mechanisms used in the industry, such as trusts? Is there a body of precedent relating to similar transactions that can provide guidance on the approach of the local courts to important issues? What are the rules around contractual interpretation – is there a role for concepts such as good faith? These sorts of issues can make a material difference to the outcome of a dispute (and, indeed, the parties' obligations throughout the life of the JV), so it is critical that they be given careful consideration at an early stage.

A further potential source of relevant law is that of the place of incorporation of the JV company (if applicable), which may be a different legal system from the contractual governing law or the law of the seat of the arbitration. A company will typically be subject to the law of its place of incorporation in respect of matters such as corporate governance, tax liability and insolvency – all areas ripe for dispute between JV partners.

5.2   Arbitrability

When drafting an arbitration agreement, parties should also consider whether, even if a particular issue in dispute falls within the scope of the parties' arbitration agreement,[62] it may still be deemed non-arbitrable – that is, not legally capable of being resolved by arbitration proceedings (as opposed to by a national court).[63] Whether an issue is arbitrable is a national law question,[64] with the result that an assessment of whether a particular claim can be referred to arbitration will be required on a case-by-case basis. However, a common theme is that the more a particular issue or remedy is likely to impact upon third parties or the general public, the less likely it is to be deemed arbitrable.[65]

The 'non-arbitrability' doctrine is recognised in various international arbitration conventions, including the New York Convention, as a basis – albeit a narrow basis[66] – for challenging the enforceability of an international

---

[62]   See N Blackaby, C Partasides, *et al*, *Redfern and Hunter on International Arbitration* (6th edn 2015), pp92–95.
[63]   The term 'arbitrable' is occasionally used by US lawyers to include broader jurisdictional questions – for example, as to the scope of the arbitration clause. See *First Options of Chicago, Inc v Kaplan*, 514 US 938, p943. The term is used in the narrow sense set out above for the purposes of this chapter.
[64]   See G Born, *International Commercial Arbitration* (2nd edn 2014), pp597–617.
[65]   G Born, *International Commercial Arbitration* (2nd edn 2014), p945 ("The nonarbitrability doctrine rests on the notion that some matters so pervasively involve "public" rights and concerns, or interests of third parties, which are the subjects of uniquely governmental authority, that agreements to resolve such disputes by "private" arbitration should not be given effect"). See generally GM Vlavianos and VFL Pappas, "Corporate Divorce: Potential Limits to Arbitral Jurisdiction over Joint Ventures" in Global Arbitration Review, *The Guide to Energy Arbitrations* (2016).
[66]   G Born, *International Commercial Arbitration* (2nd edn 2014), p955 ("[C]ourts in most [New York Convention] Contracting States have applied the nonarbitrability exception only rarely in international settings").

arbitration agreement (with respect to a particular issue)[67] and/or an international arbitral award.[68]

In a dispute arising out of an international JV, an obvious example of an issue in respect of which non-arbitrability questions may arise is termination.[69] In practice, for arbitrations seated in sophisticated jurisdictions, the overwhelming majority of disputes over termination are arbitrable. However, in an equity JV scenario, if the JV agreement itself does not provide the means for it to do so, the party may wish to look to statutory remedies for shareholders provided for by the law of the JV company, such as mandatory share transfers[70] or the dissolution or winding up of the JV company.[71] Courts in different jurisdictions have taken different approaches to determining the arbitrability of these issues – that is, whether remedies that lie outside of the parties' contract and instead arise from statute can be arbitrated. For example, under English law and Singapore law, the leading authorities have distinguished between statutory winding-up remedies (which by necessity affect the wider public and hence fall under the court's supervisory jurisdiction and are non-arbitrable) and other statutory remedies where the requested relief affects only the parties to the arbitration (which are *prima facie* arbitrable).[72] In a series of cases in the Southern District of New York, courts have held that JV termination – even dissolution remedies – may properly be ordered by arbitral tribunals, without appearing to consider the prospect that such issues may be non-arbitrable in this sense.[73] This divergence in approach illustrates again the importance of carefully considering

---

67 Such a finding does not invalidate the arbitration agreement as a whole (in the way that an argument as to the illegality or invalidity of the arbitration agreement itself might). Rather, it is an issue-specific outcome: other issues not rendered non-arbitrable may still be resolved pursuant to the arbitration clause.

68 New York Convention, Arts II(1), V(2)(A); European Convention, Art VI(2); Inter-American Convention, Art 5(2); Geneva Protocol, Art 1(b). See also UNCITRAL Model Law on International Commercial Arbitration (1985 with amendments as adopted in 2006), Arts 34(2)(b)(i) (on grounds for setting aside an arbitral award) and 36(1)(b)(i) (on grounds for refusing recognition or enforcement of an arbitral award).

69 See generally GM Vlavianos and VFL Pappas, "Corporate Divorce: Potential Limits to Arbitral Jurisdiction over Joint Ventures" in Global Arbitration Review, *The Guide to Energy Arbitrations* (2016). Other examples could include, for example, certain IP issues (going to the validity of an intellectual property right) or employment issues. See generally N Blackaby, C Partasides, *et al*, *Redfern and Hunter on International Arbitration* (6th edn 2015), pp110–124.

70 For example, under English law, this remedy may be sought under Section 994 of the Companies Act 2006.

71 For example, under English law, a shareholder may apply for the winding up of the company where it is 'just and equitable' to do so under Section 122(1)(g) of the Insolvency Act 1986.

72 *See Fulham Football Club (1987) Ltd v Richards* [2012] Ch 333 (decision of the English Court of Appeal holding that, while winding up petitions are non-arbitrable, parties were free to agree to submit shareholder claims for unfair prejudice under Section 994 of the Companies Act 2006: see p357 per Lord Justice Patten ("disputes of this kind which do not involve the making of any winding-up order are capable of being arbitrated")); *Tomolugen Holdings Ltd v Silicia Investors Ltd* [2015] SGCA 57 (decision of the Singapore Court of Appeal holding that minority shareholder oppression or unfair prejudice claims under Section 216 of the Companies Act are arbitrable, subject to certain limits – namely that all parties affected by the relief must be party to the arbitration proceedings (a third party cannot be affected), such that the winding up of a company could not be ordered); *L Capital Jones Ltd v Maniach Pte Ltd* [2017] SGCA 03 (decision of the Singapore Court of Appeal affirming the decision in *Tomolugen* as regards arbitrability of minority oppression claims).

the legal consequences that may attach to structuring choices in respect of an international JV.

5.3 Availability of investment treaty protection

As noted in the introduction to this chapter, reserves of oil and natural gas – in 2017 still the world's leading fuels in terms of overall consumption[74] – are overwhelmingly located in emerging markets.[75] Those markets are, it follows, home to a large number of JVs in the energy sector.

Where a party is entering into an international JV in such a market – in particular (though not exclusively) where its counterparty will be a state or a state-owned entity – it should consider whether the investment is, or should be, structured in a manner that will maximise its chances of being protected by an investment treaty. For example, imagine Party A, an international oil major, and Party B, the national oil company of State X, enter into a JV in State X. Party A is a national of State Y, which has not signed an investment treaty with State X. In this scenario, there may be benefit in Party A investing in the JV through a subsidiary or special purpose vehicle incorporated in State Z, which is party to an investment treaty with State X, as this may enable Party A (through its subsidiary or special purpose vehicle) to benefit from the protections contained in the investment treaty between State X and State Z (see Figure 3).

Figure 3. Structuring for investment treaty protection

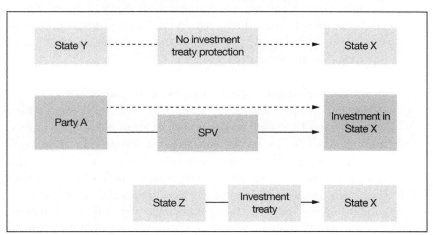

---

73   See *Millicom International VNV v Motorola, Inc*, 2002 US Dist LEXIS 5131 (SDNY), applied in *Telenor Mobile Communications AS v Storm LLC*, 524 F Supp 2d 332, both upholding challenged arbitral awards in which the dissolution of the venture had been ordered. It is perhaps significant, however, that in both of those cases the 'dissolution' of the JV ordered by the tribunal was to take place by means of a share sale from one party to the arbitration to another.

74   BP, *BP Statistical Review of World Energy* (67th edn 2018), p10.

75   BP, *BP Statistical Review of World Energy* ((67th edn 2018), pp12–13, 26–27.

Investment treaties can provide qualifying investors with protection from some of the key risks that they face when entering into JVs in or involving emerging markets, such as expropriation, dramatically increased and unfair taxation and other unfair or inequitable government regulation. Where the JV counterparty is a state or state-owned entity (whose conduct may in certain circumstances be attributable to the state for the purposes of an investment treaty claim),[76] the possibility of the investor bringing an arbitration claim against the state under the applicable investment treaty may deter the state or state-owned entity from wrongful or abusive conduct in respect of the JV and/or its JV partner(s). It could also serve as key leverage in commercial negotiations between the JV parties in the event of a dispute between them.

As a related point, where a JV involves a state or state-owned entity, issues of sovereign immunity may also be raised. Sovereign immunity is a potential bar to the initiation of proceedings ('immunity from suit') or defence against the enforcement of an arbitral award or court judgment. Parties entering into JV agreements with states or state-owned entities would therefore be well advised to include an express waiver of sovereign immunity in the relevant contract(s).[77]

Parties wishing to structure their investments so as to obtain investment treaty protection should take care to ensure that the structure adopted satisfies the applicable treaty's (or treaties') definitions of 'investor' and 'investment' – including, critically, whether the applicable treaty protects indirect investments or has any foreign ownership or control requirements for locally incorporated ventures. There is diversity among investment treaties as to what criteria must be met in order to satisfy those definitions,[78] failing which the investment and investor likely will not be protected by the treaty and may be unable to bring an arbitral claim thereunder.

6. Practicalities of managing a dispute external to the JV

While the principal focus of this chapter has been on disputes arising among the parties to a JV, a word should also be said about the scenario where a dispute arises between the JV and an outside party. Imagine, for example, that a JV company's operating permits are revoked by the local regulator. The JV company may wish to bring administrative proceedings challenging the regulator's decision. The parties will need to establish which of them will be responsible for running the proceedings (typically the operator or the incorporated JV itself) and what that party is required to do to discharge that obligation.

---

76   See generally ILC Draft Articles on Responsibility of States for Internationally Wrongful Acts, with commentaries (2001), Art 4 (and commentary thereto); J Crawford, *State Responsibility: The General Part* (2014), pp113–165.
77   See, for example, 2012 AIPN JOA, Art 18.4.
78   See Organisation for Economic Cooperation and Development Secretariat, "Novel Features in OECD Countries' Recent Investment Agreements: An Overview", 12 December 2005, para 14.

It is also advisable in these scenarios to establish a protocol for the management of the dispute among the other JV parties, covering matters such as the treatment of documents shared by JV parties for the purposes of the dispute and the rights of the various parties to review and comment on drafts of documents to be submitted in the proceedings. This can be a delicate situation: while the best interests of the JV will be served by cooperation among the venturers, the interests of the individual venturers may well be divergent. To take our revocation of permits example, the non-operator party might plan to bring proceedings against the operator alleging negligent breach of its obligation to maintain the permits in the event that the company's challenge to the regulator's decision fails.

This chapter represents only the views of the authors and not necessarily the views of Freshfields Bruckhaus Deringer LLP or any of its clients. The material in this chapter is provided for information only and is not intended to provide legal advice. The authors would like to thank Lexi Menish and Samuel Johnson for their valuable assistance in the preparation of this chapter.

LNG plant disputes

Ben Giaretta
Mishcon de Reya LLP

1. Introduction

The liquefied natural gas (LNG) industry has grown substantially in the past 50 years, since Algeria became the world's first LNG exporter.[1] There are now 29 LNG liquefaction plants across the world, half of which have been built in the last two decades; and global LNG trade reached a new record high of 258 metric tonnes in 2016.[2] Such growth is set to continue: global liquefaction capacity is due to increase by one-third by 2020[3] and the number of liquefaction sites is predicted to double by 2040.[4]

LNG disputes have also proliferated. Many of the most high-profile disputes concern price reviews; those are considered elsewhere in this book. This chapter discusses the myriad of other disputes arising in and around the production of LNG. They merit a chapter of their own because of the unique nature of LNG and LNG contracts. LNG projects operate on a massive scale using complex technology and have several decades' life expectancy; and the LNG industry has developed rapidly, while frequently using contracts that were drafted some time ago. This is all driving disputes.

This chapter considers the types of disputes associated with LNG production, the causes of those disputes and the methods to resolve such disputes. Although the focus is on LNG liquefaction plants (and in particular, the contracts for the sale of LNG from those plants), these are inseparable from the rest of the LNG supply chain, so disputes involving other parts of that chain, such as LNG shipping, are also discussed, as well as disputes which may nominally concern cargo lifting but in fact derive from the broader relationship between buyer and seller.

---

1 Algeria began exporting LNG in 1964. The first LNG delivery (from the United States to the United Kingdom) was in 1959, and the first LNG liquefaction plant became operational in 1940 (in Cleveland, United States).
2 International Gas Union (IGU), *2017 World LNG Report*, p7. Fifteen of the 29 LNG liquefaction plants have become operational since the mid-1990s.
3 As of January 2017, global nominal liquefaction capacity was 339.7 million tons per annum (mtpa), with a further 114.6 mpta under construction: see IGU 2017 report, p19.
4 International Energy Agency, *World Energy Outlook 2017*.

2. Types of disputes

2.1 Construction disputes

The increase in oil prices over the past decade has generated a boom in the LNG construction industry: projects that were previously considered uneconomic have reached final investment decision. Yet that same boon has increased prices, as commodities, labour and essential construction equipment have become scarcer through increased demand: as the International Gas Union (IGU) has observed, when commenting on the LNG construction boom, "cost escalation has been pervasive".[5] By way of example, the cost of the Gorgon LNG project in Western Australia was reported to have risen from US$37 billion to US$54 billion.[6]

The complexity of LNG projects, of course, has not diminished; while the difficulties of working in remote locations persist. This has proved a volatile mix for construction disputes. In 2015, for example, the *Sydney Morning Herald*[7] reported that CIMIC was claiming US$1.46 billion from Chevron for work on a jetty for the Gorgon LNG project; that a dispute had been settled between Murray & Roberts and Boskalis over construction of a materials offloading wharf at the same project; and that major construction disputes were also underway concerning the Ichthys LNG project in Darwin and the Gladstone LNG project in Queensland.

Construction disputes will no doubt continue in the LNG industry as more LNG liquefaction capacity is built, and particularly as technology allows natural gas reserves that were previously considered to be inaccessible or uneconomic to be tapped into, requiring more LNG plants to be built in remote locations.

2.2 Production and loading disputes

Once an LNG plant is in operation, the types of disputes during production and loading can be many and varied. Most significant, perhaps, are the disputes arising from the connection that is central to the production and delivery process: LNG plants operate continuously, but interface with shipping that operates cargo by cargo. That interface generates disputes when there is misalignment: when a ship is delayed but LNG production cannot be reduced, or when production is disrupted but the loading schedule requires that a ship leave the port without a cargo so that the next ship can berth. The question then arises of who bears the responsibility for a cargo being delayed or missed. And that question can be multiplied by time and scale, so that it becomes a central feature of the relationship between buyer and seller over the term of a

---

5   IGU 2017 Report, page 26.
6   See *Financial Times*, 12 December 2013, www.ft.com/content/282d2d02-62bb-11e3-99d1-00144feabdc0.
7   Report dated 6 July 2015, www.smh.com.au/business/lng-construction-boom-turns-to-bonanza-for-dispute-lawyers-20150611-ghm6v6.html.

sale and purchase agreement (SPA). It is a question that needs to be answered again and again – most often through negotiation, sometimes by arbitration.

A disruption that falls squarely within the preserve of one party, such as a production disruption attributable to the operator of the plant or the disqualification of an LNG vessel chartered by the buyer, is perhaps easy for the parties to deal with. A more difficult situation arises when there is some doubt over which party is responsible or when there are multiple potential causes. A ship approaching port might develop a mechanical problem at the same time as there is a production disruption at the liquefaction plant; assuming that the cargo was being sold on a free on board basis, both buyer and/or seller (potentially, depending on the contract wording) could be responsible for the cargo being missed. There is also a difficulty when multiple parties are affected: for example, several buyers could have cargoes postponed or cancelled because of a production disruption event, and a dispute can arise as to how they are to be treated subsequently – particularly when production is not stopped, but merely reduced. A dispute can then arise as to how that production is divided up – a dispute that may become more contentious depending on the demands from the buyers' own customers (the end users of the gas), or the prevailing spot market prices at the time: the immediate cost of replacement LNG might exceed the value of the compensation payable under the LNG SPA, or the value of a replacement cargo that is due to be delivered later in the year.

2.3   *Force majeure* disputes

A related category covers those losses for which neither party apparently is responsible (*force majeure*) – for example, disruption caused by a cyclone that closes the loading berth, leading to a scaling back of LNG production. Among other projects, *force majeure* notices have been issued by BG in relation to LNG production in Egypt,[8] by ENI in relation to production in Nigeria[9] and by Total in relation to production in Yemen.[10]

The party claiming *force majeure* must comply with the relevant requirements of the contract – such as the requirement to give notice – and must demonstrate that the cause of the loss is something outside of its control. The other party may have an incentive to argue against the claiming party, to show that the fault provisions of the contract apply: it might argue that the event was within the other party's control, or that the other party has not complied with its obligations to give notice or diminish the impact of the *force majeure* event. It might even argue that the event should more properly be characterised as *force majeure* affecting itself, not *force majeure* affecting the other

---

8   See www.icis.com/resources/news/2014/01/27/9747409/bg-group-declares-force-majeure-at-egypt-lng/.
9   See https://af.reuters.com/article/investingNews/idAFKBN0U41RD20151221.
10   See www.lngworldnews.com/yemen-lng-lifts-force-majeure/.

party, if different regimes apply under the relevant contract to buyer's force majeure and seller's *force majeure*. And if *force majeure* relief does apply, the issue again arises as to how subsequent production is to be divided up in a period of reduced production or during the ramp-up to full production.

2.4   Disputes after loading

A final category concerns disputes arising after the cargoes are delivered. Various issues can come to light at this stage. There may be a question over whether the LNG met the quality standard required under the contract, over the quantity taken or over how the LNG should be attributed at the end of the contract year (eg, whether there is any carry-over of the take-or-pay obligation to the following contract year as a result of an undertake of LNG, or whether a particular cargo should be classified as make-up LNG).

Within this category also fall disputes over destination restrictions within an SPA. Changing market dynamics have created differences between regions and incentives for buyers to divert or re-export cargoes for sale in other locations (see further below). This may contravene an obligation in the SPA to confine deliveries to one destination, which may accrue to the benefit of the seller because it protects the seller's activities in the other region;[11] or it may have implications for the calculation of payments between the parties under their contract. For example, *Pluspetrol Perú Corporation v Perupetro SA*[12] involved a dispute over whether LNG cargoes originally destined for the United States could be re-exported to Asia, and whether royalties should be calculated based on the original destination or the final destination of the LNG. In May 2015, an arbitral tribunal awarded US$64 million to Perupetro, which had argued that the royalties should be based on the final destination (ie, calculated on the basis of the cargoes being re-exported to Asia, rather than on the basis of being delivered to the United States).

3.   Causes of disputes

Disputes can arise for a wide range of reasons, but three of the main underlying causes of LNG plant disputes are:

- the complexity of the LNG industry;
- the rapid development of the industry in the last two decades; and
- the inadequacy of contract wording for some of the circumstances that arise.

3.1   Complexity of the LNG industry

The LNG industry and the LNG supply chain are a complex system involving

---

11   Such protection may raise competition law issues in the relevant countries.
12   ICSID Case ARB/12/28.

the interaction of many diverse components, and the failure of one component can have a significant impact on the functioning of the rest.[13] A power outage at an LNG liquefaction plant, for example, can create havoc for the scheduling of LNG cargo loadings and in turn create massive disruption for the end users' gas supply. The main components of this system include:

- the exploration and production of natural gas and transportation to the liquefaction plant, often through a challenging environment (eg, deepwater offshore exploration and production);

- liquefaction technology, with each LNG train containing multiple complex processes;[14]

- the operations of an LNG plant as a whole, which can be on a massive scale and can require substantial project management;[15]

- the regulatory environment, including safety and security; and, potentially, domestic gas market obligations that may impact on commercial sales of LNG from the plant (particularly if the host country decides to increase the domestic market take from the project);

- the natural environment, including impacts on LNG production (as a result of ambient temperatures) and LNG loading (as a result of wind strength and wave height);

- LNG cargo scheduling, which is a dynamic process that needs to be constantly monitored throughout the year to respond to changing production forecasts (both increased and reduced LNG production, compared to initial estimates) and customer demands or defaults;

- economic impacts, including project costs and market conditions, which might drive parties' behaviour (eg, leading them to seek to cut costs – see further below);

- political impacts, particularly if one of the parties is state owned or if the host state seeks to increase its tax revenue from a project;

- commercial and contractual relationships between buyers and sellers, encompassing both the present long-term contracts and any future renewals or renegotiations; and

- relationships within a group of multiple buyers and/or within a group of multiple sellers, which in some situations may be complicated further by a buyer having corporate ties to a seller as a result of an equity investment by the buyer in the LNG project.

Each of these components, by itself, can give rise to issues that might lead to disputes. Taken together, the combination can complicate or magnify any

---

13   See Scott E Page, *Diversity and Complexity* (Princeton, 2010).
14   For a description of the technology involved, see Saeid Mokhatab, John Y Mak, Jaleel V Valappil and David A Wood, *Handbook of Liquefied Natural Gas*, Chapter 3.
15   *Ibid*, Chapters 7 and 8.

dispute. For example, weather impacts might lead the plant operator to reduce production in order to comply with safety regulations, which in turn impacts on cargo scheduling, which in turn becomes a factor in a relationship between buyer and seller that is already complicated because of political pressures or price discussions. The solution to the initial issue may become lost in the maze of other factors prevailing at that time. Added to this, the parties are often bound together by long-term SPAs, and while the resolution of one cluster of problems is being sought, a separate group of issues may arise concurrently.

3.2 Development of the LNG industry

The LNG industry has undergone profound change in the past 20 years. In any other industry, such change might cause only limited disruption: contracts and relationships might be adjusted to meet the new environment. In the LNG industry, however, commitments are made over lengthy periods: construction phases from final investment decision to first LNG shipment can stretch over many years; investments in infrastructure may take a long time to see any return; and buyers and sellers can be tied into contracts that may have terms of 20 years or more. This can mean that market changes might, over time, entirely refashion the fundamental economics that underpin a contract or a project and create entirely new drivers for the parties involved, which in turn may stimulate disputes. For example, in 2016 ENI USA filed for arbitration against Gulf LNG, alleging that changes in the US gas market had "frustrated the essential purpose" of the terminal use agreement that the parties had entered into, and the plan to convert the LNG receiving terminal into a liquefaction/export facility had given rise to a right to terminate the agreement.[16]

Some of the key changes in the LNG industry include the following.

(a) Growth in the volumes of LNG sold

These reached a new high of 258 metric tonnes in 2016 (as noted above). LNG now accounts for around 10% of the global gas market (which in turn makes up around one-quarter of the world's energy supply),[17] moving it from a niche part of the energy market to a more substantial component – with particular importance in countries such as Japan and South Korea, where LNG is a key element in the energy supply. This is set to continue, as noted above, as more LNG capacity comes on stream and as demand grows, often as a result of changing political priorities. For example, the 13th Five Year Plan in China, adopted in January 2017, identified that there would be 45 billion cubic metres (bcm) of additional gas demand in China – more than the total gas demand in

---

16   This was set out in disclosures to the US Securities and Exchange Commission.
17   IGU 2017 report, p5.

the Netherlands – plus a move away from coal-fired power generation, in order to improve air quality in cities.[18]

(b) Growth in the LNG spot market and short-term sales

These now comprise around 25% of all LNG sales, up from around 2% in 1995.[19] This has created more options for both sellers and buyers, as well as promoting LNG trading, and has moved the model for the LNG industry away from exclusive reliance on long-term SPAs and long-term relationships to a more diverse mix of long-term and short-term contracts and relationships. As discussed below, long-term relationships remain the staple of the LNG industry and are a key dynamic in resolving disputes; but the spot market impacts on those relationships by creating more options and more transparency for LNG pricing, rather than this being dependent on the oil price and on disclosures of pricing agreed in other long-term LNG SPAs.

(c) Price differentials

Prices can change not only over time (the price in the Asia-Pacific market moved from around US$3 per million British Thermal Units (MMBTU) in 1998 to as high as US$17/MMBTU in 2012, before falling back to around US$7/MMBTU in 2016), but also across regions (with US prices being generally below US$5/MMBTU in the period since 2010, during which prices in Asia have reached three times that amount).[20] Such changes have created disconnects across the LNG supply chain: buyers may complain that their long-term deals, which might be linked to the oil price, are considerably more expensive than the price in the spot market. This was apparently the main reason for the renegotiation of the long-term SPA between GAIL and Gazprom in 2016: the contract price was US$7/MMBtu higher than the spot market price.[21] When the market drops, buyers may find it difficult (either contractually or politically) to pass on their costs to their downstream buyers, while sellers may find it difficult to recoup investment and to fund ongoing development. It also means that there are opportunities for arbitrage across the different markets, leading buyers to seek to avoid destination restrictions in SPAs so as to sell LNG in more lucrative regions (as in the *Pluspetrol* case, discussed above).

(d) New participants

There are not only new LNG traders, taking advantage of the spot market, but

18 *Shell LNG Outlook 2017*, February 2017.
19 IGU 2017 report, p15.
20 *BP Statistical Review of World Energy* (June 2017): average cost, insurance and freight Japan prices have been US$3.05/MMBtu (1998), US$16.75/MMBtu (2012) and US$6.94/MMBtu (2016), while Henry Hub has been below US$5/MMBtu in the period from 2011 to 2016 (the highest yearly average was US$4.35/MMBtu, in 2014).
21 See www.infracircle.in/gail-gazprom-renegotiating-lng-deal-sources/.

also new buyers and sellers in various parts of the world. There are now 35 importing countries throughout the world (most recently, since 2015, Colombia, Egypt, Jamaica, Jordan, Pakistan and Poland have all begun importing LNG),[22] and 18 LNG exporting countries.[23] In addition, the relative importance of those countries is changing: Qatar is currently the world's biggest exporter of LNG, supplying about 30% of global LNG supplies, but Australia is due to overtake it over the next few years as new production facilities come on line. It is then predicted that the United States (which currently produces around 1% of global LNG supplies) will become the world's biggest exporter by the mid-2020s as a result of the shale gas revolution.[24] Existing participants may also change their priorities: governments in particular might seek to divert more gas to domestic markets or seek higher revenue streams during price renegotiations (whether via taxes or participation in the project by a state-owned company), depending on domestic demands and politics. For example, in 2013 Statoil was awarded US$536 million by an arbitral tribunal after the Algerian government refused to give its approval to three contracts with state-owned Sonatrach.[25]

3.3   Contract wording

A third reason is the shortcomings of contractual provisions used in the LNG industry, which in some cases have proved inadequate for the circumstances that have arisen in practice. Contract drafting has improved over time, in light of experience in the LNG industry; but deficiencies in LNG contracts remain, for three main reasons.

First, parties involved in the LNG industry have tended to choose New York law or English law as the governing law of their contracts, for the commercial certainty that those laws provide; but because disputes tend to be referred to confidential arbitration or are resolved without going through a formal dispute mechanism, there is very little precedent under those laws (or other laws) for LNG disputes. Disputes in related industries, such as disputes arising from the sale of natural gas through pipelines, may overlap to some extent and provide useful analogies, but these often fall short as good precedents for LNG disputes.

Second, contractual wording may be inadequate because, when negotiating their contracts, parties may not anticipate certain issues and therefore fail to legislate for them. Such failures might be the result of not appreciating problems that arise in practice: for example, an LNG SPA might not take into account the impact on a seller's loading schedule of obligations under contracts

---

22   See *Shell LNG Outlook 2017*.
23   IGU 2017 report, page 9.
24   International Energy Agency, *World Energy Outlook 2017*.
25   See *La Societe pour la Recherche La Production Le Transport La Transformation et la Commercialisation des Hydrocarbures SPA v Statoil Natural Gas LLC* [2014] EWHC 875 Comm (challenge to the arbitration award in the English High Court).

entered into with other buyers. The various LNG SPAs entered into in relation to an LNG project might prove to be irreconcilable for the seller in practice. Alternatively, the failure to anticipate potential problems might be the result of changing technology or environments since the contract was entered into. Contracts might have been drafted and entered into 20 or 30 years (or more) in the past, and the parties may struggle to apply these to the modern environment. Many contracts are still in use in the LNG industry which date back to previous decades. For example, in 2008 Talisman Energy finally settled a dispute with CNOOC over the Tangguh LNG project in Indonesia, which derived from a contract entered into in 1968 by Talisman and CNOOC's respective predecessors in title.[26]

Finally, even when problematic situations are anticipated at the time of contract drafting, parties often use general wording to deal with these, which gives rise to debates over interpretation at a later stage. For example, in a period of reduced production, an LNG SPA might provide that the seller must make a 'fair and reasonable allocation' of available LNG among long-term buyers; but this begs the question as to what is fair and reasonable in the circumstances. It might be an allocation based on the relative size of purchases of LNG by sellers during the contract year or it might be an allocation based on need, such as the increased demand for LNG in 2011 from Japanese buyers after the Fukushima disaster.[27] As a further example, parties might agree to deal with a failure by buyer to take LNG by including a take-or-pay clause in the SPA, but fail to specify how any make-up cargo to which a buyer might be entitled after having paid the requisite amount should be scheduled. Such omission, of course, might be a deliberate choice – a seller might resist including specific scheduling obligations in an SPA so as to give it flexibility to deal with the scheduling of other cargoes – but that can still store up a problem for the future.

4.   Resolution of LNG disputes

4.1   Negotiation

Notwithstanding the growth of the spot market, the LNG industry remains founded on long-term relationships and 75% of all LNG is still sold under long-term SPAs.[28] Further, the same parties are involved across many projects and in multiple capacities. Bechtel has been involved in the construction of 41 LNG trains across the world,[29] including the three LNG liquefaction plants built simultaneously on Curtis Island, Queensland.[30] KOGAS is the largest importer of

---

26   See https://lngjournal.com/index.php/latest-news-mainmenu-47/item/609-talisman-gets-tangguh-lng-stake-from-1968-deal.

27   IGU 2017 report, page 15.

28   See footnote 20 above.

29   See www.bechtel.com/services/oil-gas-chemicals/liquefied-natural-gas/.

30   See www.bechtel.com/projects/curtis-island-lng/.

LNG, purchasing LNG from across the world, and is also an investor in eight LNG projects from which it purchases LNG, including Gladstone LNG in Australia and Donggi-Senoro LNG in Indonesia.[31] Energy majors such as Shell, Total and Chevron are investors in LNG projects across the globe, while governments such as the government of Indonesia are participants both as investors and as regulators (Pertamina, the Indonesian state-owned energy company, has investments in LNG projects which are regulated by SKKMigas, the Indonesian state regulator).

As a result, disputes under many LNG contracts are likely to be resolved through give and take over the course of a contract rather than by reference to a formal dispute process. Indeed, it might be said that resolving a dispute via a formal process such as litigation or arbitration would be entirely inappropriate for such contracts, both because the zero-sum 'yes/no' answer might have ongoing repercussions for the relationship between the parties and because a single question referred to a judge or arbitrator may not take into account all the ramifications of a dispute, as discussed above.

There has been some discussion in recent years of certain contracts being classified under English law as 'relational'.[32] In *Yam Seng Pte Lt v International Trade Corporation Ltd*,[33] Justice Legatt stated:

> *English law has traditionally drawn a sharp distinction between certain relationships – such as partnership, trusteeship and other fiduciary relationships – on the one hand, in which the parties owe onerous obligations of disclosure to each other, and other contractual relationships in which no duty of disclosure is supposed to operate. Arguably at least, that dichotomy is too simplistic. While it seems unlikely that any duty to disclose information in performance of the contract would be implied where the contract involves a simple exchange, many contracts do not fit this model and involve a longer term relationship between the parties in which they make a substantial commitment. Such 'relational' contracts, as they are sometimes called, may require a high degree of communication, co-operation and predictable performance based on mutual trust and confidence and involve expectations of loyalty which are not legislated for in the express terms of the contract but are implicit in the parties' understanding and necessary to give business efficacy to the arrangements. Examples of such relational contracts might include some joint venture agreements, franchise agreements and long term distributorship agreements.[34]*

The extent to which this categorisation might affect a party's substantive contractual obligations (eg, by the implication of a contractual duty of good

---

31   See www.kogas.or.kr/eng/contents.do?key=1557.
32   Drawing on the 'relational theory of contract', an approach developed by and most closely associated with Ian Macneil; see (among other works) *The New Social Contract* (Yale UP, 1980).
33   [2013] EWHC 111 (QB).
34   Paragraph 142 of the judgment.

faith) is controversial,[35] but the description is useful here. The nature of a long-term LNG SPA means that it might fall within the category of relational contracts and a higher degree of communication and cooperation between the parties, particularly for the resolution of disputes, would be appropriate than in relation to other types of contract. The parties have a mutual interest in reaching an amicable solution.

A formal negotiation process, written into the contract, or mediation might assist in resolving an LNG plant dispute. What may be more helpful, however, might be ongoing communication (preferably, face-to-face communication) both between those responsible on each side for the day-to-day operation of an LNG SPA and between those responsible for overall oversight of the contract. This may facilitate discussion on a near-constant basis of the issues that arise. Contract management can be more important in the LNG industry than formal dispute resolution.

4.2 Expert determination and adjudication

Despite the emphasis above on communication and negotiation, other forms of dispute resolution do have their place in LNG disputes. Expert determination might be appropriate for particular disputes – disputes confined to one technical issue, which do not impinge on other areas of the relationship between the parties. For example, a dispute over the quality of LNG might be referred to an expert for determination. Also, adjudication might be used, particularly in a construction dispute and particularly in countries where there is statutory adjudication, such as Australia – although an adjudicator's decision is often appealed to arbitration or litigation, meaning that this is not the end of the dispute resolution process.

4.3 International arbitration and national court litigation

International arbitration and national court litigation might also feature. This could be a step towards a negotiated settlement (a party might start arbitration or litigation in order to force the other party to the negotiating table), or it could be pursued to the end. A ruling by an arbitrator or a judge might be particularly useful where a negotiated outcome is impossible and a binding third-party decision is the only way forward – for example, if a group of buyers or a group of sellers cannot decide between themselves on a settlement offer, or if it might be politically embarrassing (eg, for the directors or executives of a state-owned company) for a settlement to be reached.

International arbitration is most commonly selected by parties to LNG SPAs for the final stage of the dispute resolution process, partly because of the

---

35   Recognition of relational contracts had previously been rejected in *Baird Textile Holdings plc v Marks and Spencer plc* [2001] EWCA Civ 274.

international nature of the industry and also because of the confidentiality in international arbitration that allows a party to protect sensitive commercial terms such as pricing information. However, LNG disputes are occasionally heard by national courts: the dispute between Talisman and CNOOC referred to above, for example, was heard in a court in Dallas County, Texas.

5.   Conclusion

LNG disputes reflect the nature of the LNG industry: complex, relationship driven and responsive to changes in the market. Given the massive sums required to develop LNG infrastructure, the backbone of the industry is likely to remain the long-term contract and disputes are likely to remain a function of relationship management rather than spilling over into major arbitrations. The proper conduct of disputes is important, nonetheless, because of the impact on a relationship if a dispute is handled badly. Parties need to communicate and collaborate in such a fashion as to manage the complexities of the issues and resolve the dispute constructively.

The views expressed in this chapter are those of the author alone.

The Energy Charter Treaty

Thomas K Sprange
Ben J Williams
King & Spalding International LLP

1. Introduction

When the Soviet Union collapsed in the early 1990s, the international community faced a multitude of challenges, not least in the energy sector. Put simply, overall demand outstripped supply in the western nations of Europe, whereas the former Soviet bloc was abundant with natural resources. The challenge was to encourage and protect the movement of capital from the west to the east, to facilitate the necessary investment in energy infrastructure.

To meet this challenge, the European Energy Charter was adopted in The Hague on 17 December 1991. The primary objective was to facilitate increased multilateral cooperation over transit, trade, investments, dispute resolution and energy efficiency. The charter contained a commitment to negotiate in good faith a legally binding treaty. The treaty, the Energy Charter Treaty (ECT), was adopted in December 1994 and came into force on 16 April 1998. There are currently 54 contracting states (including the European Union and EURATOM).[1]

While the ECT, even today, maintains its fundamental east/west cooperative function, the economics and politics of the 21st century have to a large extent moved on. Globalisation continues to make the world a more integrated place. Technological advances have expanded the energy sector beyond the traditional fossil fuels into clean tech and renewables. To keep pace, there is a current focus within the Energy Charter movement on geographical expansion, with accession to the ECT open to all countries and regional economic integration organisations. This attitudinal shift is reflected in the International Energy Charter, a further political declaration adopted and signed in The Hague on 20 May 2015. In total, the Energy Charter movement now involves more than 90 nations from all corners of the world.

---

[1]   Afghanistan, Albania, Armenia, Australia, Austria, Azerbaijan, Belarus, Belgium, Bosnia and Herzegovina, Bulgaria, Croatia, Cyprus, Czech Republic, Denmark, Estonia, European Union and Euratom, Finland, France, Georgia, Germany, Greece, Hungary, Iceland, Ireland, Japan, Kazakhstan, Kyrgyzstan, Latvia, Liechtenstein, Lithuania, Luxembourg, Malta, Moldova, Mongolia, Montenegro, Netherlands, Norway, Poland, Portugal, Romania, Russian Federation, Slovakia, Slovenia, Spain, Sweden, Switzerland, Tajikistan, the former Yugoslav Republic of Macedonia, Turkey, Turkmenistan, Ukraine, United Kingdom, Uzbekistan. Australia, Belarus and Norway signed, but did not ratify; hence, the treaty applies only provisionally. Italy and Russia have withdrawn, effective 1 January 2016 and 19 October 2009 respectively (albeit treaty protections apply 20 years hence).

This chapter provides an overview of dispute resolution under the ECT. It begins by providing some facts and figures relating to the arbitrations that have been brought since the treaty's inception. It goes on to explain the dispute resolution options and key protections afforded under the treaty. Finally, it discusses the key issues and trends that have emerged over the ECT's 25-year history, as demonstrated through published awards.

2.   Facts and figures[2]

Since the first case invoking the ECT in 2001, there have been a total of 114 publicly known cases (up to 18 May 2018).[3] On an annual basis, the ECT is the most frequently invoked international investment agreement. In 2015 alone, 29 cases were registered, out of a total of 80 publicly known international investment treaty cases.[4]

The investor uptake that the ECT currently enjoys was not always the case. Indeed, the initial years were slow. In the 12 years from 2001 to 2012 (inclusive), there were only 37 cases, compared to 76 in the six years from 2013 to 2018 (inclusive)(see Figure 1).

Figure 1. Investment disputes under the ECT: 114 cases (registration year of one dispute is unknown)

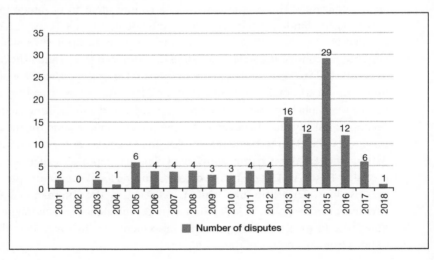

---

2   All information and graphics in this section are based on data from publicly known investment arbitrations invoking the ECT, as collated by the Energy Charter Secretariat up to 18 May 2018, https://energycharter.org/what-we-do/dispute-settlement/cases-up-to-18-may-2018/.
3   Up to 4 June 2018, a further five publicly known cases had been filed (www.energycharter.org/what-we-do/dispute-settlement/all-investment-dispute-settlement-cases/).
4   ISDS Navigator, United Nations Investment Policy Hub, http://investmentpolicyhub.unctad.org/ISDS.

The driver of the significant expansion in recent years has almost certainly been the influx of intra-EU claims (comprising the majority of cases registered in recent years and approximately 60% of all publicly known ECT cases to date), notably in the renewables sector. The growth of the renewables sector, mostly in the developed economies of Western Europe, has largely involved investors from EU member states investing in projects in other EU member states. The reversal of governmental support for such projects has led to numerous well-funded and sophisticated investors being burnt. It is hardly surprising, therefore, that a side effect of this phenomenon has been an uptick in overall case numbers, as shown in Figures 2 and 3.

Figure 2. Cases involving EU investors against EU member states (intra-EU), compared against other cases that are not intra-EU

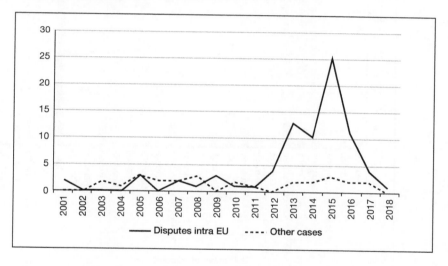

Figure 3. ECT cases by energy source

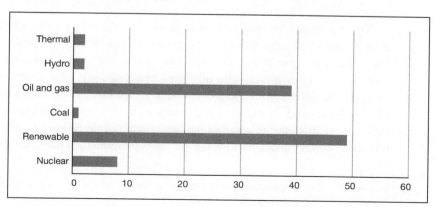

The treatment that certain states, notably Spain, has accorded to investors in the renewables sector has had a marked impact on the distribution of cases on a state-by-state basis. Cases have been brought against 26 states in total. Most states have had five or fewer cases brought against them. An intermediate category of states – comprising the Czech Republic, Italy, Russia and Turkey – have each faced five to 10. Spain, by contrast, has had 40 cases brought against it (mostly in the last four years and relating to the country's reduction or elimination of incentives offered to renewable energy producers).

Figure 4. Respondent states: 114 cases

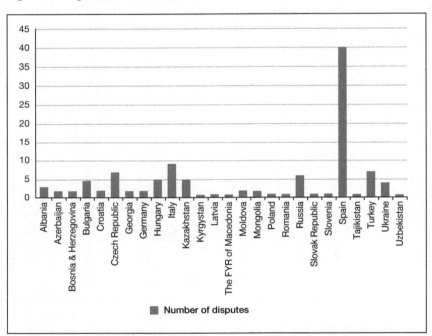

The nationality of investors bringing claims also tells a story. Claimants from a total of 32 nationalities have pursued claims. Four in particular stand out: Germany, Luxembourg, the Netherlands and the United Kingdom. Each state has had 15 or more claims advanced by its nationals. For Germany, the Netherlands and the United Kingdom – each with a mature economy and track record of outbound investment – the figures are understandable.[5] Luxembourg's inclusion at first glance is bemusing, albeit explainable bearing in mind the utilisation of the jurisdiction for tax purposes by numerous nationalities. The

---

5   With respect to the United Kingdom, the inclusion of Jersey, the Isle of Man and Gibraltar also explains the figures, given the frequent use of these jurisdictions for tax purposes by numerous nationalities.

spread across the remaining 28 nationalities is fairly uniform, with each state having five or fewer claims advanced by its nationals (with the exception of Cyprus, France, Italy and Spain, with 10 or fewer claims).

Figure 5. Nationality (or permanent residence) of claimants: 114 cases

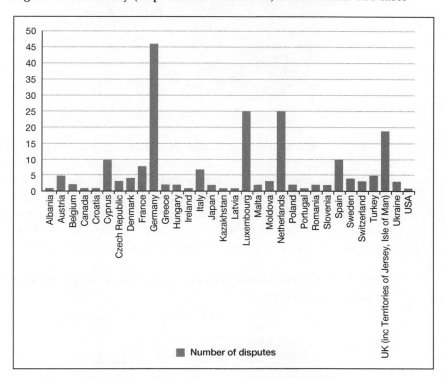

Given the uptick of cases filed in recent years, of the 114 cases filed, 66 are currently pending. Of the 48 cases that have concluded, 11 were settled, discontinued or withdrawn,[6] and 37 have resulted in final awards.

---

6   The Guide on Investment Mediation (prepared in 2016 in cooperation with the International Mediation Institute, the Stockholm Chamber of Commerce, the Permanent Court of Arbitration, the International Centre for the Settlement of Investment Disputes, the International Chamber of Commerce and the United Nations Commission on International Trade Law) encourages investors and contracting states to consider mediation on voluntary basis at any stage of the dispute.

Figure 6. Status of investment disputes under the ECT: 114 cases

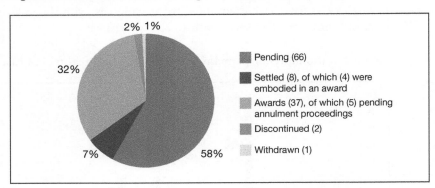

Given the relatively modest number of final awards, and leaving to one side the interaction with general principles of international law, as embodied in awards issued under other investment agreements and treaties, jurisprudence exclusively under the ECT remains in its infancy. Focusing on hard facts, 15 of the 41 final awards (including settlements embodied in final awards) have resulted in damages being awarded (mostly notably $50 billion in *Yukos Universal Limited (Isle of Man) v Russian Federation (PCA Case AA 227)*).

Figure 7. Outcome of final awards (41), including (4) settlement agreements embodied in an award

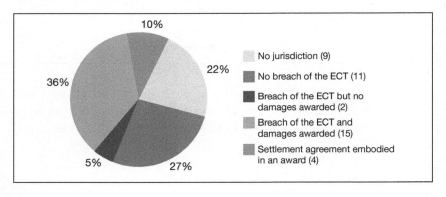

3. Dispute resolution options

Article 26(1) provides that if disputes cannot be amicably settled within three months, the parties have recourse to:

- the national courts of the contracting state;
- a previously agreed dispute resolution procedure; or
- international arbitration.[7]

(1) Disputes between a Contracting Party and an Investor of another Contracting Party relating to an Investment of the latter in the Area of the former, which concern an alleged breach of an obligation of the former under Part III shall, if possible, be settled amicably.

(2) If such disputes cannot be settled according to the provisions of paragraph (1) within a period of three months from the date on which either party to the dispute requested amicable settlement, the Investor party to the dispute may choose to submit it for resolution:

    (a) to the courts or administrative tribunals of the Contracting Party to the dispute;

    (b) in accordance with any applicable, previously agreed dispute settlement procedure; or

    (c) in accordance with the following paragraphs of this Article.

Article 26(4) allows investors to elect to submit the dispute to:

- the International Centre for the Settlement of Investment Disputes (ICSID), as long as both the state of the investor and the respondent state are parties to the ICSID Convention;[8]
- a sole arbitrator or *ad hoc* arbitration tribunal established under the Arbitration Rules of the United Nations Commission on International Trade (UNCITRAL); or
- an arbitral proceeding under the Arbitration Institute of the Stockholm Chamber of Commerce (SCC) – understandably so given the east/west genesis of the ECT and the SCC's historical role administering disputes between Western European parties and nations of the former Soviet bloc.

ICSID is by far the preferred dispute resolution procedure, with UNCITRAL (both *ad hoc* and in the Permanent Court of Arbitration (PCA)) and the SCC a broadly equal second.

Figure 8. Procedural rules applied: 114 cases

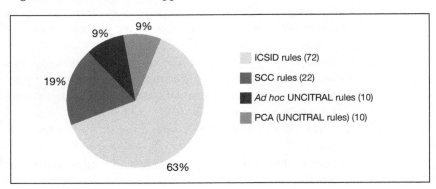

The contracting state's consent to arbitration is unconditional by virtue of its entry into the ECT.[9] The investor's consent is given pursuant to its election to submit the dispute to arbitration under one of the aforementioned procedural paths, usually by way of its request or notice of arbitration.

Article 26(6) provides that the governing law of disputes is the ECT and applicable rules and principles of international law (ie, other investment treaty jurisprudence arising from awards in cases involving other bilateral and multilateral investment treaties). While there is no binding jurisprudential precedent, tribunals are encouraged to follow the reasoning of previous decisions in accordance with the customs of international law, unless there are compelling reasons to deviate.[10]

In *Yukos* the tribunal applied the Vienna Convention on the Law of Treaties and other applicable law. More specifically, in determining the principles of international law, Article 38(1)(c) of the Statute of the International Court of Justice is instructive, referring to "general principles of international law recognized by civilized nations".

In cases involving EU member states, there is a degree of uncertainty as to the application of EU law. In *AES Summit Generation Ltd v Republic of Hungary* (ICSID Case ARB/07/22), the tribunal held that the applicable law was the ECT, with applicable rules of international law, and not EU law. In *Electrabel SA v*

---

9   With the exception of those states listed in Annex ID, where an investor is barred from bringing a claim if it has previously submitted the dispute to the national courts of the respondent state or pursuant to a previously agreed dispute resolution procedure. Such states comprise Australia, Azerbaijan, Bulgaria, Canada, Croatia, Cyprus, Czech Republic, European Union and Euratom, Finland, Greece, Hungary, Ireland, Italy, Japan, Kazakhstan, Norway, Poland, Portugal, Romania, Russia, Slovenia, Spain, Sweden and the United States. Further, those states listed in Annex IA do not allow disputes involving the last sentence of Article 10(1) (the umbrella clause) to be submitted to international arbitration. Such states comprise Australia, Canada, Hungary and Norway.

10   The Tribunal in *Electrabel SA v Republic of Hungary* (ICSID Case ARB/07/19 (2012) observed in its decision on jurisdiction, applicable law and liability at ¶4-15 that "tribunals in investor-state arbitrations should take into account earlier decisions and also should not distance themselves from an existing series of consistent decisions save for compelling reasons".

Republic of Hungary (ICSID Case ARB/07/19 (2012)), however, the opposite was the case, in circumstances where one of the parties acceded to the European Union after becoming a party to the ECT. The tribunal in *Charanne BV v Kingdom of Spain* (Arbitration 062/2012), applying *Electrabel*, went a step further and held that international tribunals not only have the power to apply EU law, but are obligated to do so (see further section 5.5).

Awards are final and binding. The ECT, pursuant to Article 26(8), requires contracting states to provide effective enforcement mechanisms in their own jurisdictions. More generally, enforcement of ECT awards under the Convention on the Recognition and Enforcement of Foreign Arbitral Awards (the New York Convention) is prevalent given Article 26(5)(b), which provides that any arbitration shall, at the request of any party to the dispute, be held in a state that is a party to the New York Convention. Of the 52 contracting states to the ECT (excluding the European Union and EURATOM), all but Turkmenistan is a signatory to the New York Convention.

4. Key protections

Part III of the ECT sets out the key protections afforded to investors.

4.1 Article 10[11]

Article 10(1) provides:

> Each Contracting Party shall, in accordance with the provisions of this Treaty, encourage and create stable, equitable, favourable and transparent conditions for Investors of other Contracting Parties to make Investments in its Area. Such conditions shall include a commitment to accord at all times to Investments of Investors of other Contracting Parties **fair and equitable treatment**. Such Investments shall also enjoy the most constant protection and security and no Contracting Party shall in any way impair by **unreasonable or discriminatory measures** their management, maintenance, use, enjoyment or disposal. In no case shall such Investments be accorded treatment less favourable than that required by international law, including treaty obligations. Each Contracting Party shall **observe any obligations it has entered into** with an Investor or an Investment of an Investor of any other Contracting Party. (emphasis added)

Article 10(1) claims can thus be broken down to invocations of one or more of the following key protections.

---

[11] This section focuses on the key protections afforded under Article 10(1). Note, however:
- the national treatment and most favoured nation protections (Article 10(7)), which ensure parity between foreign and local investors, as well as between foreign investors from different states; and
- the effective means protection (Article 10(12)), which provides that domestic law of each contracting state must provide effective means to assert claims and enforce rights in relation to investors' investments.

(a) *Fair and equitable treatment*

Given the existence of the fair and equitable treatment standard in most investment agreements, a substantial body of international law has developed around it. Common obligations that contracting states ought to abide by include:

- ensuring transparency and consistency in the treatment of investors and its investments;[12]
- acting in good faith;[13]
- refraining from acting arbitrarily or in a discriminatory manner;[14] and
- applying due process in all dealings concerning the investor and its investments.[15]

Determining whether conduct of a state falls foul of the standard is inevitably fact sensitive. In general, tribunals look for conduct which is "manifestly unfair or unreasonable (such as would shock, or at least surprise a sense of juridical propriety)".[16]

A particular issue which remains unresolved in the jurisprudence is the extent to which an investor's expectations is a barometer of whether conduct is unfair and inequitable, bearing in mind that a state has a legitimate right to regulate. While the investor's reasonable and legitimate expectation in *Electrabel* was that prices for electricity under a power purchase agreement would not materially change, and the tribunal deemed that to be a relevant factor, increases brought on by regulatory changes or operation of law in Hungary were ultimately held not to breach the standard in circumstances where they were not unreasonable, irrational or otherwise made in bad faith. By contrast, the approach in *Plama Consortium Ltd v Republic of Bulgaria* (ICSID Case ARB/03/24 (2008)) was far more restrictive. The tribunal held that only investment-backed expectations based on conditions specifically offered by the state when the investor made the investment were relevant, as opposed to legitimate expectations in general.[17]

Debate has ensued as to whether such assurances or representations by a state must be explicit or can merely be implied. In *Al-Bahloul* and *Mamidoil*, the tribunals considered that legitimate expectations can be inferred from legal orders, regulatory frameworks or other implicit assurances;[18] whereas in

---

12   *Micula v Romania* (ICSID Case ARB/05/20 (2013); *Plama Consortium Ltd v Republic of Bulgaria* (ICSID Case ARB/03/24 (2008)), Award, ¶178; *Electrabel*, Decision on Jurisdiction, ¶7.74; *Al-Bahloul v Republic of Tajikistan* (SCC Arb V064 (2008)), Partial Award, ¶¶183-184; *Mamidoil Jetoil Greek Petroleum Products Société Anonyme SA v Albania* (ICSID Case ARB/11/24), Award (30 March 2015), ¶616.
13   *Oostergetel v Slovak Republic* (UNCITRAL, Final Award (2010); Charanne, Final Award, ¶486.
14   *Electrabel*, Award (25 November 2015), ¶179; *AES Summit Generation Ltd v Republic of Hungary* (ICSID Case ARB/07/22 (2010), Award (23 September 2010), ¶¶10.3.7-10.3.9).
15   *AES Summit*; *Electrabel*, Decision on Jurisdiction, ¶7.74; *Mamidoil*, Award, ¶613.
16   *The AES Corporation v Republic of Kazakhstan* (ICSID Case ARB/10/16), Award (1 November 2013), ¶314; *AES Summit*, Award (23 September 2010), ¶¶9.3.40.
17   *Plama*, Award, ¶176.
18   *Al-Bahloul*, Partial Award, ¶202; *Mamidoil*, Award, ¶731.

Charanne, the tribunal was satisfied only with explicit statements and commitments – for example in the form of a stabilisation clause, which a regulatory landscape would not change.[19] Finally, causation will always be a critical factor. In *Al-Bahloul*, there was no breach of fair and equitable treatment where the investor was unable to establish its reliance on a legitimate expectation when making the investment that exploration licences would subsequently be granted.

(b)   Constant protection and security

This obligation requires states, as a minimum, to maintain vigilance and care to prevent and punish any activities of third parties within the territory which stand to threaten the constant protection and security of a foreign investor's investments.[20] At one end of the spectrum are actions involving force and particular physical damage.[21] At the other end is harassment, giving rise to a fear of force and particular physical harm.[22] A state's failure to afford protection from either could amount to a breach of the standard. In *Electrabel*, the tribunal held that the extent of the obligation is to exercise due diligence and where necessary take reasonable action to prevent or remedy injury of which the state is aware or ought to be aware. Hungary met this standard by affording the investor the legal means to protect its investment against the adversarial actions of third parties.

(c)   Unreasonable or discriminatory measures

As indicated above, there is some degree of overlap between the unreasonable or discriminatory measures standard and that of fair and equitable treatment (albeit that both are separate grounds of protection under the ECT). Measures that will breach the provision include those that are "not founded in reason or fact but on caprice, prejudice or personal preference".[23] In *Electrabel*, the tribunal held that the unreasonable or discriminatory measure must cause significant impairment to the investment if it is to be actionable under the treaty.[24]

In *Nykomb Synergetics Technologies Holding AB v Republic of Latvia* (SCC (Final Award) (2003)),[25] the tribunal held that when determining whether a measure is discriminatory it is necessary to consider like with like, and that the burden of

---

19   *Charanne*, Final Award, ¶490.
20   *Electrabel*, Decision on Jurisdiction, ¶7.83, applying non-ECT case *El Paso Energy International Company v Argentine Republic* (ICSID Case ARB/03/15 (2011), award ¶¶522-523); *Plama*, Award, ¶¶179-180; *AES Summit*, Award, ¶¶13.3.2-13.3.3; *Mamidoil*, Award, ¶821.
21   *Liman Caspian Oil BV v Republic of Kazakhstan* (ICSID Case ARB/07/14), in which the tribunal held that the state did not fall foul of the standard, because the investor made no allegation of force or damage to property.
22   *AES Summit*, in which the tribunal held that the standard afforded the investor legal protection in addition to physical protection.
23   *Plama*, Award, ¶184.
24   *Electrabel*, Decision on Jurisdiction, ¶7.152.
25   *Nykomb*, Award, ¶4.3.2.3.a.4.

proof lay with the state to prove that no discrimination had occurred. Discriminatory intent on the part of the state does not come into it.[26] In *Nykomb*, Latvia had discriminated against the investor, simply because it had provided double tariffs on surplus electricity to two companies in a similar position to the investor, but not to the investor. When determining whether a measure is reasonable, it is necessary to consider the existence of any rational policy objective and whether the state's actions are targeted at achieving those aims. If there is no such policy or the state's actions are otherwise aimed elsewhere, it is more likely that the conduct will be deemed to be unreasonable.[27]

(d)   Umbrella clause[28]

The umbrella clause is a catch-all provision, designed to ensure that a state's failure to adhere to an obligation it has entered into with the investor, which might not fall within one of express protections of the treaty, nevertheless produces an actionable breach. The classic example is a state's failure to perform its contractual obligations, as was the case in *Al-Bahloul* when Tajikistan failed to issue exploration and exploitation licences per its contractual obligations. See also *Khan Resources Inc v Mongolia* (UNCITRAL, PCA Case 2011/09), where Mongolia's breach of its domestic foreign investment law prohibiting unlawful expropriation was held to constitute a breach of the umbrella clause.

4.2   Article 13

Article 13(1) provides protection from expropriation:

> *Investments of Investors of a Contracting Party in the Area of any other Contracting Party shall not be nationalised, expropriated or subjected to a measure or measures having effect equivalent to nationalisation or expropriation (hereinafter referred to as "Expropriation") except where such Expropriation is:*
>
> *(a) for a purpose which is in the public interest;*
>
> *(b) not discriminatory;*
>
> *(c) carried out under due process of law; and*
>
> *(d) accompanied by the payment of prompt, adequate and effective compensation. Such compensation shall amount to the fair market value of the Investment expropriated at the time immediately before the Expropriation or impending Expropriation became known in such a way as to affect the value of the Investment (hereinafter referred to as the "Valuation Date").*

Pursuant to the first part of Article 13, expropriations can be either direct or indirect.

---

26   *Electrabel*, Decision on Jurisdiction, ¶7.152.
27   *AES Summit*, Award, ¶¶10.3.7-10.3.9.
28   Does not apply to Annex IA states: Australia, Canada, Hungary and Norway.

Direct expropriation – involving the taking of actual legal title – is rare. *Kardassopoulos v Georgia* (ICSID Cases ARB/05/18 and ARB/07/15) is one such example. The tribunal in that case held that Georgia's taking of the investor's concession to distribute oil and gas in Georgia by transferring the rights to a state-owned entity without due process or any compensation was a classic example of a direct expropriation.[29]

Much more common, however, is indirect expropriation, whereby the investor maintains legal title, but is denied any meaningful use or enjoyment of the asset. This often involves not one, but rather a series of acts on the part of a state – a creeping expropriation if you like. In *Plama*, the tribunal set out a three-part test to establish whether there has been an indirect expropriation:

- Was there a substantially complete deprivation of the economic use and enjoyment of the asset?
- Were the measures irreversible and permanent?
- Was the loss of economic value extensive?

On the facts in *Plama*, there was no expropriation where it was claimed that:
- environmental laws were amended to cast liability onto the investor;
- the investor was prevented from filing tax returns on time because of failures by Bulgaria to amend its corporate income tax laws;
- the state unlawfully privatised a port which was critical to the investment;
- the state unlawfully instigated a riot at the investor's oil refinery; and
- a state-owned bank deliberately breached a debt settlement agreement with the investor.

While such measures could conceivably constitute an indirect expropriation, the tribunal instead held that the investor had failed to demonstrate any actual harm or loss or limitation on the right to use and enjoy the investment.

By contrast, in *Yukos*, the tribunal held that while the Russian government had not "explicitly" taken the assets, it had taken steps "equivalent to nationalization or expropriation". In particular, such measures included:
- instigating criminal proceedings against in the investor's senior management;
- obstructing the investor's legal team;
- carrying out search and seizures of the investor's property;
- allegedly frustrating a merger; and
- imposing tax re-assessments of more than $24 billion and then seizing shares and other assets belonging to the investor in connection with the same.

29   *Kardassopoulos*, Award, (3 March 2010), ¶¶387-408.

These actions, the tribunal held, were part of a devious scheme to bankrupt Yukos and appropriate its assets (without explicitly expropriating Yukos or the holdings of its shareholders), and thus constituted an indirect expropriation.

When it comes to compensation, a distinction is drawn between lawful and unlawful expropriation. A lawful expropriation is one where the conditions set out in Articles 13(1)(a) to (d) are met; hence, compensation is the fair market value of the asset immediately prior to expropriation, as expressly stated in the provision. Unlawful expropriation is where the taking is completely unjustified. In such circumstances, tribunals have held that compensation "must, as far as possible, wipe out all the consequences of the illegal act and re-establish the situation which would, in all probability, have existed if that act had not been committed".[30] In practice, this can mean that damages are assessed at the date of the award, by quantifying any gain in value between the date of expropriation and the date of the award (albeit that in *Kardassopoulos*, the tribunal held that the date of the action by Georgia which amounted to the expropriation was the appropriate valuation date). Conversely, in *Yukos*, the tribunal held that if the expropriated asset can be returned to the investor, any decrease in value since the date of expropriation should be awarded in damages to the investor.

5. Key issues and trends

Over the ECT's 25-year history, certain issues have repeatedly arisen and to some extent trends are beginning to emerge. This section analyses some of the common themes – largely relating to jurisdictional objections that respondent states seek to invoke. These jurisdictional hurdles are some of the most heavily contested and adjudicated issues in arbitrations under the ECT.

5.1 Qualifying investments and investors

(a) Investments

Article 1(6) defines 'investments' broadly as all types of assets directly or indirectly controlled or owned by an investor, including:

- tangible and intangible, and moveable and immovable property and property rights (eg, leases, mortgages, liens and pledges);
- a company or business enterprise, or shares, stock or other forms of equity participation in a company or business enterprise, and bonds and other debt of a company or business;
- claims to money and claims to performance pursuant to a contract having an economic value and associated with an investment;

---

30   *The Factory at Chorzów (Germany v Poland)* (PCIJ Series A, No 17 (1928), p47, as applied in *Kardassopoulos v Georgia* (ICSID Cases ARB/05/18 and ARB/07/15).

- intellectual property;
- returns; and
- any right conferred by law or contract or by virtue of any licences and permits granted pursuant to law to undertake any economic activity in the energy sector.

The two areas that most commonly give rise to jurisdictional objections by states are:

- the ownership of shares; and
- rights conferred by contract.

With regard to shares, the question is whether the investor must be the legal or beneficial owner to qualify the shares as an investment. In *Veteran Petroleum Limited (Cyprus) v Russian Federation* (PCA Case 228 (2009), Russia's jurisdictional objection – on the basis that the investor was the legal, but not the ultimate beneficial owner of the shares – was rejected. The tribunal held that Article 1(6) contained the widest possible definition of holding an interest in a company, and that there was no limitation on ownership of shares to that of ultimate beneficial ownership. By contrast, in *Al-Bahloul*, the investor was the ultimate beneficial owner of the shares, but not the legal owner. The tribunal held that the inclusion in the definition of 'investment' of the words "owned or controlled directly or indirectly" meant that the legal ownership of shares by an intermediary company in a non-ECT state (the Bahamas) was no bar to jurisdiction when the ultimate beneficial owner was incorporated in a contracting state.

With regard to contracts, the subject matter of the agreement is critical. In *Petrobart Limited v The Kyrgyz Republic* (SCC Case 126/2003), the tribunal held that the contract itself (and a judgment founded upon the contract) were no more than legal documents containing legal rights. If the nature of such rights were related to economic activity in the energy sector – for example, the sale of gas condensate – then they would qualify as an investment. Likewise, in *Electrabel*, the investor's power purchase agreement with Hungary was a qualifying investment, separate from the investor's ownership of shares in the entity that was party to the contract. However, in *State Enterprise Energorynok v Moldova* (SCC Arbitration V 2012/175) the tribunal stressed that the investor must be directly or indirectly engaged in the economic activities comprising the contract.

An issue which remains the subject of debate is whether general indebtedness from a loan as opposed to a debt arising from a specific commercial contract qualifies as an investment. On this issue, in *Energoalians v Moldova* (UNCITRAL, Final Award (2013)) Chairperson Dominic Pellew disagreed with the party-appointed arbitrators' decision that both types of investment qualified for treaty protection. In set-aside proceedings, the Paris Court of Appeal found, consistent with Pellew's dissenting opinion, that the tribunal lacked jurisdiction, because a claim for money for an unpaid general debt for the supply of electricity was not a qualifying investment.[31]

In *RREEF Infrastructure (GP) Limited v Kingdom of Spain* (ICSID Case ARB/13/30 (2016)), the tribunal confirmed the broad definition of 'investment' as "open, general and not restrictive". It is perhaps this lack of specific language that has led to the issue being heavily arbitrated, albeit largely unsuccessfully, by states seeking to exclude any given investment from treaty protection.

(b)   Investors

Article 1(7) defines an 'investor' as either:

- a natural person having the citizenship or nationality of, or who is permanently residing in, a state that is a member of the ECT; or
- an entity organised according to the law applicable to a state that is a member of the ECT.

With regard to companies, tribunals will simply look at the place of incorporation to determine nationality. Attempts by states to pierce the corporate veil to demonstrate that the investor is in fact from a non-qualifying nationality have consistently failed.[32]

5.2   Denial of benefits

The denial of benefits provision, at Article 17(1), provides that a contracting state may deny treaty protection to companies which lack substantial business activities in the place where they are incorporated. This prevents shell companies incorporated in contracting states from availing of treaty protection. The denial of benefits clause applies where:[33]

- the company is owned or controlled by citizens or nationals of a third state, being a state that is not a contracting state; and
- the company has no substantial business activities in the contracting state in which it is incorporated.

For the purposes of the first limb of the test, it is sufficient – to negate the denial of benefits clause – that the shares in the claimant company are held through other companies in trust for a citizen or national of a contracting state. In *Plama*, the respondent state was unable to deny the claimant company treaty

---

31   Paris Court of Appeal, 12 April 2016, 13/22531.
32   *Veteran Petroleum; Charanne; Hulley Enterprises Limited (Cyprus) v The Russian Federation* (UNCITRAL, PCA Case AA 226, (2014)); *Plama; RREEF; Yukos; Energoalians;* and *Saluka Investments BV (The Netherlands) v The Czech Republic* (PCA (2006)).
33   *Plama* (Decision on Jurisdiction).

protection on the basis that it was ultimately owned and controlled by a French national.

As to the second limb of the test, the materiality of the business activity is relevant, not the magnitude. In *Amto v Ukraine* (SCC Case 080/2005), it was sufficient to negate the denial of benefits clause that the claimant company employed a small staff and conducted activities relating to the investment from offices in the contracting state where it was incorporated.

How a state, per the language of Article 17, "reserves the right" to deny investors the benefits of treaty protection has been repeatedly scrutinised by tribunals. The question is what a state must do to exercise the right and, having done so, whether the denial is retrospective as well as prospective in effect.[34] In *Plama*, the tribunal's view was that the state must give advance notice and hence a denial of benefits has only prospective effect.[35] Further, tribunals have refused to decline jurisdiction on the basis that Article 17 does not, in any event, prevent an investor's referral of the very same issue to arbitration pursuant to Article 26 (hence, technically the matter ought to be dealt with as part of a merits hearing).[36]

5.3   Tax carve-out

Article 21(1) – the so-called 'tax carve-out' – provides that the ECT does not interfere with rights and obligations concerning *bona fide* taxation in contracting states. The carve-out prevails where there is inconsistency with other treaty provisions (including Part III). The claw-back provision – at Article 21(5) – for expropriatory taxes is often challenged by states in the form of a jurisdictional objection. A state's argument is usually that the tax carve-out prevents investor claims of any kind involving taxation, which per Article 21(5) must instead be referred to competent tax authorities and exhausted in such forums first.[37]

Russia's argument in *Yukos*, that the claw-back provision applies to taxes only and not to ancillary measures, such as collection, enforcement and penalties, was roundly rejected by the tribunal. The tribunal held that:

- it had indirect jurisdiction over the Article 13 expropriation claim by virtue of the fact that the Article 21(5) claw-back brought back into play any measures carved-out under Article 21(1); and
- the Article 21(1) carve-out did not apply to measures motivated solely to destroy the investor company, rather than raising general revenue for the state; hence, prior complaint to the competent tax authorities was not a prerequisite to arbitration.

---

34   *Libananco Holdings Co Limited v Republic of Turkey* (ICSID Case ARB/06/8).
35   See also *Hulley*; *Khan*; *Liman*; *Veteran*; and *Yukos*.
36   *Plama*; and *Khan*.
37   *Plama*.

5.4 Cooling-off period

Whether the three-month cooling-off period in Article 26(2) is a precondition to arbitration is another jurisdictional objection that states often seek to raise, albeit with no real success.

In *Anatolie Stati v Republic of Kazakhstan* (SCC Arb V116/2010 (2013)), Kazakhstan argued that the investors had not provided prior notice of the dispute, let alone made any attempt to settle prior to commencing arbitration. The tribunal rejected the argument on its merits, including on the basis that it is unnecessary for investors to make specific reference to bringing a claim under the ECT in any prior attempts to resolve disputes.[38] In any event, had it not considered the objection without merit in substance, the tribunal held that the requirement was procedural not jurisdictional, meaning that non-compliance was not an automatic bar to arbitration. The arbitration was stayed for such purpose during its early stages, meaning that Kazakhstan had suffered no prejudice.

The pragmatic approach taken by the tribunal in *Stati* – albeit endorsed by the Svea Court of Appeal in the subsequent annulment action – should not lull investors into a false sense of security. Tribunals in non-ECT investment arbitrations have taken completely the opposite approach, stringently applying negotiation clauses and holding non-compliance as an absolute jurisdictional bar to arbitration.[39] Best practice is to follow such clauses to the letter unless there are compelling reasons to deviate.

5.5 Intra-EU

Given the recent spate of intra-EU claims, particularly in the renewables sector, states – with support from *amicus curiae* briefs from the European Commission – have sought to raise jurisdictional objections on the basis that the right to arbitrate contained in Article 26 of the ECT does not apply to cases involving EU investors and EU member states. The argument advanced by states and the European Commission is that intra-EU disputes ought instead to be determined exclusively by the European Court of Justice (ECJ). The ECJ has recently endorsed this position, although in the context of intra-EU bilateral investment treaties.[40]

While this is clearly a politically sensitive issue, tribunals in ECT cases have

---

38 Likewise, in *Amto* the cooling-off period was satisfied by investors' letters of claim issued three months prior to commencing arbitration, notwithstanding that they did not expressly seek amicable settlement. See also, *RREEF Infrastructure (GP) Limited v Kingdom of Spain* (ICSID Case ARB/13/30 (2016) Decision on Jurisdiction) and *Al-Bahloul v Tajikistan* (SCC Case V 064/2008, Partial Award on Jurisdiction and Liability).

39 *Burlington Resources Inc v Republic of Ecuador* (ICSID Case ARB/08/5 (2012)); *Murphy Exploration and Production Company International v Republic of Ecuador* (ICSID Case ARB/08/4 (2010)); and *Tulip Real Estate Investment and Development Netherlands BV v Republic of Turkey* (ICSID Case ARB/11/28 (2013)).

40 *Slowakische Republik v Achmea BV* (Case C-284/16), 6 March 2018, in which the ECJ held that the agreement to arbitrate in the Slovakia-Netherlands bilateral investment treaty violated EU law and was invalid.

consistently adopted a narrow legalistic approach, uniformly rejecting such objections.[41] In *Charanne* the tribunal simply held that no provision in the ECT prohibits EU member states from bringing claims against one another. Expanding on this point, the tribunal in *Eiser Infrastructure v Spain* (ICSID Case ARB/13/36 (2017)) held that there could be no such thing as 'EU investors' – only investors of individual member states. Thus, the diversity of nationalities requirement is met, notwithstanding that the European Union itself is a contracting party.

In *RREEF*, the tribunal held that international law required it to apply the ECT, there being no basis to imply a disconnection of Article 26 in respect of claims involving EU member states where conflicting principles of EU law exist. This would be the position even if there were a jurisdictional conflict between the Treaty on the Functioning of the European Union and Article 26 of the ECT (which, in the tribunal's view, there was not in any event).[42] In the subsequent renewables case of *Blusun SA v Italian Republic* (ICSID Case ARB/14/3 (2016)), Italy's intra-EU objection was rejected on similar grounds.[43]

Since the ECJ's decision in *Achmea*, tribunals have continued to reject the intra-EU jurisdictional objection, drawing on material distinctions, including the fact that *Achmea* involved an intra-EU bilateral investment treaty in which EU law was expressly incorporated into the governing law, whereas the ECT is a multilateral treaty, to which the European Union itself is a contracting party, and the governing law is the ECT, together with principles and rules of international law.[44] Notwithstanding these distinctions, a major question yet to be resolved is whether the courts of EU member states will uphold such awards in any set aside proceedings at the seat (in cases other than ICSID, where annulment is self-contained) or otherwise refuse to grant recognition and enforcement under applicable conventions, taking into account the EU law position.

Despite the European Commission's support of jurisdictional objections to intra-EU claims under the ECT and the ECJ's decision in *Achmea*, the alternative – that EU member states and the European Union withdraw from the ECT – is equally unpalatable. One-third of all ECT cases have been brought by investors

---

41   *PV Investors v Kingdom of Spain*, PCA Case 2012-14; *Electrabel SA v Republic of Hungary*, ICSID Case ARB/07/19, Award, 25 November 2015; *EDF International SA v Republic of Hungary*, UNCITRAL; *RREEF Infrastructure (GP) Limited v Kingdom of Spain*, ICSID Case ARB/13/30, Decision on Jurisdiction, 6 June 2016; *Charanne BV & Construction Investments Sarl v Kingdom of Spain*, SCC Arb 062/2012, Award, 21 January 2016; *Isolux Infrastructure Netherlands BV v Kingdom of Spain*, SCC V2013/153, 17 July 2016; *Eiser Infrastructure Ltd v Kingdom of Spain*, ICSID Case ARB/13/36, Award, 4 May 2017; *Novenergia II – Energy & Environment (SCA), SICAR v Kingdom of Spain*, SCC Arb 2015/063, Final Award, 15 February 2018.

42   Contrast with the tribunal in *Electrabel*, which held that if there are inconsistencies between EU law and the ECT, EU law will prevail, there being no principle of international law requiring harmonious interpretation of treaties.

43   See also *Isolux v Spain* (SCC Case V2013/153 (2016)).

44   *Masdar Solar & Wind Cooperatief UA v Kingdom of Spain*, ICSID Case ARB/14/1, Award, 16 May 2018; *Vattenfall AB a v Federal Republic of Germany*, ICSID Case ARB/12/12, decision on the Achmea Issue, 31 August 2018.

in EU member states against non-EU contracting states. If EU member states were to withdraw from the ECT, as Italy has recently done, their investors would lose a valuable method of effective dispute resolution against non-EU member states. Clearly, that is not something that the European Union and its member states have an interest in encouraging.

5.6   Fork in the road

Article 26(3)(b)(i) prevents investors submitting ECT claims against states listed in Annex ID if they have already submitted the dispute to the host state's national courts or to an otherwise previously agreed dispute resolution procedure pursuant to Articles 26(2)(a) and (b).[45]

The fork in the road frequently arises as a jurisdictional objection in ECT arbitrations. This is unsurprising when the complained conduct affects the investor in the host state and hence the first port of call is usually local administrative bodies and courts. However, denying jurisdiction solely on this basis would be overly simplistic.

The majority of tribunals apply a triple identity test – the fork in the road will apply only if there is identity of:

- parties;
- cause of action; and
- object of the dispute.

The test is specific and narrow. In *Charanne*, the fork in the road objection failed because the parties to the local court proceedings were different from the parties to the arbitration and Spain was unable to show that parties to the court proceedings were alter egos for the claimants in the arbitration. It is not sufficient merely to show that companies are part of the same group. In *Yukos*, the fork in the road objection failed because Russia was unable to show that the claimants had alleged in the local court proceedings specific breaches of the treaty protections.

A minority of tribunals have applied a more permissive standard, which focuses on the substance of the rights being litigated in the domestic litigation rather than requiring strict identity of parties, claims, and causes of action between the two proceedings. In *AES Corporation*, the tribunal concluded that there was a difference between the domestic litigation and the treaty arbitration, irrespective of whether the strict or permissive standard was applied.

In practice, it is seldom the case that in seeking to challenge conduct in the

---

45   The states in Annex ID are Australia, Azerbaijan, Bulgaria, Canada, Croatia, Cyprus, Czech Republic, European Union and Euratom, Finland, Greece, Hungary, Ireland, Italy, Japan, Kazakhstan, Norway, Poland, Portugal, Romania, Russia, Slovenia, Spain, Sweden and the United States.

local courts of a host state by reference to local law, an investor can be said to be pursuing relief for specific breaches of treaty protection. For example, challenging a measure by reference to local law is not the same as alleging that the measure contravenes a specific treaty protection. It is for this reason that most jurisdictional objections based on the fork in the road are bound to fail.

5.7 Provisional application

Adopting the ECT is a two-stage process (Article 44). First, the state must sign the treaty. Second, the state must ratify the treaty in accordance with its local laws, such that it comes into force. Article 45 is designed to bridge the gap between these two steps. Article 45(1) provides that all signatories shall apply the ECT provisionally from the date of signing pending its entry into force, to the extent that such provisional application is not inconsistent with its constitution, laws or regulations. When signing the treaty, a state can issue a declaration to displace provisional application (Article 45(2)(a)).[46] Likewise, a state at any time can terminate provisional application by written notification that it does not intend to become a contracting party (Article 45(3)(a)) – albeit that protections afforded to investors under the treaty shall subsist for 20 years following the date of termination (Article 45(3)(b)).[47]

A number of states have sought to raise jurisdictional objections on the basis that provisional application does not apply to them. In *Kardassopoulos* the tribunal rejected the argument that provisional application was merely aspirational. On the contrary, each signatory must apply the ECT as if has come into force before it actually does. Thus, the hurdle is high if states are to succeed on such an objection. In *Petrobart* and later in *Stati*, Kyrgyzstan and Kazakhstan respectively sought to assert that provisional application of the ECT does not extend to Gibraltar (a UK overseas territory), where certain of the claimant investors were incorporated. The jurisdictional objection was premised on the fact that when the United Kingdom signed the ECT, it made a declaration that provisional application extended to Gibraltar, but Gibraltar was not mentioned when the United Kingdom subsequently ratified the treaty. The tribunals in both arbitrations held that provisional application applied to Gibraltar in circumstances where no notification per Article 45(3)(a) had been given to terminate such provisional application. In other words, the United Kingdom's ratification of the ECT, omitting mention of Gibraltar, was not a notification under Article 45(3)(a). In separate challenges to each award, the Svea Court of Appeal has upheld this reasoning.

In *Yukos*, Russia sought to challenge jurisdiction on the basis that:

---

46 The states that did not provisionally apply the treaty were previously set out in Annex PA, but all have now fully ratified.

47 The same 20-year period applies to withdrawal from the treaty by fully contracting states under Article 47.

- its 2009 notification not to become a contracting party to the ECT severed provisional application of the treaty; and
- provisional application of the treaty violated the Russian Constitution.

The tribunal rejected both arguments. In relation to the first argument, the 20-year subsistence of the treaty protections post-termination as per Article 45(3)(b) was held to apply. In relation to the second argument, the tribunal preferred investors' evidence as to lack of conflict between provisional application and the Russian Constitution. However, in Russia's annulment action, the District Court of The Hague set aside the award on the basis that Article 26 of the ECT – providing for referral of disputes to arbitration – is inconsistent with the Russian Constitution (a decision which itself is pending appeal).

6. Conclusion

The high volume of ECT arbitrations commenced in recent years demonstrates that arbitration under the ECT is going from strength to strength, undiminished by:

- the withdrawal of states, such as Italy and Russia;
- opposition from the European Commission to the explosion of intra-EU claims; and
- the refusal of the District Court of The Hague to uphold the $50 billion *Yukos* award, the largest ECT award ever granted.

Importantly, no states other than Italy and Russia have renounced the ECT and its continuing importance is reflected in the fact that it was the most invoked international investment agreement in 2016. Further, the District Court of The Hague's decision in *Yukos*, which itself is subject to appeal, has not deterred other tribunals from finding that they have jurisdiction based on Russia's provisional application of the ECT (continuing until 2029). Several national courts have also maintained orders in support of the Yukos shareholders' continuing attempts to enforce the award.

With the spate of renewables cases in the last two to three years, the ECT has shown itself to be adaptable to changes in the international energy sector. For this reason alone, it is certain to remain, long into the future, a critical part of an investor's protective armour in cross-border investment. As the 90-nation uptake of the 2015 International Energy Charter shows, the ECT looks more likely to expand rather than shrink its geographical scope and appeal.

The role of expert evidence in energy arbitrations

Adrian Howick
KPMG LLP

1. Introduction

The energy sector consists of entities that produce or supply energy, which involves a broad range of activities:

- exploration, extraction, transportation and processing of natural resources (eg, oil, gas, coal and uranium);
- transportation and distribution of refined products (eg liquefied natural gas, petrol and mineral oils);
- electricity generation using thermal (eg, coal, gas and oil), nuclear or renewable sources (eg, solar, wind, water, geothermal, biomass); and
- the transmission and distribution of electricity to consumers.

As a result, disputes in the energy sector can arise in many different ways.

Investor-state disputes involving energy sector investments in foreign countries (as those countries might not have the financial or technical ability to exploit their country's natural resources) are increasingly prevalent,[1] where a change in government or policy might result in a shift in attitudes to foreign investment. Some of these are very significant indeed.

A wide variety of other energy disputes end up in arbitration, as one would expect in such a large industry, with capital expenditure on projects often running into billions of dollars. Without producing an exhaustive list, the author would mention:

- disputes between joint venture partners;
- construction disputes between employers and contractors or between contractors and subcontractors;
- energy pricing disputes;
- business interruption claims (eg, for a blocked pipeline or non-operating power station – or indeed for a power station not being built at all); and
- disputes over sale and purchase agreements (especially for alleged breach of warranty).

---

1   Some 41% of all 676 International Centre for the Settlement of Investment Disputes (ICSID) cases (as at 30 June 2018) involved the "Oil, Gas & Mining" and "Electric Power & Other Energy" economic sectors, and 119 cases (as at 13 July 2018) had been filed under the Energy Charter Treaty (75 with ICSID) since 2001.

It is thus unsurprising that there have been, and will continue to be, a significant number of high-value disputes arising in the energy sector, which require expert consideration of the complex issues arising.

This chapter sets out some thoughts on the role of experts and how lawyers can make the most of their expert.

2. Role of experts in international arbitration

A wide range of expertise may be needed to establish a party's case. Technical experts in, for example, the size of a natural resource, exploration and extraction or refining and processing operations might be required. However, as most arbitrations will require an assessment of the quantum of the loss suffered by the claimant, accounting and valuation experts are frequently called upon.

2.1 Expert roles

The role most commonly undertaken is as a party-appointed expert witness tasked to submit an independent opinion on specific questions. However, there are many other useful roles that an expert can fulfil.

A party might want an idea of the likely success and amount at risk for certain claims, particularly with the advent of third-party funding in arbitrations, and may ask a specialist to provide advice during the case.

In some circumstances, utilising an expert in this way will compromise his or her independence, precluding him or her from acting as an expert witness. Instead, acting solely as an adviser – also known as a 'shadow' or 'consulting expert' – he or she can assist in developing case strategy and test potential financial outcomes of claims. There will be additional costs of employing this extra expert, so this might be viable only in matters with substantial value at stake. However, the use of an expert adviser can lead to cost savings, as well as improvements in the case, by eliminating claims with little value or chance of success, providing a more focused set of instructions to the independent expert witness and challenging the expert witness's draft positions.

Where the expert evidence of both sides is particularly complex and contradictory, a tribunal may appoint its own expert to assist it.[2] Taking the idea of a tribunal-assisting expert a step further, a suitably qualified expert might be appointed as one of the arbitrators, in order to bring technical or quantum expertise to deal with the complex issues in the dispute.

Hint: If the case is largely about quantum – and commercial disputes often are, as we are not litigating boundaries – and you believe you are right, it may be

---

2   *Sempra Energy International v Argentina* (ARB-02-16, Award 28 September 2007); *National Grid plc v Argentina* (UNCITRAL Award 3 November 2008); *El Paso Energy International Company v Argentina* (ARB/03/15, Award 31 October 2011).

appropriate to appoint an accountant as an arbitrator. It will depend on the nature of the case: a straightforward debt claim or gas pricing dispute will not need an accountant (but the latter might need an expert in gas pricing). But for the right case, an expert may have more impact sitting on the tribunal than as a witness.

2.2   Role of experts through the arbitration process
Some of the tasks below could or might better be undertaken by a shadow/consulting expert, instead of (or as well as) an independent expert; it is imperative to watch the need for independence lest the testifying expert is opened to attack.

(a)   Preliminary assessment of the client's position
Engaged early enough, an expert's preliminary assessment of quantum in a case will enable the party's lawyer to identify strengths and weaknesses in both the documentary evidence and the overall claim.

(b)   Disclosure
An expert can help the client's lawyer to identify the classes of documents held by the other side that it would require to prepare an assessment of damages, as well as the information that might be available for its own side's disclosure.

(c)   Drafting memorials
An expert can ensure that the position on quantum is explained accurately in the memorial. However, an independent expert must not get involved in advocating a case and must preserve his or her professional detachment.

(d)   Expert report
The usual role of an expert is to produce a report outlining his or her opinion. The expert will also be required to comment on the expert report(s) filed by the other side and respond to positions that run counter to his or her own opinions.

(e)   Meeting of experts
Frequently, a tribunal sets a requirement in arbitrations for the opposing experts to meet and discuss their damages calculations, with the aim of narrowing the issues on which they disagree. The resulting joint report allows the tribunal to focus its attention on those areas in which the opinions of the experts diverge. The joint statement should set out where the experts agree, where they disagree and, in the latter case, in summary why.

(f)   Mediation
As the aim of mediation is to settle the issues between the parties, experts may

assist the client's lawyers in understanding the financial impact of movements in their client's position. Experts are sometimes requested to give presentations in the mediation, expressing their views to the other side with PowerPoint.

(g) Preparations for cross-examination
As the hearing approaches, as well as preparing for his or her own cross-examination, an expert can assist the client's lawyers' cross-examination preparation for the other side's expert.

(h) Oral evidence
There may be up to three distinct phases of oral testimony by experts. They may give a short presentation (with slides) to the tribunal, which can be very useful in getting across key messages and providing the tribunal with understanding of what might otherwise be quite complex. This will be followed by cross-examination and the experts may also jointly give evidence (ie, expert conferencing or 'hot-tubbing'), where the tribunal will ask questions of both experts and may invite the parties' lawyers to do likewise.

(i) Closing submissions
An expert can assist the client's lawyer with technical knowledge of relevant issues during the preparation of written closing submissions.

Deciding when to engage an expert can be difficult. Delaying the instruction can keep costs down, at least in the short term. However, instructing an expert late in the proceedings may result in insufficient time to properly consider all of the relevant issues, which may lead to a weakened expert report and expose the expert during cross-examination.

Hint: Appoint experts in good time and make full use of their assistance. Consult them and keep them informed. Respect their independence and do not push them to state things with which they do not agree.

2.3 Obligations of independent experts
Party-appointed experts should remain independent and impartial, owing an overriding duty to the tribunal.

This is crucial. Not only is it ethically important to be honest (would you like to be wrongly convicted due to a fingerprint expert trying to keep his client, the prosecution, happy?), but bias is easily detected and is counterproductive.

For example, in one large gas dispute involving drilling in a remote desert in Central Asia, the opposing expert disallowed (in a wasted costs alternative claim) air travel costs for the engineers, on the spurious ground that they had not kept their used tickets. She was not swayed by the travel agents' invoices or names on the payroll tying up with those of the passengers. The tribunal described this approach as "wholly unreasonable". Clients and their chosen lawyer have an important role in retaining experts who have a commitment to retaining their independent professional judgement. An overly supportive expert who simply echoes the client's preferred position regardless of the evidence is a serious liability and can cause significant damage to a case.

3. Assessment of damages

A claimant launches arbitration proceedings seeking compensation for the alleged wrongful conduct of the respondent. The claimant's damages claim, as it is rare for a tribunal to award specific performance, will require evidence as to the amount lost – the sum of money which will put it in the same position as it would have been in absent the wrongful conduct.

While damages are most commonly sought for the breach of a contract or the expropriation of an asset – discussed below – other types of damages also aim to compensate the claimant:

- Liquidated damages: This is an amount that parties to a contract designate at the outset as compensation for a specific breach (eg, late performance), which should be a commercially justified 'genuine pre-estimate of loss' and not intended as a punishment. The expert may be able to assist in analysing whether, at the time the contract was made, the liquidated damages amount was appropriate.
- Moral damages: These are awarded in investment arbitrations to provide compensation, in exceptional circumstances, for physical and mental suffering, or loss of reputation, which have a grave cause and effect. Increasingly, they are a component of overall damages sought,[3] although tribunals have been slow to award them.
- Restitutionary damages: These are measured by the respondent's gain rather than the claimant's loss, particularly if the claimant has suffered little or no loss. The respondent is made to surrender the profits made through its wrongful conduct (eg, for breaches of intellectual property, the claimant can seek an 'account' of the respondent's profits from its breach).
- Wasted costs: These are an alternative to lost profits, where the claimant seeks the return of money spent on a business, project or contract that has been 'wasted'. Claims for wasted costs may be brought where the venture was aborted at an early stage and anticipated profits are difficult to estimate with any degree of accuracy. One cannot normally have both the costs and the profits, as the costs would have had to have been incurred in order to earn the profits.

---

3   See, for example, *Joseph Charles Lemire v Ukraine* (ARB/06/18, Award 28 March 2011).

In evaluating quantum, much will depend on the nature of the alleged breaches and how the claimant is seeking to bring its claim. Areas in energy sector arbitrations which will be key to the assessment of loss include the following:

- Access to markets: Can the claimant sell and transport its product? In one case, a pipeline would have been needed through Afghanistan; the tribunal considered this unrealistic.
- Resource demand and pricing: There may be long-term supply agreements in place, which may include take or pay provisions; or forecasts of future demand and prices may be required.
- Size and quality of economically extractable reserves: There may be contemporaneous reserve reports or an appropriate expert may need to be engaged to identify reserves, as well as the cut-off grade. Whether a resource is economic at a point in time depends on prevailing and future prices.
- Development costs: Is further expenditure required to bring the resource to economic production levels?

Hint: Interestingly, and not always appreciated, the volume of economically reasonable reserves alters as prices alter; with higher prices, more resources become economic and can be counted.

3.1   Breach of contract/loss of profits

If the claimant's business is still operating, then losses will equate to the difference between what would have happened in its business had the breach not occurred (known as the 'but for' or 'counterfactual' position) and what actually happened following the breach. If the claimant's business failed as a result of the breach, then it will seek compensation for the loss of the entire value of their business.

To perform a loss of profits calculation, an expert prepares a realistic forecast of the financial performance of the claimant's business (ie, revenue, cost of sales and/or services performed, overheads incurred, financing costs and taxes) 'but for' the breach. Contemporaneous forecasts can be a real help and, if the circumstances were similar, more credible than optimistic forecasts of what might have happened, prepared especially for the arbitration. Assessing the business's actual performance should be (but is not always) relatively straightforward from an examination of the claimant's financial records.

Figure 1 illustrates a loss of profits calculation, with the claim comprising the lightly shaded area (where '0' equals the time of the breach).

Figure 1. Loss of profits calculation

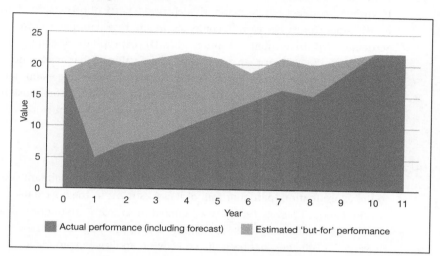

An expert will need to estimate revenue, cost of goods sold or gross profit margin and overheads,[4] with the 'but-for' revenue forecast likely to have the greatest impact on the amount claimed, and may require the most assumptions and judgements to be made. By comparison, many companies' gross profit margins may appear to be relatively consistent each year, which may be reflected in the company's forecasts.

Consideration of overheads is also important. As 'fixed' overheads do not change with business activity and revenues, they are often not saved and therefore should not be included in the assessment of lost profits. However, few costs are ever completely fixed. For example, at a certain level of activity, a business would need to expand, so rent may increase; or if production contracts sufficiently, smaller premises might be used or parts of existing premises sublet.

Despite a breach occurring, it is possible that subsequent conditions may mean that little or no loss resulted. An example is a construction project where the breach has led to a delay in, rather than a loss of, profits earned. When the author calculated the loss resulting from a two-year delayed construction of a high-rise apartment building, where the floor space also had to be reduced by about 30%, property prices had increased by enough to eliminate all but a small loss resulting from the delayed completion of the smaller building.

---

4   Overheads are costs that are incurred without having a direct relationship to the production of the company's goods. 'Variable' overheads are affected by sales levels (eg, distribution costs, utilities), while 'fixed' overheads are not (eg, rent, administrative costs).

3.2 Expropriation/loss of value

If wrongful conduct has permanently deprived a party of ownership of an asset or the opportunity to earn income, as in an International Centre for the Settlement of Investment Disputes (ICSID) expropriation claim, then to compensate the claimant, an assessment of the value of that asset is needed.

There are many books on valuation,[5] so a comprehensive examination of valuation theory is not attempted here. Rather, there follows some insight into important concepts of which recipients of an expert's valuation work should be aware.

(a) Expropriation and the date of valuation

In investment treaty cases, valuations are used to assess the claimant's loss due to the expropriation, partial or full, of its investment in the host state.

The famous *Chorzow Factory* case,[6] quoted in so many arbitrations, is seen as setting the standard of 'full reparation' for compensation in these matters. However, a distinction has been drawn between an illegal expropriation and one that would be considered legal. This distinction, which has been promulgated in many investment arbitrations since, affects the date at which the assessment should be made, as well as the information that can be used. Should an expropriation be deemed illegal, the claimant has the option to be awarded damages assessed either at the date of the expropriation or at the date of the award. This may seem unfair to a respondent, as it is a one-way bet for the claimant, but was confirmed in *Yukos*.[7] It has also been adopted in the US-Iran Claims Tribunal and by the European Court of Human Rights – though if the only fault of the respondent is that it has not paid compensation to the claimant, and so long as it negotiated in good faith, the expropriation may not be considered illegal.

The selection of the date of assessment of loss, which is matter of law, will have a significant effect on the quantum of loss calculated. It can change significantly the period over which the claimant's lost cash flows will be discounted, as well as the nature of the loss calculation. Whereas damages calculated as at the past date of the wrongful conduct (eg, expropriation) can sometimes require the lost cash flows to be discounted back to a lump sum as at this date (with usually much lower pre-award interest calculated on this lump sum to the date of the award), a damages assessment as at the date of the award would require:

---

5   Further detail is given in the following books on valuation, among others: Tim Koller *et al*, *Valuation: Measuring and Managing the Value of Companies* (McKinsey); Aswath Damodaran, *Investment Valuation: Tools and Techniques for Determining the Value of Any Asset* (Wiley); Shannon Pratt, *Valuing a Business: The Analysis and Appraisal of Closely Held Companies* (McGraw-Hill). Recently, *Global Arbitration Review* published *The Guide to Damages in International Arbitration* (2016).

6   *Factory at Chorzow (Germany v Poland)*, Merits, 1928 PCIJ (Ser A) No 17 (13 September).

7   *Hulley Enterprises Limited (Cyprus) v Russian Federation* (PCA Case No AA 226, Award 18 July 2014); *Veteran Petroleum Limited (Cyprus) v Russian Federation* (PCA Case No AA 228, Award 18 July 2014); *Yukos Universal Limited (Isle of Man) v Russian Federation* (PCA Case No AA 227, Award 18 July 2014) – together, '*Yukos*'.

- all lost future cash flows (ie, those earned after the award date) to be discounted back to a lump sum only at the award date; and
- a calculation of lost profits between the date of expropriation and the date of the award (with pre-award interest calculated on these sums to the date of the award).

Furthermore, the volatile nature of commodity prices, particularly in the energy sector, can have a significant impact on the assessment of damages – particularly when using forecasts of future prices. For example, between January 2002 and June 2008, oil prices per barrel increased from less than $30 to more than $150, then fell to less than $50 by January 2009; after increasing again to over $100, they fell to $50 between August 2014 and January 2015, and further to $30 by January 2016. Any damages calculation prepared based on oil price forecasts from early 2008 (or mid 2014) will have significantly overestimated loss.

Hint: Consider carefully whether to claim losses as at the date of the loss or as at the date or the award where it is open to the claimant to opt for a claim calculated by reference to the date of the award.

(b) *Use of hindsight*

Famous *The Times* columnist Bernard Levin once wrote that "[h]indsight is not merely the bread and butter for lawyers; it is their caviar and champagne". This is a legal issue which will be need to be considered and is not straightforward.

The date as at which a loss is calculated can be the date of damage from the wrongful conduct or the date of the award, the choice of which can greatly affect damages (in part due to discounting back future profits at one rate but adding on interest at another).

(c) *Standard of value*

While there are many different types or 'standards' of value,[8] many bilateral investment treaties (BITs) require compensation to be set at 'fair market value'. This is a common term in US valuation literature and court judgments (less so in the United Kingdom, where the authorities tend to discuss 'market value' and 'fair value'), and it can be considered the equivalent to the International Valuation Standards definition of 'market value': "the estimated amount for which an asset or liability should exchange on the valuation date between a willing buyer and a willing seller in an arm's length transaction, after proper marketing and where the parties had each acted knowledgeably, prudently and without compulsion."

---

8   These standards include market value, equitable (or fair) value, investment value, synergistic value and liquidation value, as defined in the International Valuation Standards.

Tribunals have used different definitions, but the common denominator has been that fair market value represents a reasonable price for an asset that can be paid by a willing buyer to a willing seller.

However, the other standards of value might be relevant, even in a valuation in an investment treaty dispute. For example, if a contract, tribunal order or statute requires a valuation under a different standard, then consideration will need to be given to this basis.[9]

(d) Measurement of value

There are a number of different approaches to valuing an asset. In choosing the most appropriate valuation methodology, an expert will need to have regard to:

- the availability of information (eg, lack of information will preclude certain methods);
- the stage of development of the business (eg, start-up, growth, expansion, mature); and
- whether there is a traditional or standard method (eg, comparable sales for real estate) or a method stipulated in contract or statute.

Transactions in (or serious offers for) the very asset being valued itself can be particularly good evidence of value,[10] although each case will turn on its own facts.

Income approach: The income approach is based on the premise that the value of an asset is equal to the value of the future income it is expected to generate. The most widely used method for project and acquisition appraisal in the energy sector is the discounted cash flow (DCF) methodology. Tribunals usually accept the DCF method, especially in investment treaty disputes,[11] except where data is lacking – as with a start-up without an established track record.

The DCF method requires a forecast of future cash flows, which in turn requires a reliable assessment of future revenue and costs (similar to the exercise described in section 3.1). In energy investments, projecting future revenues means relying on potentially very subjective inputs (eg, resource size, quality and prices).

However, forecasting cash flows beyond a certain period is increasingly uncertain and impractical, so a terminal value is calculated to represent the

---

9   In accordance with the valuation methodology stipulated in the sale and purchase agreement and the privatising statute, the author was required to value a business not at market value, but rather at the 'replacement cost' of the business's assets, to which an allowance for the profitability of the business was added.
10   *Ioannis Kardassopoulos v Georgia* (ARB/05/18 and ARB/07/15, Award 3 March 2010).
11   "DCF techniques have been universally adopted, including by numerous arbitral tribunals, as an alternative method of valuing business assets" – *CMS Gas Transmission Company v Argentina* (ARB/01/8, Award 12 May 2005), paragraph 416.

present value at a future point in time of all future cash flows when a stable growth rate forever is expected. It can be calculated using either the perpetuity growth model or the exit (or terminal) multiple approach. Consideration of the terminal value is critical, as it usually accounts for a large percentage of the value in a DCF valuation.

Despite its wide acceptance, a number of tribunals have decided that the DCF method was not appropriate where the investment had no track record of performance or uncertainties over its future profitability, or where its projections were too speculative.[12] In *Siag*, the tribunal rejected the DCF method, stating: "Points such as those just mentioned reinforce the wisdom in the established reluctance of tribunals such as this one to utilise DCF analysis for 'young' businesses lacking a long track record of established trading. In all probability that reluctance ought to be even more pronounced in cases such as the present where the business is still in its early development phase and has no trading history at all."[13]

However, in cases involving commodity products, there may be an exception to the rejection of the DCF method where there is no track record of profitability.[14] In *Gold Reserve*, the tribunal decided: "Although the Brisas Project was never a functioning mine and therefore did not have a history of cashflow which would lend itself to the DCF model, the Tribunal accepts … that a DCF method can be reliably used in the instant case because of the commodity nature of the product and detailed mining cashflow analysis previously performed."[15]

Forecasts of cash flows need to be reduced to a single net present value. This is accomplished by applying a discount rate, which takes into account the time value of money[16] and risk and uncertainty attaching to those cash flows.

To reflect these risks, an accepted basis upon which to discount a business's cash flows is the cost of capital, which is the expected rate of return on the sources of capital employed (ie, debt and equity). The weighted average cost of capital (WACC) weights the after-tax cost of debt (ie, interest, which is usually tax deductible) and the cost of equity by the contribution of each to overall capital employed – and is represented by the formula:

$$\text{WACC} = Kd\ (1 - t) \times (d/(d{+}e)) + Ke \times (e/(d{+}e))$$

---

12   *Amoco International Finance Corp v Islamic Republic of Iran* (Iran Award 310-56-3, 15 Iran-USCTR 189, 14 July 1987); *Asian Agricultural Products Ltd v Sri Lanka* (ARB/87/3, Award 27 June 1990); *Metalclad Corporation v Mexico* (ARB(AF)/97/1, Award 30 August 2001); *LG&E Energy Corp v Argentine Republic* (ARB/02/1, Award 25 July 2007); *Compania de Aguas del Aconquija SA v Argentine Republic* (ARB/97/3, Award 20 August 2007); *Waguih Elie George Siag v Egypt* (ARB/05/15, Award 1 June 2009); *Hassan Awdi, Enterprise Business Consultants, Inc v Romania* (ARB/10/13, Award 2 March 2015); *Rusoro Mining Ltd v Venezuela* (ARB(AF)/12/5, Award 22 August 2016).
13   *Waguih Elie George Siag v Egypt* (ARB/05/15, Award 1 June 2009), paragraphs 569-570.
14   *Occidental Petroleum Corp v Republic of Ecuador* (ARB/06/11, Award 5 October 2012); *Gold Reserve Inc v Venezuela* (ARB(AF)/09/1, Award 22 September 2014).
15   *Gold Reserve Inc v Venezuela* (ARB(AF)/09/1, Award 22 September 2014), paragraph 830.
16   Time value of money is the concept that the value of a pound or dollar to be received in future is worth less than the value of a pound or dollar in hand today.

The cost of debt (Kd) is usually measured by the effective interest rate paid on debt funding (d), although reference to a market rate might be appropriate if the cost of funds is likely to change in the near future (ie, debt with a below market rate is due to mature).

The cost of equity (Ke) can be measured using the capital asset pricing model (CAPM), which allows a company's expected rate of return to providers of equity (e) to be calculated based on observable market data and is represented by the formula:

$$CAPM = Rf + (ERP \times ß) + CRP$$

Risk-free rate (Rf) is the theoretical return on an investment with no risk of financial loss. Government bond yields are used as a proxy for risk-free rates, as there is considered to be no risk of default.

Equity risk premium (ERP) is the excess return observed in a country's equity market over its risk free rate. There are a number of studies which calculate the ERP.

Beta (ß) is a measure of the volatility of a security in comparison to the market as a whole. It reflects the degree to which a company's business might be affected by general economic conditions. Therefore, the beta modifies the ERP to reflect the expected return of investing in the subject company.

Country Risk Premium (CRP) represents the additional risk associated with investing in a less developed international market rather than in a well-developed market (eg, the United States, the United Kingdom, Germany). A common estimate for a country's CRP is the interest rate spread of the country's sovereign debt (ie, government bonds) compared with 'risk-free' countries (eg, the United States). As the CRP increases the discount rate for valuations in less developed countries, this can have a significant impact on the amount of damages awarded.

Expropriation risk is considered a component of the various risks that make up the CRP. As a result, there is some debate as to whether the CRP should be adjusted to remove this risk. One Venezuela tribunal decided that it was "not appropriate to increase the country risk premium to reflect the market's perception that a State may have the propensity to expropriate investments in breach of BIT obligations"[17] (referred to colloquially in the valuation fraternity as the 'Chavez effect').

However, a number of other Venezuela tribunals since *Gold Reserve* decided that no adjustment should be made, as a BIT does not prohibit all state taking of property, as well as not being an insurance policy or guarantee against all political or other risks associated with the investment. The claimants in these cases may have known that the risk of expropriation was high in Venezuela

---

17   *Gold Reserve Inc v Venezuela* (ARB(AF)/09/1, Award 22 September 2014), paragraph 841.

when they made their investment, but in any event a 'willing buyer' would consider this risk among all political and other risks associated with investing in the country.[18]

Often an additional element is added to the CAPM to take into account the effect on risk of the size of the subject company – the size premium. The adjustment of the discount rate for size is a contentious matter.

Hint: Consider whether the DCF approach could be challenged outright. In any event, both sides' counsel should look closely at the choice of discount rate and contentious issues such as country risk and size premiums.

Market approach: The market approach calculates value by reference to the price paid for company shares traded on stock exchanges ('trading multiples') or from recent transactions involving the acquisition of companies ('transaction multiples'). These prices are represented as multiples of key financial and operational statistics (eg, earnings before interest, tax, depreciation and amortisation (EBITDA),[19] net profit, revenues, size of reserves), with particular multiples favoured in some industries. These multiples can then be applied to the subject company's key statistics to determine its value.

There appears to be less acceptance of the market approach than of the DCF method by tribunals, as they consider that there is usually a general lack of true comparables, particularly in the oil and gas industry as it has a "unique set of value parameters".[20] However, some tribunals[21] have accepted comparable multiples when there is an inability to use the DCF method, as well as when it is used as a cross-check of the DCF method.

Accordingly, the main limitation of, and so the most important stage in, the market approach is the identification of suitably comparable companies from which to derive the valuation multiples. The expert will look to more contemporaneous transactions in companies operating in the same industry, market segment and geography, of a similar size and stage of development, with

18 *Venezuela Holdings v Venezuela* (ARB/07/27, Award 9 October 2014); *Flughafen Zurich AG v Venezuela* (ARB/10/19, Award 18 November 2014); *OI European Group BV v Venezuela* (ARB/11/25, Award 10 March 2015); *Tidewater Investment SRL v Venezuela* (ARB/10/5, Award 13 March 2015); *Quiborax SA v Bolivia* (ARB/06/2, Award 16 September 2015); and *Saint-Gobain Performance Plastics Europe v Venezuela* (ARB/12/13, Award 30 December 2016). However, *Saint-Gobain* was only a majority decision, with Charles Brower dissenting on this issue.
19 Earnings before interest, tax, depreciation and amortisation (EBITDA) are the earnings produced by the business before financing, fixed asset replacement and tax are included, and are often considered a surrogate for cash flow.
20 *El Paso Energy International Company v Argentina* (ARB/03/15, Award 31 October 2011); *Occidental Petroleum Corp v Ecuador* (ARB/06/11, Award 5 October 2012).
21 *CME Czech Republic BV v Czech Republic* (UNCITRAL Award 14 March 2003); *BG Group Plc v Argentina* (UNCITRAL Award 24 December 2007); *Ioannis Kardassopoulos v Georgia* (ARB/05/18 and ARB/07/15, Award 3 March 2010); *Hulley Enterprises Limited (Cyprus) v Russian Federation* (PCA Case No AA 226, Award 18 July 2014), *Veteran Petroleum Limited (Cyprus) v Russian Federation* (PCA Case No AA 228, Award 18 July 2014), *Yukos Universal Limited (Isle of Man) v Russian Federation* (PCA Case No AA 227, Award 18 July 2014) – together '*Yukos*'; *Crystallex International Corporation v Venezuela* (ARB(AF)/11/2, Award 4 April 2016).

similar financial and operational attributes and similar risks and future prospects.

While companies are unlikely to meet all the criteria, appropriate adjustments can be made to take into account the differences between the comparable and subject companies (eg, earnings growth, dividend pay-out ratio). An expert will prefer to have a suitable number of good comparables to work with and will consider median values (rather than averages) in order to avoid the impact of outliers in the data – unless there are good reasons to select a multiple positioned elsewhere within the comparable group. The differences between the subject company and the comparables might lead the expert to consider a multiple range to be better than a single multiple.

If they are to be used to value majority or full ownership of the subject company, multiples derived from the sale of shares in other public companies on stock exchanges will need to be adjusted to reflect that such sales are of very small parcels of shares, whereas majority or full ownership would command a premium for the control granted over the company's operations. Traditionally, this control premium is observed in the higher prices paid for shares during public takeovers – however, any element of the premium not related to control should be excluded. Similarly, if a minority or less than full ownership is being analysed, then data based on whole company values would need to be adjusted by a 'discount for lack of control'. If a private company is being valued using public company data, then a 'discount for lack of marketability' is required to reflect that selling a small parcel of shares on a stock exchange is very quick and inexpensive, whereas advertising and negotiating the sale of a private company will take considerable time and cost.

Cost approach: The cost approach relies on the economic principle that a buyer will pay no more for an asset than the cost to purchase or construct an asset of equal utility. The assessment of value is done by calculating the current replacement or reproduction cost of an asset and making deductions for physical deterioration and other relevant forms of obsolescence. This adjustment is important to ensure that the valuation is relevant to the subject asset.

An alternative asset-based valuation approach is liquidation value, being the value that can be realised upon the piecemeal sale of the asset or a group of assets (ie, not as part of a going-concern business), on an orderly or forced basis, less a reasonable estimate of the costs associated with either the eventual sale or disposal of the asset in question.

These approaches are normally used to value a recently established business without a track record of performance or to provide a floor value by way of a cross-check of other valuation methods.

4. Interest, taxation and currency

4.1 Interest

While the previous section focused on calculating the amount of damages to be awarded as at the date of loss, this date may be a number of years before the award, meaning that the claimant will have been deprived of its property for a considerable period of time.

As a result, the tribunal is likely to award interest on the damages:[22] from the date of loss until the award date (pre-award interest) and from the award date until it is paid (post-award interest).

(a) Pre-award interest

The contract between the parties, whose breach is the subject of the arbitration, may specify an interest rate to be used in cases of late payment. Investment treaties also may specify interest rates.[23]

Actual interest awards by arbitrators might be instructive; however, few international arbitration awards are made public – being one advantage of arbitration. That said, some types of arbitration awards are routinely published, including those heard under ICSID rules.

One commentator notes that pre-award interest was awarded in 60 ICSID cases he reviewed.[24] In 77% of those cases, the interest rate used was a benchmark rate (eg, the London Interbank Offered Rate (LIBOR)), with a margin added in half of these cases[25] – an interbank lending rate was used in 59% of awards, while the US Treasury bill rate was used in 28%. In the other 23% of cases, the tribunal specified its own number without reference to a market or company specific rate.

Many tribunals use LIBOR. However, some concerns over using LIBOR as a benchmark rate might be emerging, with the *Yukos* tribunal rejecting LIBOR saying it had been discredited[26] and the *Saint-Gobain* tribunal having concerns regarding the integrity of LIBOR as a reliable benchmark.[27]

---

22   *Vivendi v Argentina* (ARB/97/3), Award 20 August 2007, paragraph 9.2.3: "The object of an award of interest is to compensate the damage resulting from the fact that, during the period of non-payment by the debtor, the creditor is deprived of the use and disposition of that sum he was supposed to receive."

23   The Switzerland-Macedonia BIT specifies LIBOR (*Swisslion DOO Skopje v Former Yugoslav Republic of Macedonia* (ARB/09/16, Award 6 July 2012), paragraph 358)).

24   James Dow (professor of finance, London Business School), author of "Interest" in *The Guide to Damages in International Arbitration* (2016, *Global Arbitration Review*).

25   Financial contracts will usually refer to a benchmark interest rate, with a margin referred to as 'basis points' (equal to 0.01 of a percentage point). Common benchmarks include LIBOR, the Euro Interbank Offered Rate (EURIBOR) and the US Federal Funds Rate (which reflect the rates at which banks lend to other), and a country's bank rate (eg, Discount Rate (US), Official Bank Rate (UK), Official Cash Rate (Australia)).

26   *Hulley Enterprises Limited (Cyprus) v Russian Federation* (PCA Case No AA 226, Award 18 July 2014) ('*Yukos*'), paragraph 1679.

27   *Saint-Gobain Performance Plastics Europe v Venezuela* (ARB/12/13) Award 30 December 2016, paragraph 880.

Using a 'risk-free' rate (eg, US Treasury bill rate) to calculate interest is supported on the basis that once an award of damages has been made to compensate the claimant as at the date of the wrongful conduct, it will not suffer from economic conditions over the interest period. The purpose of interest is just to bring the amount awarded forward to the present day.

The borrowing rates of the claimant[28] and respondent[29] have also been considered.

Some claimants have attempted to claim interest using their cost of capital (ie, WACC) or a rate of return available on alternative investments, on the basis that they would have profitably invested the money deprived of in their own or another business.

(b) *Simple or compound interest*

A further consideration, which will significantly affect the amount of the interest award, is whether the interest rate is simple or compounded.

Based on recent awards, it would appear that tribunals now often accept that in order to fully compensate the claimant, it is necessary to award compound interest:[30] "The Tribunal has little difficulty accepting that interest should be compounding. In modern practice, tribunals often compound interest, and the Claimant referenced a number of such awards. ... In essence, compounding interest reflects simple economic sense."[31]

However, due to the "wide margin" of discretion enjoyed by tribunals, the award of compound interest should not be taken for granted – in *Yukos*, even though the tribunal recognised that compound interest is *"jurisprudence constante"* in investor-state expropriation cases, it chose to award simple interest instead.[32]

The currency of the award will have an impact on the choice of interest rate, as it is important not to use an interest rate related to one currency and apply it to amounts of money in another currency – for example, awards in British pounds might use LIBOR, but if in euros, EURIBOR should be used instead.

---

28 The claimant's borrowing rate has been used by tribunals on the basis that "it is appropriate and realistic to assume that the Claimant would have applied the sums received either to eliminate existing debt or to avoid incurring additional debt" – *National Grid plc v The Argentine Republic* (UNCITRAL, Award 3 November 2008), paragraph 294.

29 Rejected by the tribunal in *Railroad Development Corporation v Republic of Guatemala* (ARB/07/23, Award 29 June 2012), use of the respondent's borrowing rate is known as the 'coerced loan' theory, which posits that the respondent has had the use of the claimant's money, just as if the claimant had lent the respondent its money, so interest should be awarded to the claimant at the respondent's borrowing rate.

30 Per James Dow (professor of finance, London Business School), author of "Interest" in *The Guide to Damages in International Arbitration* (2016, *Global Arbitration Review*): since 2009, compound pre-award interest was awarded in 29 of 30 ICSID awards (in the other case the claimant did not request compound interest). Before 2010, compound interest was still awarded in 19 of 30 ICSID cases, with tribunals often awarding simple interest in other cases due to a prohibition under domestic law or for other legal reasons.

31 *Hrvatska Elektroprivreda DD v Slovenia* (ARB/05/24, Award 17 December 2015), paragraphs 555-556.

32 *Hulley Enterprises Limited (Cyprus) v Russian Federation* (PCA Case No. AA 226, Award 18 July 2014) ('*Yukos*'), paragraph 1689.

(c)   Post-award interest

Tribunals usually award post-award interest at the pre-award interest rate to ensure that the claimant does not suffer further from continuing to be deprived of its money for a period following the award. However, if the tribunal is concerned about the respondent honouring its obligations under the award, it might award a higher rate to ensure the award is paid without delay.

The interest calculation will run from the date of award or some later date (eg, if the tribunal allows a 'grace period' for payment of the award without requiring interest) until the award is actually paid.

4.2   Taxation

As the claimant's business was likely to have paid taxes on the profits or cash flows received absent the respondent's wrongful conduct, many damages calculations (for both loss of profits and value) are in effect prepared on a post-tax basis.

However, the award received by the claimant might also be subject to tax, in either its home country or its country of operation. As the goal of a damages award is to place the claimant in the same position as it would have been if the wrongful conduct had not occurred, the calculation must consider the potential impact of taxation on the award itself.

In one English High Court case,[33] the issue was that the rate of tax payable on the damages would be considerably lower than that which would have been paid on the lost profits at the time, due to a subsequent lowering of corporation tax rates. The court agreed and lowered the damages accordingly, giving full credit for this adjustment.

The assessment of tax can be quite complex, even for what might appear to be a simple set of circumstances, so the parties may benefit from obtaining advice from tax professionals.

4.3   Currency

As international arbitration addresses cross-border disputes, this may mean that the impact of different currencies will need to be considered. With free floating exchange rates, sometimes changes in currency value can be significant (eg, the depreciation of the British pound during 2016–2017).

Accordingly, one of the most important considerations will be the currency in which any award will be rendered. If the damages involve multiple currencies, a further consideration will the date(s) at which these amounts are translated into the award currency.

Damages will generally be calculated in the currency in which the loss of profits or value has been suffered. In a UK House of Lords case, *The Texaco*

---

33   *Amstrad plc v Seagate Technologies Incorporated* (1998) 86 BLR 34.

Melbourne,[34] the issue was whether the correct currency was Ghanaian cedis; while the lower courts were split on this, the House of Lords agreed in a unanimous judgment. This issue can also arise in energy arbitrations, given that so many involve different currencies.

The views expressed in this chapter are the author's personal views and not necessarily those of KPMG.

---

34   *Attorney General of the Republic of Ghana v Texaco Overseas Tankships Ltd* [1994] 1 Lloyd's Rep 473.

Arbitrating competition law claims in the energy sector

Neil Cuninghame
Max Strasberg
Ashurst LLP

1. Introduction

In the last 10 to 15 years, it has become increasingly common for competition law issues to be considered by arbitral tribunals, including in the energy sector. As we explore below, until relatively recently, there were doubts as to whether competition law claims could or should be settled by way of arbitration. These doubts have now been largely overcome.

This chapter covers the following topics:

- a brief introduction to competition law and its role in the energy sector;
- how such issues may find themselves being resolved by way of arbitration;
- the approach of the courts and arbitrators to competition law defences;
- the arbitrability of competition law disputes and the extent to which competition issues are likely to fall within the scope of arbitration agreements;
- some practical issues such as the selection of arbitrators, the role of experts and factual witnesses, the role of disclosure and how damage may be evidenced; and
- enforcement/challenge of arbitration awards.

2. Competition law and its role in the energy sector

Competition law consists of four main areas:

- prohibitions of anti-competitive agreements, such as those found in Article 101 of the Treaty on the Functioning of the European Union (TFEU) or Section 1 of the US Sherman Act 1890.[1] Such provisions

---

[1] There are also very similar provisions to Article 101 of the TFEU (and Article 102 of the TFEU) in the UK Competition Act 1998 – specifically, Sections 2 and 18. These UK provisions may become more important in international arbitration than previously, on the assumption that the United Kingdom proceeds with its plans to exit the European Union (commonly referred to as Brexit); albeit that this will depend to some extent on the form that Brexit takes. However, in most cases, whether the analysis is being done under the UK Competition Act or EU competition law is unlikely to make a material difference to the outcome, because the Competition Act is very closely based on the TFEU competition provisions. However, it is possible that there could be divergence over time – for example, on the issue of territorial restrictions, where the EU approach is very much driven by the EU single market integration goal, which does not apply at UK level.

prohibit price fixing and market sharing cartels, and other anti-competitive agreements such as output limitations, customer allocation, bid rigging and (at least in the European Union) certain types of information exchange – in particular, the exchange between competitors of future pricing information. In the European Union and other regimes, resale price maintenance is likely to be restricted and territorial restrictions pose a particular concern under EU competition law (due to the EU goal of single market integration). Other types of agreement may also infringe competition law, depending on the market circumstances (in particular, the market position of the parties and the market impact of the restrictions), including joint ventures between competitors, non-compete covenants, exclusivity provisions and minimum quantity obligations;

- prohibitions of abuse of a dominant position/market power/monopolisation, such as those found in Article 102 of the TFEU or Section 2 of the Sherman Act. Such prohibitions apply only to entities with significant market power (eg, in the European Union, usually a market share of at least 40%). Under Article 102, dominant companies have a "special responsibility" not to allow their conduct to impair genuine undistorted competition.[2] This means that actions by dominant firms such as excessive pricing, predatory (below-cost) pricing, exclusive contracts, loyalty rebates or discounts, refusals to supply, price discrimination and margin squeeze[3] may, depending on the circumstances, result in an infringement. The US approach to firms with market power is generally regarded as being less interventionist than the EU approach, as the US regime is typically more likely to take the view that the market will self-correct (eg, through new entry) in the event of 'unfair' conduct by powerful market players;

- merger control regimes designed to prevent the creation of businesses with significant market power or other adverse effects on competition as a result of M&A transactions, such as the EU Merger Regulation;[4] and

- controls on state subsidies, such as the EU state aid rules under Article 107 of the TFEU.

The energy sector has been the subject of enforcement action in each of the above four areas.

For example, under Article 102 of the TFEU, the European Commission initiated separate proceedings against RWE and ENI in 2007 for suspected

---

2   See, for example, Case 322/81 *Michelin I* [1983] ECR 3461, para 57.
3   'Margin squeeze' is the practice of charging a price in an upstream market to competitors in a downstream market in which the upstream supplier is also active which makes it impossible or very difficult for downstream competitors to make a return.
4   Regulation 139/2004/EC.

foreclosure of German and Italian gas supply markets (respectively).[5] In particular, it was alleged that RWE and ENI had restricted access to rivals to the international transportation networks which they owned to benefit themselves in downstream markets in which they operated. This resulted in binding commitments from RWE to divest its entire Western German high-pressure gas transmission network, and from ENI to divest its shares in three international pipelines to Italy (TAG, TENP and Transitas).[6] Similar action was also taken against E.ON and GDF Suez (as it then was).[7]

In 2009 the European Commission imposed its first fine (under Article 101 of the TFEU) in the energy sector against E.ON and GDF Suez (totalling over €1.1 billion) for market sharing in the French and German gas markets.[8] In particular, they had each agreed not to sell gas transported via the Megal pipeline (a pipeline running across Germany from the Czech and Austrian borders to the French border) into each other's home market. In 2014, the commission imposed a €302 million fine on 11 producers of underground and submarine high voltage power cables for participating in a price-fixing cartel from 1999 to 2009.[9]

More recently, in May 2018 the European Commission agreed binding commitments with Gazprom to resolve its Article 102 investigation concerning Central and Eastern European gas markets.[10] The commission had alleged that Gazprom had an overall strategy to partition gas markets along national borders in eight EU member states (Bulgaria, the Czech Republic, Estonia, Hungary, Latvia, Lithuania, Poland and Slovakia), and that this strategy may have enabled Gazprom to charge higher gas prices in five member states (Bulgaria, Estonia, Latvia, Lithuania and Poland). To resolve these concerns, Gazprom agreed a range of commitments, including:

- removing contractual restrictions placed on customers to re-sell gas cross-border;
- undertaking to facilitate gas flows to and from the Baltic states (Estonia, Latvia and Lithuania) and Bulgaria that are isolated from other member states due to a lack of interconnectors;
- giving Gazprom customers a tool to make sure their gas price reflects prices in competitive Western European gas markets, especially at liquid gas hubs; and
- undertaking not to act on any advantages concerning gas infrastructure which Gazprom may have obtained from customers by leveraging its market position in gas supply.

5   These investigations followed an EU-wide 'sector inquiry' into the energy sector.
6   See Case COMP/B-1/39.315 – *ENI* and Case COMP/39.402 – *RWE Gas Foreclosure*.
7   See Case COMP/39.317 — E.ON Gas and Case COMP/39.316 – *GDF*.
8   See Case COMP/39.401 – *E.ON/GDF*.
9   See Case AT.39610 – *Power Cables*.
10 See Case AT.39816 – *Upstream gas supplies in Central and Eastern Europe*.

M&A transactions in the energy sector also often fall to be considered under merger control. For example, in 2004 the European Commission prohibited the acquisition of joint control of Gás de Portugal by Energias de Portugal and ENI in 2004 on the grounds that it would have further strengthened the dominant positions of EdP and GdP in the Portuguese electricity and gas markets respectively.[11] The decision was upheld on appeal.[12] Other examples include the commission's approval of:

- EDF's acquisition of German electricity firm EnBW in 2001;[13]
- DONG's acquisition of Danish electricity companies Elsam, Energi E2, Københavns Energi Holding and Frederiksberg Elnet;[14] and
- the merger of GDF and Suez in 2006.[15]

Each of these transactions was cleared on the basis of significant commitments to remedy market power concerns.

More recently, in 2013 the commission investigated the proposed acquisition of certain refinery assets owned by Shell Deutschland Oil located in Germany by Swedish company Nynas, but ultimately concluded that blocking the acquisition would have resulted in the closure of a refinery, causing more harm to consumers than allowing the deal to proceed.[16] And in 2014 the commission opened an in-depth investigation into the proposed acquisition of DESFA (the Greek gas transmission system operator) by the State Oil Company of Azerbaijan Republic,[17] although the €400 million deal ultimately broke down in 2016 before EU approval could be obtained.

The commission has also been active in relation to state aid in the energy sector. For example, the commission has approved a variety of state support mechanisms in a number of member states to facilitate renewables (eg, UK contract for difference arrangements),[18] the availability of sufficient electricity capacity (eg, to avoid black-outs in the United Kingdom, Belgium, France, Germany, Greece, Italy and Poland),[19] and to facilitate the construction of new nuclear plants (eg, Hinkley Point C in the United Kingdom).[20]

3.   Arbitration and competition law issues in the energy sector

While a wide variety of competition law issues may arise in the energy sector, not all of these are likely to be adjudicated before arbitrators. In particular, given

---

11   See Case COMP/M.3440 – *ENI/EDP/GDP*.
12   Case T-87/05 *EDP-Energias de Portugal SA v Commission*.
13   See Case CO–MP/M.1853 – *EDF/EnBW*.
14   See Case COMP/M.3868 – *DONG/Elsam/Energi E2*.
15   See Case COMP/M.4180 – *Gaz de France/Suez*.
16   See Case COMP/M.6360 – *NYNAS/SHELL/HARBURG REFINERY*.
17   See Case COMP/M.7095 – *SOCAR/DESFA*.
18   See Case SA36196.
19   See Cases SA35980, SA48648, SA39621, SA45852, SA48780, SA42011 and SA46100.
20   See Case SA34947.

that arbitrations generally occur only where the parties have contractually agreed to submit a particular dispute, or disputes in general, to arbitration, some of the above areas of competition law are more likely than others to find themselves before an arbitral tribunal. Thus, most competition law claims which are arbitrated, including in the energy sector, relate in one way or another to allegations that contracts or contractual provisions are invalid under applicable prohibitions of anti-competitive agreements. For example, each of the following might be arbitrated if the parties have agreed to resolve disputes under their contract by way of arbitration:

- A party might seek to extricate itself from a long-term gas or electricity supply contract (or an onerous aspect of it) by alleging that the contract, or a particular provision thereof, is anti-competitive and therefore void and unenforceable. For example, it might be alleged that a contractual obligation to source gas or electricity solely or predominantly from a particular supplier for a period of several years is void and unenforceable under competition law in circumstances where the supplier has a substantial market position. Such an obligation may be unlawful either as an abuse of a dominant position or as an anti-competitive agreement: in both cases, essentially because it serves to strengthen the supplier's already powerful market position at the expense of its rivals.

- Alternatively, a party to such a long-term contract might seek to defend itself against a breach of contract claim by bringing a counterclaim that the agreement (or part of it) is void under competition law.

- Joint venture arrangements in the oil and gas industry (eg, joint operating agreements) may contain a non-compete clause to ensure that the partners focus on the joint venture during its term and that each partner does not compete with the joint venture while it is a partner or for a limited period after it has exited the joint venture. A party wishing to engage in other business opportunities which would constitute a breach of such a non-compete clause may explore ways in which it could lawfully avoid the application of the clause. Under EU competition law, non-compete obligations may be unlawful if they are not appropriately limited in product scope and temporal and geographic application. Therefore, a party wishing to circumvent the application of a non-compete clause may seek to deploy competition law arguments as a 'sword' to defeat the clause.

- Conversely, a party either responding to such a claim or discovering that its partner has been acting in apparent breach of a non-compete clause is likely to use similar arguments in support of the clause (eg, that the clause is appropriately limited in application).

- A party might decide to ignore a contractual restriction preventing it from re-selling liquefied natural gas (LNG) to customers located in different EU member states from that in which it was purchased on the basis that such a restriction is void under Article 101 of the TFEU (similar to the approach taken by the European Commission in the *Gazprom* case considered above, and in earlier LNG cases relating to Sonatrach[21] and Nigeria LNG).[22] The supplier of the LNG might then sue the buyer for breach of contract and the buyer would need to defend itself by reference to its competition law arguments.

- A party to a contract may allege that the other party has breached the contract by participating in an unlawful cartel, thereby failing to comply with a contractual obligation to observe all applicable laws.

In contrast, actions for damages to compensate for losses incurred due to a supplier's participation in a price-fixing or market sharing cartel (ie, that the effect of the cartel was that the customer was forced to pay a higher price than would have applied in a competitive market) are less likely to fall within the scope of an arbitration agreement. Although the customer will have a supply agreement with its supplier and that agreement may contain an arbitration clause, it may be the case that tortious liability for the breach of statutory duty which is involved (at least in the United Kingdom) in infringing Article 101 of the TFEU would not be regarded as falling within the scope of the contractual arbitration clause. This is considered further in section 5 below.

Similarly, since merger control is applied by national or supranational competition authorities, rather than involving a dispute between private parties, for the most part, arbitration will not be an option. However, contractual provisions between a buyer and a seller relating to obligations to obtain merger clearance could potentially be subject to arbitration, and arbitration provisions have also become relatively standard in behavioural remedies commitments offered to resolve competition concerns raised by mergers, as discussed further in section 5 below.

The EU state aid rules are also primarily applied by the European Commission. In particular, the commission has exclusive competence to rule on the compatibility of aid which has been granted with the TFEU. However, in principle, certain state aid issues can be arbitrated in the same way as they can be litigated before the courts. For example, a party which has suffered loss due to illegal state aid, such as an acquirer of a business which it subsequently transpires has received unlawful state aid that must be repaid, may in principle seek to recover that loss from the vendor of the business in the courts. If there is an arbitration agreement between the parties to the business sale transaction, depending on the scope of the clause, such an action for damages could in

---

21   IP/07/1074.
22   IP/02/1869.

principle be brought by way of arbitration. In principle, there is also no reason why an arbitral tribunal could not take a view as to whether a measure should be classified as aid and is therefore illegal for lack of notification, or whether aid falls within the scope of a block exemption such as the General Block Exemption Regulation.[23] In general, however, it would be relatively rare for a state aid issue to arise in the context of a contractual dispute between private parties subject to an arbitration agreement.

Arbitration law and state aid law have also interfaced in a different way in recent years. This relates to investment treaty arbitrations. For example, EU member states might invoke the EU state aid regime to contest their liability to honour prior commitments on the basis that to do so would involve unlawful state aid.[24] This raises interesting issues as to the relative priority to be afforded to investment treaties and EU law. Such an issue arises in relation to the European Commission's decision in *Micula v Romania*.[25] This case related to various exemptions from Romanian customs duties which had been introduced before Romania joined the European Union in 2007. As part of the accession arrangements for joining the European Union, Romania agreed to remove the exemptions in order to comply with EU state aid law.

However, that led to a claim by the Micula brothers before an arbitration tribunal under the Romanian-Swedish bilateral investment treaty (BIT).[26] Essentially, the brothers argued that the appeal of the exemptions was contrary to the BIT. The tribunal upheld their claim, notwithstanding objections from the commission to the effect that the disputed incentives were contrary to the state aid rules, and that the supremacy of EU law meant that this had to take precedence.[27] Damages were awarded and the brothers then sought enforcement of the damages award in the Romanian courts. Again, they were successful.

In response, the commission began a formal state aid investigation on the basis that payment by the Romanian state of the damages awarded by the arbitral tribunal would itself constitute state aid. This included ordering Romania to suspend any action which might lead to the execution or implementation of the part of the arbitral award that had not yet been paid, until the commission had taken its final decision on the permissibility of the aid.[28] The commission confirmed its view in its final decision, noting specifically that its analysis was not precluded by the fact that the state aid arose through

---

23   Commission Regulation 651/2014/EU. Such issues are considered in more detail in Leigh Hancher – Chapter 28: "Arbitrating EU State Aid Issues", in G Blank and P Landolt (eds), *EU and US Antitrust Arbitration: A Handbook for Practitioners*, 2011.

24   Issues relating to this were also considered in Leigh Hancher – Chapter 28: "Arbitrating EU State Aid Issues", in G Blank and P Landolt (eds), *EU and US Antitrust Arbitration: A Handbook for Practitioners*, 2011.

25   Commission Decision (EU) 2015/1470 of 30 March 2015, Case SA38517, OJ L232/43 of 4 September 2015.

26   See ICSID Case ARB/05/20, *Ioan Micula v Romania*, final award of 11 December 2013.

27   *Ibid* at paragraphs 334-335.

28   As with the subsequent final decision, that suspension injunction was appealed: see Case T-646/14.

the payment of compensation awarded by an arbitral tribunal.[29] The decision is presently on appeal before the General Court of the European Union,[30] pending which the English High Court has stayed the brothers' application for enforcement of their award in the United Kingdom and declined to order the payment of security in their favour.[31] This was also appealed by the Micula brothers before the English Court of Appeal, which recently upheld the High Court's decision not to order a stay but reversed its decision in relation to security, ordering the Romanian State to pay £150 million security to the brothers as a 'next best' option to enforcement pending consideration of the appeal before the EU courts.[32]

This issue is of importance for a wide range of BITs; as is the commission position that intra-EU BITs are contrary to EU law (a position endorsed by the European Court of Justice (ECJ) in the recent *Achmea* judgment),[33] but since it falls outside the primary scope of this chapter – namely, arbitrating competition law claims between private parties – we do not consider this further.

The deployment of abuse of dominance (monopolisation in the United States) arguments in arbitral proceedings is less common than arguments that arrangements are void under prohibitions of anti-competitive agreements. This is partly due to the fact that abuse of dominance scenarios arise less frequently, both generally and specifically in the context of an ongoing contractual relationship. Most abuse of dominance claims are brought by competitors which claim to be adversely affected by their larger rival's actions rather than by contractual counterparties. However, where dominant companies are active at several levels of the supply chain, customers may also be downstream competitors. Moreover, given the fact that in many countries, energy companies were previously (and often still are) vertically integrated monopolies, many of which were (and are) state-owned, at least at the downstream level, there is no shortage of dominant companies in the energy sector. And while there is less vertical integration than historically, at least in the European Union, as a result of the three EU energy liberalisation packages (eg, which have in principle required member states to 'unbundle' ownership of gas and electricity transmission networks from production/generation and supply businesses, albeit with certain important exceptions),[34] there remains a significant degree of vertical integration in EU energy markets.

---

29   Commission Decision (EU) 2015/1470 of 30 March 2015, Case SA38517, OJ L232/43 of 4 September 2015, at paragraph 100.
30   Cases T-694/15 and T-704/15.
31   *Micula v Romania* [2017] EWHC 31 (Comm) (stay of enforcement) and [2017] EWHC 1430 (Comm) (security).
32   *Micula v Romania* [2018] EWCA Civ 1801.
33   Case C-284/16 *Slovak Republic v Achmea BV* (EU: C: 2018: 158).
34   See Article 9 of both Directive 2009/72 of 13 July 2009 concerning common rules of the internal market in electricity and Directive 2009/73 of 13 July 2009 on common rules for the internal market in natural gas.

The analysis below focuses on arbitrations relating to competition law claims in respect of alleged anti-competitive agreements, and to a lesser extent abuse of dominance and merger control.

It is implicit in the above that competition law issues can arise in arbitrations either directly or indirectly.

For example, parties may be involved in a contractual dispute that they have agreed to arbitrate in which competition arguments are then raised – for example, by way of defence and counterclaim. If those arguments are arbitrable and fall within the scope of the arbitration agreement (see section 5), there is no reason why they should not be heard by the arbitral tribunal seised of the dispute.

Alternatively, parties may be engaged in a pure competition dispute connected with a contract that contains an arbitration clause that is sufficiently broad to encompass that dispute. Depending on the nature of the competition issues involved, this may be more or less controversial. As noted above, damages claims arising from cartel behaviour are less likely to fall within the scope of an arbitration clause, as such claims will not generally arise under contract law (eg, the tort of breach of statutory duty is relevant in the case of England and Wales).

Of course, where parties are involved in a competition dispute, as with any other dispute, they may agree after the dispute has arisen to submit it to arbitration – for example, in order to avoid publicity.

From a strategic standpoint, the deployment of competition arguments to the effect that a particular clause is anti-competitive and therefore invalid requires careful consideration. It is well understood that, while the automatic invalidity flowing from an infringement of EU competition law will only directly affect the infringing clauses of the agreement, the entire agreement may be void where the relevant clause cannot be severed from the rest of the agreement.[35] (Under EU law, whether a clause may be severed is to be determined under the applicable national law, with the rules on severance varying between EU member states.)[36] Therefore, where a potentially anti-competitive clause is central to the contract as a whole, aggrieved parties need to think carefully before raising a competition argument if they wish the rest of the contract to remain in place.

4.   The treatment of 'euro-defences'

Pleading competition arguments to avoid liability, including for breach of contract, is not a new phenomenon. This tactic, sometimes known in the United Kingdom as the 'euro-defence', enjoyed some success in the 1970s.[37]

---

35   Case C-56/65 *Société Technique Minière v Maschinenbau Ulm*.
36   Case C-319/82 *Société de vente de ciments et betons v Kerpen & Kerpen*.
37   See, for example, *Application des Gaz-v-Falks Veritas* [1974] 1 Ch 381. The term 'euro-defence' derives from the fact that, prior to 2000 when the Competition Act 1998 came into effect, as a matter of English law, a competition law defence was generally required to be based on EU competition law.

However, competition law defences were historically often subject to a restrictive interpretation by courts and arbitral tribunals and of course may be vulnerable to strike-out applications from claimants seeking to enforce the provision in question.[38]

This began to change in the late 1990s, following the ECJ's decision in *Magill*, in which the ECJ held that in exceptional circumstances, the refusal to license IP rights (and consequently the exclusive exercise of such rights) by a dominant company was capable of constituting an abuse of the dominant position enjoyed by that company.[39]

The burden on defendants arguing 'euro-defences' remained fairly high in English courts following *Magill*, which was often applied restrictively. However, importantly, it was accepted by English judges that it was an arguable defence to enforcement action in respect of a claimant's contractual right that the exercise of the right in question would amount to an infringement of competition law.[40] Nevertheless, defences based on abuse of a dominant position are unlikely to succeed where a defendant is effectively arguing that the claimant is dominant merely as a result of an IP right which the claimant is seeking to enforce.[41]

More recently, the UK Supreme Court rejected the competition law defence of M-Tech, a parallel importer of disk drives manufactured by Sun Microsystems and over which it held a number of trademarks. Sun sought summary judgment against M-Tech for trademark infringement and M-Tech argued (among other things) that the exercise of Sun's trademark rights was unlawful because it gave effect to distribution agreements containing provisions that infringed Article 101. The Supreme Court held (consistent with judgments of the ECJ) that an IP right is not itself an agreement or concerted practice that is capable of infringing Article 101 of the TFEU; and that while this right may be unenforceable where there is a sufficient nexus between its exercise and that of an agreement or concerted practice that is capable of infringing Article 101, this had not been demonstrated by M-Tech.[42]

There are insufficient reported arbitral awards in the public domain to form a clear view as to whether arbitral tribunals are particularly sceptical of 'euro-defences'. One award (given in 2007 under the International Chamber of Commerce (ICC) Rules)[43] certainly suggests that competition law defences put forward in arbitration proceedings will be scrutinised carefully. The proceedings

---

38 See N Jones, *Euro-defence: Magill distinguished*, 1998, 20(9) EIPR 352-354.
39 Joined Cases C-241-242/91P *Radio Telefis Eireann v EC Commission* [1995] 4 CMLR 718.
40 See, for example, *Philips Electronics NV v Ingman Ltd* [1998] 2 CMLR 839 (Ch D (Patents Ct)); *Football Association Premier League Ltd v QC Leisure* [2008] EWHC 44 (Ch); *Intel Corporation v Via Technologies Inc* [2003] EWCA Civ 1905.
41 See, for example, *Philips Electronics NV v Ingman Ltd* [1998] 2 CMLR 839 (Ch D (Patents Ct)).
42 *Oracle America Inc (Formerly Sun Microsystems Inc) v M-Tech Data Limited* [2012] UKSC 27.
43 *Licensor (UK)-v-Licensee (France)*, Partial Award, ICC Case 13696, 2007, partially reported at G Blanke, *Case Comment – ICC award no. 13696 – ICC tribunal rejects Euro defense*, 8(2) GCLR 46, 2015.

concerned the respondent's obligation to pay royalties to the applicant pursuant to a licence agreement relating to the manufacture and distribution of certain products developed from products discovered by the applicant. Royalties were paid to the applicant for sales in all countries except the United States and Japan, which were not expressly covered by the licence; albeit that US and Japanese patents had in fact been licensed to the respondent. In defence of its failure to pay royalties for US and Japanese sales, the respondent argued that, in circumstances where its manufacture of the product did not involve the use of licensed patents, no royalties were payable pursuant to the licence of those patents. Further, the respondent argued that paying royalties would restrict its ability to develop its own technology, in turn leading to an increase in prices for end users which would constitute a distortion of competition. In a robust rejection of this defence, the tribunal noted that the party claiming an infringement of competition law bears the burden of proof and in this case the respondent had failed to substantiate its case.

In any event, as competition arguments are increasingly considered in the context of arbitrations, and as a consequence practitioners with competition law expertise are more frequently appointed as arbitrators (see section 6), soundly based competition law arguments – whether run as a defence or otherwise – are these days unlikely to be dismissed lightly by arbitrators familiar with the relevant principles.

5.   Procedural issues

5.1   Arbitrability of competition law disputes

Historically, there was a view that, because competition law matters raise issues of a mandatory nature closely linked to public policy objectives enforced by state organs, the appropriate forum for resolving competition disputes was the courts, rather than arbitral tribunals. According to this view, arbitrators were unlikely to be attuned to the public interest goals of competition law and were more likely to focus on the narrow private interests of the parties to the arbitration. There were also concerns regarding the ability of arbitrators to deal with the complexity of competition law and concerns regarding inconsistent application of the law. In short, there was a view that competition law issues should not be arbitrable because they were either too important, too complex or both. While a key aspect of this doctrine (ie, that the enforcement of antitrust laws is important) is certainly accurate, for the most part, the view that an arbitral tribunal is an inappropriate forum to resolve competition law issues no longer holds sway. Parties are of course subject to the application of mandatory laws and able to choose the substantive law to be applied in the event of arbitral proceedings between them, which may be such that there are no applicable competition laws in the arbitration; whereas there would have been in court proceedings (albeit this is increasingly less likely to be the case as most countries have now adopted competition laws). However, this does not necessarily mean that a tribunal will not apply competition laws. In particular, arbitrators will be acutely aware of the need to produce an enforceable award and, since the *Eco Swiss* decision (considered below and in section 7), the risk is that an award that disregards competition law may be set aside or not enforced because it is against public policy.

The fact that public importance and complexity are insufficient grounds to refuse to give effect to a valid arbitration clause in a competition law context was recognised by the US Supreme Court in its 1985 *Mitsubishi* judgment, in which it referred to the flexibility of arbitral proceedings (and in particular, the ability to nominate experts as arbitrators) as reasons why the complexity factor is not in itself sufficient to preclude a competition dispute from being referred to arbitration.[44] It also reiterated the federal policy in favour of commercial arbitration, noting that "concerns of international comity, respect for the capacities of foreign and transnational tribunals, and sensitivity to the need of the international commercial system for predictability in the resolution of disputes" require the arbitration clause to be enforced.[45]

As a matter of EU law, the arbitrability question has been implicitly resolved without having ever been dealt with directly. In *Eco Swiss*, the ECJ did not deal with the issue of arbitrability *per se* (as it was not asked to do so by the Dutch Supreme Court). Instead, in line with the questions put before it, the ECJ considered whether competition law should be regarded as forming part of public policy within the meaning of the New York Convention.[46] *Eco Swiss* concerned an application for annulment of an arbitral award on the basis that the underlying contract which formed the basis for the award was in fact void under the then equivalent of Article 101 of the TFEU and therefore contrary to public policy. Specifically, it was contended that the agreement amounted to an invalid market sharing agreement, but this point had not been considered by the parties or the arbitrators during the arbitration.

The ECJ concluded that Article 101 constitutes a fundamental provision of EU law and therefore a matter of public policy under the convention. As a consequence, a national court faced with an application for annulment of an arbitration award would have to grant that application if it considered that the award were contrary to Article 101, where its domestic procedural rules required it to grant annulment on the grounds of failure to observe national rules of public policy.

The consequence of this finding is that the courts of EU member states

---

44   *Mitsubishi v Soler Chrysler-Plymouth* [1985] 473 US 614, at 634.
45   *Mitsubishi v Soler Chrysler-Plymouth* [1985] 473 US 614, at 629.
46   Case C-126/97, *Eco Swiss China Ltd and Benetton International NV*, 1 June 1999, [1999] ECR I-3055, at para 39.

(which are all New York Convention signatories) may refuse to enforce an arbitral award that, if enforced, would violate TFEU provisions relating to anti-competitive agreements.[47] In other words, as a matter of EU law, an award that fails to have regard to those provisions may be unenforceable under the New York Convention. Inherent to this logic is the principle that arbitrators may, and in fact should, have regard to EU competition law as an integral part of their duty to render an enforceable award. It follows that issues falling within those provisions must be capable of determination by an arbitral tribunal.

Legislation in several EEA member states – including Sweden, Norway and Lithuania – now expressly provides for the arbitrability of competition law disputes.[48] Subsequent domestic court rulings in various member states – including France,[49] Italy,[50] Belgium[51] and the United Kingdom[52] – have since made clear that competition law issues are arbitrable. Similar positions have been reached in Austria, Germany, Greece, the Netherlands and Spain.[53] For example, the English High Court judgment in *ET Plus* stated that "[t]here is no realistic doubt that such 'competition' claims [referring to both Article 101 and 102 of the TFEU] are arbitrable".[54] The *ET Plus* decision is perhaps of particular note as it is a rare example of a European judgment that expressly recognises the arbitrability of disputes arising in relation to Article 102 relating to abuse of a dominant position.

Accordingly, over the last 10 to 20 years, the arbitrability of competition disputes has become a largely settled principle across Europe and the issue is

---

47   The position ought logically to be the same in a post-Brexit world as regards an arbitral award which fails properly to apply UK competition law.
48   See "Is the Arbitrability of Competition Law Claims a truly settled matter?", EU Competition Law and Arbitration Joint Conference of the AI and the CEA, Stockholm, 28 April 2017, Dr Gordon Blanke, www.sccinstitute.com/media/190751/gb-2017-ai-cea-conference-stockholm-april-2017.pdf.
49   *Thales Air Defence v G.I.E. Euromissile*, Paris Court of Appeal, 10 November 2004; *Société SNF SAS v société Cytec Industries BV*, French Court of Cassation, Civ 1, 4 June 2008.
50   *Nuovo Pignone SpA v Schlumberger SA*, Florence Court of Appeal, 21 March 2006.
51   *Société SNF SAS v société Cytec Industrie*, Brussels Court of First Instance (8 March 2007).
52   *Et Plus SA v Welter* [2005] EWHC 2115 (Comm).
53   See "Is the Arbitrability of Competition Law Claims a truly settled matter?", EU Competition Law and Arbitration Joint Conference of the AI and the CEA, Stockholm, 28 April 2017, Dr Gordon Blanke, www.sccinstitute.com/media/190751/gb-2017-ai-cea-conference-stockholm-april-2017.pdf.
54   *Et Plus SA v Welter* [2005] EWHC 2115 (Comm), para 51.
55   Article 101(1) of the TFEU prohibits agreements and concerted practices which may affect trade between EU member states and which have as their object or effect the prevention, restriction or distortion of competition within the European Union. Such agreements are in principle automatically void under Article 101(2). However, Article 101(3) provides that agreements which are in void under Article 101(2) may be exempted from the prohibition if they meet certain conditions. In very simple terms, this involves demonstrating that the benefits of the arrangements outweigh their adverse effects. The European Commission has issued a number of 'block exemptions' under Article 101(3). These provide that agreements which meet certain conditions set out in the block exemption are exempt if they would or may otherwise be prohibited by Article 101(1). Block exemptions of potential relevance to the energy sector include those relating to research and development agreements (Commission Regulation 1217/2010/EU), specialisation agreements (ie, agreements under which the parties agree to produce products jointly or under which one or more parties agrees to reduce or cease production of certain goods) (Commission Regulation 1218/2010/EU) and vertical agreements (ie, agreements between parties operating at different levels of the supply chain, such as supply and distribution agreements) (Commission Regulation 330/2010/EU) .

rarely discussed in the context of specific arbitrations. This means that it is accepted that arbitrators can declare arrangements contrary to (or compatible with) Article 101 or 102 of the TFEU (and equivalent national provisions), declare an agreement compatible with Article 101(3) of the TFEU on the basis that it falls within a block exemption or can be individually exempted,[55] and draw the civil law consequences of any infringement by awarding damages to an adversely affected party.

Indeed, the 2014 EU Damages Directive[56] makes express reference to the need for national courts to encourage parties to make effective use of consensual dispute resolution procedures including arbitration.[57] To facilitate this, the Damages Directive requires member states to ensure that national courts can stay competition damages actions before them to allow parties an opportunity to resolve their dispute in accordance with a consensual dispute resolution mechanism (which may include arbitration).[58]

(a)   Commitments arbitration clauses

Outside the context of damages actions and claims that particular contractual provisions (or entire contracts) are unenforceable, another type of arbitration clause which may be encountered in matters relating to competition law concerns binding commitments given by an entity to a competition authority such as the European Commission following a competition law or merger control investigation. Such commitments may be agreed under Article 9 of Regulation 1/2003 in the case of investigations under Articles 101 and 102 of the TFEU[59] (eg, see the commitments referred to in section 2 in the *Gazprom*, *ENI*, *RWE*, *E.ON* and *GDF Suez* cases), and under Articles 6(2) and 8(2) of the EU Merger Regulation in a merger control context. In recent years, a fairly substantial number of commitments accepted by the European Commission (particularly in a merger control context) have included an arbitration clause covering disputes as to the entity's compliance with the commitments it has

---

56   Directive 2014/104 EU of 26 November 2014 on certain rules governing actions for damages under national law for infringements of the competition law provisions of the member states and of the European Union. The directive seeks to facilitate damages claims by victims of infringement of EU (and national) competition law.

57   Damages Directive, Recital 48.

58   Damages Directive, Article 18(2). However, these provisions may not have practical relevance for a number of years. For example, the Damages Directive was transposed into English law on 9 March 2017 by the Claims in respect of Loss or Damage arising from Competition Infringements (Competition Act 1998 and Other Enactments (Amendment)) Regulations 2017. Regulation 22(2) provides for the suspension of the limitation period applicable to a competition damages claim while the parties to that claim are engaged in a 'consensual dispute resolution process', which expressly includes arbitration (Regulation 6(1)). However, this regime applies only in proceedings relating to loss or damage suffered on or after 9 March 2017. See further E Burrows and M Strasberg, "England & Wales" in *ICLG Competition Litigation* 2018.

59   Council Regulation 1/2003 of 16 December 2002 on the implementation of the rules on competition laid down in Articles 81 and 82 of the Treaty (Articles 81 and 82 are now Articles 101 and 102 of the TFEU). This is the main implementing regulation governing how the European Commission enforces Articles 101 and 102.

given. Indeed, the European Commission's 2008 Notice on Remedies under the EU Merger Regulation specifically refers to this as a possibility.[60]

A defining characteristic of these arbitration commitments is that, initially at least, unlike most arbitration clauses, they are unilateral, binding only on the committing party (ie, in the case of a merger, the merged entity or acquirer). Third parties are free to refer a dispute relating to the committing party's compliance with its commitments to arbitration in accordance with the commitment or to issue proceedings in the courts. (In a merger control context, this will typically be relevant only where the merged entity has committed to behave in a particular way (or not to behave in a particular way) – for example, to provide access to a particular facility or service on fair, reasonable and non-discriminatory terms, rather than a more traditional 'structural' commitment to sell off a particular business.[61]

The use of such arbitration mechanisms in commission commitment decisions is not a recent development. For example, such an approach was used in the commitments given by News Corp to the commission in the context of its ultimately cleared acquisition of Telepiù in 2003.[62] That acquisition gave rise in 2010 to what is possibly the only known arbitration arising from EU merger commitments under the ICC rules. The dispute arose between RTI Italia SpA and SKY Italia Sri (a wholly owned subsidiary of Newscorp), and concerned the compatibility of SKY's exclusive rights to broadcast the 2010 FIFA World Cup with Newscorp's commitments. The tribunal delivered an award in SKY's favour in 2012, finding that it had not breached the commitments.[63]

There is also an arbitration provision in the recent *Gazprom* commitments referred to in section 2, although in that case Gazprom is required to offer customers a price review clause which includes the possibility for disputes to be referred to arbitration, and if such a clause is adopted, Gazprom will also have the right to refer the case to arbitration in the event of disagreement.[64]

(b)   Exceptions

There remain some exceptions to the general arbitrability of competition law disputes. In particular, matters reserved for regulatory oversight (ie, by the European Commission or by national competition or other enforcement authorities) – such as criminal liability, the imposition of fines or the approval of (non-exempted) state aid – are not arbitrable.[65] Those exceptions aside, the

---

60   Commission notice on remedies acceptable under Council Regulation (EC) No 139/2004 and under Commission Regulation (EC) No 802/2004, (2008/C 267/01) at paragraph 66.
61   However, arbitration commitments may also be given in relation to structural remedies, as noted in G Blanke, "The arbitrability of EU competition law: the status quo revisited in the light of recent developments: Part 1", 2017 10(2) GCLR 85-101, at footnote 31.
62   Case M2876 *NEWSCORP/TELEPIU*.
63   See M Marquis and R Cisotta, *Litigation and Arbitration in EU Competition Law*, Elgar 2015, p303.
64   Case AT39816, Final Commitments, 24 May 2018, paragraph 19(iv).
65   G Blanke, "The arbitrability of EU competition law: the status quo revisited in the light of recent developments: Part 1", 2017, 10(2) GCLR85-101, 85.

key question today is no longer one of arbitrability, but one of scope – does the dispute fall within the scope of the arbitration clause relied upon?

As discussed in the previous section, it is now largely uncontroversial that competition issues are arbitrable in principle. However, whether a specific competition dispute can be referred to arbitration in practice is often a more difficult question.

In theory, parties may agree to submit a competition dispute to arbitration *ex post facto* where there is no arbitration clause, but this is unlikely in practice. For example, it is not uncommon for parties to a competition dispute to deploy jurisdictional arguments for tactical gain, one example being the 'Italian torpedo'.[66] Where agreeing to submit a dispute to arbitration could remove that tactical option, parties may be unwilling to take this step.

In practice, the answer is therefore largely dependent on whether the dispute falls within the scope of an arbitration clause between the parties. Under English law, the starting point is that parties which included a valid arbitration clause in a contract intended to refer all disputes between them arising out of their contractual relationship to arbitration.[67] This is known as the 'one-stop shop' principle. The simple economic basis for this principle is that dispute resolution, to varying extents, represents a sunk cost insofar as parties will rarely recover the totality of the costs incurred in the dispute resolution process even if they are successful. In addition, there is an opportunity cost to parties involved in a dispute, representing time and resource that could have been used for other purposes but for the dispute. Those costs could increase substantially if parties are involved in multiple disputes being determined under different mechanisms. It is therefore reasonable to assume that commercial parties that agree on a particular dispute resolution mechanism in a contract also intended to resolve all disputes arising from their contractual relationship in accordance with that mechanism.[68]

The resolution of competition disputes is no exception to the 'one-stop shop' principle, in that competition claims are capable of arising out of the contractual relationship between two parties. Whether a competition claim does in fact arise out of that relationship is a question that has caused courts some difficulty in the last few years. In some cases, European courts have found that competition claims that are solely based in tort (eg, a claim for damages

---

66   A cross-border litigation tactic by which a defendant to a potential claim that would not be subject to an exclusive jurisdiction clause (often, but not always, a competition claim) commences declaratory proceedings in the courts of an EU member state that is procedurally slow or otherwise unfriendly to claimants (State A) in order to argue that any future related proceedings initiated in a different member state (State B) should either be stayed or dismissed in favour of State A. Where the claimant's claim in State B has been 'torpedoed', the defendant may obtain a more favourable settlement.
      Similar issues may also arise in relation to arbitration clauses – see, for example, Case C–185/07 *Allianz SpA v West Tankers Inc*, 10 February 2009.
67   *Fiona Trust & Holding Corp v Privalov* [2007] UKHL 40, at paragraph 13 of Lord Hoffmann's judgment.
68   See *Fiona Trust*, at paragraph 7 and P Landolt, *Arbitration Clauses and Competition Law*, 2-027 in G Blanke and P Landolt (eds), *EU and US Antitrust Arbitration: A Handbook for Practitioners*, 2011.

suffered as a result of a cartel) cannot be said to arise from the contractual relationship between the parties. A good example of this approach is the English Court of Appeal's decision in the *Ryanair* case, which considered whether a damages action for losses suffered a result of cartel behaviour evidenced by a decision of the Italian competition authority fell within a non-exclusive English jurisdiction clause. Lord Justice Rix, delivering the court's judgment, stated:

> *Such reasoning, however, does not carry over into a situation where there is no contractual dispute (by which I intend to include disputes about contracts), but all that has happened is that a buyer has bought goods from a seller who has participated in a cartel. I think that rational businessmen would be surprised to be told that a non-exclusive jurisdiction clause bound or entitled the parties to that sale to litigate in a contractually agreed forum an entirely non-contractual claim for breach of statutory duty pursuant to article 101, the essence of which depended on proof of unlawful arrangements between the seller and third parties with whom the buyer had no relationship whatsoever, and the gravamen of which was a matter which probably affected many other potential claimants, with whom such a buyer might very well wish to link itself.[69]*

While it is important to bear in mind that the *Ryanair* case did not concern an arbitration clause, the logic underpinning the decision (ie, that a claim founded exclusively in tort is unlikely to be found to arise from a contractual relationship between the parties) seems to be transferable.

This approach was taken by the ECJ in the *CDC Hydrogen Peroxide* preliminary reference.[70] The ECJ took the view that jurisdiction clauses (including arbitration clauses) which refer to all disputes arising under the relevant contract should not be considered as extending to tortious liability arising from alleged cartel behaviour. Of particular note, the court held that because a victim of an alleged cartel cannot reasonably foresee at the time of agreeing a jurisdiction clause that a dispute arising from that alleged cartel will arise in the future (because it has no knowledge of the cartel), that dispute cannot be said to arise from the contractual relationship that is subject to the jurisdiction clause.[71] At the domestic level, the same approach was taken in an earlier decision of the Helsinki District Court[72] (arising from the same facts) and a subsequent decision of the Amsterdam Court[73] applying the ECJ's judgment.

However, a somewhat different approach was taken in the English High Court's ruling in the more recent *Microsoft Mobile* case.[74] This concerned a

---

69   *Ryanair Limited v Esso Italiana Srl* [2013] EWCA Civ 1450, para 46.
70   Case C-352/13 Cartel Damage Claims (CDC) *Hydrogen Peroxide SA v Akzo Nobel NV*, 21 May 2015.
71   Case C-352/13 Cartel Damages Claims (CDC) *Hydrogen Peroxide SA v Akzo Nobel NV*, para 70.
72   CDC *Hydrogen Peroxide Cartel Damage SA v Kemira Oyj*—Interlocutory Judgment 36492, 4 July 2013, 11/16750.
73   Case C/13/500953/HA ZA 11-2560—*Kemira Chemicals OY v CDC Project 13 SA*, ruling of 21 July 2015.
74   *Microsoft Mobile Oy (Ltd) v Sony Europe Ltd* [2017] EWHC 374 (Ch).

'standalone' damages claim[75] brought by Microsoft against Sony, LG and Samsung alleging anti-competitive conduct in relation to the pricing of lithium ion batteries. Microsoft's supply agreement with Sony under which Sony supplied the batteries included a clause referring any disputes relating to the agreement to arbitration. Importantly, the supply agreement included two further clauses: an obligation to negotiate battery prices in good faith and an obligation on Sony to disclose to Microsoft events that reasonably affected Sony's ability to meet any of its obligations under the contract. Sony argued that, because participating in a cartel in relation to the contract goods would constitute a breach of both these obligations, Microsoft's claim in damages was also contractual and therefore fell within the arbitration clause. The court agreed with Sony, reconciling the *Ryanair* and *Fiona Trust* judgments by holding that contractual claims that could have been brought were sufficiently closely related to the tortious claim actually brought by the claimant "so as to render rational businessmen likely to have intended such a dispute to be decided (like a contractual dispute) by arbitration".[76] This was despite the fact that no contractual claim had actually been brought: the court found that the important point was that a good, arguable contractual claim in respect of the same conduct could have been brought.

6. Practical issues

6.1 Selecting arbitrators for competition disputes
One of the advantages often afforded to parties engaged in arbitration proceedings is the ability to choose (or at least input into) the composition of their tribunal. This is no different in the context of a dispute with a competition element, which may benefit from being considered by an arbitrator with competition and/or economic expertise.

A similar advantage can be observed in cases before the UK Competition Appeal Tribunal (CAT), a specialist court set up in 2003 to hear competition disputes. Cases in the CAT are heard by a panel of three members, comprising the president or a chairman (who will be a High Court judge) and two ordinary members (who will have expertise in specific areas including accountancy, economics, law or other fields). It is therefore common for parties in CAT cases to appear before a High Court judge, an economist and another expert.

Parties to arbitration proceedings likely to involve a material competition element may be able to replicate a similar environment by carefully selecting

---

75   That is, a claim that does not follow an infringement decision of a competition authority and therefore one in which the claimant must prove that an infringement has occurred, as well as that this has caused it loss (and the quantum of that loss). In contrast, in a follow-on action (where there is already an infringement decision of a competition authority), there is no need to prove that an infringement has occurred, with the analysis focusing on causation and quantum.

76   *Microsoft Mobile Oy (Ltd) v Sony Europe Ltd* [2017] EWHC 374 (Ch), para 72.

their arbitrator(s). Where the arbitration clause provides for three arbitrators (which frequently means that each party may select one arbitrator, with the third being nominated by an appointing body such as the London Court of International Arbitration), a party considering competition law arguments may wish to select a competition lawyer as its nominee to ensure that at least one of the three arbitrators will have a detailed understanding of competition law issues. Where there is to be a sole arbitrator, the parties may wish to ask their institution to appoint an arbitrator with competition experience.

6.2   The role of experts

The energy sector is susceptible to arbitration proceedings involving claims for very considerable sums in damages. The award in 2014 totalling over $50 billion to the former majority shareholders of the Yukos Oil Company[77] is a recent example of the potential magnitude of awards in the energy sector (although the award was overturned by the Hague District Court in 2016[78] and is presently on appeal).

One of the reasons for the frequently large amounts at stake in energy-related arbitrations is the duration of the contracts involved (eg, long-term supply contracts) combined with the volatile pricing of the product(s) that are the subject of the contract. In this context, expert evidence may be of great assistance in answering questions of liability, causation and/or quantum. In particular, the knowledge of an industry expert may help tribunals to forecast cash flows over a given period – perhaps in, or contrasted with, a counterfactual scenario. An economic expert may also be required to convert the findings of the industry expert into a quantification of damage.[79] Where volatile pricing movements are involved, a pricing expert may also be needed to assess whether, for example, prices had moved in a way that frustrated a contract or triggered a *force majeure* clause.

It is well known that economics is a central element of competition law and that, in turn, economic analysis will be essential in many contentious competition matters. In abuse of dominance cases, economic analysis will often focus on determining the relevant market and market shares (ie, to establish or rebut a dominance finding), as well as the impact of the allegedly abusive conduct on rivals and their ability to compete effectively. In cartel damages cases, economic analysis is needed to assess the level of overcharge, 'pass-on' and/or lost profits resulting from the conduct.

Other experts may also be required in connection with competition law arguments in an arbitration context. For example, industry experts may be

---

77   PCA Case No AA 227, *Yukos Universal Limited (Isle of Man) v Russian Federation*.
78   C/09/477160/HA ZA 15-1, 15-2 and 15-112, *Russian Federation v Veteran Petroleum Limited*.
79   H Rosen and M Crazier-Darmois, "Expert Evidence" in *GAR Guide to Energy Arbitrations* (2nd ed), http://globalarbitrationreview.com/edition/1001020/the-guide-to-energy-arbitrations-second-edition.

required to explain how particular aspects of an industry typically function and therefore what the market impact of particular conduct might be expected to be. Depending on the seat of the arbitration and the experience of the arbitrators, an expert in competition law itself may be required. And as in many other cases, forensic accountancy experts may be required to assess (or rebut) the level of loss incurred as a result of the infringing conduct.

6.3 The role of disclosure

In common law jurisdictions such as England and Wales, the discovery/ disclosure process in courts is typically extensive, primarily because it covers not only those documents which support a party's case, but also those which are adverse to it. In the United States, the scope of discovery is broader still, as it will frequently include depositions.

There is no real equivalent to this in civil law systems, where the exercise of establishing the relevant facts is largely entrusted to the judge. Parties will not generally be bound to disclose any more documents than those strictly required to discharge the burden of proof applicable to their arguments. The notion that a party may seek and obtain disclosure of documents adverse to its opponent's case is unusual in civil law systems.[80]

In the particular context of competition damages actions, the 2014 EU Damages Directive referred to above has considerably broadened the disclosure rules of many civil law jurisdictions within the European Union. For example, claimants may be able to obtain copies of a number of documents on a competition authority's investigation file, including information requests, statements of objections, replies to the same and even settlement submissions (if withdrawn).[81]

In arbitration proceedings involving competition law issues, to which the disclosure principles sourced from the Damages Directive are not directly applicable, the document production regime may be more limited than full English or US disclosure/discovery regimes. Of course, because parties are free to agree the rules of document production that will apply to their proceedings, it is possible for them to agree to be bound by English or US-style disclosure/discovery rules. However, in practice, it will often be the case that the document production regime in arbitration proceedings will be more aligned with civil law concepts such that parties need produce only the documents which support their case and requests for document production must be specifically framed.[82]

---

80 G Blanke, "Document production in international arbitration: from civil and common law dichotomy to operational synergies", 2017 83(4) *Arbitration* 423.
81 Article 6 of the Damages Directive.
82 G Blanke, "Document production in international arbitration: from civil and common law dichotomy to operational synergies", 2017 83(4) *Arbitration* 423.

The application of more restrictive rules of document production in arbitration proceedings may create a tension with the frequent need for broad disclosure to support arguments founded in competition law. For example, wide disclosure may be needed by a party to support an allegation that its opponent has engaged in collusive (and typically secret) behaviour with the object or effect of restricting competition. Where there is no obligation on parties to produce documents that are adverse to their case and broadly framed requests for document production are less likely to be accepted, allegations of anti-competitive conduct are likely to be more difficult to substantiate.

A compromise position is available to parties who choose to apply it. The 2010 International Bar Association (IBA) Rules on the Taking of Evidence in International Arbitration provide a document production regime which reflects aspect of both common law and civil law approaches.

The starting point under the IBA rules is that parties must produce the documents on which they rely.[83] However, the rules also state that a party may issue a request to produce documents.[84] To restrict a party's ability to conduct a 'fishing expedition' (an eventuality which the English and US disclosure/discovery regimes do not always prevent), a request to produce under the IBA rules must contain four things:

- a description of each requested document that is sufficient to identify it;
- a statement as to the relevance of the document or category to the requesting party's case and its materiality to the outcome of the same;[85]
- a statement that the requested document or category is not in the possession, custody or control of the requesting party (or, where it is, reasons why it would be unreasonably burdensome for the requesting party to produce it);[86] and
- a statement of reasons why the requesting party assumes that the requested document or category of documents is in the control of the requested party.[87]

The IBA rules go on to provide a procedure for parties to object to requests and for the tribunal to decide on contested requests.

Where parties to arbitration elect to apply the IBA rules or a similar set of bespoke rules, requests for production will often be conducted by reference to Redfern schedules.[88] The use of Redfern schedules enables parties and the tribunal to capture the entire process in a single tabular document showing the

---

83   IBA Rules, Article 3(1).
84   IBA Rules, Article 3(2).
85   IBA Rules, Article 3(3)(b).
86   IBA Rules, Article 3(3)(c)(i).
87   IBA Rules, Article 3(3)(c)(ii)
88   See A Redfern, M Hunter, N Blackaby and C Partasid, *Redfern and Hunter on International Arbitration*, 6th ed, OUP 2015.

request itself in a first column, the relevance and materiality of the request in a second column, the requested party's objection(s) in a third column and the tribunal's decision as to whether the document(s) should be produced in a fourth column.[89]

The IBA rules have been described as a "sensible middle ground between the expansive document production practices of common-law jurisdictions and the reluctance of civil-law systems to compel parties to produce documents".[90] Where the parties have decided that these rules will apply and the tribunal is sufficiently familiar with the heavier documentary requirements of many competition law issues, the tension referred to above may be eased. The IBA rules are frequently adopted in practice and their use has become almost standard. Experience shows that they produce a much more streamlined process for determining disclosure requests and in many cases lead to costs savings when compared to common law court practice.

Arbitrators will also be mindful of the need to ensure that competition law arguments have been appropriately considered, so as to avoid the risk that an arbitration award may not be enforced by a court on the grounds that, contrary to public policy, competition law has not been properly applied (see further sections 4 and 7). This, together with the increasing involvement of former judges and advocates with competition law experience in common law jurisdictions as arbitrators, may mean that – particularly where the IBA rules are used – disclosure exercises in arbitrations involving competition law issues can become very extensive and sometimes not significantly different from those which would apply in proceedings before common law courts.

6.4   The role of factual witnesses

As noted above, certain competition law arguments will be dependent on documentary evidence by their nature (eg, anti-competitive agreements are often secret). In common law systems, the party alleging that anti-competitive behaviour has taken place and/or that it has suffered loss as a result of the infringing behaviour will seek to rely on a number of factual witnesses to produce statements referring to and describing the documentary evidence in support of those allegations, which will in turn be supported by a signed/sworn statement of truth. In this context, a claimant is likely to produce witness evidence to support its allegation that, for example, the defendant participated in meetings during which anti-competitive conduct took place or was agreed.[91]

89   G Blanke, "Document production in international arbitration: from civil and common law dichotomy to operational synergies", 2017 83(4) *Arbitration* 423.

90   M McIlwrath and H Alvarez, "Common and Civil Law Approaches to Procedure: Party and Arbitrator Perspectives" in PE Mason and HA Grigera Naón (eds), *International Arbitration: 21st Century Perspectives* (2010), para 2.05 [4].

91   KPE Lasok QC, "Some Procedural Aspects of How They Could/Should be Reformed", in M Danov, F Becker and P Beaumont, *Cross-Border EU Competition Law Actions*, p47.

The defendant will adduce its own witness evidence to show the opposite (in particular, either that the alleged anti-competitive conduct never took place or that, even if it did, it did not have anti-competitive effects and/or the claimant suffered no loss as a result).

Readers may be familiar with certain basic differences in approach between civil law and common law court practice in relation to dealing with factual witnesses. In civil law systems, the judge leads the investigation into the facts, whereas in common law systems the party advocates take the lead in questioning witnesses on their evidence. As a general rule, civil law systems do not place the same emphasis on oral testimony and questioning of witnesses as the common law system. International arbitration practice, including in relation to competition law claims, may closely resemble either common or civil law litigation if all party representatives and tribunal members are from one or other legal tradition. It is quite common, however, to have lawyers (either counsel or tribunal members) from more than one tradition, in which case the procedure that will be followed may be a hybrid form reflecting both approaches. For example, it is quite common for tribunals to set strict time limits on the time counsel may spend on cross-examination. The tribunal may also be rather more interventionist than a typical common law judge, either by more extensive questioning of witnesses or by asking its own questions and requesting supplemental questioning from party representatives.

The divide between civil and common law approaches is arguably at its most noticeable at the trial itself, when witnesses are cross-examined. There is a perception in the arbitration community that civil law-trained advocates are at a disadvantage when cross-examining a witness in comparison with their common law counterparts, who will usually have greater familiarity and experience with the practice. However, the extent to which this will apply in practice will depend on the training, experience and preparation of the advocates on the one hand and the attitude of the tribunal towards cross-examination (ie, the style and extent of cross-examination it deems appropriate) on the other.

6.5   Evidencing damages

Under English law, the objective of damages for losses resulting from anti-competitive conduct is to put the claimant in the position in which it would have been had the conduct not taken place. This in turn requires the decision-maker in proceedings to assess what that position would have been in the absence of that conduct (the 'but-for' test).

The evidentiary burden on the claimant is therefore to establish the scenario which would have existed had the competition infringement not occurred. Because an infringement is either established or alleged, that scenario is by definition hypothetical. Therefore, in the absence of a 'non-infringement' scenario, the claimant must create a scenario to be used by the decision-maker as a point of reference (typically called the 'counterfactual' scenario). The parameters relied upon to construct the counterfactual scenario are likely to be a key point of contention between the parties.

As noted in section 6.2, a party claiming damages for losses resulting from anti-competitive behaviour is likely to be heavily reliant on economic evidence to show that the conduct in question put it in a worse position than that in which it would have been in the counterfactual scenario. The economic evidence presented by a claimant will therefore be concerned with comparing one or more values in the actual scenario with the corresponding value(s) in the counterfactual scenario. The value(s) chosen will depend on the head(s) of damage pleaded by the claimant (eg, price levels, volume of commerce, profit margins or input costs).[92] In this context, a typical starting point in cartel cases will involve a comparison of the prices charged to the claimant by the cartelist with non-cartel prices in order to demonstrate that a certain percentage of overcharge was applied to the prices paid by the claimant. In abuse of dominance cases, the analysis is more likely to revolve around a comparison of actual profit margins against the profit margins that would have existed but for the infringement.

The comparative analysis referred to above can be carried out in a number of ways. The simplest is likely to involve a 'before and/or after' analysis. This will essentially involve a comparison of the relevant economic value(s) before the anti-competitive behaviour began and/or after it ended with the same during the period of the infringement. An essential component of that comparison is the exclusion of all factors affecting the relevant value(s) being compared that did not result from the infringement (eg, inflation, interest rates, foreign exchange rates, raw material costs). Once those factors are 'controlled for', the resulting data should be comparable with the same data during the infringement on a like-for-like basis. Differences in the movement of the economic value(s) being compared may be *prima facie* evidence of the effect of the relevant infringement.

Another method of quantifying damages is to compare the economic value(s) in question with the same economic value(s) in respect of a product or service that is unaffected by the infringement, but sold/provided in similar market conditions. This approach is likely to be more appropriate in cartel cases than, for instance, abuse of dominance cases. In a cartel case, it may be appropriate to compare the prices of the cartelised product with the prices of a similar but unaffected product that is subject to similar market conditions.

Assuming a claimant establishes that it suffered loss, where that claimant is not an end user, a defendant is likely to seek to demonstrate that the claimant

---

92   European Commission, Practical Guide, *Quantifying Harm in Actions for Damages based on Braches of Article 101 or 102 of the Treaty on the Functioning of the European Union*, C(2013) 3440, p10.

passed on some or all of its losses to its own customers. One of the main ways to show this is to assess the movement of profit margins before, during and/or after the infringement. If a claimant's profit margins are flat during and outside the infringement period, the pass-on argument is likely to be stronger. Given the range of factors that can influence a claimant's margins, a defendant is likely to face a heavy evidential burden – particularly where the claimant has a large customer base.

While the concept of pass-on has been accepted by a number of courts, the framework of its operation as a legal defence has yet to be properly considered and determined in many of them. There is a general perception that where pass-on has been considered by courts, the burden of proof faced by defendants has been extremely difficult to discharge. The question of whether an arbitral tribunal would be more open to considering arguments around pass-on is likely to be heavily dependent on the background of the arbitrator(s).

7. Role of national courts in enforcing/challenging arbitral awards

The New York Convention regulates the enforcement of arbitral awards in the courts of its party states. In this context, the convention provides that each of its contracting states shall recognise awards as binding and enforce them in accordance with the procedural rules of the place where the award is relied upon.[93] This enables parties to enforce arbitral awards in the courts of any member of the convention (of which they are currently 159) in which the award is enforceable.

However, the New York Convention also provides certain grounds on which the enforcement of an award may be refused by a national court. These include situations in which it is demonstrated that:

- the arbitration agreement in question was invalid;
- the party against which enforcement is sought was not given proper notice of the appointment of the arbitrator or of the proceedings, or was otherwise unable to present its case;
- the award addresses matters outside the scope of the arbitration agreement;
- the composition of the tribunal was not in accordance with the arbitration agreement and/or the law of the seat; or
- the award has not yet become binding or has been set aside or suspended by the courts of the country where it was made.[94]

Enforcement may also be refused at the discretion of the court in which it is sought where the court considers that:

---

93   Convention on the Recognition and Enforcement of Foreign Arbitral Awards 1958, Article III.
94   Convention on the Recognition and Enforcement of Foreign Arbitral Awards 1958, Article V(1).

- the subject matter of the arbitration was in fact not capable of settlement by arbitration under the law of the country in which enforcement is sought; or
- enforcment of the award would be contrary to public policy.[95]

The inclusion of a 'public policy' exception giving a court fairly broad discretion not to enforce an arbitral award may appear odd against the background of an instrument that is designed to facilitate the enforcement of awards. This has led some commentators to refer to this exception as the 'public policy paradox'.[96]

While courts tend to take a restrictive approach when considering public policy arguments put forward by unsuccessful parties resisting enforcement of arbitral awards, it does not follow that they are not seriously and properly considered. In a recent example, the English High Court considered a 2013 award arising from a Swedish seated arbitration conducted under the Energy Charter Treaty which resulted in an order for over $500 million in damages. The unsuccessful defendant applied to the High Court to resist enforcement of the award on the basis that, because the claimant had dishonestly misled the tribunal as to the value of a bid it relied upon to assess the level of damages awarded, enforcement of the award would be contrary to public policy in England and Wales, as it gave effect to fraud. The application has yet to be determined, but the High Court has allowed it to proceed to trial.[97] This may demonstrate a willingness to hear public policy arguments against enforcement in circumstances where the US and Swedish courts previously seised of the same question were not so willing.[98]

Competition law arguments may also form the basis of resistance of an arbitral award on public policy grounds. In the seminal *Eco Swiss* judgment referred to in section 4, the ECJ considered a question from the Supreme Court of the Netherlands as to whether, if an award is found to have been made pursuant to an agreement that was anti-competitive (ie, contrary to Article 81 of the EC Treaty, now Article 101 of the TFEU), enforcement of that award should be refused on public policy grounds. Importantly, the ECJ responded that considerations of EU law may be relevant for the purposes of determining whether an award is enforceable and, in particular, Article 101 was of such fundamental importance as to amount to a rule of public policy for the purposes of the New York Convention.[99]

---

95   Convention on the Recognition and Enforcement of Foreign Arbitral Awards 1958, Article V(2).
96   W Ma, "Recommendations on public policy in the enforcement of arbitral awards", 2009, 75(1) *Arbitration* 14.
97   *Anatolie Stati v Kazakhstan* [2017] EWHC 1348 (Comm).
98   See the judgment of the US District Court for the District of Columbia in *Stati v Republic of Kazakhstan* [2018] Docket No 1: 2014cv01638 and the judgment of the Stockholm District Council of 24 January 2018, both upholding the award.
99   *Eco Swiss China Time Ltd v Benetton International NV* (C126/97) [1999] ECR I-3055 (ECJ).

It has since become clear (within the European Union at least) that competition law matters are capable of standing in the way of the enforcement of an arbitral award on public policy grounds. The corollary of this is that arbitral tribunals should consider carefully whether the claim before them raises any competition law issues that could potentially threaten the enforceability of the award. In other words, arbitrators should consider competition law issues to the extent they fall within the scope of the arbitration agreement on the basis that this is inherent to their obligation to deliver a binding and enforceable award.[100] In practice, this generally means that arbitrators are keen to ensure that competition law issues are given a proper airing so as to guard against a risk of subsequent challenge under the New York Convention. As noted in section 6, this can have a knock-on effect on, for example, the approach to disclosure, as the nature of competition law issues may lead arbitrators to mandate a more expansive approach to disclosure than would apply in cases which do not involve competition law arguments.

8. Conclusion

It is increasingly common for competition law issues to be considered by arbitral tribunals, including in the energy sector. Historic concerns as to the suitability of arbitration to resolve competition law disputes have now largely been overcome. These days, a more likely bone of contention is whether the particular competition dispute falls within the scope of an arbitration clause.

The effect of the increasing number of competition law arbitrations is that an increasing number of practising arbitrators have competition law expertise. This – together with the nature of competition law issues, which typically require an understanding of how the relevant markets operate – means that, as in competition proceedings pursued before the courts, expert evidence may often be crucial. It may also mean that disclosure becomes more extensive than would typically be seen in a 'standard' arbitration. While such developments may reduce the cost advantage of arbitration over court proceedings, they are unlikely to lead to a significant change in the belief of many companies that arbitration is a desirable means of resolving their disputes. Accordingly, it is likely that a significant number of competition law disputes in the energy sector will continue to be resolved by way of arbitration.

The authors would like to thank Tom Cummins for his comments on an earlier draft of this chapter.

---

100   JW Barratt and D Foster, "European Law and International Arbitration" in *European & Middle Eastern Arbitration Review* 2010.

Dispute funding and the energy sector

Oliver Gayner
Tom Glasgow
Nathan Landis
IMF Bentham Ltd

1. Introduction

The energy sector is steeped in complex, international, capital-intensive projects and transactions. Long-term commercial cooperation, political instability and cultural differences prompt a desire for commercial certainty and neutrality, which can be met by the reference of commercial disputes to international arbitration. One leading arbitrator has described the energy sector as "the poster boy of arbitral globalisation", noting that "there is scarcely a major energy sector contract (whether oil, gas, electric, nuclear, wind or solar) that does not call for disputes to be resolved before an independent and neutral arbitral tribunal".[1]

As the use of international arbitration in the energy sector has grown, so too have the complexity, cost and associated risk of international arbitration as a form of dispute resolution.[2] Users of the arbitral process are increasingly looking for innovative ways to finance their cases, manage risks and reduce costs. This has contributed to an exponential rise in the use of third-party dispute finance – a progressively sophisticated global industry, with an estimated worth of over $10 billion and growing.[3]

Given the prevalence of arbitration in the energy sector, it is reasonable to assume that the industry will also become the 'poster boy' for arbitration funding. It is appropriate, therefore, that any modern guide to international arbitration in the energy sector include a discussion of third-party dispute funding.

This chapter is intended to provide a practical guide to the use of dispute funding in the energy sector. The first part provides an overview of the development of the dispute funding industry, the characteristics of those seeking funding and what one may expect to happen during the dispute

---

1   J William Rowley QC (2017), "The Guide to Energy Arbitrations", *Global Arbitration Review*, 2nd Edition, Editor's Preface, pvii.
2   In the *2018 International Arbitration Survey: The Evolution of International Arbitration*, conducted by Queen Mary University of London and White Case LLP, 67% of participants cited cost as the "worst characteristic of arbitration". The cost of arbitration is often compounded by the international nature of the dispute, requiring multi-jurisdictional and often specialist legal teams, as well as institutional fees, arbitrator costs and hearing venue hire.
3   International Council for Commercial Arbitration-Queen Mary Taskforce on Third-Party Funding in International Arbitration (April 2018), p17.

funding process. The second part briefly considers specific types of energy-related disputes and how their characteristics may or may not appeal to a dispute funder.

2. Dispute funding

2.1 What is dispute funding?

Parties to international arbitration can obtain funding or reduce their risks in many ways. These include traditional means such as insurance, bank loans, corporate finance and retaining lawyers on a success or contingency fee basis. A broad definition of 'dispute funding' could therefore encompass numerous risk mitigation tools.[4]

In the modern context, however, references to third-party funding or dispute finance are typically to a non-recourse financing arrangement where an otherwise uninterested party agrees to meet the costs of a party to a dispute in exchange for a share in the commercial benefit obtained on a successful outcome. The non-recourse nature of the arrangement means that the funder has no recourse against the funded party if the case is unsuccessful: the funder must meet the costs of the dispute and possibly the adverse costs ordered against the funded party.

2.2 Development of the industry and rising demand

The concept of commercial dispute funding was pioneered in Australia in the 1990s, in the insolvency sector. IMF Bentham Limited became the world's first publicly listed funder in 2001. Dispute funding soon caught on in the United Kingdom and more recently the United States, where funding by contingency fees has been prevalent for many years. In these jurisdictions, well-established, sophisticated and competitive dispute funding markets now exist.

Elsewhere, the use of dispute funding continues to develop, led by international centres for dispute resolution. In 2017 Asia's principal international arbitration hubs, Hong Kong and Singapore, both passed legislation expressly permitting third-party funding of international arbitration and associated court proceedings – a clear recognition of the global trend towards dispute finance and the need to adapt to meet the demands of commercial parties.[5]

Supply is also increasing, as investors seek meaningful returns from investments that are not directly correlated with volatile and unpredictable financial markets. The past years have seen numerous new entrants in the

---

4   Indeed, the definition of 'third-party dispute finance' has been the subject of considerable debate among commentators, regulators, lawyers and funders. In a recent report produced by the International Council for Commercial Arbitration-Queen Mary Taskforce on Third-Party Funding in International Arbitration (April 2018), the taskforce dedicated some 30 pages to the consideration of various definitions.

5   Civil Law Act (Cap 43), ss 5A and 5B and associated regulations (Singapore); and Arbitration Ordinance (Cap 609), Part 10A and Mediation Ordinance (Cap 620) Part 7A (Hong Kong).

dispute finance market and established players are continuing to raise additional capital for investment.

2.3 Who is seeking funding and why?

Despite its origins in helping impecunious claimants to obtain access to justice, modern dispute finance is not just for those who cannot pay. Recent industry growth has been driven, in part, by well-resourced, financially capable parties simply seeking to shift, or share, the cost and risk of commercial disputes to a third party.

Funded costs might include some or all of the following:

- legal costs and disbursements;
- expert fees;
- institutional costs;
- arbitrator fees; and
- payment of security for costs or adverse costs if a case is unsuccessful.

Shifting responsibility for these costs to the funder means that the litigation expenses no longer drag down the profit and loss of the business. In this way the business can mitigate its potential downside risk, while retaining the bulk of any commercial benefit and freeing up cash to be spent elsewhere. Such arrangements are increasingly used by both large and small companies as a flexible tool to help manage cash-flow and legal budgets as well as risk.

(a) Claimants

Claimants are the most easily identifiable candidates for dispute funding. Claims in damages or for a clearly defined and measurable commercial benefit provide a simple platform to calculate and assign the funder its costs and agreed return on a successful resolution.

A claimant may seek funding at various stages of a dispute. Funders can add most value prior to initiation of proceedings, so that the financial arrangements can be set as an integral part of the overall dispute strategy from the outset; however, funding is often sought partway through a case (as costs escalate or as the merits of the case become more defined), or at the enforcement stage, once an award is obtained.

(b) Respondents

Although respondents represent 50% of the disputes market, funding of respondents is less common.

The most likely opportunity to secure funding is where the respondent has a meritorious counterclaim such that the likely net outcome is an amount payable to the respondent. A portfolio financing arrangement (discussed below) might also permit the allocation of costs to a defence within a wider portfolio.

Other than by legal expenses insurers, standalone respondent funding is currently rare. Although there may be a measurable commercial benefit retained by a successful respondent (ie, retention or reduction in the amount claimed by the claimant), there is no flow of money in favour of the respondent (aside from the recovery of costs) from which the funder might derive its return on investment. However, as the sophistication of the industry develops, the use of innovative funding solutions by respondents is expected to grow.

(c) Dispute portfolios

The financing of dispute portfolios (ie, claims grouped together) is increasingly common and is used by large corporates and law firms.

Although any portfolio arrangement will be tailored to the circumstances and may take many forms, the additional benefits to the funder and the funded party are usually derived from some form of cross-collateralisation throughout the portfolio. The funder's return will be linked to the overall performance of the portfolio rather than individual claims and its risk is therefore spread across a range of disputes carrying different risk profiles. In such cases, the funder may accept a lower overall return and the arrangement enables quicker deployment of funds to individual cases, often on pre-arranged terms.

For corporates, a portfolio arrangement may also allow greater flexibility to offset defence costs and the costs of disputes with non-monetary claims. The funder will recover its costs and return from the revenue-generating claims within the portfolio. In some cases, the business might also secure an advance on working capital against the claim value of the portfolio, to deploy within the business or simply to declare as profit.

These benefits can be applied in any combination of disputes and need not involve large portfolios. For example, a construction contractor may have a claim against a subcontractor while also defending a claim from the project owner. The contractor might seek dispute funding and cross-collateralise to fund both its claim and defence costs.

For law firms, similar arrangements can be structured to support the firm's portfolio of contingency or success fee cases. The funder essentially assists the firm to meet its regular overheads as well as case-specific disbursements. In exchange, the funder is paid from the contingency or success fees generated by the firm.

2.4 The dispute funding process

The features of a dispute finance arrangement can vary greatly from case to case. Individual funders will have different assessment processes, although commercial dispute funders will typically apply the following basic investment criteria.

(a) Basic investment criteria

At a minimum, a funder will want to ensure that:

- the case is meritorious;
- the economics of the investment and the claim are likely to provide a reasonable return to all parties; and
- there is a high prospect of recovery.

Merits: The degree of merit required to satisfy a funder's board or investment committee is highly subjective. Some funders or their brokers may require prospects of success expressed in percentage terms, often so that it may be incorporated into some form of algorithmic risk assessment or pricing model. For this reason, lawyers are often now asked to ascribe percentage figures to the prospects of success (although what makes a case 60% likely to succeed as opposed to 62% or 65% is often not clear).

Funders will give greater weight to documentary evidence and clear points of law which provide predictability. Cases heavily reliant on contested facts and oral evidence are likely to carry greater risk.

Economics: Assessing the 'economics' of a case will involve weighing the funder's likely exposure (ie, the legal and other costs to be invested, as well as potential exposure to adverse costs) against the likely recovery on resolution of the matter. Approaches will vary considerably; however, large commercial funders such as IMF Bentham will typically seek to fund cases where the economics permit the funded party to retain more than half of the resolution sum. For this reason, funders often require a minimum ratio between the likely resolution sum and costs of investment. The wider the ratio, the more attractive the economics of the case to the funder. A typical benchmark in the funding industry is 10:1, meaning a project budget of up to $1 million for a meritorious case worth $10 million.

A funder will tend to focus on the conservative likely outcome, rather than the maximum potential claim value, considering the legal, factual and technical issues that might reduce the headline figure in any final award. The prospect of settlement and the respondent's ability to pay will also factor into the likely level of recovery. Those seeking funding should therefore avoid overselling the value of their claim. A balanced, realistic approach will better assist the funder in the assessment process.

A similar, measured approach will be taken to the assessment of the project budget. The funder will likely require a detailed budget that accounts for legal and associated costs, arbitrator fees, institutional costs, experts, travel, disbursements, general file management and prospective contingencies. This provides an accurate estimate of the funder's total investment. Some funders may require a fee cap or fixed fee from the legal team, or an agreement on the treatment of budget overruns, to provide further certainty over the budget.

Recoverability: The non-recourse nature of a typical arrangement means that the funder does not receive its costs or a return unless there is a successful recovery. For this reason, the counterparty must have the ability to meet any award made against it or to settle at a figure that supports the economic assessment of the case (discussed above). If enforcement action is likely to be required in order to recover, the counterparty must have identifiable assets in jurisdictions where funded enforcement action is permissible and likely to be effective.

The relatively simple and wide-ranging enforceability of arbitral awards across jurisdictions pursuant to the New York and International Centre for the Settlement of Investment Disputes Conventions allows funders and funded parties to plan an enforcement strategy at the outset of a matter. It is not uncommon to draw on asset-tracing and financial investigation expertise in developing these strategies, which often involves a multi-asset, multi-jurisdictional approach.

(b)   The investment – types of costs funded
In general, the types of costs met by funders can be characterised as follows.

Seed funding: Expenses required to allow a prospective case to be fully investigated. These costs might include:
*   an opinion from counsel on the legal merits;
*   an investigative report on the financial position of the counterparty;
*   in insolvency cases, public examination of directors; or
*   an initial quantum assessment by a forensic accountant or quantity surveyor.

These costs are often incurred prior to finalising an unconditional funding agreement and recovered by the funder (from the recoveries) if the case is funded.

Case-related costs: Legal fees, arbitrator fees, institutional costs, expert fees, travel costs and other incurred towards the funded matter.

Adverse costs: Some, but not all, funders may provide a contractual indemnity against adverse costs payable to the counterparty if the case is unsuccessful. Others may seek to cap any adverse costs exposure or insist that the funded party takes out an adverse costs (ATE) insurance policy.[6]

---

6   'ATE' stands for 'after the event'. The approach varies considerably among funders and if insurance is required, that additional cost should be considered in evaluating the commercial benefit of the funding arrangement to the funded party. Even if the funder absorbs the cost of the ATE policy premium, that cost is likely to be recovered from any resolution sum and possibly multiplied to calculate the funder's return on investment.

Security for costs: If security for costs is ordered by a tribunal, the funder may agree to pay the amount of security required or to issue a bank guarantee.

Working capital: Where the economics of a case allow it and the relevant jurisdiction permits, funders may be prepared to advance capital (repayable from the recoveries in the arbitration) to the funded party for use generally within its business or other interests. This may be required simply as a means of alternative financing for a solvent organisation; or alternatively, it may be needed to keep an impecunious party afloat pending the outcome of the dispute.

(c)   *Return structures*
A funder will expect a return commensurate with the risk of the investment.

There are many ways in which the funder's return might be calculated. It may include a fixed fee component, a multiple of invested capital, a percentage of the recovered sum or a combination of these methods. In a recent example found to be representative of standard market rates, the funder was entitled to a return equal to the higher of three times its invested capital or 35% of the recovered sum.[7]

The funder's return will likely increase over set time increments or by reference to anticipated stages in the project, making the return proportionate to the length of time its capital has been at risk.

The wide range in approaches to return structures and the complexities created by combined calculation methods, incremental returns and/or additional ATE insurance costs mean that the comparison of funding arrangements may require, at a minimum, some form of basic financial modelling. While one funder may propose a lower percentage-based return than its competitor, the ultimate outcome may be less favourable to the funded party when other aspects of the arrangement are considered. Prospective parties to funding arrangements should take care to properly analyse the impact of all variables in the return calculation.

(d)   *Case assessment process*
The process typically begins with a self-assessment of the suitability of a matter for funding and investigation into available dispute finance providers. Deciding which funders to approach should involve careful consideration of a funder's basic investment criteria, business model, financial stability and source of funds. Any reluctance to provide insight into the funder's track-record and source of funds should be met with caution.

Once a decision has been made to approach a funder, time should be taken to prepare the case for presentation. As a preliminary step, the applicant should

---

7   *Norscott v Essar* [2016] EWHC 2361 (Comm), paras 22 and 25. In ordering that the respondent pay the claimant's dispute funding costs in that case, the arbitrator had heard and accepted expert evidence that this funding structure reflected standard market rates.

consider producing a short briefing memorandum from its lawyers to address the basic considerations:

- details of the claimant and respondent;
- the basis of the claim and its perceived strength;
- any likely defences;
- the claim value or settlement range; and
- the likely cost of pursuing the claim to resolution.

Key supporting evidence can be attached. A well-prepared memorandum of this sort will enable prospective funders to form a preliminary view on whether the case is likely to fit the funder's investment criteria.

Based on its initial assessment of the case, an experienced funder should be able to provide indicative commercial terms or decline to fund. Indicative terms are often recorded in a term sheet or in the form of a conditional funding offer. If the funder's further due diligence is likely to require significant time or expense, the funder may ask for an exclusivity period in which to carry out its assessment. The time needed will depend on the complexity of the case, the degree to which the applicant has prepared and the efficiency with which the applicant, funder, legal team and any experts can work together.

This detailed assessment of legal, factual and expert issues at the outset of the case can be beneficial in its own right. If significant issues are identified, the wasted cost of pursuing the case may be avoided. If the case continues, funded or not, it will have had the benefit of stress-testing and a refined case strategy to see it through to resolution efficiently.

In many cases, the final decision to offer formal funding terms will be taken by an investment committee or the funder's board on recommendation from the case assessment team.

(e) Confidentiality and privilege

The assessment of a case will necessarily require confidential and privileged information to be shared with the funder for due diligence. In some cases, highly sensitive commercial information or trade secrets may be at issue. Ensuring that confidentiality and privilege are maintained is important.

Steps can and should be taken to document the funder's interest in receiving any information. This should help to ensure that privilege attaches to or is maintained in any communications with the funder; however, the concerns and protocols will vary depending upon local laws. In many common law jurisdictions, well-established rules of privilege can be relied upon to draw comfort that the disclosure of communications with funders is unlikely to be compelled if appropriate protocols are followed.[8] In civil law jurisdictions,

---

8   See, for example, *Hastie Group Ltd (in liq) v Moore* [2016] NSWCA 305; (2016) 339 ALR 635.

where discovery is not readily available, the risk of compelled disclosure is lower. However, caution should be exercised and appropriate measures should be taken to protect privilege and confidentiality in the specific circumstances of each case.

(f) Funding agreement

There is no standard form of arbitration funding agreement; however, long-established funders will have well-established precedents that have evolved over years of use.

A range of guidelines have now been produced by a number of arbitration bodies in Asia to assist those entering funding arrangements.[9] One commendable example, endorsed by international funders, is the Singapore Institute of Arbitrators Guidelines for Third Party Funders. These guidelines provide a clear and succinct checklist for an arbitration funding agreement.

(g) Involvement during the matter

A critical feature of any funding agreement is the definition of the parties' respective roles over the life of the proceedings. The extent to which funders are involved in day-to-day and strategic decision making has been a source of some debate among users of arbitration, lawyers, regulators and the judiciary.

Parties should be careful to ensure that funding agreements are structured appropriately to avoid or minimise any risk of challenge to their lawfulness on the ground that the funder has undue control of the proceedings. Parties to international transactions may also have regard to the legal framework for dispute finance when considering their choice of arbitral seat for dispute resolution.

(h) Control and reporting

Most funding agreements are structured to maintain a clear separation between the duties owed by lawyers to the funded party (which remain as they would in a typical lawyer-client relationship) and the financial or other interest of the funder. 'Soft-law' guidance serves as a helpful reminder to lawyers and funders to ensure this distinction of responsibilities is clearly defined and maintained.

In situations where a funder's involvement is passive, the funder will rely on regular reporting and monitoring of its investment. In any case, most funders will expect to be consulted on key strategic matters, have direct access to the legal team and be involved in settlement decisions (discussed below).

Where the parties agree and the legal framework permits, the funded party may wish to involve the funder to a greater extent. A well-established

---

9   See, for example, guidelines published by the Singapore Institute of Arbitrators, CIETAC Hong Kong and the Law Society of Singapore, among others.

commercial funder will possess valuable insights into legal and technical issues, procedural and commercial strategy, arbitrator appointments and more. Funded parties often seek to draw on this expertise to add value to the legal team at no further cost. In some circumstances, day-to-day project management of the case may be passed to the funder, subject always to the funded party's overarching control. Such arrangements are common in funded class actions in Australia, for example. Whatever the intended arrangement, parties should take care to clearly identify respective roles in their funding agreement.

(i) Settlement

As a prudent measure to protect its investment, a funder will typically insist that it retains a say in any proposed settlement. In the event that a case is discontinued or settled at an inappropriate figure, the funder may be unable to recover its investment or any return. For this reason, a funding agreement will typically require that the funder be notified of any settlement offer, and that any disagreement between the funder and the funded party as to the reasonableness of that offer be referred to a specified dispute resolution mechanism.

(j) Termination

A funder will also typically safeguard its investment by retaining the ability to cease funding in appropriate circumstances. The funding agreement is unlikely to be an unconditional agreement to fund the case to its conclusion; rather, continued funding will be subject to an ongoing assessment of its merits and the likelihood of successful recovery.

Termination of any funding arrangement is unlikely to be taken lightly. In most cases, especially if the case is withdrawn, the funder will lose its investment up to termination and potentially remain accountable for adverse costs to that point. For this reason, termination is likely only where there is a material deterioration in the merits or prospects of recovery or in circumstances where the funded party is in breach of the funding agreement.

(k) Disclosure, conflicts of interest and security for costs

International guidance suggests that an arbitrator should disclose any interest (whether actual, potential or perceived) in a third-party funder once he or she is aware of the funder's involvement in the case.[10]

In some jurisdictions, parties or counsel to funded arbitrations, are obliged by law to disclose the existence and identity of any funder.[11] In other

---

10   See, for example, Singapore International Arbitration Centre Practice Note 01/17 (31 March 2017), *Note to Parties and Arbitral Tribunals on the Conduct of the Arbitration Under the ICC Rules of Arbitration*; ICC International Court of Arbitration, s 24; and International Bar Association *Guidelines on Conflicts of Interest in International Arbitration* (2014), General Standards 1-6.

11   Legal Profession (Professional Conduct) Rules 2015, Rules 49A (Singapore); and Arbitration Ordinance (Cap 609) (Hong Kong), s98U (passed into law, but not yet in force at the date of this publication).

jurisdictions, there may be a strategic decision to be made in this regard. The disclosure of the existence of funding may prompt an application for security for costs (discussed below). However, disclosure may help to avoid any actual, potential or perceived conflict of interest, with the potential to undermine any successful award. Disclosure can also send a signal to the other side that the claim has been approved by an objective commercial funder and that the party is well resourced to see it through. These sentiments are often strong drivers for settlement and, in some cases, a reason why a party seeks funding.

The relevance of third-party funding to questions of security for costs is case dependent. Some tribunals have argued that the simple existence of third-party funding could constitute grounds for ordering security for costs in an investment arbitration.[12] This principle is controversial and has not been followed by subsequent investment arbitration tribunals.[13] As noted above, many solvent and well-resourced claimants choose dispute funding simply to manage cash flow and risk. Even in the case of an impecunious funded party, the existence of a funder may, in fact, improve the likelihood of a respondent recovering any adverse costs, particularly if the funder (or ATE insurer) is willing to provide an undertaking to the court or tribunal to meet such costs on the funded party's behalf.

Funded parties disclosing their means of meeting an adverse costs award at the same time as disclosing the existence of third-party funding may avoid a security for costs application.

(l) *Resolution, payment, priority and waterfalls*

Upon the successful recovery of any commercial benefit, the funder's costs and return will be distributed in accordance with the funding agreement. Typically, the funder will take an assignment of the proceeds of the case and may hold the right to register a security interest over other commercial benefits received. Most funders will require priority of payment or payment pursuant to an agreed waterfall structure with the funded party and other stakeholders entitled to share in the proceeds of the case.

3. Dispute funding in the energy sector

3.1 Suitability and current trends

Many international arbitrations in the energy sector are suitable for dispute finance insofar as they satisfy the criteria identified above. Common disputes include disagreements about the construction or operations of oil and gas

---

12 *RSM Production Corporation v Saint Lucia* (ICSID Case ARB/12/10), Assenting Reasons of Gavin Griffith (12 August 2014).

13 *EuroGas Inc v Slovak Republic*, (ICSID Case ARB/14/14), Procedural Order 3 (23 June 2015); *South American Silver Limited v The Plurinational State of Bolivia*, (PCA Case 2013-15), Procedural Order 10 (11 January 2016), para 77.

extraction projects and power production projects, commodity contract disputes and joint venture disputes.

The Energy Charter Treaty (1994),[14] under which a number of investor-state disputes in the energy sector have arisen,[15] contains no prohibitions on a claimant (or indeed a state[16]) utilising dispute finance. The current trend appears to be to accept dispute funding but seek to regulate it – the Comprehensive Economic Trade Agreement entered into between Canada and the European Union is an example of this.[17]

One driver of change in the energy sector is the transition of energy supply away from higher-carbon (oil and coal) projects towards lower-carbon and renewable energy projects, although the pace of that transition is somewhat uncertain.[18] This change is producing a new range of disputes being presented for funding which raise novel issues for the energy sector.[19] The challenge for dispute funders is to properly assess these new cases without the benefit of existing precedents and prior experience.

Despite these ongoing changes, disputes common to the energy sector are frequently referred to funders and certain categories of disputes present unique risks and considerations. Some of the most common categories of energy sector arbitrations are considered below in this context.

3.2 Considerations in specific energy sector cases

(a) Investor-state cases

The energy and mining sector is the largest source of cases registered by the International Centre for the Settlement of Investment Disputes (ICSID).[20]

Many investor-state cases in the energy sector involve an investor whose primary investment is in assets located in a single jurisdiction. When a state violates an investor's treaty-based protections and that violation affects the investor's ability to generate cash flow from its assets, dispute funding gives the investor the financial ability to prosecute its claims against a state.

---

14   The Energy Charter Treaty entered into force in April 1998. It presently has 54 signatories (including the European Union and Euratom).

15   The *ICSID Caseload – Statistics* (Issue 2017-2) indicates that 13% of cases commenced in fiscal year 2017 as at 30 June 2017 relied on the Energy Charter Treaty as the basis for establishing ICSID's jurisdiction. That proportion dropped slightly in fiscal year 2018, with only 9% of cases relying on the Energy Charter Treaty.

16   Although unusual, one example of a state utilising dispute finance was *RSM Production Corporation v Grenada* (see para 5 of the decision in ICSID Case ARB/05/14 Annulment Proceedings).

17   Article 8.26 specifically deals with third-party funding in the context of investor-state disputes.

18   BP Energy Outlook 2018, www.bp.com/en/global/corporate/energy-economics/energy-outlook.html.

19   A recent example of these novel issues was the investor-state dispute in *Eiser Infrastructure Ltd v Kingdom of Spain* (ICSID Case ARB/13/36), which concerned the effect of electricity market reforms implemented by the Spanish government which removed incentives to solar energy projects. The claimants were partially successful in that case (obtaining an award of €128 million), although the award is the subject of pending annulment proceedings.

20   The *ICSID Caseload – Statistics* (Issue 2017-2) indicates that 41% of cases commenced in fiscal year 2017 as at 30 June 2017 are from those economic sectors. In fiscal year 2018, the proportion was 37% of cases.

Although such activities are a relatively recent phenomenon, there is a body of case law in investment treaty cases where third-party funding has been considered and largely accepted.[21] There is also an emerging trend of not-for-profit funding of states defending claims, particularly those involving public health issues.[22]

As claims made in investment treaty arbitrations are unsuccessful more often than not,[23] they are likely to be considered relatively high risk. Nonetheless, the potential rewards are high, with the average claim size in investor-state cases estimated to be in the region of $490 million.[24]

These types of cases are distinguishable from commercial arbitrations in terms of their length (ICSID cases run longer than commercial arbitration cases) and costs (parties incur an average of $8 million running cases heard by ICSID tribunals as opposed to parties to commercial arbitration cases, which have an average spend of £1.5 million).[25] This increases the funder's investment and potential time to recovery.

These cases are generally factually intensive and may require preliminary expert evidence to assist the funder to understand the claim. In particular, investors' claims often seek damages for the loss of anticipated profits from the investment in question. Quantifying this loss can be difficult, frequently resulting in high-value headline figures which are substantially reduced by the tribunal in any award.[26] A funder may well require the help of experts to properly assess the viability of such claims at the outset.

Further complications may arise when dealing with developing countries as respondents, particularly where government institutions may not be as robust as is usually the case in developed countries. The prospects of recovery may not be as strong and the potential for settlement may be at the whim of political influences. Risks of influence or intimidation may also arise in circumstances where key witnesses reside in the jurisdiction against which the claim is asserted. All of these factors may add to the funder's perception of risk and the required level of due diligence.

---

21   See, for example, *Oxus Gold plc v Republic of Uzbekistan*, UNCITRAL, Final Award, 17 December 2015 at [127].

22   In 2015, Bloomberg Philanthropies and the Bill and Melinda Gates Foundation announced the creation of the Anti-Tobacco Trade Litigation Fund, to provide financial support for low and middle-income countries that have been sued by tobacco companies in investor-state cases.

23   See *Investment Treaty Arbitration: Cost, duration and size of claims all show steady increase* (2017), a survey by Allen & Overy LLP, www.allenovery.com/publications/en-gb/Pages/Investment-Treaty-Arbitration-cost-duration-and-size-of-claims-all-show-steady-increase.aspx.

24   *Ibid.*

25   O'Reilly, Michael, "Costs in International Arbitration: London, September 27–28 2011" (2012) 78 *Arbitration*, Issue 1.

26   Although the average claim size in investor-state arbitration is above $490 million, the average award is approximately $76 million. See *Investment Treaty Arbitration: Cost, duration and size of claims all show steady increase* (2017), a survey by Allen & Overy LLP, www.allenovery.com/publications/en-gb/Pages/Investment-Treaty-Arbitration-cost-duration-and-size-of-claims-all-show-steady-increase.aspx.

(b)   ***Construction cases***

With a global construction sector worth $10 trillion per year,[27] it is inevitable that a sizeable number of disputes arise in the industry. Construction projects typically involve multiple parties (project owners, contractors, subcontractors and government authorities), all with competing interests. This provides fertile ground for disputes, which are often referred to arbitration.

At the outset, a potential funder will be interested in understanding whether the parties intend to maintain ongoing commercial relationships. This information is important because the funder will need to factor into its review the potential that settlement may be subject to a 'relationship discount', or granting future contracts in place of damages.

As with investor-state disputes, construction cases often require extensive due diligence, given their factually intensive and technical nature. These cases may require preliminary expert evidence on questions of both liability and quantum to assist the funder to understand the basis for the claim and to assess likely recovery. The likelihood of a counterclaim or cross-claim will also be relevant, given the prevalence of competing claims within construction projects.

(c)   ***Long-term supply contracts and gas price reviews***

Gas price reviews will generally occur several times over the life of a contract and require both specialist counsel and specialist experts. A funder in such a case may need to accept a relatively passive role because of the strategic importance of the review to the funded party (be it the buyer or seller). Although a funder will need to factor in a higher cost associated with the legal team and experts, such costs may be offset by the limited factual matters in dispute. The commercial emphasis of gas price review arbitrations means that the funder will need to take into account both legal and commercial considerations when assessing the likely outcome.

Generally, disputes over long-term supply contracts (including gas price reviews) do not rely on a binary outcome. Settlement is a real possibility, which may make such claims attractive to dispute funders. However, a resolution to a dispute over a long-term supply contract often involves agreement to revised ongoing prices or quantities. The commercial benefit to the funded party may therefore accrue over time and the funding arrangement will need to allow for the calculation and distribution of the funder's return accordingly.

(d)   ***Joint venture disputes***

Although joint ventures are an extremely common form of ownership in the

---

27   "The construction industry's productivity problem", *The Economist*, 17 August 2017, www.economist.com/news/leaders/21726693-and-how-governments-can-catalyse-change-construction-industrys-productivity-problem.

energy sector, they are productive of disputes – approximately 25% of joint ventures in the construction industry end up in a dispute.[28]

Some joint venture disputes may not be suitable for dispute funding, particularly those cases where declaratory relief is sought (eg, removal of the operator or manager of the joint venture), or where the relief may be difficult to value for the purposes of calculating the funder's entitlement (eg, where the claimant seeks the transfer of shares in the joint venture).

Joint venture disputes also present challenges common to other energy sector disputes, including the following:

- They are often factually intensive (failed joint ventures, in particular, are likely to involve hotly contested mutual allegations of repudiatory conduct);
- One joint venture party may be a local entity in a developing nation or a state-owned enterprise (which raises similar issues to investor-state claims, above); and
- Claims arising from failed joint ventures often seek damages for lost profits, the calculation of which may be speculative and may require an early expert assessment if the case is to be considered for funding.

4. Conclusion

The dispute finance industry is growing in size and sophistication to cater to the needs of modern-day corporations and users of international arbitration. The result is a highly adaptive, innovative tool to manage risk, reduce cost, raise capital and control cash flow. The nature and prevalence of disputes in the energy sector provide ample opportunity to secure the benefits of dispute finance. International disputes lawyers and industry participants should actively investigate financing options for current and future disputes, develop familiarity with the various offerings and stay informed of developments. There is no doubt that dispute finance is becoming and will remain a mainstay of the international arbitration landscape.

---

28   Global Construction Disputes Report 2016, Arcadis, www.arcadis.com/media/3/E/7/%7B3E7BDCDC-0434-4237-924F-739240965A90%7DGlobal%20Construction%20Disputes%20Report%202016.pdf.

Enforcement of awards

Rajinder Bassi
Jon Newman
Kirkland & Ellis

1.   Introduction

1.1   The importance of enforcement to international commercial arbitration

Over the past few decades, international commercial arbitration has become firmly established as a means for commercial entities to resolve their disputes. As a form of dispute resolution, it appeals to such parties for a number of reasons, including:

- the ability it gives the parties to agree the procedure to resolve the dispute beforehand;
- the final and binding nature of arbitration;
- the confidentiality of the process; and
- most notably, an almost worldwide enforcement regime which allows parties to readily enforce an arbitral award rendered in one country in another country where the party against which the award is sought to be enforced may have assets.

The fact that the parties to an arbitration can have some certainty that they should be able to enforce an award almost anywhere in the world has arguably done more than anything else to support and foster the development of international commercial arbitration.

This certainty derives from the United Nations Convention on the Recognition and Enforcement of Foreign Arbitral Awards (the New York Convention), signed in New York in 1958. As of November 2018, 159 countries had become contracting states according to the status table published by the United Nations Commission on International Trade Law (UNCITRAL).[1] While this means that approximately 40 states are not parties to the New York Convention, by far the vast majority of all countries involved in material international commerce are contracting states. So important is the New York Convention to the viability of international commercial arbitration, allowing as it does international parties to effectively have their awards recognised and

---

1   www.uncitral.org/uncitral/en/uncitral_texts/arbitration/NYConvention_status.html.

enforced around the world, it is usually considered the cornerstone of international commercial arbitration.[2]

The New York Convention sets out the general obligation on contracting states to recognise and enforce non-domestic arbitral awards. It also sets out certain grounds for refusal of enforcement, which, if a party against which an award is sought to be enforced can prove existed, entitles the domestic court in the contracting state in which enforcement is sought to refuse enforcement. These grounds have in some cases been interpreted differently by courts in different contracting states, which is discussed further below. However, enforcement of arbitral awards in practice is not necessarily as easy as the New York Convention framework might suggest.

This chapter:

- provides an overview of the framework for the enforcement of arbitral awards pursuant to the New York Convention; and
- discusses the grounds which may entitle a court to refuse to enforce an award under the New York Convention, and how those grounds may be interpreted differently in different jurisdictions.

1.2   Recognition and enforcement

At the outset, and although this chapter is principally concerned with issues of enforcement, it is important to note the difference between 'recognition' and 'enforcement' of arbitral awards. The New York Convention provides, at Article III, that "Each Contracting State shall recognise arbitral awards as binding and enforce them in accordance with the rules of procedure of the territory where the award is relied upon".

Recognition of a foreign arbitral award involves seeking to secure from a court in a contracting state in which enforcement is sought a declaration or acceptance that the award has the same status as a domestic award. It is a defensive mechanism, which prevents new proceedings being brought on the same issues in dispute. Once recognised, an award may be enforced or, where applicable, used as a defence in, or set-off against, other legal proceedings. An award may be recognised without necessarily being enforced, but to enforce an award it first needs to be recognised. Seeking recognition as a first step in circumstances where a party refuses to voluntarily comply with an award after it is made may be enough to spur that party into compliance (or, where circumstances allow, into making a settlement offer on the award).

Enforcement of a foreign arbitral award involves seeking the domestic court's assistance in compelling the party against which the award was made to

2   Dr Reinmar Wolff (ed), "New York Convention on the Recognition and Enforcement of Foreign Arbitral Awards – Commentary", Verlag CH Beck oHG, 2012, p4; Nigel Blackaby, Constantine Partasides, Alan Redfern and Martin Hunter, *Redfern and Hunter on International Arbitration* (Sixth Edition), Oxford University Press, 2015, p617.

comply with that award. Under English law, for example, this means that an award is given the same effect as a domestic court judgment and the enforcing party has access to all legal means available to it to ensure that the party against which the award was made complies with its obligations (often, to pay damages and costs to the enforcing party).

Generally speaking, the rules of most arbitral institutions expressly state that an award is binding on the parties, and that the parties undertake to carry out an award without delay. Such an undertaking may also be included in arbitration agreements. As a result, most arbitral awards are complied with voluntarily, without the need for enforcement proceedings.[3] However, if an unsuccessful party refuses to carry out the award, the successful party may take enforcement steps to compel performance.

1.3 Final awards versus interim orders

It is also worth briefly discussing the difference between final awards and interim orders, and the enforcement implications of the latter. While the remainder of this chapter focuses on the enforcement of final awards, there is some debate over whether courts can and should enforce interim or provisional measures in the same manner as final awards.

Where a tribunal has issued a binding temporary order (designed to preserve the status quo pending the final award), it has no power directly to compel compliance with that order (other than perhaps to draw inferences or impose costs sanctions in the final award if the order is violated). Parties may therefore need to seek a court's assistance in compelling compliance. However, the New York Convention does not apply to interim provisional and conservatory measures. The UNCITRAL Model Law on International Commercial Arbitration 1985 (with amendments as adopted in 2006) provides at Article 17(H) that: "An interim measure issued by an arbitral tribunal shall be recognized as binding and, unless otherwise provided by the arbitral tribunal, enforced upon application to the competent court, irrespective of the country in which it was issued." Not all states, however, have incorporated the UNCITRAL Model Law (as discussed further below), or this particular article thereof, into their domestic arbitration legislation. Commentators have indicated that this situation is illogical. It violates common sense to enforce a final award under the New York Convention, but deny enforcement of an interim or preliminary order issued by the same tribunal presumably for the purposes of ensuring that the final award, when it is ultimately issued, is effective.[4]

---

3   *Redfern and Hunter*, p605.
4   *Wolff*, p48.

2. Framework for the enforcement of arbitral awards – the New York Convention

As noted above, in the opinion of many commentators and members of the international arbitration community, the New York Convention has done more than anything else to render international commercial arbitration a viable alternative means for resolving disputes. Articles I to IV of the New York Convention set out:

- the obligations on contracting states;
- the reservations that contracting states may make; and
- the requirements for recognition and enforcement.

2.1 Obligations on contracting states

Article I of the New York Convention provides that the convention "shall apply to the recognition and enforcement of arbitral awards made in the territory of a State other than the State where the recognition and enforcement of such awards are sought, and arising out of differences between persons, whether physical or legal". Article II obliges contracting states to recognise written arbitration agreements. It provides that: "Each Contracting State shall recognise an agreement in writing under which the parties undertake to submit to arbitration all or any differences which have arisen or which may arise between them in respect of a defined legal relationship, whether contractual or not, concerning a subject matter capable of settlement by arbitration." It also requires courts of contracting states to refer disputes to arbitration on the application of a party where the parties have entered into a valid arbitration agreement. Finally, Article III provides that contracting states recognise and enforce arbitral awards, and that there should "not be imposed substantially more onerous conditions or higher fees or charges on the recognition or enforcement of [international] arbitral awards...than are imposed on the recognition or enforcement of domestic arbitral awards".

2.2 Reservations

Article I (3) of the New York Convention allows contracting states, on the basis of reciprocity, to declare that they will apply the convention to the recognition and enforcement of awards made only in the territory of another contracting state (as opposed to any other state). More than half of all contracting states have adopted this reservation.[5]

This article also allows contracting states to declare that they will apply the convention only to differences arising out of legal relationships (whether contractual or otherwise) which are considered 'commercial' in nature under

---

5   See the UNCITRAL status table, notes (a) and (b), at www.uncitral.org/uncitral/en/uncitral_texts/arbitration/NYConvention_status.html.

their own domestic law. Slightly under half of all contracting states have adopted this reservation.[6]

2.3 Requirements for recognition and enforcement

Article IV of the New York Convention sets out what is required to obtain recognition and enforcement of an award. It provides that the party seeking recognition and enforcement shall, at the time of the application, supply to the court the duly authenticated original award (or a duly certified copy thereof), and the original arbitration agreement (or a duly certified copy thereof). Where either of these materials is not made in an official language of the country in which recognition and enforcement is sought, the applicant is required to supply a certified translation.

While the New York Convention sets out these basic requirements, and also provides that the recognition and enforcement of awards should not be subject to substantially more onerous conditions than those on the recognition and enforcement of domestic awards, each contracting state will have its own procedural requirements pursuant to domestic legislation and rules of procedure. These may include different requirements in respect of notice, service, limitation periods and other procedural steps. This is because the New York Convention obliges contracting states to enforce awards in accordance with the rules of procedure of the territory where the award is relied upon.

3. Grounds for refusing enforcement under the New York Convention

Article V(1) of the New York Convention sets out the exhaustive list of grounds on which a domestic court may refuse recognition and enforcement, if the party seeking to defend recognition and enforcement can prove the existence of one or more of those grounds. The Article V(1) grounds include the following:

- A party did not have capacity or the arbitration agreement is invalid under the law to which the parties have subjected it or, failing that, the law of the country where the award was made;
- A party was not given proper notice of the appointment of the arbitrator or was otherwise unable to present its case;
- The award deals with a difference not contemplated by or not falling within the terms of the submission to arbitration or contains decisions on matters beyond the scope of the submission to arbitration;
- The composition of the tribunal or arbitral procedure was not in accordance with the parties' agreement or, failing such agreement, was not in accordance with the laws of the courts where the arbitration took place; or

---

6   See the UNCITRAL status table, note (c), at www.uncitral.org/uncitral/en/uncitral_texts/arbitration/NYConvention_status.html.

- The award has not become binding or was set aside or suspended at the seat.

Article V(2) sets out the exhaustive list of grounds on which a domestic court may refuse recognition and enforcement if that court finds the existence of those grounds. The Article V(2) grounds include the following:

- The subject matter of the dispute was not capable of submission to arbitration under the law of the enforcement country; or
- Recognition and enforcement of the award would be contrary to the public policy of the enforcement country.

Certain commentators have pointed out that the Article V grounds are to be, and indeed have been, construed narrowly. For example, van den Berg notes that the Article V(1) grounds are accepted "in serious cases only", and that the Article V(2) grounds are accepted "in extreme cases only".[7] The manner in which these grounds have been accepted is discussed further below.

Before discussing the specific grounds themselves, however, it is worth providing some brief analysis as to courts' general approach to considering the grounds.

3.1   Prevalence of the grounds

The grounds have been widely incorporated into states' domestic arbitration legislation. The grounds are incorporated in the UNCITRAL Model Law at Article 36. The UNCITRAL Model Law was designed as a draft law for states to adopt, either wholesale or in part, when developing their own domestic arbitration laws. Around 80 states have now either wholly adopted the UNCITRAL Model Law or enacted legislation which is based on it.[8] The United Kingdom's Arbitration Act 1996, for example, contains many elements from the UNCITRAL Model Law, but does not incorporate it wholesale into domestic legislation. It does, however, specify (at Section 103) the circumstances in which an award may not be recognised or enforced (as based on the New York Convention and the UNCITRAL Model Law).

3.2   Exhaustive nature of the grounds

The list of grounds set out in Article V is exhaustive. Article V(1) expressly states that recognition and enforcement may be refused "only" if proof of the existence of one of the listed grounds is provided (although no express limitation is contained in Article V(2)). The exhaustive nature of this list has been confirmed

---

7   Albert Jan van den Berg, "The New York Convention of 1958: An Overview", www.arbitration-icca.org/media/0/12125884227980/new_york_convention_of_1958_overview.pdf, p13.
8   See the UNCITRAL Model Law status list at http://www.uncitral.org/uncitral/en/uncitral_texts/arbitration/1985Model_arbitration_status.html.

in case law internationally, which has generally recognised the pro-enforcement bias of the New York Convention. In England, the principle has been espoused in *Kanoria v Guinness*, in which Lord Justice May stated that: "The limited circumstances in which an English court could be persuaded to refuse recognition or enforcement of an arbitration award to which the New York Convention applies are those to be found in ss. 103(2) and (3) of the Arbitration Act 1996. The authorities make clear that the court is not concerned to investigate the merits of the dispute which is the subject of the award."[9] It was further upheld in *Diag Human SE v The Czech Republic*, in which Justice Ede held that "under the Convention, the grounds for refusing enforcement are restricted and construed narrowly: enforcement may be refused only if one of the listed grounds, which are exhaustive, is satisfied".[10] Similar findings have been made in Switzerland, Canada, the United States, Germany and Russia, among many others.[11]

3.3   Courts' discretion

International case law has further held that the courts in the country in which recognition or enforcement is sought are not permitted to engage in a review of the merits of the case or consider whether there has been an error of law or fact. In *Cukurova Holding AS v Sonera Holding BV*, the UK Privy Council reiterated that "the court cannot refuse to enforce an award on the ground of error of law or fact".[12] Other jurisdictions have taken a similar approach. The US Court of Appeals for the Federal Circuit has similarly held that legal or factual error is not a ground for disturbing an arbitral award: "In numerous ways, the relevant federal statutes and precedents make clear that ordinary legal or factual error is not a ground for disturbing an arbitral award."[13]

Some questions remain as to whether courts have discretion to refuse enforcement of an award if one of the Article V grounds exist or whether the courts must, if the existence of a ground is proven, refuse to enforce an award. This uncertainty derives from the drafting of Article V, which provides that recognition and enforcement may be refused if the party seeking to defend enforcement furnishes proof of the existence of one of the Article V(1) grounds. Typically, the standard meaning given to the word 'may' indicates a discretion. In the main, therefore, domestic courts interpret this language as discretionary (eg, courts in the United Kingdom, the United States and Canada have all exercised discretion when determining whether to refuse enforcement when a ground exists).[14] Even French courts have exercised discretion on this point

---

9   *Kanoria v Guinness* [2006] EWHC Civ 222 at 29.
10   *Diag Human SE v The Czech Republic* [2014] EWHC 1639 (Comm) at 12.
11   For a useful summary of these cases, see Gary B Born, *International Commercial Arbitration* (Second Edition), Wolters Kluwer, 2014, Volume III, pp3426–3427.
12   *Cukurova Holding AS v Sonera Holding BV* [2014] UKPC 15 at 4.
13   *Bayer CropScience AG v Dow Agrosciences LLC* 680 Fed Appx 985 (Fed Cir 1 March 2017)), at III.A.
14   Wolff, pp264–265.

(despite the French translation of the New York Convention actually replacing 'may' with slightly more mandatory language translatable as "will only be refused if...".[15] Other countries, such as Germany, mandatorily refuse to enforce awards where the existence of a ground for refusal is proven (although German courts do tend to interpret those grounds very narrowly).[16]

Parties to arbitration would do well to consider potential enforcement jurisdictions during the arbitral process (and indeed beforehand). Where it is possible that a party seeking to defend enforcement may have an arguable defence, parties seeking enforcement may be better served seeking enforcement from an enforcing court which allows discretion, so as to maximise the prospects of an award being enforced, notwithstanding the potential existence of a ground for refusal.

The specific grounds to refuse recognition and enforcement are discussed below.

3.4 Article V(1)(a) – incapacity and invalidity of the arbitration agreement

Article V(1)(a) provides as follows: "The parties to the [arbitration agreement] were, under the law applicable to them, under some incapacity, or the [arbitration agreement] is not valid under the law to which the parties have subjected it or, failing any indication thereon, under the law of the country where the award was made."

Incapacity has not been regularly used as a ground to defend enforcement. Whether a party had capacity to enter into an arbitration agreement will be judged according to the law governing the personal status of the party at the time the agreement was made. This applies equally to individuals and corporate entities.

In respect of the validity of the arbitration agreement, this may mean that the arbitration agreement is not compliant with necessary requirements as to form (eg, it does not comply with the form requirements set out in Article II of the New York Convention, requiring that the arbitration agreement be in writing). It may also mean that the arbitration agreement is not valid under mandatory rules of law. For example, certain countries impose restrictions on the ability to include arbitration agreements in certain types of consumer contracts. In the United States, the Dodd-Frank Wall Street Reform and Consumer Protection Act of 2009 provides that certain consumer finance disputes cannot be subject to pre-dispute arbitration agreements.

Article V(1)(a) provides that the validity of the arbitration agreement should be judged pursuant to the law governing the arbitration agreement or, if no governing law is cited, under the law of the country where the award was made.

---

15   Herbert Kronke *et al* (eds), "Recognition and Enforcement of Foreign Arbitral Awards: A Global Commentary on the New York Convention", Wolters Kluwer, 2010, p208.
16   Wolff, p265.

3.5   Article V(1)(b) – improper notice and inability to present a case

Article V(1)(b) provides as follows: "The party against whom the award is invoked was not given proper notice of the appointment of the arbitrator or of the arbitration proceedings or was otherwise unable to present his case."

This ground essentially seeks to guarantee basic principles of procedural fairness and due process. According to some commentators, it is one of the most regularly cited and most important grounds for seeking to defend enforcement,[17] and is an extremely broad ground.[18] It falls into two basic parts – enforcement can be refused if:

- a party was not given proper notice of the appointment of an arbitrator or of the proceedings; or
- a party was otherwise unable to present its case.

Of course, a causal link between the failure in due process and the outcome of the arbitration is required. A party cannot seek to rely on this as a ground to defend enforcement if the failure or procedural irregularity in fact had no bearing on the fact that an award was made against it. Despite the frequency with which Article V(1)(b) has been invoked, courts have generally taken a narrow view on what constitutes a violation of procedural fairness and due process, and thus rarely refuse enforcement pursuant to Article V(1)(b). Indeed, some reports have suggested that as few as 10% of all applications for refusal of enforcement based on this ground have succeeded.[19]

It is generally the case that court will not refuse enforcement based on this defence where a party has failed to 'help itself'. For example, if a party has waived a procedural irregularity (by conduct or otherwise), or has failed to object to an irregularity during the arbitral proceedings themselves, it may be unable to rely on that irregularity when seeking to defend enforcement. In a recent case before the English High Court, a party sought to rely on this defence when defending enforcement proceedings in relation to an award issued by a Russian arbitration at the International Commercial Arbitration Court (ICAC) of the Russian Chamber of Industry and Commerce. In that case, the parties had entered into an arbitration agreement which provided for the language of the arbitration to be Russian. When the arbitration was commenced, documents in respect of the proceedings were transmitted to the party in the Russian language. The party then sought to defend enforcement of the award ultimately issued on the grounds that it had not received proper notice, as the documentation it had received was largely in Russian. The court held that as the

---

17   Wolff, p280; Redfern and Hunter, p627.
18   Gary B Born, pp3494–3495.
19   See Herman Verbist, "Challenges on Grounds of Due Process pursuant to Article V(I)(b) of the New York Convention", in E Gaillard and D Pietro (eds), *Enforcement of Arbitration Agreements and International Arbitral Awards, the New York Convention in Practice*" quoted in Wolff, p280.

documentation (which was not voluminous) could have been easily translated, and was clearly on the ICAC's letterhead (and that, absent a dispute, there was no reason for the ICAC to write to the parties), it should have been obvious that arbitration had commenced. The court held that 'notice' for these purposes "is such as is likely to bring the relevant information to the attention of the person notified, taking account of the parties' contractual dispute resolution mechanism, including any applicable institutional arbitration rules".[20] In this case, despite the language barrier, the party seeking to defend enforcement was, in the court's view, given proper notice of the proceedings. The party had simply not sought to clarify the position in respect to the dispute once it had received Russian language documents, which it would have easily been able to do, and thus had not helped its own cause. As van den Berg points out, it is generally accepted that "arbitration being a private manner of settlement of disputes, the notice need not be in a specific (official) form as is laid down in certain laws for domestic arbitration or court proceedings".[21]

The second element of this ground – that is, that a party was otherwise unable to present its case – seeks to guarantee the fundamental principle of 'equality of arms', or equal treatment. Generally, this requires that what is granted to one party must not be refused to the other and vice versa. It does not, however, require the tribunal to provide reasons for its decisions where it is otherwise not required to do so.

A failure by the International Chamber of Commerce (ICC) court to give reasons for rejecting a challenge to an arbitrator does not, pursuant to a Swiss judgment, give rise to an argument that a party was unable to present its case. In that case, a party sought to defend enforcement of an ICC award, arguing that as the ICC court had not given reasons for its decision, its right to be heard was violated and due process had not been followed. The Swiss court, quite reasonably, dismissed this argument, holding that the relevant ICC rules did not require that the ICC court communicate reasons for its decisions, and that this is not unusual in international arbitration.[22]

3.6 Article V(1)(c) – an award on matters outside the scope of the submission to arbitration

Article V(1)(c) provides as follows: "The award deals with a difference not contemplated by or not falling within the terms of the submission to arbitration, or it contains decisions on matters beyond the scope of the submission to arbitration, provided that, if the decisions on matters submitted to arbitration can be separated from those not so submitted, that part of the

---

20   *Zavod Ekran OAO v Magneco Metrel UK Ltd* [2017] EWHC 2208 (Comm), at 12.
21   van den Berg, p15.
22   Decisions 5A 68/2013 and 5A 69/2013 of the Swiss Supreme Court, at 4.2.2.

award which contains decisions on matters submitted to arbitration may be recognised and enforced."

Unlike defences to enforcement based on procedural irregularity pursuant to Article V(1)(b), defences based on matters falling outside the tribunal's authority are rarely raised.[23] Generally, there is a presumption that awards rendered by a tribunal are made within the confines of the tribunal's authority.[24] As such, any refusal to enforce is limited to circumstances in which the party seeking to defend enforcement can prove that the tribunal exceeded its powers under the arbitration agreement. By way of example, the Singapore court has set out a two-stage test to determine whether an award should be set aside for falling foul of this article (as incorporated into Article 34(2)(a)(iii) of the UNCITRAL Model Law, which is in force in Singapore). This is that the court should consider:

- what matters were within scope of the submission to the arbitral tribunal; and
- whether the arbitral award involved such matters or whether it involved "a new difference...outside the scope of submission to arbitration and...irrelevant to the issues requiring determination".[25]

The Singapore court also held that there is no requirement to show real or actual prejudice as a result. The mere fact that the tribunal has made an award on a subject matter outside the scope of the arbitral award is enough to refuse enforcement of that award (or part thereof, insofar as other parts of the award deal with matters which were within the scope of the submission to arbitration and can be separated from the award and recognised and enforced).

However, if, in pleadings or during the hearing, a party makes submissions which go beyond the scope of the submission to arbitration, and all parties either expressly or tacitly agree to such an expansion, this may serve to broaden the scope of the submission to arbitration.[26] Parties should therefore be alive to such matters during the pendency of proceedings to ensure that, insofar as they deem it necessary, they object at the time to any attempted expansion of the submission to arbitration, to avoid potentially forgoing the possibility of seeking to rely on this ground when defending enforcement.

3.7 Article V(1)(d) – composition of tribunal or arbitral procedure not as agreed by the parties

Article V(1)(d) provides as follows: "The composition of the arbitral authority or the arbitral procedure was not in accordance with the agreement of the parties,

---

23   Wolff, p309.
24   Wolff, p310.
25   *GD Midea Air Conditioning Equipment Co Ltd v Tornado Consumer Goods Ltd* [2017] SGHC 193 at 39.
26   van den Berg, p15.

or, failing such agreement, was not in accordance with the law of the country where the arbitration took place."

Insofar as this article is to be used as a ground to defend enforcement proceedings, the enforcing court must rely on the arbitration agreement or, where the issue itself was not addressed in that agreement, must consider the law of the seat of the arbitration.

Issues of composition and arbitral procedure can include issues relating to challenging the appointment of arbitrators, the number of arbitrators, their qualifications and their impartiality. They can also include issues of arbitrator capacity. This ground requires a serious violation which results in prejudice to a party. It cannot be relied on in circumstances in which a minor breach of the parties' agreement or arbitral procedure occurred, which in reality cannot be said to have prejudiced a party or influenced the outcome of the award.[27] As with issues of procedural irregularity, a party cannot generally rely on this defence if it has done nothing to 'help itself' – for example, by failing to raise objections when the issue arose.[28] By way of example, a German court granted enforcement in circumstances where a party had sought to defend enforcement on the ground of failures in arbitral procedure where a tribunal member in an ICC arbitration seated in the United States had reportedly fallen asleep on several occasions during proceedings. The German court found that this was an issue which should have properly been raised with the tribunal's chairman during the arbitral proceedings.[29] This case should serve as a reminder to parties that if a party does not raise objections to actual or potential procedural flaws at the time they arise, that party may struggle to rely on the issue when seeking to defend enforcement.

3.8 Article V(1)(e) – the award is not binding or was set aside at the seat

Article V(1)(e) provides as follows: "The award has not yet become binding on the parties, or has been set aside or suspended by a competent authority of the country in which, or under the law of which, that award was made."

This ground is unique among the Article V grounds, in that it requires not only that an award have been made, but also that such award have been considered by a court in the seat of arbitration and, following such consideration, set aside or suspended. Parties against which an award has been rendered may view this as affording them a potential 'second bite of the cherry'. They may seek to set aside the award at the seat before enforcement proceedings are started elsewhere, as well as to adduce evidence of one or more grounds for refusal in that enforcing court.

---

27   Born, p3564.
28   Wolff, p343.
29   Higher Regional Court of Karlsruhe, Docket 9 Sch 02/09, published on 4 January 2012, summarised by Stephan Wilske and Christian Leisinger in "Germany: Higher Regional Court of Karlsruhe rules on sleeping arbitrator", Thompson Reuters 2012, https://uk.practicallaw.thomsonreuters.com/5-520-2180?originationContext=document&transitionType=DocumentItem&contextData=(sc.Default)&firstPage=true.

Seeking to set aside an award at the seat may also be a useful delaying tactic, given that Article VI of the New York Convention provides that: "If an application for the setting aside or suspension of the award has been made [at the seat], the authority before which the award is sought to be relied upon may, if it considers it proper, adjourn the decision on the enforcement of the award."

Moreover, pursuant to Article VII(1) of the New York Convention, none of the grounds for refusal to enforce an award should "deprive any interested party of any right he may have to avail himself of an arbitral award in the manner and to the extent allowed by the law of the treaties of the country where such award is sought to be relied upon". As such, parties seeking enforcement can rely on the law of the jurisdiction in which enforcement is sought where such law is more favourable than the rules of the New York Convention.

Courts have taken varying approaches to dealing with the issue of awards set aside at the seat. Indeed, courts of the same country have reached different conclusions on whether to enforce awards which have been set aside at the seat (depending on the facts of the case in question). A court's approach will be influenced by the circumstances in which the award was set aside. For example, if an award is set aside by a foreign court because the arbitration itself was conducted improperly, this is likely to be a more compelling reason to refuse enforcement than, say, if an award is set aside by a foreign court where that court can be said to be acting in a partisan manner. Two relatively recent decisions from the United States illustrate this contrast.

First, in *Getma Int'l v Republic of Guinea*,[30] the US Court of Appeals for the District of Columbia affirmed a decision of the district court to refuse enforcement of a €39 million award made against the Republic of Guinea. The case involved a dispute under a port development and operation contract, which, Getma argued, had been terminated by the Republic of Guinea without compensation. The tribunal agreed and awarded Getma damages of €39 million. However, the Republic of Guinea argued before the Common Court of Justice and Arbitration (CCJA), being the competent court pursuant to the OHADA treaty which was relevant in that case, that the arbitrators had improperly sought enhanced fees. As a result, the CCJA annulled the award. The US court found that in order to override the annulment made by the CCJA and enforce the award, it would need to find the CCJA's actions in annulling the award "to be repugnant to the United States' most fundamental notions of morality and justice".[31] It was not convinced, in this case, that such a high standard had been met (as the annulment decision was made in response to the improper actions of the tribunal), and thus refused to enforce the award.

Second, in *Corporación Mexicana de Mantenimiento Integral v Pemex-Exploración y*

---

30   *Getma Int'l v Republic of Guinea* (DC Cir 7 July 2017), at p2.
31   *Getma Int'l v Republic of Guinea*, at p2.

Producción,[32] a US court found that where a decision of a foreign court to set aside an award offends domestic notions of fairness, it has discretion to set aside that decision and enforce an award. This case related to a contract for the construction of offshore gas platforms, which provided for disputes to be heard by arbitration seated in Mexico City pursuant to the ICC rules. There was also a provision allowing Pemex to rescind the contract if certain obligations were not met. After disputes developed, Corporación Mexicana commenced arbitral proceedings and Pemex attempted to rescind the contract. While ICC proceedings (which ultimately resulted in an award of around $400 million in favour of Corporación Mexicana) were underway, the Mexican Supreme Court held that Pemex was entitled to rescind the contract. Pemex challenged the award before the Mexican courts and had it set aside on the basis that administrative rescission is not arbitrable, pursuant to Mexican policy. The court, in granting the order to set the award aside, applied a statute which had only come into effect after the dispute began. When Corporación Mexicana sought enforcement of the award in the United States, the US court found that while it does have discretion to refuse to enforce awards set aside at the seat, where the set-aside decision has been made in violation of fundamental domestic notions of justice and fairness, it also has discretion to ignore that decision and proceed to grant enforcement. In this case, it found that the Mexican court's actions were unfair (in applying a statute retroactively) and also favoured a Mexican state enterprise over a commercial enterprise.

In other jurisdictions, courts have granted enforcement of awards set aside at the seat on the basis that an international arbitration award is 'separate' from, and not integrated within, the legal system of the seat, and so remains extant even when set aside at the seat. For example, this is the view generally taken in France (pursuant to Article VII of the New York Convention), where the French Civil Code does not include as a ground to refuse enforcement the fact that an award has been set aside at the seat. The French court has held that an award rendered abroad "is an international award which is not integrated in the legal system of that State, so that it remains in existence even if set aside and its recognition in France is not contrary to international public policy".[33]

In the United Kingdom, recent case law has confirmed that where an award which has been set aside at the seat is sought to be enforced in the United Kingdom, the English court is not required to recognise the decision to set aside the award if it violates basic principles of justice. In *Yukos Capital SarL v OJSC Oil Company Rosneft*, Yukos sought to recover interest on sums awarded in four arbitral awards made in a Russian seated arbitration.[34] The awards were set aside by a Moscow court. The English court considered whether these set-aside decisions had the effect that the awards could not be enforced in England under

---

32 *Corporación Mexicana de Mantenimiento Integral v Pemex-Exploración y Producción*, (SDNY 2013).
33 *Hilmarton v Omnium de Traitement et de Valorisation*, extracted in *Redfern and Hunter*, p637.
34 *Yukos Capital Sarl v OJSC Oil Company Rosneft* [2014] EWHC 2188 (Comm).

common law. The court held that the awards were *prima facie* enforceable at common law, as the fact the awards had been set aside was simply a defence to a claim to enforcement, and that it was open to the claimant to show that no effect should be given to those set aside decisions "based on conventional English conflict of law principles, for example on the basis that the judgments were obtained by fraud, that it would be contrary to public policy to enforce the judgments, or that the judgments were obtained in breach of the rules of natural justice".[35] Justice Simon found that:

> *In my judgment the answer to the question is not provided by a theory of legal philosophy but by a test: whether the court in considering whether to give effect to an award can (in particular and identifiable circumstances) treat it as having legal effect notwithstanding a later order of a court annulling the award. In applying this test it would be both unsatisfactory and contrary to principle if the court were bound to recognise a decision of a foreign court which offended against basic principles of honesty, natural justice and domestic concepts of public policy.[36]*

In many contracting states, whether a party seeking to defend enforcement can rely on a set-aside decision will depend on whether the party seeking enforcement can show that such set-aside decision offended basic principles of justice pursuant to the laws and norms of the jurisdiction in which enforcement is sought. If it can show this, the enforcing court may – but is not bound to – ignore the set aside decision and grant enforcement.

3.9 Article V(2)(a) – arbitrability of the dispute

Article V(2)(a) provides as follows: "The subject matter of the difference is not capable of settlement by arbitration under the law of that country."

As mentioned above, the grounds for refusal under Article V(2) differ slightly from those under Article V(1), in that they do not need the party seeking to defend enforcement to request that they be considered. The enforcing court is entitled to consider these grounds of its own volition.

Article V(2)(a) essentially covers issues of arbitrability – that is, what matters can be resolved by arbitration and what matters must, on a mandatory basis, be resolved by national courts. Each contracting state will have its own laws governing which matters must be resolved by the courts and cannot, for policy reasons of that state, be resolved by arbitration. Commentators have pointed out that the scope of issues which can be subject to arbitration has broadened in contracting states over the years, and that this ground is very rarely successful in defending enforcement of an arbitral award.[37] Matters which certain countries may consider not arbitrable include issues of antitrust law, consumer rights, family and probate, insolvency and intellectual property.

---

35   *Yukos*, at 12.
36   *Yukos*, at 20.
37   Wolff, pp380-381; van den Berg, p19.

3.10 Article V(2)(b) – public policy

Article V(2)(b) provides as follows: "The recognition or enforcement of the award would be contrary to the public policy of that country."

Public policy as a ground to refuse to recognise and enforce arbitral awards is regularly pleaded, but in the view of some commentators, seldom successfully. Statistics prepared by Felix Dasser show that in Switzerland, between 1989 and 2009, public policy was invoked as a ground in applications to refuse enforcement on 142 occasions, but was successful on none of those occasions.[38] Of course, this is only one jurisdiction, but it can perhaps be taken as indicative of a broader pattern.

Of all of the Article V grounds, public policy has perhaps proven to be the most controversial and open to interpretation and, some might say, misuse. This is because 'public policy' is not defined in the New York Convention. It is left to courts in contracting states where enforcement is sought to determine their own interpretation as to what that means. However, despite this, a significant number of national courts apply a very narrow definition of 'public policy', essentially equating it with internationally accepted questions of morality and justice, rather than specific domestic public policy concerns.

In the English case of *Lemenda Trading Co v African Middle East Petroleum Co Ltd*, the court held that 'public policy' in the context of enforcement of arbitral awards will only amount to issues which infringe a "universal principle of morality".[39] This was further developed in *Westacre Investments Inc v Jugoimport SDPR Holding Co Ltd*, in which "universally condemned activities" were defined by example as "terrorism, drug-trafficking, prostitution and paedophilia".[40] It was further held that if these fundamental principles are not invoked, the court should not refuse to enforce an award on public policy grounds. In *Pencil Hill v US Citta di Palermo SpA*,[41] the court noted that there is a strong policy in favour of enforcement of arbitral awards, and that this policy outweighs other policy objectives of English law (in that case, the policy against penalty clauses which are otherwise unenforceable pursuant to English law).

Similarly, in the United States, there is a line of case law which follows this approach. The courts there have held that public policy will be used as a ground to refuse enforcement only where there are "basic notions of morality and justice" in play (see *Bayer CropScience v Dow Agrosciences and Parsons & Whittemore Overseas Co*).[42]

In Singapore, courts have confirmed that an award obtained by "corruption, bribery or fraud" would violate basic notions of morality and justice, and may

---

38 Felix Dasser, "International Arbitration and Setting Aside Proceedings in Switzerland – An Updated Statistical Analysis", *ASA Bulletin* 1/2010 (March), pp87 *et seq*.
39 *Lemenda Trading Co Ltd v African Middle East Petroleum Co Ltd* [1988] LRC (Comm) 444 at 454.
40 *Westacre Investments Inc v Jugoimport SDPR Holding Co Ltd* [1998] 4 All ER 570 at 601.
41 *Pencil Hill v US Citta di Palermo SpA* [2016] EWHC 71 (QB), at 32.

therefore not be enforced; but that this would not extend to "erroneous legal reasoning or the misapplication of law" (see *Beijing Sinozonto Mining Investment Co Ltd v Goldenray Consortium (Singapore) Pte Ltd*).[43] In India, courts have also adopted a narrow interpretation of the meaning of 'public policy', with the Supreme Court finding that enforcement will be refused on grounds of public policy only if the award is contrary to a fundamental policy of Indian law, the interests of India and justice or morality (see *Shri Lal Mahal Ltd v Progetto Grano Spa*).[44]

Some jurisdictions, conversely, have tended to adopt a slightly wider interpretation of the meaning of 'public policy'. In China, courts consider issues of Chinese judicial sovereignty to fall within its definition. For example, in *Hemofarm v Yongning*,[45] a Chinese court had issued an asset preservation order prior to an ICC arbitration, in which the tribunal found that the party which had taken out the asset preservation order had breached the arbitration agreement by so doing. However, when the award was sought to be enforced before the Chinese court, the court found that an award which decided against the court-ordered asset preservation order was an interference in Chinese judicial sovereignty. A similar decision was made in *Wicor Holding AG v Taizhou Hope Investment Co Ltd*,[46] in which a Chinese court had declared an arbitration agreement to be invalid prior to ICC proceedings being brought pursuant to that arbitration agreement. When the consequent award was sought to be enforced in China, the Chinese court held that as the Chinese court had declared the arbitration agreement invalid prior to the arbitration proceedings, to enforce it would contravene Chinese public policy.

Parties to arbitration would therefore do well to consider the likely enforcement jurisdiction prior to commencing proceedings. Where enforcement of an award would contravene generally accepted norms in respect of morality and justice, enforcement may be difficult anywhere and may be further refused in certain other countries for broader reasons.

4. Conclusion

With the emergence of increased international trade and globalisation, the New York Convention has played a pivotal role in providing a relatively reliable international framework for the enforcement of arbitral awards.

---

42 *Bayer CropScience AG v Dow Agrosciences* LLC 680 Fed Appx 985 (Fed Cir 1 March 2017)) at III.A; *Parsons & Whittemore Overseas Co Inc v Societe Generale de L'Industrie du Papier* (RAKTA), 508 F 2d 969 (2nd Cir 1974)), per J Joseph Smith.

43 *Beijing Sinozonto Mining Investment Co Ltd v Goldenray Consortium (Singapore) Pte Ltd* [2013] SGHC 248, at 41.

44 *Shri Lal Mahal Ltd v Progetto Grano Spa*; Civil Appeal 5085 of 2013, at 22.

45 *Hemofarm v Yongning* (Case (2008) Min Si Ta Zi Di 11), discussed in Nuo Ji, Yanhua Lin, Vincent Mu and Lingqi Wang, "Enforcement of judgments and arbitral awards in China: overview", Thompson Reuters, 2017, https://1.next.westlaw.com/Document/I52fc15496d6311e598dc8b09b4f043e0/View/FullText.html?contextData=(sc.Default)&transitionType=Default&firstPage=true&fromAnonymous=true.

46 *Wicor Holding AG v Taizhou Hope Investment Co Ltd* ((2015) Tai Zhong Shang Zhong Shen Zi 00004 Civil Ruling), also discussed in Nuo Ji, Yanhua Lin, Vincent Mu and Lingqi Wang.

However, contracting states' differing approaches to interpreting the Article V grounds means that a degree of variability remains when it comes to enforcement, depending on the state in which enforcement is sought. Some critics have been pushing for an update of the New York Convention, highlighting both how uncertain and how short it is for a convention of such international importance. However, while there are valid arguments as to why the New York Convention should be modernised, it is unlikely that any updated New York Convention would result in a seamless and uniform regime for the enforcement of arbitral awards. The reality remains that national courts will invariably have different approaches to interpretation and (in some instances) different motivations when considering enforcement issues.

About the authors

Peter Ashford
Partner, Fox Williams LLP
pashford@foxwilliams.com

Peter Ashford is a partner in the litigation and dispute resolution department and head of international arbitration at Fox Williams LLP.

He is a fellow of the Chartered Institute of Arbitrators and the author of the *Handbook on International Commercial Arbitration* published by Juris Publishing of New York in 2014. He has also written a guide to the International Bar Association (IBA) Rules on the Taking of Evidence in International Arbitration and a guide to the IBA Guidelines on Party Representation in International Arbitration, both published by Cambridge University Press in 2013 and 2016 respectively. He is working on a companion guide to the IBA Guidelines on Conflicts.

Mr Ashford has been appointed by the London Court of International Arbitration (LCIA) and the president of the Law Society as arbitrator, and is also recognised in the third edition of *Best Lawyers in the United Kingdom* for Litigation. He has been recommended and listed by *Chambers* and *Legal 500* for many years.

Rajinder Bassi
Partner, Kirkland & Ellis International LLP
rajinder.bassi@kirkland.com

Rajinder Bassi co-founded and is a partner in the international arbitration and litigation group in the London office of Kirkland & Ellis International LLP. She has represented multinational corporations, government entities and high-profile individuals in high-stakes international arbitrations and litigations around the world. These cases have involved a wide range of complex subject matter, applicable laws and venues, and have covered many industry sectors, including telecoms, energy, pharmaceuticals and financial services.

Ms Bassi also serves as an arbitrator. She is listed as a leading international arbitration lawyer in *Chambers UK 2018*, where she is described as "excellent, very client focused and really gets her hands dirty in a case"; and in *Legal 500 2017*, where she is described as a "superb tactician and tough negotiator".

Rachael Bewsey
Regional counsel, Southeast Asia, Ophir Energy plc
rachael.bewsey@ophir-energy.com

Rachael Bewsey has more than 18 years' experience in oil and gas law, having joined Premier Oil plc in 2000 and more recently

Ophir Energy plc in July 2018. She qualified as a solicitor in 1996 at Simmons & Simmons and worked in Hong Kong, London, Abu Dhabi and New York. She was first listed in *Legal 500* in 2007. Based in London for more than 10 years, she relocated to Singapore in 2011 to become regional counsel. There, she headed up all M&A activity for Premier Oil in Asia, managed all legal and compliance issues for over one-third of Premier Oil's total production, and was responsible for recruiting and managing national legal teams in Vietnam and Indonesia. Ms Bewsey has extensive experience negotiating with foreign governments and regulators and senior management in other oil companies and private equity negotiating production sharing contracts with various governments and state regulators; international and domestic gas sales agreements; and managing disputes.

Luke Carbon
Senior associate, Ashurst
luke.carbon@ashurst.com

Luke Carbon is a senior associate in the dispute resolution group at Ashurst Australia. He specialises in the resolution of disputes in the energy, resources, construction and infrastructure sectors. He provides advice and representation in respect of domestic and international litigation, international commercial arbitration and alternative dispute resolution. Mr Carbon has particular experience in the resolution of international disputes. His experience includes disputes across the Asia-Pacific region, Africa, the Americas and Europe.

Neil Cuninghame
Partner, Ashurst LLP
neil.cuninghame@ashurst.com

Neil Cuninghame is a partner in the competition and EU law group in Ashurst LLP's London office. For more than 20 years, he has specialised in providing advice on all aspects of EU and UK competition law. This includes advising on EU, UK and other merger control regimes, acting for clients in relation to alleged anti-competitive practices and agreements before the European Commission, the UK Competition and Markets Authority and other regulators, and advising on competition disputes (including those resolved through arbitration), market investigations, competition law compliance and state aid issues.

Mr Cuninghame also advises on regulatory issues in the energy sector, including price control regimes, and unbundling and third-party access obligations.

Mr Cuninghame advises clients across a wide range of industries, including energy and resources, infrastructure, metals and mining, financial services, media and property services.

Oliver Gayner
Investment manager, IMF Bentham Ltd
ogayner@imf.com.au

Oliver Gayner is an investment manager at international litigation funding group IMF Bentham in Sydney, and head of the company's Europe, Middle East and Africa (EMEA) office in London. Mr Gayner investigates, finances and manages litigation and arbitration cases in various jurisdictions including Australia, the United Kingdom, Hong Kong and Singapore.

While in private practice, Mr Gayner was

a solicitor at Freshfields Bruckhaus Deringer and Olswang in London, specialising in dispute resolution across a variety of industries, including banking and finance, energy, telecoms, media and IT. He has degrees in English and law and is a frequent author on issues relating to law, economics and civil justice.

Ben Giaretta

Partner, Mishcon de Reya LLP
ben.giaretta@mishcon.com

Ben Giaretta is a partner at Mishcon de Reya LLP. He is a solicitor advocate, a chartered arbitrator and a fellow of the Chartered Institute of Arbitrators. Educated at Oxford University and Queen Mary University of London, from which he has a diploma in arbitration, he is also a fellow of the Singapore Institute of Arbitrators. He represents clients on international arbitrations throughout the world, particularly in the energy, projects and construction sectors. He has extensive experience of working on liquefied natural gas (LNG) disputes, including pricing, production, LNG sale and purchase agreements, joint ventures and shipping disputes. In addition, he is frequently appointed as arbitrator, having served as sole arbitrator, party-nominated arbitrator, presiding arbitrator and emergency arbitrator, under the rules of many institutions. Now based in London, he was previously based in Singapore and has worked for clients throughout Asia, as well as in Europe and Africa.

Tom Glasgow

Chief investment officer (Asia),
IMF Bentham Ltd
tglasgow@imf.sg

As chief investment officer (Asia), Tom Glasgow leads IMF Bentham's regional investment activity and business expansion in Asia. He is responsible for assessing and managing IMF Bentham's portfolio of funded cases throughout the region, including international commercial and investment treaty arbitrations involving Asian parties.

Prior to joining IMF Bentham, Mr Glasgow was a senior member of Allen & Overy's international arbitration and disputes practice in Asia, where he handled complex multi-jurisdictional commercial matters for leading global businesses across a range of sectors. He holds dual degrees in law and international relations, and is a qualified lawyer in both New Zealand and Hong Kong. He has a strong interest in international disputes, litigation finance and the development of legal services. He frequently speaks and publishes on these topics.

Adrian Howick

Director, KPMG LLP
Adrian.Howick@KPMG.co.uk

Adrian Howick is a director in the dispute analysis services practice of KPMG in London. He holds degrees in commerce and law, and a graduate diploma in applied finance and investment.

Mr Howick has specialised in forensic accounting for the last 20 years, principally on accounting disputes and the quantification of loss and damage. He provides an expert assessment of the loss of profits and the value of businesses and shares for claims relating to breaches of tort and contract and the expropriation of assets, as well as in shareholder, partnership, infrastructure and construction disputes, including those involving the oil and gas industry. He has also worked on insolvency and restructuring assignments in the UK, Europe and Australia.

Mr Howick has been appointed as an independent expert witness, and given testimony, in disputes in the UK High Court and in London-seated arbitrations. He has led many expert engagements involving both court proceedings (in the United Kingdom, Ireland and Australia) and arbitrations (under the International Centre for the Settlement of Investment Disputes (ICSID), International Chamber of Commerce (ICC), LCIA, Singapore International Arbitration Centre (SIAC) and United Nations Commission on International Trade Law (UNCITRAL) rules).

M Imad Khan
Senior associate, Hogan Lovells
imad.khan@hoganlovells.com

Imad Khan is a senior associate in Hogan Lovells' international arbitration and international law practice groups. He represents and advises companies across diverse economic sectors, including energy, oil and gas, electricity, renewables and mining in international treaty and commercial arbitrations. Mr Khan has represented both foreign investors and host states in investment disputes before the International Centre for the Settlement of Investment Disputes at the World Bank, well as under the rules of the United Nations Commission on International Trade Law. He also represents clients in construction and commercial arbitrations under the rules of the International Chamber of Commerce, the International Centre for

Dispute Resolution (ICDR) and the Hong Kong International Arbitration Centre.

Mr Khan currently teaches courses in international law and arbitration at Washington University School of Law in St Louis, and previously taught courses in international law at the University of Houston Law Center. He is currently serving as a Global Advisory Board member of the ICDR Young & International group.

Ronnie King
Managing partner Tokyo, Ashurst LLP
ronnie.king@ashurst.com

Ronnie King is the managing partner of Ashurst Tokyo. Ronnie graduated from Cambridge University (MA, LLM), prior to joining Ashurst in 1984. He has acted on energy sector disputes for over 25 years, including on some of the highest value sector disputes in the market, and was one of the first law firm partners in London to identify energy sector dispute resolution as a separate discipline. His client mandates include Centrica, Total, Tullow, E.ON, National Oil Company (Libya), Kuwait Petroleum and Hess Corporation in work that spans many of the types of dispute covered in this text. Mr King represents clients as counsel in arbitrations and sits as an arbitrator. He has been ranked consistently in independent commentaries as a legal expert in relation to energy disputes.

He has had the privilege of working with, or opposite, most of the contributors of this book, each of whom has genuine expertise in the subjects which they address.

Nathan Landis
Investment manager, IMF Bentham Ltd
nlandis@imf.com.au

Nathan Landis is an investment manager based in the Perth office of IMF Bentham. He joined IMF Bentham from the Western Australia Bar, where his practice focused on the energy and resources sector. While at the Bar, he advised on a number of disputes involving energy projects. Prior to joining the Bar, he was a counsel in the litigation and dispute resolution department at Clifford Chance, where he was also part of the firm's global oil and gas industry group. He has worked in the Middle East and with a top-tier law firm in Australia.

During his career, Mr Landis has appeared in a range of courts and tribunals within Australia and the Middle East. He is a member of the Chartered Institute of Arbitrators. In 2015 he was recognised by *Doyle's Guide* as a recommended barrister for Dispute Resolution in Western Australia.

Ghislaine Lawless
Associate, Ashurst LLP
ghislaine.lawless@ashurst.com

Ghislaine Lawless is an associate at Ashurst LLP specialising in international commercial arbitration, with a particular focus on the energy and resources sector. She has experience of both *ad hoc* and institutional arbitration, including pursuant to the LCIA and UNCITRAL rules. Ms Lawless has acted for a variety of clients in the energy, defence, finance and resources sectors, as well as for large corporates, and has a particular interest in African disputes. A keen linguist, she speaks Italian and French and continues to do battle with Mandarin following her completion of a postgraduate diploma at Shanghai Normal University.

Nicholas Lingard
Partner, Freshfields Bruckhaus Deringer
nicholas.lingard@freshfields.com

An experienced international arbitration counsel and advocate, Nicholas Lingard heads Freshfields' international arbitration practice in Asia. He has a particular focus on oil and gas and politically delicate negotiations in the energy sector, and leads probably the most active treaty arbitration practice in Asia. He also represents clients in commercial disputes across a variety of industries, under all the major arbitral rules and under all major systems of law.

Mr Lingard is an expert member of the Energy Charter Treaty Secretariat's Legal Advisory Task Force. He is co-author of the leading Japanese practice text on international arbitration and *A Guide to the SIAC Arbitration Rules* (2nd ed, Oxford University Press, 2017).

Mr Lingard was educated at the University of Queensland and Harvard Law School. He is admitted to practise in New York and New South Wales, Australia. He is also a registered foreign lawyer at the Singapore International Commercial Court.

James MacDonald
Associate, Ashurst LLP
james.macdonald@ashurst.com

James MacDonald is an associate in Ashurst's dispute resolution team based in Dubai. He has acted in a number of large and complex commercial disputes, and regularly advises clients on drafting effective arbitration clauses and on the enforcement of arbitration awards.

Mr MacDonald has experience acting for clients in a range of industries, including energy, resources and construction in the Middle East and globally. His experience advising clients in the energy sector includes advising on both contractual and regulatory issues.

Tim Martin
Managing director, Northumberland Chambers
tim@timmartin.ca

Tim Martin has more than 40 years' experience in the international oil and gas industry where he has been general counsel, country manager, finance director, commercial manager, corporate director and petroleum economist, working in more than 50 countries. He has been president of the Association of International Petroleum Negotiators and other industry organisations.

Tim's peers have selected him as one of the leading International Who's Who of Oil & Gas Lawyers and Commercial Arbitrators, where he has been described as the "best around for energy disputes", as "a true expert in the [oil & gas] sector" and as a "true innovator" in international oil and gas law.

Mr Martin has extensive experience as an arbitrator, counsel and expert in international arbitration, transborder litigation and boundary disputes. He has provided advice on some of the largest energy and infrastructure projects in the world.

Mr Martin is a fellow and chartered arbitrator of the Chartered Institute of Arbitrators, a council member of the AAA, and a member of the LCIA, IAI and Energy Arbitrators List. He is also on the arbitrator panels of the ICDR, SIAC, KLRAC, SCCA and BCDR. More information can be found on Tim's website: www.timmartin.ca.

Patrese McVeigh
Associate, Ashurst LLP
patrese.mcveigh@ashurst.com

Patrese McVeigh is an associate in Ashurst's dispute resolution team based in Singapore. She has experience in dispute resolution and international arbitration, with a particular focus on high-value disputes in the construction, resources and energy sectors. Her work includes advising corporations on complex commercial disputes and assisting clients through the dispute resolution processes.

Jon Newman
Partner, Kirkland & Ellis International LLP
jonathan.newman@kirkland.com

Jon Newman is a partner in the international arbitration and litigation group in the London office of Kirkland & Ellis International LLP. He has represented numerous multinational corporations, financial institutions and high-net-worth individuals in international commercial arbitrations, including under the ICC, LCIA, Hong Kong International Arbitration Centre, SIAC and UNCITRAL rules. He has also represented multinational corporations and financial institutions in complex litigations in the English courts, and in international internal and regulatory investigations. Such cases have involved various business sectors, including financial services, telecoms, healthcare, real estate, heavy industry and consumer goods.

Dyfan Owen

Partner, Ashurst LLP

dyfan.owen@ashurst.com

Dyfan Owen is a partner at Ashurst and leads the Middle East dispute resolution team. He specialises in complex disputes arising out of the infrastructure, energy and resources sectors, and has advised on a number of multimillion-dollar disputes in these sectors for clients in the Middle East and globally. In addition to acting for clients in international arbitration, Mr Owen is well versed in other forms of dispute resolution, including expert determination, adjudication and mediation. Recent matters on which he has acted include disputes and international arbitration relating to the operation of a power plant in the United Arab Emirates, the construction of an airport in a Gulf Cooperation Council state, the construction of telecommunications infrastructure in Saudi Arabia, investments in renewable energy projects in Egypt and a dispute relating to a landmark downstream oil and gas project.

Rob Palmer

Partner, Ashurst LLP

rob.palmer@ashurst.com

Rob Palmer is a partner in Ashurst's dispute resolution team in Singapore and managing partner of Ashurst's Singapore office. He has a particular focus on dispute resolution in international energy, construction and infrastructure projects.

Mr Palmer has been based in Southeast Asia since 2003 and during that time has conducted arbitrations under the rules of all major regional and international arbitral institutions including the SIAC, AAA, ICC, LCIA, KLRCA, TAI and BANI. He also sits as arbitrator, and is a panel member of the ACICA, KLRCA, TAC and BANI, as well as having been appointed by the SIAC. Mr Palmer is admitted to practise in England, New South Wales (Australia) and New Zealand and is a registered foreign lawyer at the Singapore International Commercial Court.

Georgia Quick

Partner, Ashurst

georgia.quick@ashurst.com

Georgia Quick is a partner in the litigation and dispute resolution group at Ashurst Australia in Sydney. She specialises in dispute resolution and risk management in the areas of energy, construction and major projects and is joint head of the Australian international arbitration practice. She is dual qualified (Australia and the United Kingdom, having practised international arbitration in London for seven years). She was named as the Alternative Dispute Resolution Practitioner of the Year at the 2017 Australian Alternative Dispute Resolution Awards.

Matthew Saunders

Partner, Ashurst LLP

matthew.saunders@ashurst.com

Matthew Saunders is a partner in the dispute resolution practice in London. He focuses on international arbitration relating to international projects and the energy and resources sectors and leads the global international arbitration practice at Ashurst.

Mr Saunders has a particular focus on disputes in the gas sector including pricing and supply issues in both natural gas and LNG sectors. He also has particular experience of treaty claims involving bilateral investment treaties and the Energy Charter and Energy

Community treaties. He is a member of the London Court of International Arbitration, the Chartered Institute of Arbitrators and the Association of International Petroleum Negotiators. His practice covers both contract and investment treaty arbitration.

Jennifer Smith
Partner, Hogan Lovells
jennifer.smith@hoganlovells.com

Jennifer Smith, a partner at Hogan Lovells in Houston, has significant experience in international dispute resolution. A recognised leader in her field, she has advocated for companies involved in complex international commercial disputes for more than 25 years.

Dual-qualified in England and Texas, she is well versed in the business and cultural realities of cross-border disputes and has a deep understanding of almost every facet of the energy industry. Ms Smith advises corporations on disputes concerning a wide range of issues, from those involving drilling rigs, reservoir management, LNG, production sharing agreements and floating production storage and offloading facilities to issues of corporate governance and joint ventures.

Ms Smith serves on the executive committee of the Institute of Transnational Arbitration, on the international advisory committee of the ICDR, on the advisory council of the Kay Bailey Hutchison Centre for Energy, Law and Business, on the executive committee of the World Affairs Council of Houston and as a trustee of Wellesley College.

Thomas K Sprange QC
Partner, King & Spalding International LLP
TSprange@KSLAW.com

Thomas K Sprange QC is partner in King &

Spalding's trial and global disputes group based in London, England. He provides advocacy and strategic advice in significant high-value and complex commercial disputes, in particular in the energy sector. He has acted as lead counsel in more than 100 international arbitrations in the leading arbitration institutes, including the ICC, LCIA, AAA, SCC and ICSID. He also regularly sits in three-member arbitration tribunals and as a sole arbitrator. He is ranked in the latest editions of *Chambers Global, Chambers UK, Chambers Europe, Legal 500 UK* and *Who's Who of Commercial Arbitration, Asset Recovery* and *Construction* directories for Arbitration and Dispute Resolution.

Emily Stennett
Associate, Freshfields Bruckhaus Deringer
emily.stennett@freshfields.com

Emily Stennett is an associate in Freshfields' dispute resolution group, with a focus on commercial disputes and international arbitration.

Ms Stennett advises clients across various sectors on a broad range of complex, high-value commercial disputes, both in the English courts and in arbitration proceedings under all major institutional rules and systems of law. She regularly advises clients in the oil and gas and construction sectors, and has also represented both investors and states in a number of high-profile investment treaty arbitrations in Asia and around the world.

Ms Stennett studied at Cambridge University and graduated in 2011 with a BA in law. She is qualified as a solicitor-advocate in England and Wales.

Max Strasberg
Associate, Ashurst LLP
max.strasberg@ashurst.com

Max Strasberg is an associate in the dispute resolution department in Ashurst LLP's London office. He has advised clients on a wide range of contentious matters before the High Court and Competition Appeal Tribunal. His experience includes investigations by competition authorities, competition damages actions (including follow-on and collective actions), public procurement disputes (including judicial review), as well as oil and gas and general commercial disputes and arbitration. Mr Strasberg was recently recognised in *Legal 500 UK* as a recommended practitioner in competition litigation.

Ben J Williams
Senior associate, King & Spalding
International LLP
bwilliams@kslaw.com

Ben Williams is a solicitor-advocate in England and Wales and an attorney and counsellor at law in New York state. He is a member of King & Spalding's trial and global disputes group based in London, England. With more than a decade of experience handling and resolving complex commercial disputes, he focuses his practice on the energy sector and frequently represents clients in national courts and international arbitrations, including in proceedings brought under the Energy Charter Treaty.

Related titles

Globe Law
and Business

Go to **www.globelawandbusiness.com**
for full details including free sample chapters